151 DIVES

**in the protected waters
of Washington State and British Columbia**

Betty Pratt-Johnson

151 DIVES

in the protected waters
of Washington State and British Columbia

THE MOUNTAINEERS BOOKS

THE MOUNTAINEERS BOOKS
*is the nonprofit publishing arm of The Mountaineers Club, an organization
founded in 1906 and dedicated to the exploration, preservation, and
enjoyment of outdoor and wilderness areas.*

1001 SW Klickitat Way, Suite 201, Seattle, WA 98134

Nautical chart portions for dives in Canada:
© Her Majesty in Right of Canada, Department of Fisheries and Oceans (2007)
Sa Majesté du Chef du Canada, Ministère des Pêches et Océans (2007)

First edition, 2007. Originally published in Canada
by Betty Pratt-Johnson Adventure Publishing.

Credits for Illustrations: see page 456.

FRONT COVER DESIGN
Laura Redmond

FRONT COVER PHOTOGRAPH
Safety stop on ascent line
Barb Roy

BACK COVER PHOTOGRAPH
Snakelock anemones
Neil McDaniel

SPINE
The red-and-white dive flag marks an area where scuba diving is in progress, and is flown
from a float. It is recognized throughout North America.
   The blue-and-white dive flag is flown from a vessel when scuba divers are in the water.
It is recognized throughout the world.

Manufactured in China

A Library of Congress Cataloging-in-Publication record is on file at the Library of Congress.

Thanks

to all divers, to First Nations,

federal, provincial and municipal individuals and agencies

and interested non-divers

who continue working to protect

our priceless, irreplaceable marine life heritage

in the Pacific Northwest.

I love you.

It matters. It's coming – keep going!

Protection of marine life must become legal and permanent.

CONTENTS

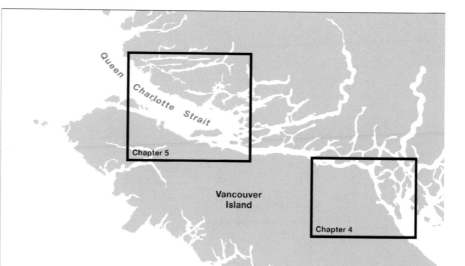

KEY TO CHAPTER MAPS
Strait of Georgia, Queen Charlotte Strait and Puget Sound

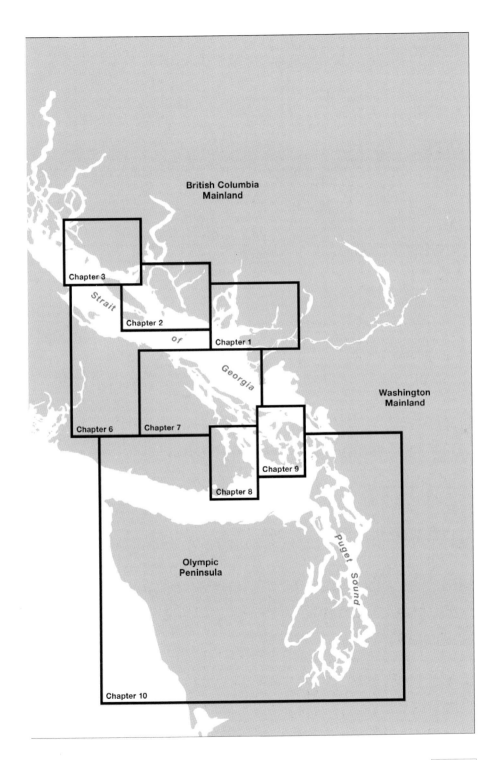

British Columbia
Mainland

Chapter 3

Strait

Chapter 2

of

Chapter 1

Georgia

Washington
Mainland

Chapter 6

Chapter 7

Chapter 9

Chapter 8

Olympic
Peninsula

Puget Sound

Chapter 10

Come Dive With Me

Scuba diving continues to grow and change – so, once again, I have fully updated and expanded this guide that started as *141 Dives in the protected waters of Washington and British Columbia*.

Today diving is easier and more complex. More options exist in every aspect of diving: equipment, training, boat charters, resorts.

When I learned to dive, we scrambled to try the one single-hose regulator provided for the class. For early dives I invested in a skin-two wet suit, weight belt, tank with J-valve to pull when my air was gone. A depth gauge, knife – and the lusted-after single-hose "reg". Two years later I got a pressure gauge and compass, the next year a horse-collar buoyancy compensator.

Step-by-step training for recreational divers did not exist – we learned the basics, were certified with one open water dive. Then tried things, learned from other divers. It's one way to develop skills. But since those early exciting years, diving instruction has leapt forward along with the development of sophisticated equipment.

Today my gear includes a dry suit, console with multiple gauges, and an analyzer to check my nitrox mix just before each dive. No, I don't have to pull a J-valve. But I'd better watch the gauges. One piece of equipment has not changed for me over the years: I still wear my original

weight belt from 1967. Complex, simple.

One thing about diving that has not changed for me is that whether I walk quietly into the shallows or roll off a boat, I know something new will soon come into my life. It has to be the same for technical divers laden with gear going down a descent line. The newness of each dive is the magic experienced by all divers and snorkelers. It's what keeps us diving.

I personally have enjoyed every dive included in this guidebook. All dive descriptions are within sport diving limits, none are for greater depth than 130 feet (40 meters). Many sites are suitable for snorkeling or skin diving as well as scuba diving. Some dive descriptions in this guide at deeper sites serve a triple function – they are also useful for technical divers.

What's different about Pacific Northwest diving? What's old? What's new?

What's old:
- A kaleidoscope of color – hot pink, red, yellow and orange; cool blue, mauve, purple and white – covers the ocean floor. The emerald sea is bursting with life.
- Another permanent feature of diving in the Pacific Northwest inland sea is the sheer magnitude of coastline protected from surf, making it one of the safest

and most accessible diving areas in the world.

What's new:

- Diving has become a mainstream recreation; charter boats and all dive facilities have increased in sophistication and numbers to meet the need.
- There is no more needless depletion of marine life – almost-forgotten octopus wrestling contests, spearfishing and collecting of marine life at well-known sites are "out".
- Adventuring by diving or snorkeling to see wild creatures like Steller sea lions, Pacific white-sided dolphins and sixgill sharks is "in".
- Wreck divers today are ardent preservers of our underwater heritage. They don't pillage wrecks and tear them apart, they document them.
- Artificial reefs are very popular; six are described in this guide. They are destinations for divers of all skill levels: new divers explore outside the hull; experienced divers training in penetration are taught in predictable interiors; expert wreck divers experienced in penetration find challenges.
- Technical diving is creeping up on us. Nitrox, or enriched air, is popular and widely available; for me, it is one more margin of safety. Full-fledged technical diving is another way to grow, to reach for new frontiers. It is a strong trend.
- Many sites in this guide are suitable for technical divers – namely, the ones deeper than 125 feet (38 meters), and the wrecks and artificial reefs.

After diving a location in *101 Dives* and now in *151 Dives* one technical diver wrote that it was "a site worthy of both technical and recreational exploration".

Who can dive where?

All dives described are rated for skill and experience required. This skill level requirement cannot be measured by the number of years you have been diving. It can only be measured by the variety of diving situations you have encountered. Any certified diver should be able to attempt the dives classified "All Divers". Beginners and visitors should have experience with a number of these dives before doing any of the more difficult ones. When a dive site has some complications but does not require intricate planning, I have rated it for "Intermediate Divers". An intermediate should know how to use tide and current tables and how to dive in straightforward currents. Dives that require precision because of extreme current or depth or boat traffic or any other variable described in hazards, dives that require great strength and fitness, dives that present several difficult hazards are classified for "Expert Divers".

When I state that a dive is suitable for all divers, or intermediate divers "with guide", I indicate that divers who go under water with an experienced guide can enjoy a site that is otherwise above their skill and experience level: this presupposes that the guide will have a great deal of local knowledge and will be capable of summing up the visiting diver to help him or her deal with the dive situation.

Kayak-divers will find 17 kayak dives described in this guide that can also be reached by larger boat, 3 from shore.

Divers who use wheelchairs will find 11 shore dives noted that might be accessible to them, 15 more for those who paddle dive-kayaks. I say "might" because I could have misjudged suitability. Not all of these locations have been checked by divers with wheelchairs.

Be aware that I have made no value judgments about the capabilities of any dive guides or charter operators – I simply list them. I have tried to present a balanced number of dives for divers of all skill levels in each locale. The greatest number of dives are in and around cities where there are the most divers looking for places to get wet.

How I obtained data,
how to use it

To obtain information for this updated guide I talked with local divers about each site dived earlier; where changes were reported I dived those sites again. Many old favorites are still in this new guide but with enhancements as at Porteau Cove Marine Park. And it has been a thrill to experience many new sites: the *Capilano,* a choice heritage wreck in British Columbia; Bell Island in the San Juans, a site nourished with current but divable at most times on one side or other of the island; newly accessible and easy-but-excellent shore dives like Ansell Place in British Columbia and Rockaway Beach in Washington State where new divers can go, and experts will also want to.

The book format is deliberately designed with each dive described on two opposing pages. You can easily photocopy a write-up and when you dive, take just the photocopy.

My marine life observations are those of an interested layperson. I refer to all animals by common names. If no authoritative common name is apparent, I use the common name most descriptive to me.

Tide tables and/or current tables are listed for every site. When possible, time corrections are simple rule-of-thumb figures. Corrections derived from locals can be more reliable than calculating dive time from the current tables. Currents are often measured mid-channel, not where you are diving.

A portion of nautical chart in the actual chart size is included in each site description. These charts are for diving reference only – not to be used for navigation. A scale bar is beneath each chart and an arrow on it to indicate the dive-entry point described.

Global Positioning System (GPS) datum are included for every boat dive in this edition, an excellent tool to help locate a dive. But not perfect. GPS readings vary: the number of satellites the information bounces off changes from minute to minute. Buoys swing with the current. Rough water can make it difficult to hold a position and wait

for more satellites to collect. In addition, programming of GPS devices differs. My readings often disagreed with readings on boats I was on. All the same variables apply to the user, which could double the error. Still, rather than taking readings off a chart, I offer you my readings from my Garmin 48 with 12 channels, "warts" and all.

I have been there. All readings except one are mine – I did that dive too but was

Pacific white-sided dolphins: two swim, two frolic as they migrate

so enthralled I forgot to record the location. I prefer to trust the location of a reef or wreck to my readings rather than to a nautical chart. Yet even my errors are inconsistent.

As I take readings my GPS tells me its degree of error, usually ranging from 10 to 40 feet (3 to 12 meters) but it does not note in which direction. Double that, and you have the diameter of the circle you might have to search in – the user has the same variables which might double the error again. Difficult, especially if diving in turbid conditions. Sometimes GPS readings are spot on; I would not go without this help. But be aware. Use everything you've got – hand-held depth sounders are another excellent aid for locating sites.

Service Information in this Edition

Dive shops usually offer air fills, instruction, equipment sales and repairs. Air stations usually offer only air fills, so these facts are not included in the descriptions of services – they are assumed.

Technical training and gas availability are included in this guidebook even though no specific descriptions of technical dives are in it. Many recreational divers now use nitrox – it's the "toe in the door" to technical diving – and some recreational divers have trained for trimix. So sources of tuition and mixed gases are listed.

Training disciplines referred to in the service information are as follows:
1. Recreational instruction: teaching divers to use compressed air to sport-diving depth of 130 feet (40 meters).
2. Nitrox instruction: teaching divers to use enriched air to sport-diving limit.
3. Rebreather instruction: training divers to use rebreathers to dive within sport-diving limit or sometimes deeper.
4. Technical instruction: training divers to use mixed gases for one or more of the following purposes: to enable them

a) to dive to greater depths than 130 feet (40 meters)
b) to dive for long duration
c) to dive in overhead environments such as caves and deep wrecks to greater depths than 130 linear feet (40 linear meters)
d) to work under water – and who knows where else it's going!

Water Salinity

All sites covered in this book, except one, are in salt water. Divers accustomed to diving in fresh water will find they need to wear 1 to 4 pounds (½ to 1¾ kilograms) more weight when diving in the sea. Probably most divers should start by adding 2 pounds (1 kilogram) to accommodate for the increased density of salt water. Experiment until you find the right amount.

Water Temperature

Water temperature is affected by several factors including depth and currents. Surface temperature of Pacific Northwest waters varies from 39° to 46° Fahrenheit (4° to 8° Celsius) in winter to 54° to 64° Fahrenheit (12° to 18° Celsius) in summer, depending upon location. However, below a depth of 30 to 40 feet (9 to 12 meters) the temperature varies little, winter or summer, from about 45° Fahrenheit (7° Celsius).

It's just a matter of where the thermocline, or temperature drop, comes – at 30, 40, 50 or 60 feet (9, 12, 15 or 18 meters), usually not deeper than that. A factor for wet-suit divers to consider is that you will probably feel the cold more quickly when diving where there is current. The current constantly forces a change of water under any gaps in your suit. And the water itself will probably be colder because shifting water never becomes warm.

Most local divers dive comfortably year-round in all locations wearing custom-fitted dry suits. Some wear custom-fitted wet suits of neoprene. Wet-suit divers usually wear the "farmer Jane" or "farmer John" style of suit which covers the trunk of the body with a double thickness. Some divers wear lightweight neoprene five-finger gloves in summer and ¼ inch (6½ millimeter) neoprene mitts in winter. In very cold weather, wet-suit divers warm themselves for entry by pouring warm water into their gloves and hoods.

Many wet suits manufactured in California and other warmer parts are of less than ¼ inch (6½ millimeter) neoprene and will not be comfortably warm in winter waters of this region. Visiting divers may want to rent a dry suit or buy or rent a vest or an Arctic hood for added warmth while diving in the Pacific Northwest.

Seasons

Year-round diving is enjoyed in the Strait of Georgia and Puget Sound. Winter is best for photography since low plankton activity and low river runoff levels make visibility best then. In summer, you will find good visibility in northerly waters in the Port Hardy area. Throughout the rest of the inland sea, summer visibility can be poor: it is a good time to combine a dive with a picnic on an unspoiled beach, or pursue some diving activity like bottle collecting. Because much bottle collecting is done at muddy sites by touch alone, visibility does not matter. Sunny September days are considered best all-round by some, as it is often most beautiful both above and below the surface.

Visibility

Water clarity is the most significant variable in Pacific Northwest diving. It can vary from "faceplate" visibility when you cannot see 1 foot (⅓ meter) ahead, up to a crystal clear 100 feet (30 meters). Poor visibility may be the result of several factors: the type of bottom, river runoff, industrial pollution and plankton growth.
• Type of bottom – Muddy substrates are

Photographer descending into clear emerald sea in winter

liable to be stirred up when current is running, or when many divers are swimming close to the bottom. In many locations, diving at the end of the outgoing tide will help you obtain the best possible visibility; yet at sites where beach litter is pulled into the sea when the tide recedes, visibility is better at high tides. At a silty site near a wall, if possible, go down at one level and up at a shallower level. A buoyancy compensation device should be worn at all times and is essential in murky waters.
• River runoff – Both melting snow and rainstorms cause murky water, especially near rivers and creek mouths. In spring, early summer and after rainstorms, check your chart and avoid sites near large rivers like the Fraser or Skagit. A small, clear stream of fresh water flowing into the sea creates a shimmery appearance like scotch and water, but does not impede vision or match the taste!
• Industrial pollution – Effluents, tailings and other solid wastes from the mines, factories and logging operations can impair visibility. Avoid these areas.
• Plankton growth – Two waves of plankton growth or "bloom" come to protected waters of Pacific Northwest seas each spring and summer. Prolonged sunny weather encourages these blooms. The spring bloom invariably occurs each year throughout the Strait

5

*Bull kelp on surface
at slack water*

of Georgia and Puget Sound. It begins any time from March through April or May, and clouds the top 20 to 30 feet (6 to 9 meters) with a green growth of plankton making the water look like pea soup. Later, the plankton aggregates in white clumps and looks like a snowstorm in the water. This may last only two weeks or a month. However, often just as the plankton bloom fades away, river runoff comes to cloud surface waters.

The second wave of plankton is less predictable and more localized. It may come in late summer, August through September or October, making the water look slightly red. This second bloom may come to one area and not to another, usually lasting a very short while. The water may be turbid one day and clear the next. Therefore, at easily accessible sites, it is always worth checking to see if the water is clear. The best summer visibility comes on a sunny day after a week of overcast weather.

Sometimes the only way to find good visibility in the late spring and early summer is to select a dive site deep enough that you can descend through the surface murkiness until the visibility improves. When diving in turbid water, use a compass; swim with your hands touching and extended forward to protect your head and face; and surface with a good reserve of air so that you

can meet any emergency poor visibility might create.

One of the most beautiful dives I ever made was on a sunny day in May at Lookout Point in Howe Sound. Excessive Fraser River runoff and a healthy bloom of plankton had combined to make the surface almost opaque. There was only faceplate visibility until my buddy and I reached 50 feet (15 meters). Suddenly we were in a garden of fluffy white plumose anemones shimmering with bioluminescence. Spectacular! Like a night dive, only better, because it came as such a complete surprise.

Bull Kelp

Beauty or beast? If you have never been diving in kelp you should know something about it.

Experienced Pacific Northwest divers are lured to bull kelp for many reasons. For instance, it can help orient you. On the surface, bull kelp gives an indication of depth – in the Strait of Georgia kelp usually grows in less than 30 feet (9 meters) of water. Kelp shows you the direction the current is running. When it pops to the surface, the current is slowing down.

Under water, kelp gives a handhold in difficult current. In areas with a great many boats, if the kelp itself is not too thick to penetrate, it is a relatively traffic-free place to ascend. It provides a rich habitat for marine life. You will often find crabs hiding under it, fish swimming through it. Urchins eat it as a favorite food.

Bull kelp is a seasonal plant which nearly dies off over the winter and grows again in spring and summer, sometimes as much as 6 inches (15 centimeters) in a day.

It can be a hazard, though, if you are caught in it and panic. When diving near bull kelp, be particularly careful at the surface. Kelp is easier to swim through under water. Enter the water by surface-diving down, feet first, to avoid entanglement. Always ascend with a reserve of air so that you can descend again, if necessary, and come up at another spot. Bull kelp has a strong stem which is very difficult to break by hand. Wear a knife you can reach with either hand, so that if caught you can calmly cut your way free. I have never been caught in the kelp, but one time my buddy and I decided to find out how difficult it would be to cut. Our knives cut it like butter. Try it. Find out if your knife works. A few unprepared divers have drowned as a result of entanglement, and most of these drownings were on the surface.

Do not avoid kelp because of its dangers, but use its positive points. Be careful when diving in it, and respect its strength.

Currents and Riptides

The strongest tidal streams in the world occur in passages of the Strait of Georgia and Puget Sound. In some locations near islands and narrows there are tidal currents with massive kinetic energy – some race at the rate of 16 knots. No person can command this element; you must work with it. But you can glance at a chart and predict areas where current will be a serious consideration. And, where there is current there is also abundant marine life because the moving water provides food for many animals. It is well worth learning to dive safely at current sites in order to enjoy the rich scenes that open to you.

• Before you dive:

1. Always ask local divers for advice about sites and times.
2. Use your tide and current tables, charts and other tools and plan carefully.
3. Always think for yourself – do not rely on the expert in your crowd. Do not rely on the pickup boat, yet on some dives you must also have a pickup boat standing by. And do not rely on your charter operator to put you in at the right time. All divers should learn to deal with currents and think for themselves on every dive. Ask your buddy to make

a dive plan, too, then check to see if you have planned for the same time.

• In the water:

1. Wear a watch. When diving high-current sites of the Pacific Northwest it is important to know the actual time.
2. Use a small volume mask. It is less likely than a large mask to be dislodged by the current.
3. If caught in a rip current, an upwelling or downwelling, do not try to swim against it. Swim across it and gradually work your way out.
4. Wear a whistle in the event you are swept away on the surface.
5. When diving where the current is not too strong, you do not necessarily have to dive precisely on slack but somewhere near slack.
6. On all dives where the current never stops, go upcurrent at the start of your dive, and when half of your air is gone, turn and drift downcurrent to your entry point.
7. If caught by unexpected extreme current, hold onto rocks and pull yourself along. Crawling upcurrent saves energy and air. On a sandy bottom you could "knife it". But both of these tactics should be avoided if possible to protect marine life. Even holding onto rocks should be avoided. Try not to disturb the marine life nor even the rocks.

Bull kelp flowing with current

• When diving from a boat in current:

1. Use the anchor line as a descent/ascent line and surface near the bow. Trail a floating line that is 200 feet (60 meters) long behind. If you miss the boat you can catch onto the line. With a 2-knot current you travel just over 3 feet (1 meter) per second. Thus 200 feet (60 meters) of line "buys" nearly one minute to swim across the current to reach the line. Attach a float or plastic bottle to the end of the line or use a polypropylene line which floats.

2. When diving in an area subject to strong currents, a fairly safe rule for timing your dive is to get wet 30 minutes before slack tide, the period when the water is still and the tide is neither coming in nor going out. Remember that tides and currents do not always fit with the tables. Depend upon your common sense. Look at the water and sum up the situation visually before entering the water. For instance, at Sechelt Rapids be ready at the site an hour before slack, watching and waiting for the water to slow down. Then complete your dive shortly after the tide has turned.

3. When diving in a location with very strong currents, such as Deception Pass or Gabriola Passage, plan to have a "live" boat – a vessel under power and not anchored – ready to pick up all divers, if necessary.

4. At some sites described in this guide, divers deliberately play with the current, enjoy the ride – fly through tidal rapids at Agate Passage, glide through Tzoonie Narrows. A floating buoy with dive flag should mark the group of divers so that the following boat can follow easily and other boats can avoid the divers.

Every year divers stretch the limits – dare more, dive where bigger, more radical tidal currents flow. Many charter operators have learned to dive their "home" big-current sites safely, and they take divers there at the right time. When you dive a big-current site on complete slack and on one of the best days of the year for it, it feels easy. It isn't. Many operators have great skill and local knowledge. Each diver should strive to acquire those skills. Divers should ask questions, learn everything you can.

Do not become complacent about current. Finally, remember that all predictions are just that – only predictions. Whatever the source, do not accept current or tide information as infallible. No predictions are. Wind and barometric pressure can radically alter the time of the turn. According to the *Canadian Tide and Current Tables* published by the Canadian Hydrographic Service, "Currents are particularly sensitive to the effects of wind. The times of slack water can be advanced or retarded considerably by strong winds. In some instances, particularly if the following flood or ebb current is weak, the direction of current may not change and slack water may not occur".

When you reach a site, check it out: look at the kelp, throw in a stick, float a bottle. If the current is not doing what you expected, trust what you see. Be prepared to watch and wait for the right moment to dive – if you have missed slack, call off the dive. And enjoy it another day.

Sources of Tide and Current Information

Sources of tide and current information for regions in this guidebook are given in the service information of each chapter: a greater number of current tables are included in the Canadian tables than used to be. It has become possible to dive with a degree of confidence at wild current sites such as Sechelt Rapids, Race Rocks, Seymour Narrows and Nakwakto Rapids even though the "window of time" to dive is not great. The accuracy of the predictions at these sites is especially good since the dives are close to or at the current stations.

At most stations in the current tables you can expect slack within 30 minutes of their predictions 80% of the time.

Boats and Log Booms

Thousands of boats also use the inland sea waters described in this guide. Areas where boat traffic is particularly heavy are noted in the detailed site descriptions, and you should be especially careful at these places. But a boat could appear at any time over any site. Dive defensively:
1. Dive with a dive flag – it is required. Use it but do not count on it to protect you.
2. Ascend with a reserve of air:
   a) Where the bottom is featureless, dive with a compass and stay close to the bottom all the way to shore.
   b) In open water, listen for boats, spiral as you ascend in order to see as much of the surface as possible and look up for boats.
   c) At other sites, ascend near a rock wall, or a boat dive-flag anchor line or in a kelp bed, being careful not to become caught in the kelp. Larger vessels usually steer clear of kelp.
3. If you hear a power boat, stay down until it passes. If you hear a really big ship, hang onto rocks or wedge yourself between boulders on the bottom.
4. When diving near log booms, ascend with a large reserve of air; then if you surface under the log boom you will have time to descend and come up at another place. Spiral, look up and extend one arm above you as you ascend.

Broken Fishing Line

Beware of broken bits of fishing line under water. It is very strong and difficult to see. Look for it where you know there are many fishermen and at rocky points near heavily populated areas. Carry a diver's knife; if you become entangled you can cut yourself free.

Surge and Surf

Since the scope of this guide is limited to inland sea and inlets protected from the open ocean, surge and surf are usually not factors to consider at the sites described except when big winds blow across broad stretches.

Marine Life

The color and variety of marine animals living in the Strait of Georgia and Puget Sound are astonishing. I carry an underwater light on every dive in order to see all of that color. The sea is teeming with life, all of it fascinating, and practically none of it dangerous to the diver.

Pacific Northwest waters are unrivaled for colorful invertebrates. Soft corals found in few parts of the world are in several locations in British Columbia – more than 6,000 species of invertebrates have been identified and new species are still being described with regularity, many found by sharp-eyed divers.

In 1997 a sport diver shot a video of a field of "freshwater corals" in Pavilion Lake, British Columbia, gave it to the Underwater Research Laboratory at Simon Fraser University and provoked a serious ongoing investigation. These pyramid-, mound-, and turret-shaped microbialites range in height from $\frac{1}{2}$ inch (1 centimeter) to $9\frac{3}{4}$ feet (3 meters). It is estimated they grow at the rate of 1 to 10 inches ($2\frac{1}{2}$ to $25\frac{1}{2}$ centimeters) per 1,000 years and that the tallest ones in Pavilion Lake began growing 11,000 years ago.

At the time of writing a full collection of the various microbialite shapes can be seen within sport diving depths. Divers may photograph but not touch these fragile structures: each one is a "beehive-like city" for tiny bacteria, the minuscule unicellular microorganisms, too small to see, that built them and live in them. The structures are delicate like cloud sponges but take much longer to grow. So . . .

Exquisite buoyancy control and correct

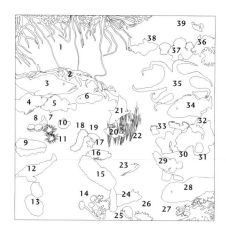

WHAT TO LOOK FOR

ROCK REEF
1. Bull kelp
2. Bottom kelp
3. Lingcod
4. Kelp greenling
5. Black rockfish
6. Cabezon
7. Swimming scallops
8. Abalones
9. Rock scallop
10. Red Irish lord
11. Giant urchins
12. Painted greenling
13. Chitons

SAND
14. Plume worms
15. Sea pen
16. Dungeness crab
17. Leather star
18. Sea cucumber
19. Striped seaperch
20. Seaperch
21. Dogfish
22. Eelgrass
23. Flounder
24. Orange peel nudibranch
25. Moon snail
26. Alabaster nudibranch

ROCK WALL
27. Basket star
28. Wolf-eel
29. Chimney sponge
30. Grunt sculpin
31. Giant barnacles
32. Sailfin sculpin
33. Dahlia anemones
34. Copper rockfish
35. Octopus
36. Sunflower stars
37. Plumose anemones
38. Ratfish
39. Sea peaches

weighting are required to dive this site. The latter is different in fresh water than in salt water; when calculating bottom time consider altitude. No additional information on the site is in this volume as it is not within the scope of the book. I include this mention because of the significant scientific work being done that was made possible by an alert sport diver – keep your eyes open. You might make the next discovery.

I have not dived this site yet and want to! I repeat: we must dive with extreme care and retain our welcome at this site that could relate us to outer space.

In 2004 the National Aeronautics and Space Administration and the University of British Columbia (NASA–UBC) began a joint study at Pavilion Lake. It is hoped these studies will lead to a greater understanding of early life on the earth and possibly Mars.

For more information see page 21; also http://supercritical.civil.ubc.ca/~pavilion. Go to Information, select Lake Protection; then click on Management Direction Statement, select Pavilion Lake and go to page 10 to learn where the Natural Environment Zone in Pavilion Lake is – where recreational diving is permitted. No diving in the Special Features Zone. In the water and on shore take care: the Ts'kway'laxw Band recognizes Pavilion Lake as their traditional territory. They are stewards of the land, air and water.

But back to earth and salt water. The greatest number of sea stars found in any one area of the world is here. Probably 400 species of fish live in the region. Not only are animals abundant but seaweeds are as well; nearly 650 kinds have been recorded in the Pacific Northwest.

At shallow sandy sites you will probably find large Dungeness crabs revealed only by a pair of eyes and a slight indentation in the bottom. Moon snails that look like something from another planet. And sometimes the bottom itself takes off like

a flying carpet – starry flounders in flight!

When diving deep look for yelloweye rockfish beneath ledges. You might find prawns – especially at night, or discover ancient ghostly clumps of cloud sponges with a small rockfish peeping from each tuberous appendage. No one knows how to gauge for sure, but some say a clump as tall as a man must be hundreds of years old.

At rocky reefs you will find red Irish lords, kelp greenlings skittering away spookily into crevices, tiny grunt sculpins looking like precisely painted tropical fish. Lingcod that sometimes grow to 30 or 40 pounds (14 or 18 kilograms) – and more – in the rocky current-swept depths. Or you might meet a 2,000-pound (900-kilogram) Steller sea lion. Large marine mammals abound: from Pacific white-sided dolphins to harbor seals, California sea lions and killer whales. Gorgeous giant red nudibranchs, delicate as tissue paper, waft through the water near newly laid eggs cascading over rocky cliffs like an intricate lace shawl. Also many small nudibranchs live in these waters.

And the Pacific Northwest is home to some of the world's largest octopuses. For many years octopuses had the reputation of being dangerous to divers, but this is a myth. The octopus can be handled quite easily. If one grabs onto you, simply tickle it and it will release you and slip away. And if you must touch one, be gentle. Octopuses are fragile and easily damaged as well as being much more frightened of you than you are of them.

What animals *are* potentially dangerous in Pacific Northwest waters? The following creatures are sometimes considered dangerous, or simply bothersome, by divers.
• Dogfish – Dogfish are not known to attack people, but most divers leave the water when they circle in a pack.
• Jellies – More of a nuisance than a hazard, the lion's mane, brown, yellow and water jellies can leave a painful sting. If you have seen any jellies, you and your

buddy should check one another for stinging tentacles before removing masks and gloves. Even after removing gear be cautious as the stingers stay active on your gear for hours. I have been told that urine is an antidote, and also that canned milk neutralizes the sting. Jellies are seasonal and usually appear in fall and early winter.

- Killer whales – Killer whales or orcas are not known to attack people, but most divers leave the water when killer whales appear. Again, some divers try to meet them under water. Viewing Guidelines for appropriate behavior around killer whales are available at www.pac.dfo-mpo.gc.ca, click on Marine Mammals, select Viewing Guidelines.
- Lingcod – Though not generally considered dangerous, the lingcod has a formidable set of teeth and has been known to attack divers. Males may be aggressive when guarding eggs during winter.
- Ratfish – The ratfish has a poisonous spine just in front of its dorsal fin. Avoid this spine. Once a ratfish bit my leg on a night dive. The only attack I have heard of yet, but beware.
- Sea urchins – Urchins have sharp spines and can cause nasty puncture wounds as well as damage dry suits. A couple of antidotes I have heard of are urine and meat tenderizer.
- Sea lions and harbor seals – These animals are sometimes sought, sometimes avoided. One diver told me he saw a seal dislodge a diver's mask in play, and cause the diver to panic. Another told me of a friend whose daily dive companion is a harbor seal.

Sea lions may approach divers and some divers have reported injuries. Yet I include a write-up in *151 Dives* with guidelines for a winter dive with Steller sea lions for those who choose it. Even in winter, do not dive close to haulouts, do not touch sea lions. And if you meet a bull in summer, watch out. It will be aggressive. Viewing Guidelines for behavior around harbor seals and sea lions are available at www.pac.dfo-mpo.gc.ca, click on Marine Mammals, select Viewing Guidelines.

- Sixgill sharks – Sixgills have not harmed people to date, but have been noted to be more aggressive at dawn and dusk. They are meat eaters and they have very large mouths with exceedingly sharp teeth. In spite of their sluggish appearance they can react with startling speed when annoyed. It is safer not to touch. Yet, again, I include a write-up in this volume with guidelines for a summer dive with sixgill sharks.
- Wolf-eels – The wolf-eel with its very strong teeth and jaws could inflict a bad bite. These fish are not known to attack without provocation, and if you shine a light into dark holes and beneath ledges to look before sticking your hand in, you will probably never tangle with one. Be wary but not dismayed if a wolf-eel lunges out of a cave at you. Many divers hand-feed wolf-eels causing them to approach divers looking for handouts.

Public Access

"You can't drive 20 minutes without reaching water in Washington" one dive buddy says. Access is limited only by our imagination. I hope readers of this guidebook will use it as a starting point, learn to use reference materials and then throw the guidebook away.

Find your own sites: use everything you can to find public access to the water. Look for parks on maps. Find launch ramps on the web; study nautical charts for nearby drop-offs and reefs: then use an inflatable or dive-kayak to go there. No limits!

However, be aware that in Washington State you cannot always land on the beach or even in shallow water. Privately owned property often extends below mean tide level to the extreme low-water mark. In addition, go carefully and honor wildlife reserves.

In Washington State, whenever you see this official public access logo on a sign you may walk to the water.

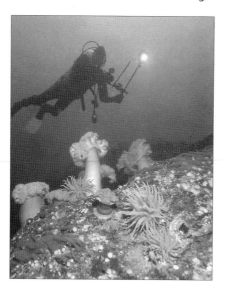

Photographing plumose topped rock

Diver Traffic

Divers have become part of the marine life scene. Diving etiquette on shore as well as under water is more and more important. We need to be considerate when parking, be discreet when changing, take care not to trespass when entering and exiting the water, and go quietly. When night diving, avoid shining lights into the windows of private homes and save wild parties for the wilds – enjoy quiet après-dive parties at beaches in the city.

And what about the affect of divers on the sea, the fish? Diver damage from dropping anchors on reefs and wrecks, kicking fragile cloud sponges, dragging equipment consoles on the bottom, snagging and breaking hydrocoral – it happens. Divers can wreak havoc on the marine environment without even being aware of it. Yet if we dive carefully we can look forward to returning again and again to pristine sites.

Also, I believe we should look, not touch, and leave the sea and fish as we find them. I do not believe in feeding fish or any wildlife, as it alters their natural behavior. They become too trusting.

Feeding a wolf-eel could result in the death of the animal. A friendly wolf-eel might lunge from its den looking for handouts, frighten a visiting diver and be killed.

When diving, we are favored guests in a special place, let's just go for a visit.

Dive Flag Regulations

In British Columbia:
- Shore divers: when diving, fly your red-and-white diver-down flag from a float. It is required under the *Canada Shipping Act.* This diver-down flag is recognized throughout North America as marking an area where scuba diving is in progress.
- Boat divers: the federal Collision Regulations require all vessels engaged in diving operations to fly the blue-and-white international Code Flag "A" from the boat, and fly the red-and-white diver-down flag from a float on the water. Refer to www.boatingsafety.gc.ca.

In Washington State:
- Shore divers: when diving, fly your red-and-white diver-down flag from a float. It is required by law in some counties and unless you know the regulations where you are, it is simpler always to fly it. This diver-down flag is recognized throughout North America as marking an area where scuba diving is in progress.
- Boat divers: fly your blue-and-white international Code Flag "A"or Alpha flag on all dives. The Alpha flag is required under the federal Regulations for the Prevention of Collisions, also referred to by the short titles "The Collision Regulations", or "COL REGS" – or as "The Rules of the Road". The Alpha flag is a navigational signal indicating the vessel's restricted maneuverability and does not pertain to the diver. In addition, therefore, also fly your red-and-white diver-down flag from a float. Refer to www.uscgboating.org.

Underwater Photography

What's different about underwater photography in the Pacific Northwest sea? Winter is the season for it as visibility is then at its best. Artificial light is usually required, as available light is almost always insufficient to produce good photographs. Endless subjects are at hand, particularly to photographers interested in close-up work, as there are so many colorful invertebrates in these waters. Even after years of photography, an enthusiast may find new subjects on every dive.

Marine Life Conservation

In the Pacific Northwest you will be "one of the crowd" if you do not collect marine life at popular sites and if you dive carefully to avoid damaging fragile marine life. I believe there is no longer a place to take marine life at any dive site described in any diving guidebook – and that goes for this one. If each diver takes even one empty shell we will eventually destroy what we love.

In 1970 in Washington State, Edmonds became the first underwater park on the west coast. In 1993, Washington State Senate Bill 5332 was passed committing the state "…to conserve and protect unique marine resources of the state of Washington". It was an excellent legal precedent.

In British Columbia, divers have pressed for conservation since 1976. Many sectors of the non-diving population have found imaginative ways to express their concern: I believe the first was in the early 1970s at Maple Bay on Vancouver Island where, I was told, a non-diving little old lady waved her umbrella at divers who came onto the dock with fish in their goodie bags, and she was supported by the municipality of North Cowichan. In the late 1970s wooden signs were planted by divers at Whytecliff Park declaring it a federal reserve; some individual federal fisheries personnel checking boaters for their catch also voluntarily checked divers for theirs. In the 1980s charter boat operators joined the bandwagon: most, if not all of them, now voluntarily forbid spearfishing and taking of marine life by their guests. Individuals have noticed the need for conservation – yes! But have governments?

It's going global. The United Nations definition of a marine protected area is "…any area of intertidal or subtidal terrain, together with its overlaying water and associated flora, fauna, historical and cultural features, which has been reserved by law or other effective means to protect part or all of the enclosed environment".

On May 4, 1971, British Columbia became the first province in Canada to give permanent protected status to ecological reserves by a legal Order-in-Council and in 1971 twenty-nine land-based reserves were established. In 1975 two were established to protect marine life: one unsuitable for diving; the other, at Ten Mile Point, a dive described in this guidebook. In 1980 Race Rocks, also in this book, was established as an ecological reserve and as such has been a no-take zone for a quarter of a century. In 2005 it is the first dive site that has been noted by the Canadian federal government as a Candidate Marine Protected Area within the federal Oceans project.

The U.S. federal government too is planning Marine Protected Areas. Their official definition of marine protected areas expressed in U.S. Executive Order 12158 speaks to me: it states that a marine protected area is "…any area of the marine environment that has been reserved by federal, state, territorial, tribal or local laws or regulations to provide lasting protection to part or all of the natural or cultural resources therein". At present there is not one Marine Protected Area that I know about – they are all Marine Managed Areas (MMAs).

Definitions, definitions, talk talk talk talk talk – but where is the action?

The best marine conservation website I have found uses ordinary language I can understand and the site contains details of marine life to be careful of and where it is. The information has been collected and presented by a volunteer group of citizens who care: the San Juan County Marine Resources Committee. Visit their Marine Stewardship Area Map Workbook: www.sjmrc.org/programs/stewardship_MPAs.htm. Details are on color-coded maps.

Urge your government agencies at all levels to take a look – nudge governments to make the next, very important, absolutely necessary step that only governments can make: protection must become legal and permanent.

Bottle, China and Junk Collecting

"I'm diving for history!" That's the exuberant way one diver describes his passionate pursuit of everyday relics of the past: bottles, cups and saucers, foot warmers, mining artifacts. Try it. Diving for bottles opens a whole new world on land, stirs you to learn about pioneer days on Pacific shores, appeals to divers who like to explore, and it could become lucrative. I love to explore but was still slow to catch onto the fun of diving for junk. I also soul-searched and wondered if bottle collecting is an unacceptable inclusion in a guidebook as I now believe collecting marine life to be. Are we destroying our heritage by taking old bottles buried in the muck?

I think not. No one would ever have seen the bottles I found if I had not gone down to look: those bottles could not have been photographed on the ocean floor, they were buried in silt. Items tossed overboard are not protected and are fair game. The only bottles and china you should not take are those within the vicinity of a shipwreck as they could be part of the wreck.

Having thought about it hard, I happily allowed myself to become hooked. To really get into "diving for dishes", you can take each step dedicated artifact divers do:
1. In the library: look at old maps, charts and photos, and read regional histories to locate former passenger-steamer wharves, logging camps and settlements. Learn where the Mosquito Fleet and Union Steamships called in.
2. At the site before diving: go to local museums, coffee shops, art galleries, libraries. Talk with people, look for old photographs of terrain and buildings. Before diving, make a plan in the event you and your buddy are separated. You are almost on your own when diving for junk because of so much silt.
3. In the water: take a light. Dive on the ebb, if possible, on days with an extreme tidal exchange. Usually best because the tide carries away silt that you kick up. At deeper sites that slope off rapidly on the chart, start deep and work your way up. At shallow sites, dive in a small area and gradually enlarge it. Fan the bottom gently to stir up silt and reveal hidden relics. Or, if digging, wear gloves to protect yourself from broken glass. Scan the tops of mounds. Look for barnacles and geometric shapes, the most obvious sign of china and bottles.

Archaeological Diving

Ancient relics and fossils are hidden beneath the seas. In 1992 a barbed harpoon point made of antler bone was found at Galiano Island, probably crafted 6,800 years ago.

Middens, petroglyphs and artifacts that were once on the surface of the earth are beneath the water today because sea level has risen as a result of the warm interglacial climactic period we are in now.

If you make a find, the most important thing to do is leave it where it is and contact the appropriate agency. If you discover any old or new underwater shipwrecks, wrecked aircraft, artifacts or underwater fossils that are not well known, avoid any disturbance of the site, note the location and report your finds to the following agencies:

History weaves into the present: one bottle diver's memorabilia includes an old British Columbia Coastal Steamships photograph, an original Union Steamships Limited stock certificate and, on the certificate, a medallion made of the china logo from a Union steamship plate he found. The logo was probably from the 1920s to 1940s.

1. In British Columbia
   Archaeology and Registry Services
      Branch
   Ministry of Sustainable Resource Mgmt.
   PO Box 9375
   Station Provincial Government
   Victoria BC V8W 9M5
   (250)952-5021
   www.gov.bc.ca/arch/
   They are interested in any old wrecks with possible heritage value found in British Columbia that are not well known.

   Director
   Royal British Columbia Museum
   675 Belleville Street
   Victoria BC V8W 9W2
   (250)356-7226
   1-888-447-7977: Toll-free throughout
      North America
   www.royalbcmuseum.bc.ca
   They are interested in all underwater fossils.
2. In Washington State
   State Historic Preservation Officer
   Department of Archaeology & Historic
      Preservation
   Mailing address: PO Box 8343
   Olympia WA 98504-8343

(360)586-3065
www.oahp.wa.gov
They are interested in any underwater fossils, relics, shipwrecks and submerged aircraft with possible heritage value found in Washington State. A permit may be required from this office and from the Department of Natural Resources (DNR).

Wreck Diving

If you've ever discovered a wreck, you know what "wreck fever" means. Our group found the steamship *Ravalli* wreck in Lowe Inlet off Grenville Channel in 1976: intact compacted salmon can wrappers from 1918 were near it. The paper still had color and you could read the fine print. More than 2,000 wrecks in 200 years are known to have sunk off British Columbia.

Formal training in wreck diving is available through certifying bodies. Divers also might want to become a member of the Underwater Archaeological Society
   of British Columbia (UASBC)
c/o Vancouver Maritime Museum
1905 Ogden Avenue
Vancouver BC V6J 1A3
www.uasbc.com

In British Columbia report finds to:
Fisheries and Oceans, Receiver of Wreck
401 Burrard Street, Suite 200
Vancouver BC V6C 3S4
(604)775-8867
www.ccg-gcc.gc.ca/nwp-pen/receivers/
ReceiverOfWrecks-htm.
*(Salvage laws in Canada require you to
report the find of any wrecks of ships or aircraft that are not well known. Ask for the
pamphlet* A Guide to Reporting Wreck.*)*

In Washington State report finds to:
Commander
13th Coast Guard District (oan)
US Coast Guard, 915 Second Avenue
Seattle WA 98174, (206)220-7237
d13lnm@Pacnorwest.uscg.mil
*(Salvage laws in the USA require that you
report the find of any shipwreck or wrecked
aircraft that is not well known.)*

Artificial Reefs

Preparing artificial reefs for diving provides
a new specialty for many recreational divers.

Edmonds Underwater Park in Washington unleashed the creative fancy of a
myriad divers since its creation in 1970.
The concrete-block-and-steel dinosaur at
Edmonds is a far cry from early days when
most artificial reefs were made of old tires.

In British Columbia, sinking of the *G.B.
Church* followed by five more naval vessels,
then a Boeing 737, demanded imagination,
research and dedication of another sort.
Before sinking, the vessels and aircraft
were made environmentally safe by removing insulation and hydrocarbons; made
safe for diving by removing entanglement
hazards and providing openings for light,
entry and exit.Stringent standards set by
Environment Canada are followed and
these standards have been adopted as the
benchmark for artificial reefs in
many other countries.

All artificial reefs are described
in *151 Dives* except the Boeing 737,
scuttled after this volume went into
production. To learm more about
artificial reefs and possibly helping
to prepare future ones, contact:
The Artificial Reef Society
    of British Columbia
c/o Vancouver Maritime Museum
1905 Ogden Avenue
Vancouver BC V6J 1A3
www.artificialreef.bc.ca

Special Interest Association

Pacific Northwest Scuba Challenge
    Association
14286 - 72nd Avenue
Surrey BC V3W 2R1
(604)591-9042
*(This association makes diving
accessible to handicapped persons.
It offers scuba instruction and spon-
sors dives. Membership is open to
able-bodied divers – ABs – as well as
to divers with disabilities.)*

*Chaudière Artificial Reef,
ten years after sinking*

Night Diving

If you've been disappointed in the marine life in an area, or by the diving in any way, or if you're looking for an extra thrill – a new dimension – then try a night dive. Bioluminescence is present in some animals year-round. In autumn, you'll see underwater fireworks.

Nothing else can match it for me. Many more animals come out at night. Some, like prawns, come up shallower and can be seen more easily then. The old, familiar life takes on a new look. The eyes of ratfish glow like sapphires. When you switch off your light the smallest crab glows in the magical biolu-minescent night sea; orange sea pens shimmer neon green in the dark; and, if lucky, you might see an octopus – fantastic in the night sea – coiling and uncoiling in a sparkle of light.

Specialty courses are offered for night diving. Don't wait – do it now!

Mackenzie Artificial Reef, five years after sinking

Saskatchewan Artificial Reef, day of sinking

19

How to Go

Highways, ferry boats and airplanes converge on Vancouver from all sides.

You can reach Vancouver by road on Trans-Canada Highway 1, Highway 99 or Highway 7. Arriving by road on the mainland, bridges are the key to know where you are.

- Heading north on Highway 99 into Vancouver, know you are almost in the city when you cross Oak Street Bridge.
- Arriving from the Fraser Valley on Trans-Canada Highway (Highway 1), notice when you cross the Port Mann Bridge. If you plan to dive Indian Arm, be alert for the turnoff for some dives immediately across the Port Mann Bridge; for others immediately across Ironworkers Memorial Bridge (Second Narrows Bridge). If diving Howe Sound, continue on Highway 1 to Horseshoe Bay.
- In the heart of the city, Lions Gate Bridge reaches from Stanley Park to North and West Vancouver. You can pick up a provincial road map on your way into town, and it will be easy to find your way around. Use the bridges.

Tourist Information

Tourism BC
- Toll-free throughout North America: 1-800-435-5622
- From all other international locations: (250)387-1642
- In Vancouver: (604)435-5622
www.hellobc.com

Ferry Information

British Columbia Ferry Services (BC Ferries)
- Toll-free throughout North America: 1-888-223-3779
- From all other locations: (250)386-3431
www.bcferries.com
At the time of writing the following information applies – but frequent changes occur; it would be wise to check current requirements on BC Ferries web page before every trip.

Rules Regarding Scuba Tanks on BC Ferries
Persons transporting scuba tanks containing compressed air, full or partially full, are required under Canadian law to declare dangerous goods at the terminal or to a vessel officer. Persons transporting scuba tanks with the valves removed do not need clearance. All pressurized tanks with a UN 3156 sticker, indicating nitrox or mixed gases, are taboo – remove the valve.

Expedite Dangerous Goods clearance at the ferry ticket booth – complete a Dangerous Goods Shipping Document prior to arrival. Obtain it from the web at home or a library: Go to www.bcferries.com: select Travel Planning; click on Carrying Dangerous Goods, then For the General Public. Download Dangerous Goods Shipping Document and complete it: include your name, home address and phone number; Class 2; UN 1002, which indicates compressed air; the number of cylinders you are transporting and quantity in each one: most tanks are 80 cubic feet/2.27 cubic meters.

(To calculate quantity in scuba tanks: 1 cubic foot=0.0283168466 cubic meters.)

Arrive at least 45 minutes prior to intended sailing time. However, it might save you from missing a ferry if you phone the terminal you will travel through and ask when they suggest you should arrive.
1. Tsawwassen: (604)943-9331
2. Horseshoe Bay or Bowen Island: (604)921-7414

Prearranged Dangerous Goods Clearance Requires 48 Hours
Complete a Dangerous Goods Shipping Document as described above and fax it at least 48 hours before intended sailing time to the terminal manager responsible for the terminal of your departure.
1. Tsawwassen: fax (604)943-3028
2. Horseshoe Bay or Bowen Island: fax (604)921-7238

• DIVE SHOPS

VANCOUVER

Deeper Aquatics
1782 Alberni Street
Vancouver BC V6G 1B2
(604)662-3337
1-866-955-3337: Toll-free throughout
    North America
www.deeperaquatics.com
(Recreational dive shop.)

BC Dive and Kayak Adventures
1695 West 4th Avenue
Vancouver BC V6J 1L9
(604)732-1344
1-800-960-0066: Toll-free throughout
    North America
www.bcdive.com
*(Recreational and technical dive shop. Nitrox
and intermediate trimix instruction. Also
nitrox and trimix fills. Day charters.)*

Rowand's Reef Scuba Shop
1512 Duranleau Street, Granville Island
Vancouver BC V6H 3S4
(604)669-3483
www.rowandsreef.com
*(Recreational, nitrox and technical instruction.
Nitrox and trimix fills.)*

The Diving Locker
2745 West 4th Avenue
Vancouver BC V6K 1P9
(604)736-2681
1-800-348-3398: Toll-free throughout
    North America
www.divinglocker.ca
(Recreational and nitrox instruction.)

International Diving Center (IDC)
2572 Arbutus Street
Vancouver BC V6J 3Y2
(604)736-2541
1-866-432-3483: Toll-free in Canada
www.diveidc.com
*(Recreational, nitrox, technical and rebreather
instruction. Supply nitrox, trimix, soda-lime.)*

Blue Zone Diving
#109 - 2040 York Avenue
Vancouver BC V6J 1E7
(604)537-1767
www.bluezonediving.com
*(Recreational and nitrox instruction. Nitrox
fills. Also day charters on Manatee II.)*

Aqua Society (Aqua Soc)
University of British Columbia
6138 SUB Boulevard
Student Union Building
Vancouver BC V6T 2A5
(604)822-3329
www.ams.ubc.ca/clubs/aqua
*(Recreational and nitrox instruction.
Nitrox fills.)*

NORTH VANCOUVER AND SQUAMISH

The Great Pacific Diving Company
1236 Marine Drive, at Pemberton
North Vancouver BC V7P 1T2
(604)986-0302
www.greatpacific.net
*(Recreational and nitrox instruction.
Nitrox fills.)*

Sea to Sky Ocean Sports
37819 Second Avenue, downtown
PO Box 2179
Squamish BC V0N 3G0
(604)892-3366
www.seatoskyoceansports.com
*(Recreational dive shop. Also dive-kayak
rentals.)*

BURNABY, COQUITLAM, NEW WESTMINSTER AND SURREY

Ocean Quest Water Sports
#107 - 3790 Canada Way, at Boundary
Burnaby BC V5G 1G4
(604)436-1157
www.diveoceanquest.com
*(Recreational, nitrox and technical
instruction. Nitrox and trimix fills.)*

Dive & Sea Sports Ltd.
#2 - 825 McBride Boulevard
New Westminster BC V3L 5B5
(604)524-1188
www.diveandsea.com
(Recreational and nitrox instruction.
Supply nitrox and soda-lime.)

The Great Pacific Diving Company
10020 - 152nd Street
Surrey BC V3R 8X8
(604)583-1700
www.greatpacific.net
(Recreational, nitrox and rebreather instruction. Supply nitrox and soda-lime.)

Scubatech 2000
13036 - 98A Avenue
Surrey BC V3T 1C6
(604)219-8847
www.scubatech2000.com
(Private tuition only: technical instruction;
and recreational instruction for disabled
persons.)

Ocean Pro Divers
#2 - 3189 King George Highway
Surrey BC V4P 2B8
(604)538-5608
www.oceanprodivers.com
(Recreational and nitrox instruction.
Supply nitrox.)

• DAY CHARTERS
For Howe Sound
Adventure II
BC Dive and Kayak Adventures
1695 West 4th Avenue
Vancouver BC V6J 1L9
(604)732-1344
1-800-960-0066: Toll-free throughout
    North America
www.bcdive.com
(Out of Sunset Marina, and out of Mosquito
Creek for Indian Arm. Also dive shop.)

Golden Eye
See King Charters
1995 West 42nd Avenue
Vancouver BC V6M 2B2
(604)737-2628
1-877-734-2628: Toll-free throughout
    North America
www.seekingcharters.com
(Out of Granville Island to Howe Sound.)

Manatee II
Blue Zone Diving
#109 - 2040 York Avenue
Vancouver BC V6J 1E7
(604)537-1767
www.bluezonediving.com
(Out of Horseshoe Bay; also dive shop.)

MV *Sea Dragon*
Blue Adventure Scuba Diving Charters
Sewell's Ocean Adventure Center
6409 Bay Street, Horseshoe Bay
West Vancouver BC V7W 3H5
(604)329-3486
www.blueadventure.ca
(For individuals or groups up to 12 divers.)

DAY CHARTERS (CONTINUED)
For Indian Arm
Adventure II
BC Dive and Kayak Adventures
1695 West 4th Avenue
Vancouver BC V6J 1L9
(604)732-1344
1-800-960-0066: Toll-free throughout
  North America
www.bcdive.com
(Out of Mosquito Creek in Vancouver Harbour for Indian Arm; and out of Sunset Marina for Howe Sound. Also dive shop.)

Sarah L
Sarah L Charters
#43 - 1486 Johnson Street
Coquitlam BC V3E 3J9
(604)944-6996; cell (604)999-5510
E-mail: c.neill@shaw.ca
(Out of Ioco for Indian Arm. Wheelchair divers welcome.)

• MULTIPLE-DAY CHARTERS
Golden Eye
See King Charters
1995 West 42nd Avenue
Vancouver BC V6M 2B2
(604)737-2628
1-877-734-2628: Toll-free throughout
  North America
www.seekingcharters.com
(Guided getaway diving trips with land-based accommodation – great for out-of-town divers and local divers. Escape to Victoria, Sidney or Nanaimo on Vancouver Island; the Gulf Islands, Sunshine Coast or Barkley Sound.)

• LIVEABOARD CHARTERS
Nautilus Explorer
Lever Diving
PO Box 97182, Richmond Main Post Office
Richmond BC V6Y 4H4
(604)657-7614
1-888-434-8322: Toll-free throughout
  North America
www.nautilusexplorer.com
(Seven- to fourteen-day charters out of Steveston to Port Hardy and Hakai Pass. Circumnavigate Vancouver Island, dive the Queen Charlottes, Alaska and more. Nitrox and trimix available with advance notice.)

• BOAT RENTALS
Sewell's Ocean Adventure Center Ramp
6409 Bay Street, Horseshoe Bay
West Vancouver BC V7W 3H5
(604)921-3474
www.sewellsmarina.com
(Rental boats with motors for Howe Sound; boat tender required. Wheelchair-accessible restrooms at Lookout Coffee Shop. Telephone beside restrooms in the park. Fee for parking.)

Sea to Sky Ocean Sports
37819 Second Avenue (downtown)
PO Box 2179
Squamish BC V0N 3G0
(604)892-3366
seatoskyoceansports.com
(Dive-kayak rentals; also dive shop.)

Empress Boat Sales and Rentals
7249 Curragh Avenue
Burnaby BC V5J 4W1
(604)433-3985
(Car-top and trailerable boats; also trailers and motor rentals.)

• LAUNCH RAMPS

For Howe Sound and Strait of Georgia

Sewell's Ocean Adventure Center Ramp
6409 Bay Street, Horseshoe Bay
West Vancouver BC V7W 3H5
(604)921-3474
www.sewellsmarina.com
(Launch year-round for a fee: concrete ramp, good at tides greater than 2 feet [⅔ meter]. Wheelchair-accessible restrooms at Lookout Coffee Shop. Telephone beside restrooms in park. Fee for parking.)

Sunset Marina
34 Sunset Beach
West Vancouver BC V7W 2T7
(604)921-7476
www.sunsetmarina.ca
(Launch year-round for a fee: paved ramp, good at all tides. Restrooms and take-out food at marina, telephone at top of ramp.)

Porteau Public Ramp
Porteau Cove Marine Park
(Launch year-round for a fee: concrete ramps, good at all except minus tides. Wheelchair-accessible restrooms beside parking lot – open except in freezing weather. Telephone at entrance to campground; turn right when leaving parking lot and go 150 yards [140 meters]).

Located on Sea to Sky Highway (Highway 99),15 miles (24 kilometers) north of Horseshoe Bay, 12 miles (19 kilometers) south of Squamish.

For Indian Arm

West Cates Park Public Ramp
North Vancouver
(Launch year-round for a fee; asphalt ramps, good at all except extreme low tides. Restrooms at concession stand; no telephone at Cates Park. Two outdoor telephones at Dollar Shopping Centre.)

Located in North Vancouver – 3 miles (5 kilometers) east of Ironworkers Memorial Bridge (Second Narrows Bridge). Follow signs toward Deep Cove on Dollarton Highway to West Cates Park. Enter the park, drive straight to the ramps.

Rocky Point Park Public Ramps
Foot of Moody Street
Port Moody
www.cityofportmoody.com
(Launch year-round for a fee: concrete ramps, good at all tides. Restrooms across park, open April to October. Pay parking space for boaters launching. Telephone next to parking area.)

• COMPRESSOR RENTALS

Fraser Burrard Diving Ltd.
3521 River Road West
Delta BC V4K 3N2
(604)940-9177
www.fbdiving.com
(Compressor rentals.)

All of this Service Information is subject to change.

PORTEAU COVE MARINE PARK

SHORE DIVE

SKILL
All divers

TIDE TABLE
Point Atkinson

WHY GO

Easy-to-find sunken ships for divers with all levels of skill to explore.

The SS *Granthall* is 95 feet (29 meters) long. It was built by the Canadian Pacific Railway in Montreal in 1928, cut into sections and shipped over land: first to Kootenay Lake where it hauled railway barges and carried passengers, then to Great Slave Lake, then to New Westminster. It was sunk at Porteau Cove in 1992. It's shallow and easy to dive.

The *Centennial III* is a steel dredge tender, 33 feet (10 meters) long. It was scuttled at Porteau in 1991. Also for all divers.

The *Sinbad el Marino*, a 48-foot (15-meter) ferroconcrete sailboat, was also scuttled in 1991 along with old tires, pipes, concrete blocks and steel H-beams that form the artificial reef close to the dive entry. The reef extends from the sailboat, which is south of the *Centennial III,* to the "Leaning Tower of Porteau" nearer the entry point. Shallow and easy to dive.

The *Nakaya*, a YMS-Class minesweeper, was active in World War II. The wooden hull is 130 feet (40 meters) long. It was sunk at Porteau in 1985. It's a long swim to it, and often there is surface current. It's deep – for intermediate and expert divers only.

The other artificial reefs in the park are often used for open-water certification dives. All artificial reef features of the park are in a boat-free zone reserved for divers. White boundary buoys rim this protected area: fishing and collecting of marine life are forbidden here – also it's a safe place to practice underwater navigation.

And the marine life? It's becoming richer all the time. Divers have seen as many as six octopuses on one dive in shallower parts of the reef. Galatheid crabs lurk in the shadows of the *Nakaya*.

"Outrageous!" one diver exclaimed, "I saw a 6-foot (2-meter) lingcod in the sailboat. Plumose anemones are everywhere."

But the artificial reefs are what most divers go for.

BOTTOM AND DEPTHS

Silty sand scattered with small rocks slopes gradually to the artificial reefs. The *Granthall, Centennial III* and "Leaning Tower of Porteau" range in depth from 30 to 50 feet (9 to 16 meters). The *Nakaya* rests on the bottom slightly skewed from northeast to southwest with the bow in 90 to 100 feet (27 to 30 meters), the stern in 60 to 70 feet (19 to 21 meters), depending on tide height.

HAZARDS

Silt, visibility, some current and the artificial reefs themselves. Often poor visibility spring and summer because of Squamish River runoff as well as plankton bloom. However it is always worth checking to see if visibility is good. The site is mostly current free except for surface current when swimming to the *Nakaya*: plan your dive to use the current. The wheelhouse of the *Nakaya* has collapsed; do not enter.

TELEPHONE

Porteau Cove Marine Park campground entrance: when going out of the parking space for divers and boaters, turn right and drive 150 yards (140 meters) to it.

FACILITIES

Changehouse for divers across railway tracks near park entry – lit at night. Wheelchair-accessible toilets, cold showers for rinsing gear – year-round.

Beside parking lot, more wheelchair-accessible restrooms, open except when weather is extremely cold. Boat ramp. Waterfront campsites with wheelchair-accessible toilets and hot showers except in freezing weather, picnic tables and fire rings. Advisable to reserve.

Air fills in North Vancouver, Squamish and throughout Greater Vancouver. Dive-kayak rentals in Squamish.

ACCESS

Porteau Cove Marine Park is on Howe Sound beside Highway 99 (Sea to Sky Highway) between Squamish and Horseshoe Bay. Driving to it takes 20 minutes from Squamish, the same from Horseshoe Bay.

At Porteau Cove Marine Park turn toward the water. Cross the railway tracks and park. The dive entry point is near the launch ramp. A map locating artificial reefs is between the boat ramp and concrete steps to the beach. Easier to enter with higher tides. Do not enter down the launch ramp.

The yellow buoys mark the shallower artificial reefs; and a resting buoy with handles marks the *Nakaya*. Snorkel out to the buoy of your choice and go down. Or, if you want the challenge, follow a compass heading from vessel to vessel.

To dive the *Nakaya*: best to swim to it on the flooding tide, dive on slack and drift back with the ebb; allow 20 minutes to reach it. The vessel is easy to find with the resting buoy present, and there is a chain to descend to it. But beware. The decking is wood and has almost completely rotted away. Descending, do not drop into the hull. Do not enter the *Nakaya* at any point as it could collapse on you.

Wheelchair access is at the launch ramp. However, at high tide most wheelchair divers "bum it" down the stairsteps rather than enter at the ramp which can be busy. Disabled divers can obtain permission to paddle a dive-kayak or other small boat from the launch ramp to the resting buoy at the *Nakaya*. Write to British Columbia Parks, Box 220, Brackendale BC V0N 1H0, noting the date, names of persons in the party, telephone number to contact: permission will be telephoned back to you.

To get to Porteau Cove Marine Park
• From Horseshoe Bay go north 15 miles (24 kilometers) on Sea to Sky Highway (Highway 99). When heading downhill and close to the water, you will see a signpost: turn left into the park.
• From Squamish, at the head of Howe Sound, drive 12 miles (19 kilometers) south on Sea to Sky Highway (Highway 99) and turn right into Porteau Cove.

NOTES

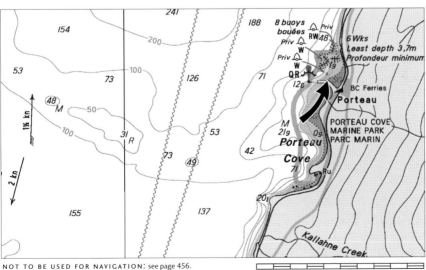

NOT TO BE USED FOR NAVIGATION: see page 456.
Use CHS chart #3526 for navigation; for information on obtaining navigational charts see page 456. Soundings are in meters.

1 NAUTICAL MILE

—PAM ROCKS—

BOAT DIVE
GPS
49°29.237' N
123°17.970' W

SKILL
All divers and snorkelers

TIDE TABLE
Point Atkinson

WHY GO

Pam Rocks flaunts flamboyant displays of oversized life starting with the harbor seals usually lying on the rocks.

Under water much of the life is oversized, too. Three-foot (1-meter) white plumose anemones, tube-dwelling anemones with 8-inch (20-centimeter) purple plumes, big sea peaches and transparent tunicates are all over the place. Orange dead man's finger sponges poke from the kelp-covered rocks in the shallows. You may see a rose star. In spring you'll see lots of nudibranchs. Fish life is not so big, but copper rockfish are abundant. Sometimes you'll see flounders, tiger rockfish, an octopus, lingcod and red Irish lords. Splendid cloud sponges start at 80 to 90 feet (24 to 27 meters). Pam Rocks is a favorite site for underwater photographers in winter.

But the big thrill at Pam Rocks comes when you've been in the water a long while and the seals have forgotten you're there. Sometimes you can come up and be part of their group.

For appropriate diving and boating behavior around seals, see www.pac.dfo-mpo.gc.ca, click on Marine Mammals, select Viewing Guidelines.

BOTTOM AND DEPTHS

On the east side of the marker undulating rocky bottom, clean-swept by the current, ranges from a depth of 20 to 30 feet (6 to 9 meters) to 90 to 100 feet (27 to 30 meters). White sand between the rocks. In some places, deep canyon-like slots between the rocks.

HAZARDS

Current, wind and broken fishing line. Boats and poor visibility in summer because of Squamish River runoff. Dive near the slack. Use your compass, be aware of your direction and watch the

See "devilfish" peaks on head of giant octopus

current. Be particularly careful if you go down into the deep slots because the current can be strong. It is wise to leave a boat tender on the surface. Carry a knife. Listen for boats. If you hear a boat you can stay down until it passes.

TELEPHONES
- On the water: VHF radio; if no VHF, try a cell phone.
- On land: at Porteau Cove Marine Park campground entrance: when going out of the parking space for divers and boaters, turn right and drive 450 feet (137 meters) to it.

FACILITIES
None. Charters out of Horseshoe Bay and Vancouver. Launch ramps at Porteau Cove, Sunset Beach and Horseshoe Bay.

ACCESS
The Pam Rocks site is in Howe Sound just over 1 nautical mile south of Anvil Island and 6½ nautical miles north of Horseshoe Bay where Ramillies and Montagu channels meet. It is 5 nautical miles southwest of Porteau Cove; about the same distance north of Sunset Marina.

Charter or launch your own boat at Sunset Beach or Horseshoe Bay and go north to Pam Rocks; or launch at Porteau Cove and head south to Pam Rocks. On the surface the water can become choppy very quickly at this exposed site. A difficult anchorage. Small boats can anchor southeast of the marker, between the two rocks, in 20 to 30 feet (6 to 9 meters).

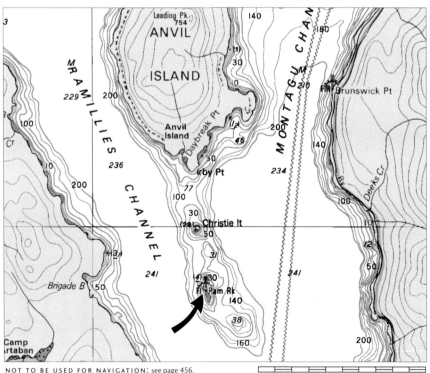

NOT TO BE USED FOR NAVIGATION: see page 456.
Use CHS chart #3512 for navigation; for information on obtaining navigational charts see page 456. Soundings are in meters.

2 NAUTICAL MILES

NOTES

KELVIN GROVE

SHORE DIVE or BOAT DIVE

GPS
49°27.026′ N
123°14.390′ W

SKILL
All divers

TIDE TABLE
Point Atkinson

WHY GO

Octopuses, wolf-eels and red brotulas are resident at this site. That was enough to lure me. Two tanks are not enough.

Tank 1: Purple sea stars. Red slipper cucumbers. Orange sea cucumbers. A juvenile wolf-eel in a crack at 45 feet (14 meters) – it was peach colored. Pink dahlia anemones, tube-dwelling anemones, white plumose anemones. Quillback rockfish. A gray-and-maroon striped convict fish, or painted greenling. Sea lemons, an octopus in a deep indentation at 70 feet (21 meters). Two red brotulas in a crevice. A ratfish. And chimney sponges, sometimes called boot sponges.

Tank 2: Sailfin sculpins. Alabaster nudibranchs. California sea cucumbers. Giant sunflower stars, white with orange spots. White sea cucumbers feathering between the cracks in the rocks. Two orange sea pens in the sand. One of the red brotulas, once again. And I had thought once in my life might never happen. This slim, sinuous brilliant fish is like a shiny red satin ribbon.

If you need more reasons: easy entry; easy to dive. I've been told there are grunt sculpins. And it's a great beach for a picnic.

Red brotula

BOTTOM AND DEPTHS

The bottom slopes gently from the beach. Eelgrass in the bay. Vertical cracks and crevices for creatures to hide in along the rock wall, bottoming out to sand at 110 to 120 feet (34 to 37 meters) at the point. Also a wall to the south.

HAZARDS

Boats; sometimes poor visibility, in summer, because of Squamish River runoff. But worth checking if visibility is good. Listen for boats and ascend along the contours of the bottom all the way to the surface well out of the way of boats.

TELEPHONES

- On the water: VHF radio; if no VHF, try a cell phone.
- Beside the water: Sunset Marina, outside.
- On land: café and grocery store in Lions Bay, outside. Go to Highway 99 and head north. Take the next exit to Lions Bay: follow signs to the café and store.

FACILITIES

Charters out of Horseshoe Bay and Vancouver. Boat rentals at Horseshoe Bay. Launch ramps at Horseshoe Bay and Sunset Beach.

ACCESS

Kelvin Grove is in the village of Lions Bay on Howe Sound. It is off Sea to Sky Highway (Highway 99) between Horseshoe Bay and Squamish: 10 minutes from Horseshoe Bay, 30 minutes from Squamish.

At Lions Bay, turn off Highway 99 toward the water into Kelvin Grove Road, the *southernmost* of two exits to Lions Bay. Various roads go off Kelvin Grove Road: stay far left. Curve down the hill; cross the railway tracks and drop gear beside the path to the water. Return across the tracks and immediately turn right into a large parking lot.

Walking to the dive, do not wear your hood crossing the tracks. Small railway scooter cars race by: with a hood on you cannot hear them. This beach park is signposted "Members Only, Lions Bay Beach Park". Divers who don't live in Lions Bay have been going there for many years with no problem. But if divers do not behave well or if the numbers of divers should overwhelm the beach to the detriment of Lions Bay residents, someone might ask you if you are a resident of Lions Bay or ask you to leave.

Be aware: the beach is not privately owned below high water mark – no beaches in British Columbia are. But the village of Lions Bay *does* own the path of 100 paces and the 16 steps down to it, as well as the restroom in the beach park.

So, if entry through the beach park becomes prohibited, charter out of Horseshoe Bay or Sunset Beach, or rent a boat and go north 5 nautical miles to Kelvin Grove. Land on the beach, gear up and dive. Gentle entry from the cobbled beach with silvered logs on it. Swim out over eelgrass and around to the point on your right.

NOTES

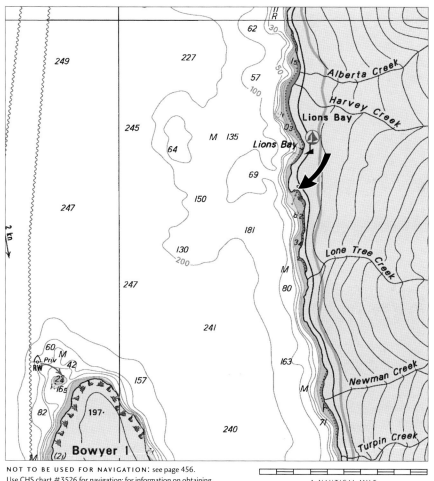

NOT TO BE USED FOR NAVIGATION: see page 456.
Use CHS chart #3526 for navigation; for information on obtaining navigational charts see page 456. Soundings are in meters.

1 NAUTICAL MILE

BOWYER ISLAND

BOAT DIVE

GPS
49°19.529' N
123°07.735' W

SKILL
All divers

TIDE TABLE
Point Atkinson

WHY GO

An easy-to-dive reef with slots and crevices down the wall beneath it where octopuses and wolf-eels hide. Take a light even in the day – it helps when looking for them.

Swimming scallops, sea pens, red dahlia anemones, quillback rockfish, gum boot chitons, tube-dwelling anemones are at this site. We also saw the often-present, ever-glamorous white plumose anemones, a blood star, a giant silver nudibranch and lingcod, too. Lots of chimney sponges starting at 50 feet (15 meters). Cloud sponges starting at 70 feet (21 meters). Feather stars all over the wall.

My buddy and I saw an octopus but no wolf-eel for us that dive. However, other divers that night saw one. If you poke around, there's a good chance to see them.

A rich, safe site for open-water certification dives. Perfect for diving at night. And be sure to turn off your light, touch gently to see the incredible neon-green bioluminscence ripple through the fronds of a sea pen.

BOTTOM AND DEPTHS

A rocky reef is at the southern tip of Bowyer Island. Sandy patches between the rocks. Over the reef edge, a wall drops to however deep you want to go. The chart shows a ledge at 100 feet (30 meters) then plunges to 400 feet (120 meters). We went to 80 feet (24 meters).

HAZARDS

Boats and transparent fishing line. Listen for boats and ascend up the side of the island out of the way of boats, then swim out to your boat. Carry a knife.

TELEPHONES

- On the water: VHF radio; if no VHF, try a cell phone.
- On land: outside Horseshoe Bay ferry terminal.

Sea Dragon tied up at buoy, divers down

FACILITIES

None at Bowyer Island. Charters out of Horseshoe Bay, Fisherman's Cove, Sunset Beach and Greater Vancouver. Boat rentals in Horseshoe Bay. Launch ramps in Horseshoe Bay and Sunset Beach.

ACCESS

Bowyer Island is located in Howe Sound 2½ nautical miles north of Horseshoe Bay and 1 nautical mile northwest of Sunset Beach. Charter or launch at Sunset Beach or Horseshoe Bay and go to Bowyer Island. Usually a buoy is in place: tie up to the top heavy eye on the buoy; if not present, use your GPS and depth finder to locate your anchorage at the southeast tip of Bowyer. If windy, leave a boat tender on the surface. The water can become choppy quickly at Bowyer, but the anchorage is well protected from northern Squamish winds.

NOTES

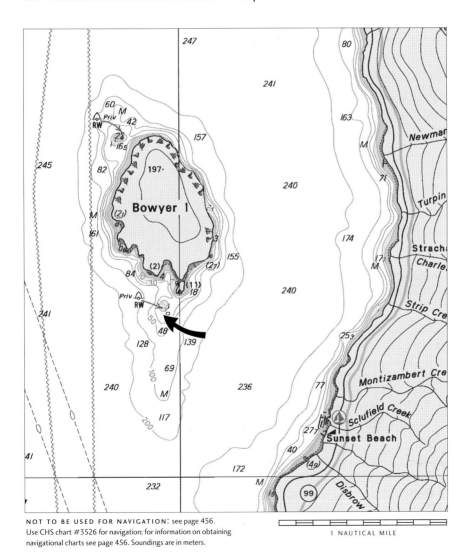

NOT TO BE USED FOR NAVIGATION: see page 456.
Use CHS chart #3526 for navigation; for information on obtaining navigational charts see page 456. Soundings are in meters.

1 NAUTICAL MILE

— ANSELL PLACE —

SHORE DIVE

SKILL
All divers with guide, at
northern wall

Intermediate and expert
divers, at southern wall

TIDE TABLE
Point Atkinson

WHY GO

Two walls. A cave. Critters galore – we saw octopuses in the cracks, a pair of mated wolf-eels, timid, peeking from their den beneath a narrow ledge. Juvenile lingcod and kelp greenlings darting about, spearnosed poachers. Quillback, copper and yellow rockfish. Lots of little scraggly tube worms on the wall. A decorator crab. Anemones: a scattering of pale orange dahlias; bright orange plumose, some white ones. A swimming anemone.

Sea cucumbers on the bottom. Orange sea pens. Red and green sea urchins. Both walls are dotted with small cloud sponges. At the base of the deep wall, we saw small boot or chimney sponges at 100 feet (30 meters). One wall section on each side is stark and dark, except for clusters of orange sea peaches. We saw feather stars, shallow and deep. A comb jelly with delicate electrodes pulsing through open water. A cushion star on the wall. A five-rayed white star. Brittle stars in the shallows.

Ansell Place is a wilderness, vital with new-feeling life. Mature life: my buddy saw a lingcod nearly 3 feet (1 meter) long. Unusual life: red brotulas are seen here. It's a two-tank site – no way you can enjoy the whole scene in one dive, especially if you want to reach the cave.

BOTTOM AND DEPTHS

The northern wall bottoms out to sand at 30 to 40 feet (9 to 12 meters), deepens gradually to 80 to 90 feet (24 to 27 meters), depending on tide height. There is a break in the wall, and then a large rock at 50 to 60 feet (15 to 18 meters). Look for an octopus in a crack before you turn around.

If diving both sides, cut across open water to the southern wall which starts at 30 to 40 feet (9 to 12 meters), deepens to 120 to 130 feet (37 to 40 meters), again, bottoming out to sand. This wall is undercut at places. And then the cave. It is 25 feet (8 meters) wide, 10 feet

(3 meters) high; and goes back 15 feet (4½ meters). A school of rockfish in it.

HAZARDS

Waves from ferries; depth; boats and fishing lines; long walk to the site. Gear up and, if no ferry waves, enter quickly. Carry a knife for fishing line. Throughout your dive, be aware of depth at all times. Ascending, listen for ferries and boats; look up for boats; and hug the bottom all the way to shore.

TELEPHONE

Top of Sunset Marina ramp: go ½ mile (¾ kilometer) north on Highway 99 to the marina turnoff and head downhill.

FACILITIES

None. Toilets at Sunset Marina, go north on Highway 99 to the turnoff.

ACCESS

Ansell Place is on Howe Sound in West Vancouver. It is off Sea to Sky Highway (Highway 99) and 5 minutes north of Horseshoe Bay. Plan to dive at high tide when entry is easier.

Go to Citrus Wynd: turn left and curve downhill and through the tunnel beneath the railway tracks. Turn right. Park at the turnaround at the end of the road. Space for six to eight cars. The water is far below; this access is not for the faint-hearted. Go down 64 wooden steps with handrails. Climb down rock steps; then cross tidal rocks to the water. From here, entry is easy as it deepens quickly.

To reach Citrus Wynd
• Heading north, when 2⅓ miles (3¾ kilometers) north of Horseshoe Bay, exit at Ansell Place, turn left across a bridge toward the water; then turn left along Ansell Place.
• Heading south, when ½ mile (¾ kilometer) past the turnoff to Sunset Marina, exit at Ansell Place and turn left.

Swimming anemone

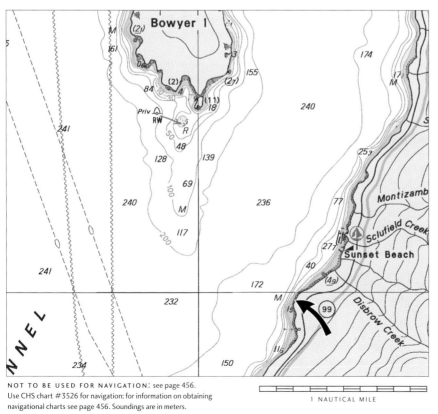

NOT TO BE USED FOR NAVIGATION: see page 456.
Use CHS chart #3526 for navigation; for information on obtaining
navigational charts see page 456. Soundings are in meters.

1 NAUTICAL MILE

NOTES

— MANNION BAY [DEEP BAY]

SHORE DIVE

SKILL
All divers and snorkelers

TIDE TABLE
Point Atkinson

WHY GO

Bottles new and old – thousands of them. Plus frequent sightings of the small Pacific red octopus, *octopus rubescens,* which often live in the bottles. The dive is shallow, with easy entry and a short swim.

During one 60-minute exploratory dive my buddy and I found seven bottles that were "keepers" – at least they were keepers for a beginner like me. We had just reached a rich source – heaps of bottles – when it was time to come up. We discovered an embossed bottle from the Silver Springs Brewing Company, Victoria. It was probably produced between 1908 and 1913. We found another bottle with Black Bear Brand on it, two blue bottles with air bubbles in the glass, a dark amber one, a ginger ale bottle, vintage 1940s or '50s, and a dark green tapered one with an applied lip probably created in the early 1900s.

Before the dive I pored over history books for clues about where to go and what we might find. In 1889 a brick works was at the property we dived in front of. A year later Joseph Mannion built his

Bottles found at Mannion Bay

home there. It was bought by Terminal Steamship Lines in 1900 to be a hotel. In 1920 the Union Steamship Lines added cottages and a lodge. People used to row out from the cottages and dump their garbage. When you find a treasure-trove of bottles, you have probably happened onto the old resort dump.

Fascinating stuff. We did not find old dock pilings nor any Terminal or Union Steamship china at Mannion Bay – not yet. But the potential is

there. It is all around Bowen Island, as well as up the coast of British Columbia.

The old hotel and hotel float located on Mannion Bay [Deep Bay] are in the "Happy Isle" Historic Walking Tour brochure about Crippen Park. This brochure is provided by the Greater Vancouver Regional District (GVRD) parks department with the cooperation of the Bowen Island Historians. The dive is not in Crippen Park and, of course, the brochure does not mark the dive. But you can figure out where to look for bottles from the map in the brochure showing historic locations.

Old maps, historic photographs, history books and tourist brochures all provide clues – they're everywhere. This diving for history could become a wonderful obsession!

BOTTOM AND DEPTHS

Silty bottle-covered sand that slopes very gently to a depth of 45 to 60 feet (14 to 18 meters). We came across one slight mound on the bottom.

HAZARDS

Silt, small boats and water-skiers in summer. Weight yourself adequately so you can hover above the bottom. Listen for boats; if you hear a boat, stay down until it passes. Allow time for a water-skier to pass as well.

TELEPHONES

• At Miller Road and Bowen Island Trunk Road, northwest corner.
• One block west of Snug Cove ferry landing, south side of road.

FACILITIES

None at Mannion Bay; even roadside parking is very limited. At Snug Cove, restrooms in the ferry terminal on the south side of road. No camping and no hotels on Bowen – Union Steamship Lines closed theirs in 1957. But some bed and breakfast accommodations and cabins.

ACCESS

Mannion Bay, formerly Deep Bay, is on the east side of Bowen Island. It is the first bay north of Snug Cove ferry landing. Travel 20 minutes by ferry from Horseshoe Bay to Bowen; then drive 1 ½ miles (2 ½ kilometers) from Snug Cove to the dive. Safer to dive in winter when fewer boats are moving in Mannion Bay.

From Snug Cove ferry landing on Bowen, go ¾ mile (1 ¼ kilometers). Turn right at Miller Road and go ½ mile (¾ kilometer) to Melior Road. Turn right into Melior, and right again following Melior to a "T" junction at Senator Road. Turn left. Then right at the next road – it's steep. Drop your gear beside the water; return uphill and park at the roadside. Scramble over a few logs on the beach to the water.

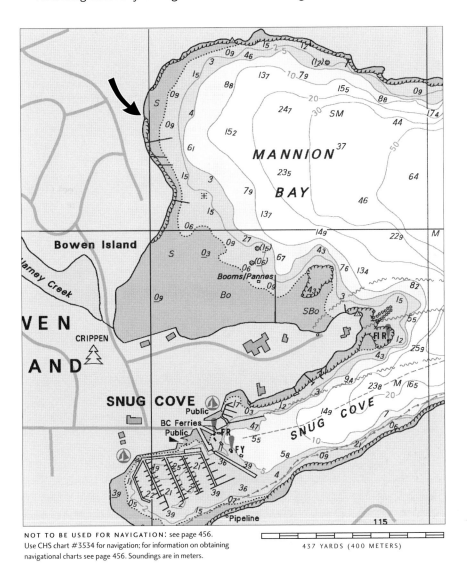

NOTES

NOT TO BE USED FOR NAVIGATION: see page 456.
Use CHS chart #3534 for navigation; for information on obtaining navigational charts see page 456. Soundings are in meters.

437 YARDS (400 METERS)

41

COPPER COVE

SHORE DIVE

SKILL
All divers and snorkelers

TIDE TABLE
Point Atkinson

WHY GO

Copper Cove is especially good for night diving enthusiasts because of the easy entry.

If you're in the mood for a relaxed dive you'll enjoy the shallow rocky shores rimming the cove where you can see a variety of life. Bright orange dead man's finger sponges poke from the bottom kelp. Huge sunflower stars and masses of smaller ones cling to the rocks. Pale orange sea peaches and small brown and beige anemones cluster beneath the overhangs. Brown sea cucumbers, rockfish, barnacles, California sea cucumbers and lingcod live along the rock-rimmed cove.

Night diving over the sand and eelgrass yields a whole new experience. We saw a variety of flatfish: a mottled sand dab, lemon sole and C-O sole; a whiting, a small white curled-up eelpout, a midshipman with golden eyes. And sculpins – a grunt sculpin, sailfin sculpins and a roughback sculpin, a small fish with an intricate dorsal fin that reminded me of a miniature tropical lionfish. Spider crabs, prawns, hermit crabs, shrimp and lots of small ratfish come out on the sand at night.

And in autumn, I love snorkeling back through the shimmering bioluminescent night sea.

BOTTOM AND DEPTHS

Rocks covered with bottom kelp rim the cove bottoming out to smooth white sand at 20 to 30 feet (6 to 9 meters). The sand slopes gradually to whatever depth you might want to go. There are three deep rocky reefs just left to center of the cove, the first at 70 to 80 feet (21 to 24 meters). To find the reefs go to the point on your left and follow the bottom to the right.

Sunday afternoon at Copper Cove

HAZARDS

Wind, and wash from ferries. Poor visibility, in summer, because of Fraser/Squamish rivers runoff. However, the water may be turbid one day and clear the next; worth checking. A "Squamish" wind from the north can blow up the surf making entry and exit difficult. If you heard a ferry pass, when you ascend watch for logs being tossed about in the wash near shore.

TELEPHONE

In Horseshoe Bay, outside ferry terminal. To get there, return to Marine Drive, go east to Nelson Avenue, turn left and head downhill. Nelson Avenue runs into Royal Avenue; turn right to ferry terminal.

FACILITIES

None.

ACCESS

Copper Cove is the first cove west of the Horseshoe Bay ferry terminal.

In Horseshoe Bay, head west on Marine Drive and go through the roundabout: go out at the third roundabout exit and continue west ½ mile (¾ kilometer) to Copper Cove Road. Turn right and go to the end of the road. Parking is limited: unload gear, park, and return to walk down 41 concrete steps to the beach. Dive towards the point on your left.

To get to Marine Drive
• From West Vancouver, Park Royal Shopping Centre (west of Lions Gate Bridge), 20 minutes to the site: go on Highway

1A West/99 North up Taylor Way, then left onto Highway 1 (Upper Levels Highway). Go 7½ miles (12 kilometers) following signs toward Whistler and Squamish. Stay right. Pass the ferry toll booth on your left-hand side, and take the first left across the Overpass Bridge onto Marine Drive North.
• From Horseshoe Bay ferry terminal, take Exit 0 following signs to Horseshoe Bay, Squamish and Whistler. Turn right toward Marine Drive North, and immediately left toward Horseshoe Bay.
• From Squamish, follow Highway 99 south to Horseshoe Bay. The turnoff is signposted: turn right across the Overpass Bridge to Marine Drive in Horseshoe Bay.

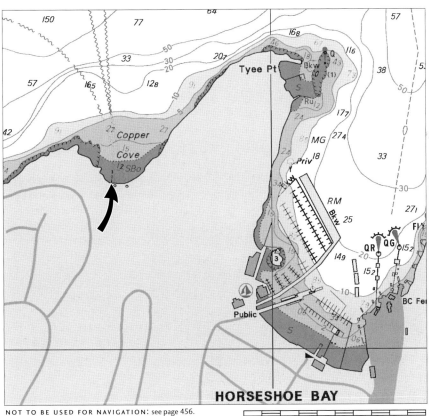

HORSESHOE BAY

NOT TO BE USED FOR NAVIGATION: see page 456.
Use CHS chart #3534 for navigation; for information on obtaining navigational charts see page 456. Soundings are in meters.

437 YARDS (400 METERS)

NOTES

LOOKOUT POINT

SHORE DIVE

SKILL
All divers and snorkelers

TIDE TABLE
Point Atkinson

WHY GO

Lookout Point, the western extreme of Cliff Cove, commonly called Telegraph Cove, is ideal for open-water certification dives, photography, night dives – almost anything you can think of except collecting marine life. It is a no-take zone. Part of Whytecliff Park municipal marine protected area.

So much life around Lookout Point that local divers keep coming back again and again. It's easy to choose your level and dive shallow or deep. When diving here I like to move down quickly to the second ledge at 50 to 60 feet (15 to 18 meters) where lovely clusters of white anemones are piled like mushroom caps on top of the rocks, spilling over into the valleys below. The walls are covered with small, anemone-like zoanthids. Octopuses live in the area. Lingcod, red Irish lords, urchins, rockfish, grunt sculpins, sea pens, ratfish, shrimp, sea peaches, hermit crabs and giant barnacles. Look for dogfish and harbor seals. For viewing guidelines see www.pac.dfo-mpo.gc.ca, click on Marine Mammals.

Once on a night dive at Lookout Point I even saw a vermilion rockfish, a fish more commonly found on the west coast of Vancouver Island. Deeper, you will see cloud sponges and small solitary cup corals.

BOTTOM AND DEPTHS

The point drops in rocky tiers. First a ledge at 30 to 40 feet (9 to 12 meters), another at 50 to 60 feet (15 to 18 meters) and another at 110 to 120 feet (34 to 37 meters). Bottom kelp covers broken rocks down to 30 to 40 feet (9 to 12 meters). Pockets of sand in the ledges.

HAZARDS

Current, broken fishing line, wash from the ferries, and small boats. Poor visibility in summer because of Fraser River runoff. The water may be turbid one day and clear the next; it is always worth checking it out. Visibility is best on a rising tide. Both flooding and ebbing tides can be overpowering. Dive near slack, especially on large tidal exchanges. Carry a knife. When ascending, and especially if you heard a ferry pass, watch for logs being tossed about in the wash near shore. Listen for boats and ascend close along the wall all the way to the surface.

TELEPHONES

- Whytecliff Park, east of the refreshment stand.
- Horseshoe Bay, outside ferry terminal.

FACILITIES

None. Roadside parking very limited. Be considerate of local residents. If parking is full, unload gear beside the path to Cliff Cove and park at the overload lot.

Grunt sculpin, two times life-size

ACCESS

Lookout Point juts into Queen Charlotte Channel west of Horseshoe Bay.

In Horseshoe Bay, head west on Marine Drive and go into the roundabout: go out the third roundabout exit, and continue west on the curvy road to Whytecliff Park. From the park entry, follow the sign toward Overload Parking. Take the upper road on your right; go ⅓ mile (½ kilometer) on Cliff Road. At the confluence of Cliff Road, Arbutus Road and Arbutus Place, look for a small sign on the right-hand side saying "Beach Access". A gravel path follows the telegraph line on your right down to Cliff Cove. It is 100 yards (90 meters) from road to beach; 35 stairsteps make access easy. At the beach you might have to climb over logs to reach the water. Snorkel to the point on your left and descend.

To get to Marine Drive
- From West Vancouver, Park Royal Shopping Centre, 20 minutes to Horseshoe Bay. Go up Taylor Way, then left onto Highway 1 (Upper Levels Highway). Go 7½ miles (12 kilometers) following signs toward Whistler and Squamish. Stay right. Pass the ferry toll booth on your left-hand side, and take the first left across the Overpass Bridge onto Marine Drive North.
- From Horseshoe Bay ferry terminal, take Exit 0 following signs to Horseshoe Bay, Squamish and Whistler. Turn right toward Marine Drive North, and immediately left toward Horseshoe Bay. Continue west on Marine Drive.
- From Squamish, follow Highway 99 south to Horseshoe Bay. The turnoff is signposted: turn right across the Overpass Bridge to Horseshoe Bay.

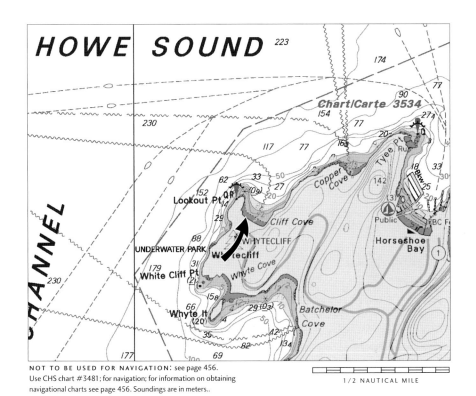

NOT TO BE USED FOR NAVIGATION: see page 456.
Use CHS chart #3481; for navigation; for information on obtaining navigational charts see page 456. Soundings are in meters..

1/2 NAUTICAL MILE

WHYTECLIFF PARK, DAY MARKER

SHORE DIVE

SKILL
Intermediate and expert
divers

All divers with guide

TIDE TABLE
Point Atkinson

*Wall of plumose anemones
past the Day Marker*

WHY GO
Incredible to have this wild and wonderful
seascape right in the city. Even more
unbelievable to expect it will continue to be
with us – forever we hope, because
removal of marine life is forbidden at this
municipal marine protected area.

The reef at the Day Marker is home for
several marine animals so familiar to divers
they're like old friends. Two octopuses are
well known. Almost every time I dive here I
meet one old grandfather lingcod. You'll
see rockfish, red Irish lords, seaperch, sea
pens, urchins, grunt sculpins and sea stars.
Ratfish and sailfin sculpins, at night. Also
on a night dive we saw a small stubby squid
shimmer from blue to green to white like
an opalescent teardrop pendant. Masses
of white plumose anemones cascade down
the sheer rock wall. At 80 feet (24 meters)
fluffy white cloud sponges lure you farther,
lighting up the dark cliff below. And as you
drop into the depths lit with these puffs
of white you think that Whytecliff Park
must have been named by divers.

The most seasoned diver will enjoy the
rocky reef and fantastic drop-off past the
Day Marker in Whytecliff Park.

BOTTOM AND DEPTHS
Rocky reef around the Day Marker, dropping off north of it. The wall plunges to
700 feet (200 meters).

HAZARDS
Depth, current and broken fishing line.
Old cables from boat moorings if you swim
out from the beach. Small boats and poor
visibility, in summer, because of Fraser
River runoff. However, if you dive deep
you can get beneath it. There can be con-
siderable surface current past the Day
Marker and along the wall. On large tidal
exchanges, dive near slack. Carry a knife. If
caught in transparent fishing line you can
cut your way free. Listen for boats and
ascend up the rocks at the marker or along
the wall all the way to the surface, out of
the way of boats.

TELEPHONES
• Whytecliff Park, east of the refreshment
  stand, by paved path to beach.
• Horseshoe Bay, outside ferry terminal.

FACILITIES
Beach, large grassy area, picnic tables, a
playground and restroom near the View
Point at west end of the park. In summer,
a refreshment stand, and just west of it,
a freshwater tap to wash gear.

ACCESS

The Day Marker – and The Cut – at Whyte-cliff Park are on Queen Charlotte Channel, southwest end of Horseshoe Bay.

In Horseshoe Bay, head west on Marine Drive and go into the roundabout: go out the third roundabout exit. Continue west on the curving road for 1 ¾ mile (3 kilometers) to Whytecliff Park. At Whytecliff, drive completely around the park to the refreshment stand where a variety of rock steps and paved paths go to Whyte Cove – at high tide each path is about 100 paces to the water. From the beach, swim out close beside the shore on the right. Go 100 yards (90 meters) to the point and the Day Marker that marks the reef. Continue a short way northwest past the reef to the drop-off.

The Day Marker and The Cut can also still be reached by way of steps and a path down the narrow ravine to The Cut. This entry is at the southwest end of the park and east of the View Point. Pass some picnic tables to the steps where you can climb down to the sea. Then go straight to the Day Marker, or turn right and dive the sheer wall. Since the path can be very slippery when wet, most people are glad now to be able to use one of the easier access points to the beach, followed by a short swim to the wall.

To get to Marine Drive
- From West Vancouver, Park Royal Shopping Centre (west of Lions Gate Bridge), 25 minutes to the site: go on Highway 1A West/99 North up Taylor Way, then left onto Highway 1 (Upper Levels Highway). Go 7½ miles (12 kilometers) following signs toward Whistler and Squamish. Stay right. Pass the ferry toll booth on your left-hand side, and take the first left across the Overpass Bridge onto Marine Drive North.
- From Horseshoe Bay ferry terminal, take Exit 0 following signs to Horseshoe Bay, Squamish and Whistler and almost immediately turn left toward Horseshoe Bay. Continue west on Marine Drive.
- From Squamish, follow Highway 99 south to Horseshoe Bay. The turnoff is signposted: turn right across the Overpass Bridge to Horseshoe Bay.

NOTES

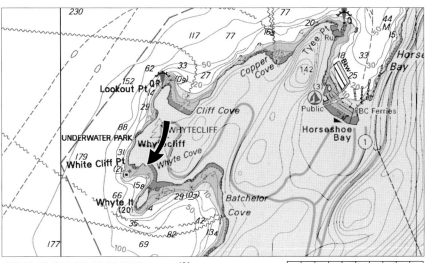

NOT TO BE USED FOR NAVIGATION: see page 456.
Use CHS chart #3481 for navigation; for information on obtaining navigational charts see page 456. Soundings are in meters.

1/2 NAUTICAL MILE

WHYTECLIFF PARK, WHYTE ISLET

SHORE DIVE

SKILL
All divers and snorkelers

TIDE TABLE
Point Atkinson

WHY GO

Whyte Islet is a popular open-water certification site within Whytecliff Park marine protected area where you can easily skin dive to see flounders and crabs, or enjoy a shallow dive. But resist: just look, don't touch – it is a no-take zone.

The smooth rock walls of Whyte Islet provide homes for a variety of marine animals. You'll see lots of little things: calcareous tube worms attached to shallow rocks, sea lemons, leather stars and purple sea stars. Sea cucumbers all over the bottom. You're sure to see orange plumose anemones tilting their ruffled fronds to the current. You might see an octopus. Lingcod often cruise around the islet. Look for dogfish, and on almost every dive, resident seals come buzzing by. I've even seen a feather star at Whyte Islet.

In the event you might see a seal, go to www.pac.dfo-mpo.gc.ca, click on Marine Mammals, select Viewing Guidelines.

BOTTOM AND DEPTHS

A rock groin, which dries on most low tides, leads up to Whyte Islet. Beside the islet a smooth rock wall drops to sand at 10 to 20 feet (3 to 6 meters), sloping gradually to a depth of 50 to 60 feet (15 to 18 meters) at the tip of Whyte Islet.

HAZARDS

Small boats and poor visibility, in spring and summer. Some current. Large cables protruding from the rocks. Wear extra weight, listen for boats and ascend close along the bottom all the way to the surface. Current can be quite strong at the tip of Whyte Islet. If you feel current, stay under water and pull yourself along on the rocks; watch for cables.

TELEPHONE

Whytecliff Park, east of the refreshment stand, beside paved path to beach.

FACILITIES

In summer, a refreshment stand, and just west of it a freshwater tap to wash gear. At the time of writing, changerooms near the rock groin out to Whyte Islet are open mid-May to October.

And you will meet many divers at this popular site.

ACCESS

Whytecliff Park is on Queen Charlotte Channel, west end of Horseshoe Bay.

In Horseshoe Bay, head west on Marine Drive and go into the roundabout: go out at the third roundabout exit. Continue west on Marine Drive and follow signs to Whytecliff Park, 1 ¾ miles (2 ¾ kilometers) on the curving road. At Whytecliff, drive completely around the park to the refreshment stand. Walk down an easily inclined paved path and steps on the left-hand side to the water.

To get to Marine Drive
- From West Vancouver, Park Royal Shopping Centre (west of Lions Gate Bridge), 25 minutes to the site: go on Highway 1A West/99 North up Taylor Way, then left onto Highway 1 (Upper Levels Highway). Go 7½ miles (12 kilometers) following signs toward Whistler and Squamish. Stay right. Pass the ferry toll booth on your left-hand side, and take the first left across the Overpass Bridge onto Marine Drive North.
- From Horseshoe Bay ferry terminal, take Exit 0 following signs to Horseshoe Bay, Squamish and Whistler. Turn right toward Marine Drive North, and immediately left toward Horseshoe Bay. Continue west on Marine Drive.
- From Squamish, follow Highway 99 south to Horseshoe Bay. The turnoff is signposted: turn right across the Overpass Bridge to Horseshoe Bay.

*Whyte Islet on left,
Day Marker around
point on right*

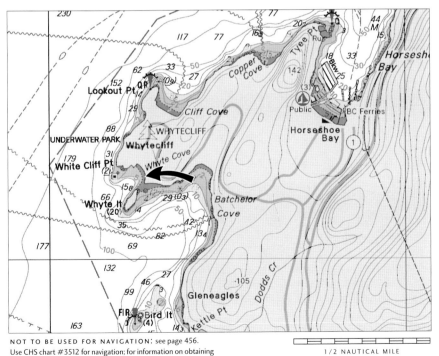

NOT TO BE USED FOR NAVIGATION: see page 456.
Use CHS chart #3512 for navigation; for information on obtaining
navigational charts see page 456. Soundings are in meters.

1/2 NAUTICAL MILE

NOTES

BIRD ISLET

WHY GO

Anemones are the highlight. Huge white plumose anemones cluster on top of the rocks and billow between the crevices and beneath the overhangs. Delicate pink snakelock anemones and calcareous tube worms are on the walls, transparent tube-dwelling anemones in the sand.

Green urchins, nudibranchs, swimming scallops and bright yellow knobby encrusting sponges are more marine animals you might see at Bird Islet. It is in town, but feels like wilderness.

Also look for lead cannonball weights to salvage at this popular fishing site.

BOTTOM AND DEPTHS

The rounded rock of Bird Islet bottoms out to sand at 20 to 30 feet (6 to 9 meters) at the north end. The rock walls are smooth – not much to hold onto. Deeper, south of the islet, the walls are undercut and riddled with slits, caverns and hiding places. The islet is deceptive. An under-water plateau runs southward to the marker. Diving on a low tide, we reached a depth of 70 feet (21 meters).

HAZARDS

Fishing boats, sailboats that are soundless, current and transparent fishing line. Use a compass. Do not ascend in open water. Return to the islet where you can hug the wall all the way to the surface. Dive on or near slack. Carry a knife. If caught in fishing line, you can cut your way free.

TELEPHONES

• On the water: VHF radio; if no VHF, try a cell phone.
• Beside the water: by paved path to beach at Whyte Islet.
• On land: Horseshoe Bay, outside ferry terminal.

FACILITIES

None at Bird Islet. Charters out of Horseshoe Bay in West Vancouver, and Vancouver. Boat rentals in Horseshoe Bay. Launch ramps at Horseshoe Bay. Dive-kayak rentals in Squamish.

ACCESS

Bird Islet is in Queen Charlotte Channel ½ nautical mile south of Whytecliff Park.

From Bird Islet Marker,
looking northeast

Charter, rent a boat and launch at Horseshoe Bay or go by dive-kayak. Boats can anchor at the southwest side of the islet. Dive out and back on the west side at different depths – do not circle the island. The east side is shallow and not as interesting as the west wall.

Bird Islet is an excellent place for a first kayak-dive: at low tides, a narrow cove is at the northeast side of the islet where it is easy to gear up and leave a kayak. At higher tides anchor, climb on the rocks and gear up. A choice of two launch points – both reached by Marine Drive, then paddle 15 to 20 minutes.

Kayak-diver launch points:
• Whytecliff Park is the easiest place to launch because a great deal of parking space is available – even then, go early, especially on weekends. There are both stairsteps and a graduated paved path to the beach (see directions to Whytecliff on page 47).
• Batchelor Cove, at the foot of Dufferin Avenue, is the access with the least distance to carry gear. Sixteen shallow stairsteps go to the beach. At high tide, you're there. At low tide, 36 paces to the water across cobbled beach. The difficulty is that no parking space is available at the end of the road. However, you could drop gear, then park back up the hill. To reach Batchelor Cove, turn left down Dufferin when just past Copper Cove Road and go ⅓ mile (½ kilometer) to the water (see directions to Copper Cove Road on page 43).

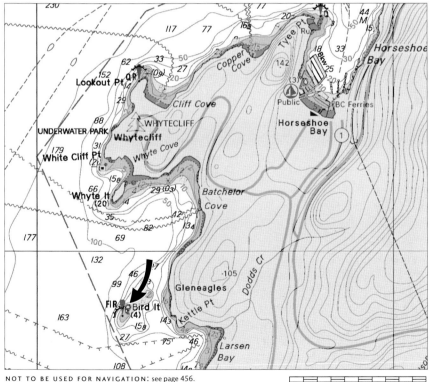

NOT TO BE USED FOR NAVIGATION: see page 456.
Use CHS chart #3481 for navigation; for information on obtaining navigational charts see page 456. Soundings are in meters.

1/2 NAUTICAL MILE

NOTES

PASSAGE ISLAND REEF

BOAT DIVE
GPS
49°20.494' N
123°18.813' W

SKILL
Expert divers

Guided intermediates
with descent line

TIDE TABLE
Point Atkinson

WHY GO

Passage Island Reef is a magnificent underwater mountain for sightseeing.

Rising to within 20 to 30 feet (6 to 9 meters) of the surface, this large mound covered with boulders lies in current-swept Queen Charlotte Channel. All of the water flowing between Bowen Island and West Vancouver pours over this large reef which snags nutrients to feed the fish.

Diving here you drop onto piles of white plumose anemones tumbling one over the other like a gigantic feather bed. I was tempted to lie in it and luxuriate in the fluffy white fronds. Moving down the side of the small seamount we saw lingcod lying on their chins, looking out of dark seams in the rock. Each nook and cranny conceals another large fish or octopus. Transparent sea squirts hang from boulders like clusters of plastic grapes. Sea cucumbers, calcareous tube worms, crevice-dwelling cucumbers, sunflower stars and urchins are on the reef.

At the southern end of the reef, we swam through a field of sea pens into a ghostly garden of tall, slim white sea whips.

BOTTOM AND DEPTHS

The reef rises like a huge mound scattered with boulders. Sloping muddy bottom surrounds the base of the reef at 50 to 60 feet (15 to 18 meters). The top of the reef is always 20 to 30 feet (6 to 9 meters) below the surface.

HAZARDS

Current, small boats and wind. Poor visibility, in summer, because of Fraser River runoff. Dive on the slack, especially on large tidal exchanges. Listen for boats and ascend on your anchor line or the buoy line, if present, well out of the way of small boats. Wind from almost any direction can make anchoring impossible in this very exposed site; if windy take a boat tender. Visibility best in fall and winter, and on an ebbing tide.

TELEPHONES
- On the water: VHF radio; if no VHF, try a cell phone.
- On land: Fishermans Cove, Thunderbird Marina at top of ramp.

FACILITIES
None. Charters out of West Vancouver and

Sea whips twisting from muddy bottom

Vancouver. Launch ramps at West Vancouver, Horseshoe Bay and Sunset Beach. Air fills in North Vancouver, Squamish and throughout Greater Vancouver.

ACCESS

Passage Island Reef is in Queen Charlotte Channel between Point Atkinson and Bowen Island.

Charter out of West Vancouver or Vancouver. Or rent a boat or launch your own boat at Horseshoe Bay and go

4 nautical miles to Passage Island, then to the reef that is ¼ nautical mile west of its southern tip.

To find the reef, look for a buoy that is in place at the time of writing. It is maintained by the Underwater Council of BC. If you do not find it, go out from Passage Island: head south down the west side of it and as soon as you see Point Atkinson lighthouse between Passage Island and the islet at its southern tip, go west. Then use your depth sounder to find the reef.

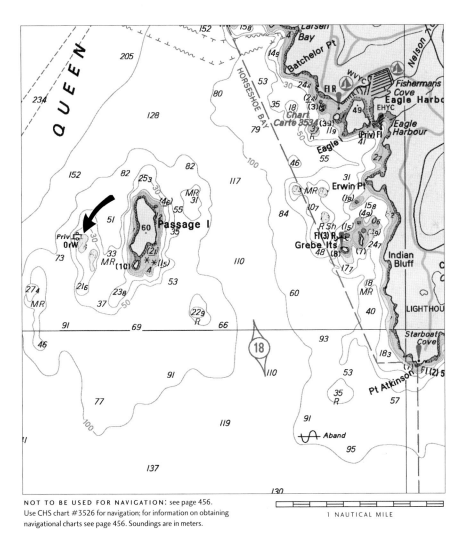

NOTES

NOT TO BE USED FOR NAVIGATION: see page 456.
Use CHS chart #3526 for navigation; for information on obtaining navigational charts see page 456. Soundings are in meters.

1 NAUTICAL MILE

LIGHTHOUSE PARK

**SHORE DIVE or
KAYAK DIVE**

SKILL
Intermediate and expert
divers

CURRENT TABLE
Second Narrows

WHY GO

Lighthouse Park has the wildest underwater seascape and the most fantastic variety of marine life in the Vancouver area.

One dive at Lighthouse Park reveals an incredible amount of life. Large, gray warty cabezons and delicate shimmering kelp greenlings live side-by-side. Orange sea pens burrow in pools of sand between ledges covered with purple and pink sea stars. Schools of black rockfish swim past. Copper rockfish and lingcod live along the wall. We saw a huge octopus hiding under a ledge, little hairy lithode crabs and small bryozoans which look like pale pink Christmas trees. Boulders smothered with orange anemones so thick you can't see the rock. One-inch (2½-centimeter)

slipper cucumbers flame from the wall next to 5-inch (13-centimeter) orange trumpet sponges and giant barnacles. Crevices overflowing with large white plumose anemones slice the dark slope. Cloud sponges start at 65 feet (20 meters). There are green and red urchins, dahlia anemones and red Irish lords at Lighthouse Park.

It's the richest dive in Vancouver. But the people who know it intimately say the marine life is noticeably declining – even here. Please leave your spear guns at home.

BOTTOM AND DEPTHS

Flat sand scattered with rocks and brown bottom kelp gently tiers off, then drops in dramatic ledges with huge boulders poised at the edge. Light silt over all.

HAZARDS

Current, wind and broken fishing line. Small boats; poor visibility, in summer, because of Fraser River runoff; and the dangers of overheating and exhaustion hiking between the parking lot and the site. Dive on slack using current tables for Second Narrows. Even though seemingly illogical, it works. Enter 15 or 20 minutes before the turn of the tide. Do not dive at Lighthouse Park if a strong west wind blows up surf. Carry a knife. Listen for boats and ascend close to the rocks and ledges all the way to the surface.

Divers hiking to the site and kayak-divers should allow plenty of time to reach it for slack. Then rest before heading back, because of the possible danger of bringing on bends by overexertion after diving.

TELEPHONES
• Marine Drive/The Dale Shopping Centre; it is ⅕ mile (⅓ kilometer) east of Marine Drive and Beacon Lane.
• Cypress Park Shopping Centre, 1½ miles (2½ kilometers) east on Marine Drive.

*Point Atkinson
Lighthouse,
Point Grey behind*

FACILITIES

Air fills in North Vancouver. Many private residences around this little cove and no place for a picnic. Good for the dive only. After the dive go to Cates Park or the park at Deep Cove.

ACCESS

White Rock, or Strathcona, is on the *west* side of Indian Arm near Second Narrows. It is in North Vancouver, 4 miles (7 kilometers) east of Second Narrows Bridge off Trans-Canada Highway 1. From Second Narrows Bridge, 15 minutes to the dive.

At Mount Seymour Parkway, go east 3¾ miles (6 kilometers). Turn left onto Deep Cove Road; then right into Strathcona Road, the first road on the right. Go ⅓ mile (½ kilometer) to the water where one car may park by the wharf. Do not

jump off wharf unless it is very high tide, as the beach beneath it dries at low tide. Snorkel 100 yards (90 meters) to White Rock, go down and dive around it.

To get to Mount Seymour Parkway
• On Highway 1 West: heading *north* across Second Narrows Bridge, move to the right-hand lane. Immediately across the bridge, take Exit 23B. Cross the Seymour River and follow signs to Mount Seymour Park. Turn left onto Riverside Drive, then right onto Mount Seymour Parkway.
• On Highway 1 East: from Horseshoe Bay, West Vancouver and North Vancouver, go east on Highway 1 but *do not cross* Second Narrows Bridge. Take Exit 22. Follow signs to Mount Seymour Park and go onto Mount Seymour Parkway.

NOTES

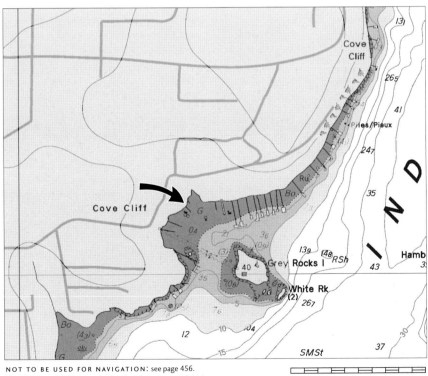

NOT TO BE USED FOR NAVIGATION: see page 456.
Use CHS chart #3495 for navigation; for information on obtaining navigational charts see page 456. Soundings are in meters.

1/5 NAUTICAL MILE

─WOODLANDS─

WHY GO

Woodlands provides opportunity for a deep dive or a shallow dive at one site. As the name suggests, there's a real wilderness feeling both above and below water.

Look for hairy lithode crabs which are not seen everywhere but are quite often present in this part of Indian Arm. Lots of decorator crabs and rockfish on the wall. Flounders on the flat sand. And an unequalled cascade of Johnnie Walker whiskey bottles kept me speculating for months about the kind of parties once held at Woodlands!

Perhaps some old bottles here, too.

Woodlands Wharf

BOTTOM AND DEPTHS

Hard sand, 20 to 30 feet (6 to 9 meters) deep, slopes from the wharf to the island. At the marker and around to the left, a rock wall drops off to a depth of 110 to 120 feet (34 to 37 meters). A cascade of small broken rock and rubble is down it.

HAZARDS

Boats, especially in summer. Lion's mane jellies, in the fall. Poor visibility. Listen for boats and if you hear a boat, stay down until it passes. Extremely important to use a dive flag at this site. Use a compass and ascend close to the bottom all the way to shore. If you have seen any jellies, you and your buddy should check one another for stinging tentacles before removing your masks and gloves. For the best visibility dive on an outgoing tide.

TELEPHONE

Mount Seymour Parkway and Mount Seymour Road, at small shopping center on northeast corner.

FACILITIES

Limited parking space at site.

ACCESS

Woodlands is on the *west* side of Indian Arm in a remote corner of North Vancouver. It is 7 miles (11 kilometers) from the north end of Second Narrows Bridge. From Highway 1 to the dive takes 20 minutes.

At Mount Seymour Parkway in North Vancouver go east 2 miles (3¼ kilometers) to Mount Seymour Road at a traffic light; a shopping mall is on the left-hand side. Turn left toward Mount Seymour Park. Go for ½ mile (¾ kilometer). Just before the park gates, turn right into Indian River Drive. Again go ½ mile (¾ kilometer); at the "Woodlands" sign, turn left up Indian River Crescent. Pass a few homes, then drive through the woods on this narrow, winding road. It is a narrow paved road all the way but sometimes

(4 kilometers) to First Avenue with a church on the left-hand side, a school on the right-hand side. Turn right. First Avenue becomes Bedwell Bay Road; continue on it. Pass White Pine turnoff and the regional park turnoff. Go through the village of Belcarra to the end of Bedwell Bay Road. Turn right on Belcarra Bay Road and go ½ mile (¾ kilometer): pass Turtle-head Road, pass mail boxes and go up a hill to a parking space on the left-hand side of the road just before Whiskey Cove Lane. Space for five or six cars to park: beside it notices to scuba divers: "Park hours are 8 am until 6 pm. Special use permits are required for after hours access to Whiskey Cove". Telephone on a weekday one week in advance: (604) 432-6352.

Then, walk down a short trail – 100 paces through the woods, to a log-covered crescent of beach. Snorkel to the left or to the rock wall on the right.

• To get to Port Moody
From downtown Vancouver, go east on Hastings Street (Highway 7A) to Highway 1. When across Highway 1, continue 3 miles (5 kilometers) more on Hastings to Inlet Drive. Bear left on Inlet which becomes Barnet Highway, still Highway 7A, and go to Port Moody. At St. Johns Street, turn left and continue nearly through Port Moody. Follow a sign to Ioco, turn left.

• From North Vancouver (Highway 1 East): head south across Second Narrows Bridge, and move to the lane sign-posted Hastings Street 7A Bridgeway. Take Exit 26 and follow signs to Hastings Street East. Head east through Burnaby on Hastings (Highway 7A) for 3 miles (5 kilometers) to Inlet Drive. Bear left on Inlet which becomes Barnet Highway, and go to Port Moody. At St. Johns Street, turn left and continue nearly through Port Moody to a sign to Ioco. Turn left.

• From Highway 1 in the Fraser Valley: take Exit 44 at *north* end of Port Mann Bridge. Follow the signposts: go to Port Coquitlam on Highway 7 East (Lougheed Highway) for 4 miles (7 kilometers). Turn left to Port Moody onto Highway 7A East (Barnet Highway), 1¼ miles (2 kilometers). Turn right following signs to Ioco Road.

NOTES

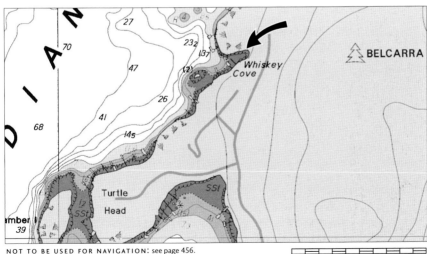

NOT TO BE USED FOR NAVIGATION: see page 456.
Use CHS chart #3495 for navigation; for information on obtaining navigational charts see page 456. Soundings are in meters.

1/5 NAUTICAL MILE

WRECK OF THE VT-100

SHORE DIVE

SKILL
All divers

TIDE TABLE
Vancouver

WHY GO

Shallow, close to shore and obviously in the shape of a ship – much of this 136-foot (41-meter) wooden hull and steel superstructure remains intact. A forward gun platform, which once held the 3½-inch (90-millimeter) cannon, is plainly visible.

The *VT-100* is great for a first wreck dive, a natural for practicing compass navigation, a favorite of divers for years. And, to add to the fascination, this old wreck has recently acquired a new identity. Until 1983 it was known as Canadian minesweeper HMCS *Cranbrook.* Then a local diver discovered the wreck to be an American Yard Class Minesweeper (YMS) built during World War II. After the war, the vessel was brought to Bedwell Bay and was made into a wood-chip barge; it was redesignated as the *Vancouver Tugboat-100* or *VT-100.* In 1956 vandals started a fire on board and the vessel burned to the water line and sank.

Diving the wreck we saw lacy white nudibranchs tipped with blue, spider crabs, calcareous tube worms, white and orange plumose anemones. Seaperch, pile perch and rockfish, large and small, congre-

gating inside the hull as though contained in a fishbowl. Swimming back to shore over sandy bottom crawling with Dungeness crabs, snails and flounders, galaxies of moon jellies billowed around us like a whole miniature universe under water.

BOTTOM AND DEPTHS

The *VT-100* lies on gently sloping, muddy bottom. The bow is 55 to 65 feet (17 to 20 meters) deep at the south end; the stern is 42 to 52 feet (13 to 16 meters) deep at the north end.

HAZARDS

The wreck itself, small boats and poor visibility. Water-skiers, in summer. Lion's mane jellies, in the fall. The wreck is intact but crumbling dangerously – it should not be entered even by the most experienced wreck divers. Listen for boats; if you hear a boat, stay down until it passes. Allow time for a water-skier to pass, as well. Or use a compass and navigate to shore under water. Try not to stir up the silt. If you have seen any lion's mane jellies, you and your buddy should check one another for stinging tentacles before removing masks and gloves.

TELEPHONE

Return the way you came for 1¼ miles (2 kilometers) through the village of Belcarra. At the stop sign, turn right and go another 2½ miles (4 kilometers) to Belcarra Picnic Area to the telephone beside the parking lot.

FACILITIES

None at the site. Restrooms at Belcarra Picnic Area. A site plan of the *VT-100* is in *Vancouver's Undersea Heritage,* a book published by the Underwater Archeological Society of British Columbia (UASBC).

Moon jellies

ACCESS

The wreck of the *VT-100* is in Bedwell Bay, east side of Indian Arm in the village of Belcarra. It is reached by way of Port Moody off Highway 7A.

In Port Moody, turn north off St. Johns Street (Highway 7A) following signs to Ioco. Turn left at signal lights on Ioco Road. Almost immediately turn left again, following signs to Belcarra and Ioco Road. Continue on Ioco Road 2½ miles (4 kilometers) to First Avenue with a church on the left-hand side, a school on the right-hand side. Turn right. First Avenue becomes Bedwell Bay Road; continue on it for 2 ¾ miles (4½ kilometers) to Kelly Road. Turn right on Kelly and wind down a short way to Marine Avenue. At Marine, turn sharply left and go 200 yards (185 meters). Park by the roadside but well off the pavement, just past stairsteps down to a wharf. Walk down one of the short, steep trails to the rocky beach – 27 paces to the water. Do not trespass on wharves and boathouses. All are privately owned property constructed on leased water-lots. Respect all "No Parking" signs.

Enter and follow a 330° compass bearing toward the middle of the opposite shore. One hundred yards (90 meters) offshore you should come to the *VT-100* lying north to south.

To get to Port Moody

- From downtown Vancouver, go east on Hastings Street (Highway 7A) to Highway 1. When across Highway 1, continue 3 miles (5 kilometers) more on Hastings to Inlet Drive. Bear left on Inlet which becomes Barnet Highway, still Highway 7A, and go to Port Moody. At St. Johns Street, turn left and continue nearly through Port Moody. Follow a sign to Ioco, turn left.
- From North Vancouver (Highway 1 East): head *south* on Ironworkers Memorial Bridge (Second Narrows Bridge), and move to the lane signposted Hastings Street 7A Bridgeway. Take Exit 26 and follow signs to Hastings Street East. Head east through Burnaby on Hastings (Highway 7A) for 3 miles (5 kilometers) to Inlet Drive. Bear left on Inlet which becomes Barnet Highway, and go to Port Moody. At St. Johns Street, turn left and continue nearly through Port Moody to a sign to Ioco. Turn left.
- From Highway 1 in the Fraser Valley: take Exit 44 at *north* end of Port Mann Bridge. Follow the signposts: go to Port Coquitlam on Highway 7 East (Lougheed Highway), 4 miles (7 kilometers). Turn left to Port Moody onto Highway 7A East (Barnet Highway), 1 ½ miles (2½ kilometers). Turn right following signs to Ioco Road.

NOTES

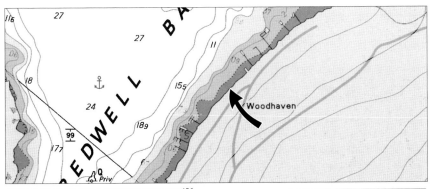

NOT TO BE USED FOR NAVIGATION: see page 456.
Use CHS chart #3495 for navigation; for information on obtaining navigational charts see page 456. Soundings are in meters.

1/5 NAUTICAL MILE

RACOON ISLAND

**BOAT DIVE or
KAYAK DIVE**

GPS
49°20.524' N
122°54.309' W

SKILL
All divers and snorkelers

TIDE TABLE
Vancouver

WHY GO

Racoon Island is a picturesque undersea garden – ideal for open-water certification dives as well as photography – and it drops off too. A variety of both sand and rock dwellers live here.

The first time I dived at Racoon Island we anchored over the white gravel bottom. As we jumped in a pair of harbor seals were playing, but they disappeared rapidly. We were soon into picturesque terrain with a rocky reef on either side. Gorgeous white and orange plumose anemones which are 1 and 2 feet (⅓- and ⅔-meter) tall cluster on top of each reef. We saw a few rockfish, one decorator crab and a variety of other crabs. We looked over the edge of the dark drop-off and turned back towards the sand.

Snails scurried away. Tube worms snapped in. We saw egg cases of moon snails, Oregon tritons and flounders. Millions of minute transparent fairy shrimp. Back at shore, little colorful anemones fill the tide pools. For information on how to behave with harbor seals go to www.pac.dfo-mpo.gc.ca, click on Marine Mammals, select Viewing Guidelines.

BOTTOM AND DEPTHS

Two rocky reefs undulating from 30 to 40 feet (9 to 12 meters) deep parallel the northern shore. At the eastern end of the reefs, a sheer drop-off to 282 feet (86 meters). One of the darkest drop-offs I've seen. It stopped us at 80 feet (24 meters). At the western end of the reefs, eelgrass and coarse white broken-shell bottom.

HAZARDS

Boats, including silent sailboats, more numerous since Racoon became part of Indian Arm Marine Park. Lion's mane jellies, in the fall. Use a compass and ascend up the side of the island or spiral and look up as you ascend. If you have seen any jellies, you and your buddy should check

one another for stinging tentacles before removing masks and gloves. Kayak-divers who have dived deep: to avoid bringing on bends by overexertion, rest before paddling back.

TELEPHONES

- On the water: VHF radio; if no VHF, try a cell phone.
- On land: Deep Cove, above dock at foot of Gallant Avenue.

FACILITIES

None at Racoon Island, but nearby at Twin Islands you will find camping space, a pit toilet and walking trails. Air fills are available in Burnaby, Coquitlam, New Westminster, Langley, Surrey and North Vancouver. Dive-kayak rentals in Squamish.

ACCESS

Racoon Island is in Indian Arm Marine Park near the southern end of Indian Arm: it is 2 nautical miles northeast of Deep Cove, and 3 nautical miles northeast of Cates Park in North Vancouver.

Charters available out of Ioco and Vancouver; rental boats in Burnaby. Launch ramps in North Vancouver and Port Moody. Or, launch dive-kayaks at Woodlands or Deep Cove and go to Racoon Island.

Anchor near the northwest shore, just north of the widest bulge of the island, in 30 to 40 feet (9 to 12 meters) of water. Or land on the island and enter from the pebble beach. Swim straight north and down to the two rocky reefs.

*Looking north toward
sailboat approaching
Racoon Island*

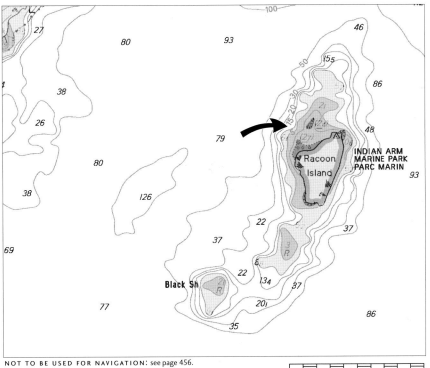

NOT TO BE USED FOR NAVIGATION: see page 456.
Use CHS chart #3495 for navigation; for information on obtaining
navigational charts see page 456. Soundings are in meters.

1/5 NAUTICAL MILE

NOTES

BUNTZEN POWER PLANT

BOAT DIVE
GPS
49°22.208' N
122°52.407' W

SKILL
Intermediate and expert divers

TIDE TABLE
Vancouver

WHY GO

Beautiful rock formations plummet to a depth of 110 to 120 feet (34 to 37 meters). The wall by Buntzen Power Plant is renowned as *the* drop-off of Indian Arm. It's brightest in the afternoon.

As we dived through the shallows, schools of bright blue and yellow seaperch glinted in the sun. Millions of moon jellies throbbed through the water. Then there were no more. Spindly spider crabs and hairy lithode crabs – two specialties of Indian Arm – were clinging to the smooth rock wall. Little else. It felt barren. We saw a few scattered rockfish. At 80 feet (24 meters), a pale white blenny. Suddenly, a lion's mane jelly streaming tentacles that were 10 feet (3 meters) long. Beautiful! And bright red slipper cucumbers decorating the dark wall sweeping…down…down…to a yelloweye rockfish deep along the wall.

BOTTOM AND DEPTHS

Broken rock covered with lettuce kelp gives way immediately to sheer rock wall with loose gravel spilling over it. Beautiful rock formations drop to a depth of 110 to

Divers at Buntzen Power Plant

120 feet (34 to 37 meters). Slightly farther out the bottom drops to 90, 300 then 600 feet (27, 90, 180 meters).

HAZARDS

Extreme depth and tail-race from the dam. Lion's mane jellies in the fall. At any time, day or night, the power plant gates might be opened without warning and a huge volume of water discharged between the dock and dive site. The discharge is above the surface and is extremely turbulent. Because the gates are remotely controlled, divers will not be warned even when flying their diver's flag. Do not swim under water past the gates. Snorkel past. If you have seen any jellies, check for stinging tentacles before removing your masks and gloves.

TELEPHONES
• On the water: VHF radio; if no VHF, try a cell phone.
• On land: Deep Cove, above dock at the foot of Gallant Avenue.

FACILITIES

The dock and land by the powerhouse are owned by BC Hydro and Power Authority. As long as we leave the property as we find it and use it at our own risk, BC Hydro will continue to allow divers to use the area. Charters out of Port Moody, Vancouver and North Vancouver. Water taxi out of Deep Cove or wherever convenient for pickup. Launch in North Vancouver or Port Moody. Air fills throughout Greater Vancouver.

ACCESS

Buntzen Power Plant is halfway up the east side of Indian Arm. It is 4 nautical miles northeast of Deep Cove, 5 nautical miles northeast of Cates Park in North Vancouver; 9 nautical miles northeast of Rocky Point in Port Moody.

Charter, rental boat or launch your own boat and go to Buntzen. Tie up by the big concrete power station, referred to by BC Hydro as Buntzen Number Two; another power plant is slightly north, but Buntzen Number Two is the first one on

your right as you go up Indian Arm. From the dock, snorkel north around the corner to the right and go down.

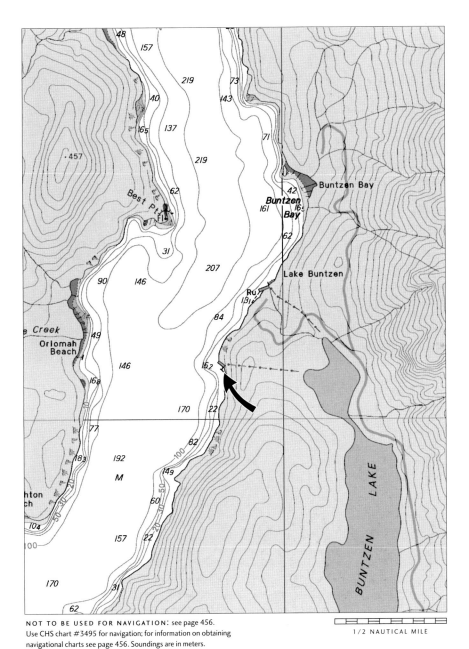

NOTES

NOT TO BE USED FOR NAVIGATION: see page 456.
Use CHS chart #3495 for navigation; for information on obtaining navigational charts see page 456. Soundings are in meters.

1/2 NAUTICAL MILE

69

CROKER ISLAND

BOAT DIVE

GPS

Southeast corner:
49°25.773' N
122°51.785' W

Northwest corner:
49°26.819' N
122°52.461' W

SKILL
All divers and snorkelers

TIDE TABLE
Vancouver

WHY GO

"Paradise", one experienced diver calls this area, maybe because you can find almost anything you can name somewhere around Croker Island.

Clumps of anemones and sea stars overflow the south point. We saw small dahlia anemones, chitons, green urchins, painted greenlings and sea cucumbers. Lingcod and rockfish haunt the ledges and overhangs shelving down from the bay. As you move to the eastern side below the light, the water is thick with small shrimp. Tarantula-like hairy lithode crabs hang by a leg from the sheer smooth cliff which plunges l00 feet (33 meters).

At the northwest corner, we anchored in the small cove south of the point and first went deep. Emerald green water like I've seen nowhere else in British Columbia was here at the northwest corner of Croker – on a sunny day in late September. I was lured to this dive because I was told there were swimming scallops. We saw one swimming scallop, but what hooked me was the visibility and the drop-off.

Dark and deep and green. Curvaceous rock formations, as if sculpted by current, ripple down the dark steep wall. We saw four big lingcod, spider crabs, a sturgeon poacher and crimson slipper cucumbers, also called creeping pedal cucumbers – they look like red lace. On the way up plumose anemones brighten the scene from 20 to 40 feet (6 to 12 meters). In the cove shallows, we saw a sand dab with a shrimp in its mouth. Lots more shrimp, too.

At the northern end of Croker, beautiful variety again: masses of cucumbers, sea stars, small barnacles, tube worms, seaperch, kelp greenlings and an occasional octopus and grunt sculpin. A forest of sea whips. Sometimes huge schools of herring and salmon grilse.

Because little current stirs up the silt, in winter visibility ranges up to 100 feet (30 meters) all around the island. Indian Arm is usually calm winter and summer.

BOTTOM AND DEPTHS

The cove at the northwest corner of Croker is rocky with pockets of sand in the shallows of the bay at 15 to 25 feet (5 to 8 meters). Heading down, a ledge at 65 to 75 feet (20 to 23 meters); then the wall sheers off deeper than we wanted to go – to a depth of 130 to 140 feet (40 to 43 meters). At the northern tip, rocky bottom undulates to a depth of 60 to 70 feet (18 to 21 meters).

At the southwest corner rock formations, large overhangs, caves and ledges drop to 100 feet (30 meters) and more to whatever level you choose.

HAZARDS

Boats in summer. Lion's mane jellies in the fall. Listen for boats and keep close to the bottom all the way to the surface. If you have seen any jellies, check with your buddy for stinging tentacles before removing masks and gloves.

TELEPHONES

- On the water: VHF radio; if no VHF, try a cell phone.
- On land: Deep Cove, above the dock at foot of Gallant Avenue.

FACILITIES

None at uninhabited Croker Island. Launch in North Vancouver or Port Moody. Charter out of Ioco or Vancouver.

ACCESS

Croker Island is at the head of Indian Arm. It is 10 nautical miles northeast of Cates Park in North Vancouver. Farther from Rocky Point in Port Moody.

Charter, go by rental boat or launch your own boat at North Vancouver or Port Moody and go to the top of Indian Arm to Croker Island. If diving the south side of the island, anchor west of the light. If diving the northwest corner, anchor in the small cove south of the point.

Sarah L, off to Croker Island

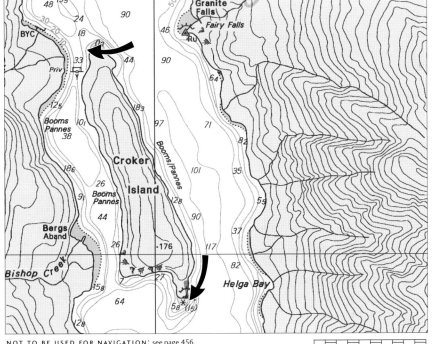

NOTES

NOT TO BE USED FOR NAVIGATION: see page 456.
Use CHS chart #3495 for navigation; for information on obtaining
navigational charts see page 456. Soundings are in meters.

1/2 NAUTICAL MILE

Sechelt Peninsula

Sechelt Rapids, looking north to Sutton Islets

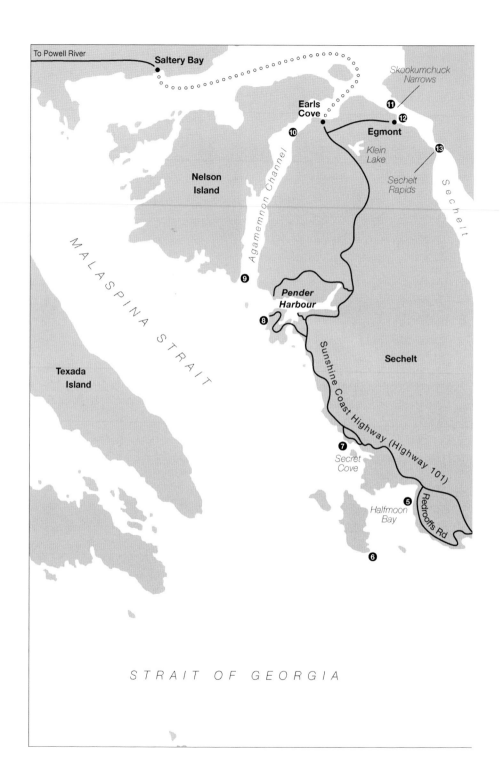

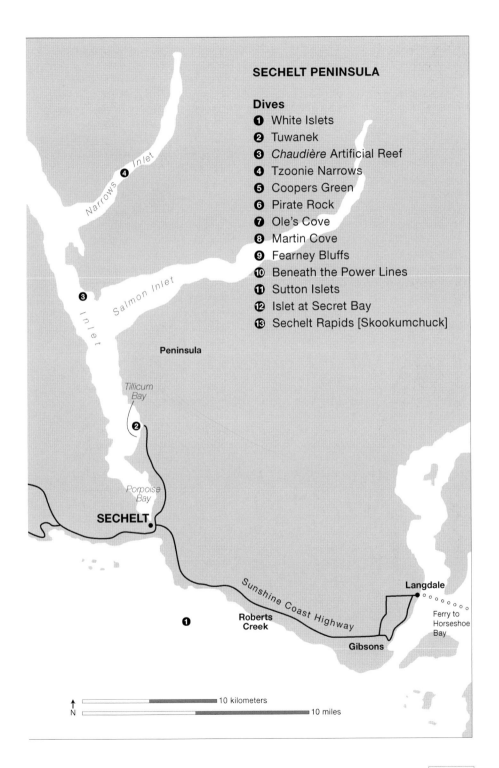

SECHELT PENINSULA

Dives

❶ White Islets
❷ Tuwanek
❸ *Chaudière* Artificial Reef
❹ Tzoonie Narrows
❺ Coopers Green
❻ Pirate Rock
❼ Ole's Cove
❽ Martin Cove
❾ Fearney Bluffs
❿ Beneath the Power Lines
⓫ Sutton Islets
⓬ Islet at Secret Bay
⓭ Sechelt Rapids [Skookumchuck]

SERVICE INFORMATION

Tide and Current Information

- *Tide and Current Tables, Volume 5: Juan de Fuca Strait and Strait of Georgia,* Canadian Hydrographic Service print annual
- *Current Atlas: Juan de Fuca Strait to Strait of Georgia,* purchase one time. Use with *Murray's Tables* or *Washburne's Tables,* purchase annually; privately produced publications available at marine equipment and supplies stores.
- www.lau.chs-shc.gc.ca: Tide and Current Tables for all of Canada. Go to the web site: click on Pacific; General Information; Tide and Currents, Data Available; then Tide Tables available in PDF form. Select Volume 5 and click on the tide or current table desired – both are on the same list on the pdf.

Weather Information

- Canadian Coast Guard: Speak with a person, 24 hours; telephone Comox (250)339-3613.
- Canadian Coast Guard (Victoria Coast Guard Radio): continuous Marine Broadcast (CMB) recorded, 24 hours; listen for weather in the Strait of Georgia and Merry Island, telephone Vancouver (604)666-3655.
- Environment Canada: recorded, 24 hours; telephone Vancouver (604)664-9010
    Press 1 for Weather Line
    Press 2 for Marine Weather, press 1 and listen for weather in the Strait of Georgia and Howe Sound.
- www.weatheroffice.ec.gc.ca

Tourist Information

Tourism BC
- Toll-free throughout North America: 1-800-435-5622
- From all other locations: (250) 387-1642
www.hellobc.com

Diving Emergency Telephone Numbers

On land and water:
- Call 911, request "ambulance" and say, "I have a scuba diving emergency".
- Vancouver General Hospital; for 24-hour, 7-day-a-week response: telephone (604)875-5000 and say, "I want the hyperbaric physician on call".

On the water:
- VHF radio: Call Coast Guard radio, Channel 16 and say, "I have a scuba diving emergency".
- Cell phone: 911, *16 or *311 and say, "I have a scuba diving emergency".

If emergency or medical personnel are unfamiliar with scuba diving emergencies, ask them to telephone DAN (Divers Alert Network) at (919)684-4326. No money for a long distance call? Dial DAN collect at 011-919-684-4326 and say, "I have a scuba diving emergency".

Mark emergency location before leaving scene: other divers might be down.

How to Go

Sechelt Peninsula is connected to the mainland of British Columbia by 1,100 yards (1,000 meters) of land. It's "water country" – getting there is half the fun.

The southern tip of Sechelt at Langdale is a quick-trip-away from Horseshoe Bay in West Vancouver – 40 minutes by ferry.

The northern tip of Sechelt Peninsula is a leisurely-trip-away from Vancouver Island: two ferry boat rides plus driving. The ferry from Comox to Powell River takes 1¼ hours; next drive 30 minutes to Saltery Bay; then ride the ferry for 50 minutes to Earls Cove at the north end of Sechelt.

Ferry Information

British Columbia Ferry Services (BC Ferries)
- Toll-free throughout North America:
  1-888-223-3779
- From all other locations: (250)386-3431
www.bcferries.com
At the time of writing the following information applies – but frequent changes occur; it would be wise to check current requirements on BC Ferries web page before every trip.

Rules Regarding Scuba Tanks on BC Ferries
Persons transporting scuba tanks containing compressed air, full or partially full, are required under Canadian law to declare dangerous goods at the terminal or to a vessel officer. Persons transporting scuba tanks with the valves removed do not need clearance. All pressurized tanks with a UN 3156 sticker, indicating nitrox or mixed gases, are taboo – remove the valve.

Expedite Dangerous Goods clearance at the ferry ticket booth – complete a Dangerous Goods Shipping Document prior to arrival. Obtain it from the web at home or a library: Go to www.bcferries.com: select Travel Planning; click on Carrying Dangerous Goods, then For the General Public. Download Dangerous Goods Shipping Document and complete it: include your name, home address and phone number; Class 2; UN 1002, which indicates compressed air; the number of cylinders you are transporting and quantity in each one: most tanks are 80 cubic feet/2.27 cubic meters.

(To calculate quantity in scuba tanks: 1 cubic foot=0.0283168466 cubic meters.)

Arrive at least 30 minutes prior to intended sailing time. However, it might save you from missing a ferry at Langdale if you phone the terminal and ask when they suggest you arrive.
1. Langdale: (604)886-2242
2. Earls Cove: (604)487-9333

Prearranged Dangerous Goods Clearance Requires 48 Hours
Complete a Dangerous Goods Shipping Document as described and fax it at least 48 hours before intended sailing time to the terminal manager responsible for the terminal of your departure.
1. Langdale: fax (604)886-7468
2. Earls Cove: fax (604)487-9396

SECHELT AND GIBSONS

• DIVE SHOP

Suncoast Diving and Watersports
5648 Teredo Street, Highway 101
Mailing address: PO Box 1914
Sechelt BC V0N 3A0
(604)740-8006
1-866-740-8006: Toll-free throughout
    North America
www.suncoastdiving.com
(Recreational, nitrox, technical and rebreather instruction. Nitrox, trimix and soda-lime available. Also dive-kayak rentals and boat charters.)

• RESORTS

Porpoise Bay Charters
PO Box 2281
5718 Anchor Road, next to Lighthouse Pub
Sechelt BC V0N 3A0
(604)885-5950
1-800-665-3483: Toll-free throughout
    North America
www.porpoisebaycharters.com
(Resort packages include day, weekend and midweek diving in Sechelt Inlet off Hel-Cat I, Narrows Mist II *and the* Foggydart; *waterfront accommodation in cabins; and air fills. Custom packages could include canoeing and sea kayaking – not sit-on-top kayaks but ocean kayaks.)*

Tzoonie Outdoor Adventures
PO Box 157
Sechelt BC V0N 3A0
(604)885-9802
1-866-340-0543: Toll-free throughout
    North America
www.tzoonie.com
(Wilderness resort accommodation in Narrows Inlet close to the Chaudière *and Sechelt Rapids, Tzoonie Narrows; a sunken wreck 11 yards [10 meters] from the resort float. Sauna, meals provided or do your own cooking. Inquire early so the resort can arrange in advance with a dive shop for air fills, guided boat charters to sites and equipment if needed. Minimum of two nights for groups of two to six divers.)*

• DAY CHARTERS

Atria Star and a go-anywhere Zodiac
Suncoast Diving and Watersports
5648 Teredo Street, Highway 101
Mailing address: PO Box 1914
Sechelt BC V0N 3A0
(604)740-8006
1-866-740-8006: Toll-free throughout
    North America
www.suncoastdiving.com
(Day dive charters from a covered boat or a Zodiac. Dives offered around the entire Sechelt Peninsula – in Sechelt Inlet, Agamemnon Channel and the Strait of Georgia.

Also charters, guiding and air fills for 2 to 6 people, by pre-arrangement, for wilderness camping or resort trips. Tank rentals if needed.)

Hel-Cat I, Narrows Mist II and *Foggydart*
Porpoise Bay Charters
PO Box 2281
5718 Anchor Road, next to Lighthouse Pub
Sechelt BC V0N 3A0
(604)885-5950
1-800-665-3483: Toll-free throughout
    North America
www.porpoisebaycharters.com
(Day charters for groups of 6 to 30 for Sechelt Inlet: dives range from the Chaudière *to Tzoonie Narrows and Sechelt Rapids. Dives in Agamemnon Channel include Beneath the Power Lines; in Jervis Inlet, Captain's Island, Miller Rock and more. Waterfront and roadside air fills for drop-ins – with advance notice.)*

• LAUNCH RAMPS
For Strait of Georgia

Gibsons Marina
675 Prowse Road, PO Box 1520
Gibsons BC V0N 1V0
(604)886-8686; VHF-68
E-mail: gibsonsmarina@uniserve.com
(Launch for a fee for Strait of Georgia: concrete ramp, good at all except extreme low tides. Restrooms and hot showers; telephones outside, on waterfront side of marina office.)

LAUNCH RAMPS (CONTINUED)
For Strait of Georgia
Coopers Green Public Ramp
Halfmoon Bay
(Launch free year-round for Strait of Georgia: concrete ramp, good at all except extreme low tides. Chemical toilet year-round, restrooms in summer; telephone outside restrooms.)

Located north of town of Sechelt.

- Heading north on Highway 101: when 5½ miles (9 kilometers) past the sharp turn at Wharf Road and the highway in the center of Sechelt, take Redrooffs Road. Go north on Redrooffs for 5½ miles (9 kilometers) to foot of Fisherman's Road.
- Heading south on Highway 101 when just over ½ mile (¾ kilometer) past turnoff to Smugglers Cove, follow Redrooffs Road. Go 1 mile (1½ kilometers) south on Redrooffs to foot of Fisherman's.

For Sechelt Inlet
Porpoise Bay Ramp, next to Sechelt wharf
(Launch for a fee at the head of Sechelt Inlet: concrete ramp, good at all except extreme low tides. Chemical toilet at wharf. Telephone top of ramp, outside pub.)

From Highway 101: turn north at traffic light in Sechelt town center and go ⅔ mile (1 kilometer) to foot of Wharf Road.

Tillicum Bay Marina
5794 Naylor Road
Sechelt BC V0N 3A4
(604) 885-2100
(Launch for a fee at Tillicum Bay, Sechelt Inlet: concrete ramp, good at all tides for small boats only. Pit toilets; telephone outside marina office.)

Located on Sechelt Inlet: from Sechelt, follow signs toward Porpoise Bay Provincial Park: go north on Wharf Road to Porpoise Bay Road. Turn right onto Porpoise Bay Road, which becomes Sechelt Inlet Road, and go 5 miles (8 kilometers) along the east side of Sechelt Inlet to Naylor Road. Turn left downhill to the marina.

PENDER HARBOUR AREA
Pender Harbour area is near the middle of the Sechelt Peninsula: access is from three roads off Highway 101:

1. Francis Peninsula Road turnoff is 19 miles (31 kilometers) north of the right-angle left-hand turn on Highway 101 in the heart of the town of Sechelt. It is 14 miles (23 kilometers) south of Earls Cove ferry landing.
2. Madeira Park Road turnoff is 20 miles (32 kilometers) north of the right-angle left-hand turn in the heart of the town of Sechelt. From Earls Cove go south 13½ miles (22 kilometers) to it.
3. Garden Bay Road turnoff is 24 miles (38 kilometers) north of the heart of the town of Sechelt, and 10½ miles (17 kilometers) south of Earls Cove.

• DAY AND LIVEABOARD CHARTERS
Seaborne
Seaborne Adventure Tours
4749 Francis Peninsula Road
PO Box 343
Madeira Park BC V0N 2H0
(604) 883-9120
1-888-844-0099: Toll-free throughout North America
www.sunshinecoastcharters.com
(Day charters, boat rentals and The Beach House accommodation.)

Mamro
Mamro Adventures
1 - 5765 Turner Road, Suite 203
Nanaimo BC V9T 6M4
(250) 756-8872
www.mamro.com
(Liveaboard charters out of Madeira Park, Pender Harbour, in winter. Dives range from Agamemnon Channel, Sechelt Inlet, Jervis Inlet to Lund; for small groups — up to 7 divers. Also out of Nanaimo to the Gulf Islands, summer and winter; out of Port Hardy in spring and fall.)

PENDER HARBOUR AREA (CONTINUED)

• LAUNCH RAMPS

For Malaspina Strait and Agamemnon Channel

Seafarer Millennium Park Public Ramp
Madeira Park
(604) 883-2234
www.haa.bc.ca/SCH_Services_Directory/
Madeira_Park.htm
(Launch for a fee year-round: concrete ramp, good at medium and high tides only. Chemical toilet year-round; flush toilets in summer across Madeira Park Road at Tourist Infocentre. Telephone top of dock beside parking lot.)

Pender Harbour Resort
4686 Sinclair Bay Road, RR1, S-15, C-13
Garden Bay BC V0N 1S0
(604) 883-2424
1-877-883-2424: Toll-free throughout
   North America
www.penderharbourresort.com
(Launch for a fee year-round: concrete ramp, good at all except extreme low tides. Hot showers available for divers. Camping in area surrounded by trees with full hook-up RV sites, self-contained cottages and outdoor swimming pool. Telephone outside marina office.)

• BOAT RENTALS AND LAUNCH RAMP

For Malaspina Strait and Agamemnon Channel

Fisherman's Resort & Marina
PO Box 68
Garden Bay BC V0N 1S0
(604) 883-2336
www.fishermansresortmarina.com
(April through October 15: launch for a fee at Garden Bay, Pender Harbour. Hot showers for divers who launch and/or rent boats. Also power-boat rentals, cottages and RV sites.)

EGMONT

Egmont is at the top of Sechelt Peninsula: the turnoff into Egmont Road is ½ mile (¾ kilometer) south of Earls Cove ferry landing. It is 33 miles (53 kilometers) north of the right-angle left-hand turn on Highway 101 in the heart of the town of Sechelt.

• AIR STATION

Egmont Marina Resort
General Delivery
Egmont BC V0N 1N0
(604)883-2298
1-800-626-0599: Toll-free throughout
    North America
www.egmont-marina.com
(Air fills; also ramp, toilets, hot showers and laundry. Telephone outside, beside air station behind Backeddy Pub. Camping, RV sites, camper cabins and pub.)

• DAY AND MULTIPLE-DAY CHARTERS

Topline and *B-line*
Sunshine Coast Tours
RR1, S-9, C-1
Garden Bay BC V0N 1S0
(604)883-2280
1-800-870-9055: Toll-free throughout
    North America.
www.sunshinecoasttours.com
(Day, weekend and week-long charters out of Egmont and Pender Harbour: dives range from Agamemnon Channel to Skookumchuck Narrows, Sechelt Rapids and the Chaudière in Sechlet Inlet. Transportation only; with prior notice a dive master can be made available.)

• BOAT RENTALS AND WATER TAXI

Bathgate General Store, Resort & Marina
6781 Bathgate Road, beside the wharf
Egmont BC V0N 1N0
(604)883-2222
www.bathgate.com
(Boat rentals, water taxi, tent camping and RV sites. Hot showers with restrooms during store hours; telephones outside store.)

• LAUNCH RAMPS

For Skookumchuck Narrows, Agamemnon Channel, Sechelt Inlet
Egmont Marina Resort
General Delivery
Egmont BC V0N 1N0
(604)883-2298
1-800-626-0599: Toll-free throughout
    North America
www.egmont-marina.com
(Dirt and gravel ramp, good at all tides, available for a fee. Also air fills.)

Egmont Public Ramp
Egmont BC
(Launch free in Egmont: tarmac ramp, good at high tides only. Telephones nearby, outside Bathgate General Store, Resort & Marina.)
    Just before reaching the wharf at Egmont, turn north into Maple Road. Turn right into Bradwynne Road and immediately turn right again. Go downhill to the ramp.

All of this Service Information is subject to change.

—WHITE ISLETS—

**BOAT DIVE or
KAYAK DIVE**
GPS
49°25.080' N
123°42.658' W

SKILL
Intermediate and expert
divers

TIDE TABLE
Point Atkinson

*Sheltered cove at
White Islets*

WHY GO
Wilderness above and below water. Blue
sky, white rock and green depths where
fish are a specialty – we saw at least 40
medium-sized lingcod on one summer
dive. This site is a lingcod breeding ground.
Quillback rockfish line the vertical crevices
in the rock, noses up, as if in formation.
Lots of kelp greenlings cruise in the open.
We saw tiger rockfish hiding in deep, dark
crevices.

Anemones, sea stars, chimney and cloud
sponges are spaced out on the stark rock
as if on display. Snakelock anemones, also
called crimson anemones, fling long, fleshy
flamboyant red fingers into the current.
Also white snakelocks. Christmas anemones
cling to the rock with brilliant mottled red
and green stalks. Peach-colored carnivo-
rous anemones are on the rock. Isolated
plumose anemones, orange ones and white.

Red urchins and green ones. You might find
an octopus or two. Tube worms are under
ledges. Transparent tube-dwelling anemones
and sea pens are on the sand. We saw purple sea stars, slime stars, blood stars, a rose
star and tiny yellow stars. Sea lemons, a
frilly orange and white nudibranch. Plus a
very special treat, a first-time sighting for
me: two mating pairs of box crabs.

You might meet a harbor seal. At the
end of our dive as we headed up over the
shell bottom, a seal swooped around us,
repeatedly came within 5 to 10 feet (1½
to 3 meters).

BOTTOM AND DEPTHS
White shell and gravel bottom gently but
quickly slopes off to smooth, dark rock
creased with vertical crevices. The rock
wall rolls down into darkness, bottoms
out to sand at 105 to 115 feet (32 to 35
meters), depending on tide height.
South of it, a boulder field; more gravel
and clam shells at the southern tip.

HAZARDS
Current, small boats and poor visibility
near shore from bird droppings which wash
off the islets. Danger of overexertion after
the dive for kayak-divers. Dive on slack.
Current is reasonably unpredictable at this
site. When windy, current is probably
more predictable on larger exchanges
when the tidal movement overrides the
effect of winds. Kayak-divers should rest
before paddling back to avoid the possibility of bringing on bends after the dive.

TELEPHONES
• On the water: VHF radio; if no VHF,
  try a cell phone.
• On land:
1. Roberts Creek store, 2 miles (3¼ kilometers) east at other end of Beach Road.
2. Highway 101 opposite Roberts Creek
   campground entrance: return up
   Flume Road to Highway 101, turn left
   and go ¾ mile (1⅓ kilometers).

FACILITIES

None at White Islets. Dive shop with inflatable charters and dive-kayak rentals in Sechelt. Or take your own dive-kayak or inflatable. Picnic tables and pit toilets at Roberts Creek picnic site on Beach Road at foot of Flume Road.

ACCESS

White Islets are in the Strait of Georgia southeast of the town of Sechelt and immediately south of Wilson Creek. Westerly and southeasterly winds can make access difficult – pick a calm day.

Charter out of the town of Sechelt; or launch an inflatable at the beach at Davis Bay which is south of the town of Sechelt; or launch a dive-kayak at the west end of Beach Road where there is space for three or four cars to park. Carry across 30 to 50 yards (27 to 46 meters) of sand and cobble beach, depending on tide height, and go 1½ nautical miles to the White Islets.

It takes 25 to 30 minutes by dive-kayak.

Land in the narrow cove – it is a sandy beach at low tides – and gear up. The cove is sheltered from most winds and is a good place to leave your dive-kayak or inflatable.

To get to west end of Beach Road
• Heading north on Highway 101, go nearly ½ mile (¾ kilometer) past Roberts Creek Road to Flume Road. Turn left and go 1 mile (1½ kilometers) on Flume to Beach Road. Turn right. Go ½ mile (¾ kilometer) to the end of Beach Road.
• Heading south on Highway 101, when south of the town of Sechelt and ¾ mile (1⅓ kilometers) past Roberts Creek Provincial Park campground, turn right into Flume Road. Go for 1 mile (1½ kilometers) on Flume to Beach Road. Turn right. Go ½ mile (¾ kilometer) to the end of Beach Road.

NOTES

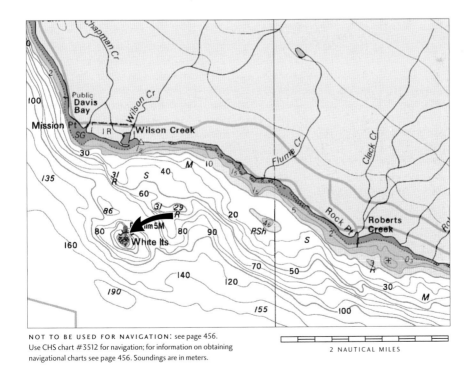

NOT TO BE USED FOR NAVIGATION: see page 456.
Use CHS chart #3512 for navigation; for information on obtaining navigational charts see page 456. Soundings are in meters.

2 NAUTICAL MILES

TUWANEK

WHY GO

The shallow waters around three small islands at Tuwanek are like a large aquarium. It's beautiful for first open-water dives. Beautiful for fish. Beautiful for available light photography.

Small fish are everywhere. You'll see schools of black-and-white striped pile perch. Lots of reddish pink and yellow-tinged rockfish apparently totally unafraid. I touched one with my light. Delicate yellow-and-blue striped seaperch school everywhere in the sunny shallows. Hundreds of tube-snouts, too. You're bound to see maroon-and-gray vertically striped painted greenlings, sometimes called convict fish. Lots of these very ter-ritorial and colorful 4- to 5-inch (10- to 13-centimeter) convict fish live here. They'll probably try to chase you from their particular portion of the sea.

Many other creatures at Tuwanek, as well. Red hydroids – or heart tunicates, which look like little tulips, cling to the rocks. Sea lemons and alabaster nudi-branchs eat bottom kelp. Angular orange dead man's finger sponges twist out of the rocks. A small crab menaced me from under a leaf of kelp. Sea peaches and transparent sea squirts hang like grapes from the wall.

Sun shines through the shallow water and lights it all.

BOTTOM AND DEPTHS

Shallow undulating rocky bottom encir-cles the islands. Rocks and boulders are scattered about. At 50 to 75 feet (15 to 23 meters) the bottom turns to silty sand. South of the point near the creek the bottom drops off swiftly to muddy bot-tom, scattered with a series of logs fallen to look like pick-up-sticks.

HAZARDS

Small boats in summer. Listen for boats and ascend along the contours of the bottom all the way to shore.

TELEPHONES

• Tillicum Bay Marina: do not go down Tillicum Bay Road. From Tuwanek, go 1 mile (1 ¾ kilometers) back toward Sechelt to Naylor Road and to the water.
• At Porpoise Bay Park: go 3½ miles (6 kilometers) back toward Sechelt to the turnoff to Porpoise Bay Park. Telephone is at the park entrance.

FACILITIES

Cobbled beach for a picnic but no restrooms or pit toilets at Tuwanek. Camping year-round 3½ miles (6 kilometers) back at Porpoise Bay Provincial Park with picnic tables, pit toilets and fire rings; hot showers in summer. Air fills at Sechelt.

ACCESS

Tuwanek is north of the town of Sechelt on the protected waters of Sechelt Inlet. The dive is a 10-minute drive from the town of Sechelt which is 35 minutes from the ferry at Langdale, 55 minutes from Earls Cove.

In Sechelt, follow signs toward Porpoise Bay Provincial Park: go north on Wharf Road to Porpoise Bay Road. Turn right onto Porpoise Bay Road, which becomes Sechelt Inlet Road, and go 6 miles (10 kilo-meters) along the east side of the inlet. Pass turnoffs to Porpoise Bay Provincial Park and Tillicum Bay. Continue down a hill to where the road comes close to the water. Two or three cars can park at the roadside near the "No Parking" signs that mark the public access point. You'll see lots of overturned dinghies on the beach. High tides are best for all; wheelchair accessible at high tide for those who can get across 10 feet (3 meters) of sand.

Swim to the island. When swimming, don't give up. Keep going past the log-dump debris covering the bottom near shore. At the south end of the island directly out from the point, large rocks and boulders are tumbled in 25 to 30 feet (8 to 9 meters) of water, making hiding places for all kinds of life.

Leave this neighborhood beach cleaner than you find it; come and go quietly in small groups – no noise pollution – so the people of Tuwanek will welcome divers.

Painted greenling or convict fish

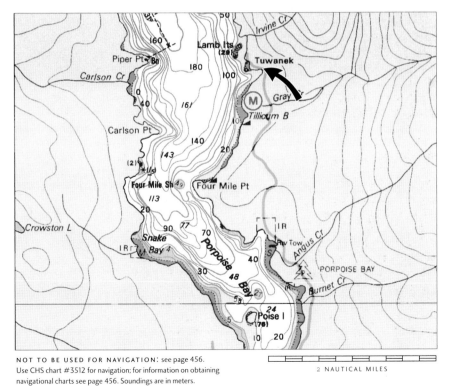

NOT TO BE USED FOR NAVIGATION: see page 456.
Use CHS chart #3512 for navigation; for information on obtaining navigational charts see page 456. Soundings are in meters.

2 NAUTICAL MILES

NOTES

CHAUDIÈRE ARTIFICIAL REEF

BOAT DIVE
GPS
49°37.713′ N
123°48.590′ W

SKILL
Exterior: intermediate and expert divers and all divers with a guide

Interior: expert divers well-experienced with wreck penetration

TIDE TABLE
Point Atkinson
• Slack before flood: Add 2 hours

• Slack before ebb: Add 3 hours

WHY GO

The "Everest of Wreck Diving" – an apt description of the *Chaudière* immediately after sinking. This warship is big, easy to find, pale military gray – spooky when you descend onto the ghostly hull in clear winter water.

A superb vessel for practicing and teaching penetration techniques but make no mistake – exploration is a challenge. It lies on its side, is deep and complex with 67 rooms on the four decks open for diving.

Much equipment remains on board to photograph and play with. At the "ops" (operations) level below the bridge, look for radar equipment with knobs to turn. A bathtub, toilet and sink are in the Captain's quarters. Ovens with working doors in the galley on the "Burma Road" level that has 42 rooms.

Recreational divers will find interest on the exterior. When I dived the *Chaudière* the day after sinking my buddy and I went to the ocean floor at the stern, then up and cruised the starboard exterior. Pulled along the rails almost to where the bow overhangs the dropoff.

Glass tunicates and orange plumose anemones surrounded the stern where the vessel came to rest on the bottom. The second day the ship was down, penetration divers saw shrimp, a gunnel and sculpins sheltering inside the hull, a feather star in the officers' mess. Six months later, feather duster worms, quillback and yelloweye rockfish, lingcod, prawns, millions of glassy tunicates living on it and in it.

Shaped like a great big canoe, the hull is tall and slim. It is 65 feet (20 meters) high, with a beam of 45

Plumose anemones on Chaudière hatch cover

feet (14 meters) and is 366 feet (112 meters) long. The HMCS *Chaudière* was commissioned as a destroyer escort on November 14, 1959; decommissioned in 1974. The ship was prepared by the Artificial Reef Society of British Columbia and scuttled on December 5, 1992.

BOTTOM AND DEPTHS

The *Chaudière* lies on its port side. The bow points south. All decks are accessible at about the same depth on the starboard side. At high tide, depth at the top of the hull at the stern is 60 feet (18 meters); at the bow, 100 feet (30 meters). The stern rests on gently sloping rock bottom at 90 feet (27 meters) at high tide. Beneath the bow, 145 feet (44 meters) on the chart.

HAZARDS

Depth, the temptation to explore, disorientation because of the 90° list, and some surface current. The ship is vast: just diving the length of it on the outside, you could easily stay down too long. Ascend at one of the marker-buoy chains: then, if current, you can make a safety stop out of the way of boats and under control. Pay attention to surface current, and go down to get out of it.

Only expert wreck divers trained in penetration and with full information about the *Chaudière* should enter. A plasticized Dive Slate Add-on Page of the *Chaudière* including information on exits and depths can be obtained from dive shops and www.aquatic-realm.com.

TELEPHONES
• On the water: VHF radio; if no VHF, try a cell phone.
• On land: *south* of Sechelt Rapids
1. Tillicum Marina Resort, east side of Sechelt Inlet and two-thirds of the way back to Porpoise Bay, outside marina office.
2. Porpoise Bay: outside Lighthouse Pub, top of the wharf.

• On land: *north* of Sechelt Rapids
1. Bathgate's Marina, above the wharf at Egmont.
2. Backeddy Pub at Egmont Marina, north of Egmont.

FACILITIES

Charters, air fills and launch ramps in Sechelt and Egmont. In Sechelt: a resort dive package that includes diving, air, land-based accommodation.

ACCESS

The *Chaudière* is in Sechelt Inlet in the bay north of Kunechin Point. It is 9 nautical miles north of the town of Sechelt, the same distance south of Egmont. Approach from north or south depending on tidal currents.

Charter or launch out of Tillicum Bay or Porpoise Bay – both at the *south* end of Sechelt Inlet and go north. Tillicum Bay is part-way up the inlet and cuts travel time on the water by one-third.

Or, charter or launch out of Egmont, *north* of Sechelt Inlet and go south to the bay north of Kunechin Point.

The *Chaudière* is 220 yards (200 meters) offshore. Usually three buoys mark the vessel at the bow, amidships and stern. All are used for mooring and diver access.

To get to the bay north of Kunechin Point
• From Tillicum Bay or Porpoise Bay, go *north* up Sechelt Inlet. The first opening you pass is Salmon Inlet on your right-hand side. Immediately north of it, again on the right-hand side, pass the Kunechin Islets; then you are at Kunechin Point.
• From Egmont, go *south* through Sechelt Rapids [Skookumchuck] – plan your passage in advance. Refer to the current table for Sechelt Rapids. You might need slack, depending on speed of your vessel. Currents up to 16 knots race through this narrows. Once through Skookumchuck, pass the mouth of Narrows Inlet on your left-hand side and continue south toward Salmon Inlet. Kunechin Point is on the left-hand side immediately north of the mouth of Salmon Inlet.

If you reach the Kunechin Islets you have gone too far.

NOTES

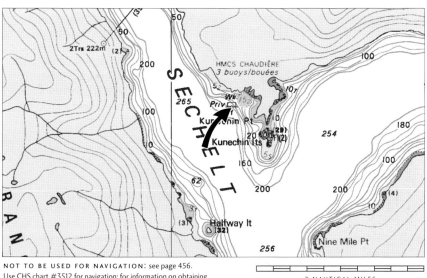

NOT TO BE USED FOR NAVIGATION: see page 456.
Use CHS chart #3512 for navigation; for information on obtaining navigational charts see page 456. Soundings are in meters.

2 NAUTICAL MILES

BOAT DIVE
GPS
49°42.793′ N
123°46.290′ W

SKILL
Intermediate and expert divers

All divers with guide

CURRENT TABLE
Sechelt Rapids:
Add 10 minutes

WHY GO

Remote, protected, perfect "intro" to drift diving.

On a slow cruise through we saw large clusters of tiny almond-shaped lampshells, millions of them! Leafy hornmouth snails heaped on one another, a forest of short-stemmed brown kelp ribbons. Tube-dwelling anemones. A sea lemon. Two large lingcod, kelp greenlings, silvery pile perch, striped seaperch, and quillback, blue and black rockfish. Big rock scallops. Feather stars, giant barnacles, orange solitary cup corals, white encrusting sponges, cemented tube worms which look like popcorn balls, and bands of small white plumose anemones. The bottom feels bright. You might see a wolf-eel which sometimes comes out in the open. When my buddy tickled a brown Irish lord on eggs, then pointed out an 8-inch (20-centimeter) long deco-rated warbonnet with a spike on its head, my day was made.

Charter boats even drift this site at . Tzoonie Narrows is 50 yards (46 meters) wide at its narrowest point. At night,

remember to take a light-stick as well as an underwater light.

Winter or summer Tzoonie's great. Safe too because of fewer boats than at most narrows and because it is protected from wind. We dived it during a December snowstorm on a day when all power on Sechelt Peninsula was knocked out by wind, snow and ice. The dive was not affected. The boat trip *was* a bit cold and bumpy, but hot chocolate back at the pub while rehashing the dive and we were warm again.

BOTTOM AND DEPTHS

Boulders and kelp. Maximum depth, 50 to 60 feet (15 to 18 meters).

HAZARDS

Current and boats. Maximum current, 4 knots. Diving, stay close to the bottom or wall; ascend at the side, out of the way of boats.

TELEPHONES

• On the water: VHF radio; if no VHF, try a cell phone.

• On land, at Sechelt Inlet, south end:
  1. Tillicum Bay Marina, east side of Sechelt Inlet and two-thirds of the way back to Porpoise Bay, outside marina office.
  2. Lighthouse Pub, outside, at top of Porpoise Bay wharf.

• On land, at Egmont: Bathgate's Marina, above the wharf.

FACILITIES

Dive shop, dive resort, charters and launch ramp at Sechelt; another ramp partway up the inlet at Tillicum Bay. Rustic camp-ing east side of Narrows.

Decorated warbonnet

Camping year-round at Porpoise Bay Provincial Park with picnic tables, pit toilets – hot showers in summer.

Charters, air station, launch ramp, camper cabins, camping and a pub at Egmont.

ACCESS

Tzoonie Narrows is more than halfway up Narrows Inlet, a finger of water that branches off Sechelt Inlet. Tzoonie is 19 nautical miles northwest of Porpoise Bay in the town of Sechelt, 11 nautical miles southeast of Egmont. To go from deeper to shallower water, plan to drift through on the ebb.

At Narrows Inlet, go northeast to Tzoonie Narrows and through it. Enter on the southern side of the Narrows. Drift through on an ebbing current with a "live" boat following.

To get to Narrows Inlet by boat
- From Egmont, go *south* through Sechelt Rapids [Skookumchuck] – plan your passage through Sechelt Rapids in advance. Refer to the current table for Sechelt Rapids. You might need slack, depending on the speed of your vessel. Currents up to 16 knots race through Skookumchuck.
- From Porpoise Bay or Tillicum Bay go north through Sechelt Inlet to Narrows Inlet and Tzoonie. The distance is greater than approaching from Egmont, but the approach is easier to plan from Porpoise Bay as no rapids must be considered.

NOTES

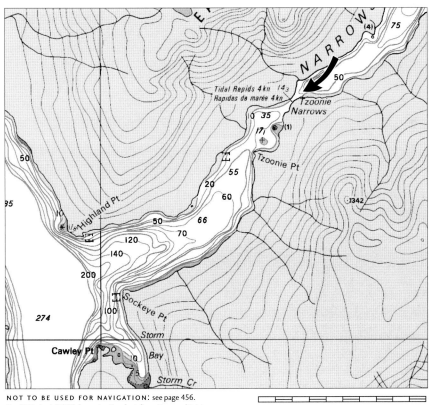

NOT TO BE USED FOR NAVIGATION: see page 456.
Use CHS chart #3512 for navigation; for information on obtaining navigational charts see page 456. Soundings are in meters.

2 NAUTICAL MILES

COOPERS GREEN

SHORE DIVE

SKILL
All divers and snorkelers

TIDE TABLE
Point Atkinson

WHY GO

Nice and easy entry and swim. Pleasant park for a picnic after diving.

Marine life? Look for a wolf-eel, an octopus, huge white plumose anemones. We saw sunflower stars, blood stars, a vermilion star, sea pens, sea peaches and sea cucumbers. Orange dead man's finger sponges and even a vase sponge. Delicate white petals of a nudibranch, a few kelp greenlings and a 1-foot (⅓-meter) lingcod. Lettuce kelp and clams in the shallows.

An excellent place for a first dive with a new diving partner or to check out gear. It's shallow. On the outside of the rock, no deeper than 60 feet (18 meters). No current here, so you can dive anytime day or night but go carefully: the site is next to a launch ramp. Safest in winter.

BOTTOM AND DEPTHS

Slopes gently. Around the rock, it bottoms out to coarse sand and pebbles at 50 to 60 feet (15 to 18 meters), depending on tide height.

HAZARDS

Boats – lots of them in summer, and there could be poor visibility because of silt. Log booms are sometimes tied to the rock. Best as a winter dive. Always fly a dive flag at this multi-purpose site. Listen for boats, and ascend on the west or south side of the rock and close to it. Then snorkel to shore. If you dive when a log boom is tied up to the rock, be aware of it. If the water becomes dark, head out from beneath the boom to the light. Try to stay off the bottom, so you do not stir up silt.

TELEPHONES

- Coopers Green, outside beach house.
- Halfmoon Bay General Store, down Mintie Road – 1 mile (1¾ kilometers) north off Redrooffs Road. Telephone inside: at the time of writing, only available from 9 am to 9 pm.

FACILITIES

Restrooms in summer, chemical toilet year-round. Picnic tables and lots of room to spread out at Coopers Green. Keep the groundskeeper happy by not wearing your wet suit or dry suit into the restrooms, and by taking care not to track mud and gravel into them.

ACCESS

Coopers Green is on Halfmoon Bay, Strait of Georgia side of Sechelt Peninsula. It is on Redrooffs Road (north end). Redrooffs cuts off of Sunshine Coast Highway 101 between Sechelt and Halfmoon Bay – the dive is midway on the peninsula between Langdale and Earls Cove. Allow 1 hour from each ferry to reach it.

At Coopers Green, dive or snorkel out to the rock on the left-hand side of the ramp and rock as you face the water. The diving area is marked. Dive around the south end of the rock and the ocean side of it, staying down out of the way of boats.

To get to Redrooffs Road and Coopers Green
- From Langdale, Gibsons and Sechelt head north on Highway 101: when 5½ miles (9 kilometers) past the sharp turn in the center of Sechelt at Wharf Road and Highway 101, turn left into Redrooffs Road. Drive north on Redrooffs for 5½ miles (9 kilometers) to Coopers Green. Go past it up the hill to Fisherman's Road, turn left and drive down Fisherman's to drop gear. Then return to Redrooffs to the parking area on the right-hand side, or roadside parking on Redrooffs down the hill.
- From Egmont and Pender Harbour, go south on Highway 101: when just over ½ mile (¾ kilometer) past the turnoff to Smuggler Cove Provincial Park at Brooks Road, bear right down Redrooffs Road. Go 1 mile (1½ kilometers) to Fisherman's Road – it is at the top of the hill. Drive down Fisherman's to the boat

ramp and drop gear. Then return to Redrooffs to the parking area on the right-hand side, or roadside parking downhill at Coopers Green.

Sunflower star

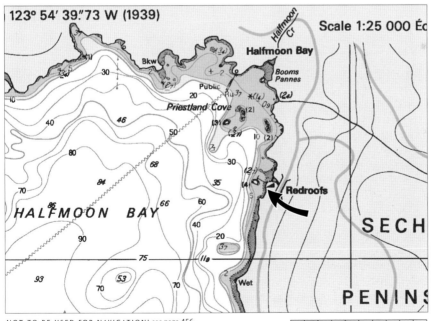

NOT TO BE USED FOR NAVIGATION: see page 456.
Use CHS chart #3535 for navigation; for information on obtaining navigational charts see page 456. Soundings are in meters.

1/2 NAUTICAL MILE

NOTES

PIRATE ROCK

BOAT DIVE
GPS
49°27.997' N
123°56.978' W

SKILL
Expert divers

TIDE TABLE
Point Atkinson:
Add 10 minutes

WHY GO

Pirate Rock sits "king-of-the-castle" on top of a series of irregular ledges, boulders and arches. Anchor heaven. It's one of the most dramatic pinnacles of rock I've dived.

And there's more than an average amount of life around it. Quillback rockfish – smallish to medium-sized – crowd the cracks of the rocks. Tube worms, sea peaches and plumose anemones hold tight under the overhangs. Sea pens tilt out of pools of sand between the ledges. Greenlings hide in the bottom kelp. Lingcod move in and out of the shadows.

Deeper, ratfish slide past big gray immobile chimney sponges, also called boot sponges. A wolf-eel hides in a hole under the rocks, while snakelock anemones, thick like fringe on a Spanish shawl, test the current with sticky fingers. And cloud sponges 1 foot (1/3 meter) wide float below like fluffy summer clouds in a beautiful reverse world.

Look for anchors.

Quillback rockfish

BOTTOM AND DEPTHS

Bull kelp is attached to irregular rocky bottom around Pirate Rock which is 20 to 30 feet (6 to 9 meters) deep, depending on tide height. Ledges, overhangs and arches which you can swim through surround the rock. The arches are formed by boulders tumbled one over the other. The north side drops off quickly. Narrow ledges tier down to 10 to 20 feet (3 to 6 meters), to 60 and 80 feet (18 and 24 meters) and on.

HAZARDS

Current and wind. Small fishing boats, bull kelp and broken fishing line. Dive on slack. Even then it is difficult. Currents come in streaks on the surface. One streak from Welcome Pass side. Then dead water. Then another streak of current from the west side of Thormanby Island. A pickup boat is advisable. Pirate Rock is popular with salmon fishermen. Be especially careful of small-boat traffic in salmon fishing season. Because the bottom undulates irregularly it is difficult to find your anchor line to use as an ascent line. If you cannot find it, ascend close to the rock all the way to the surface. Listen for boats and ascend cautiously; if you hear a boat, you can stay down until it passes. Carry a knife.

TELEPHONES

- On the water: VHF radio; if no VHF, try a cell phone.
- On land:
  1. Merry Island Lighthouse radiotelephone.
  2. Coopers Green, outside beach house.
  3. Halfmoon Bay General store, inside; near the Halfmoon Bay Wharf.

FACILITIES

None at Pirate Rock. Inflatable charters out of Sechelt. Launch ramp at Halfmoon Bay. A wilderness provincial park at Smuggler Cove, northeast end of Welcome Passage. No drinking water, but pit toilets and a place to pitch your tent.

ACCESS

Pirate Rock is ¼ nautical mile off the southeast tip of South Thormanby Island near Welcome Passage beside Sechelt Peninsula.

Allow 55 minutes from Langdale and 40 minutes from Earls Cove to drive Highway 101 to Secret Cove or Halfmoon Bay.

Charter out of Sechelt and go to Pirate Rock. Or launch your own boat at Halfmoon Bay and go 3 nautical miles southwest to Pirate Rock. Anchor anywhere around the rock, but do not tie onto the marker. It is a federal offense to make fast to a marker or tamper with any aid to navigation. Anchor carefully. In winter, south wind might blow you onto the rocks.

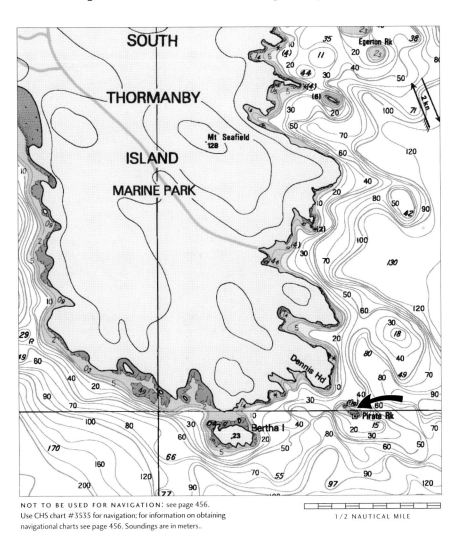

NOT TO BE USED FOR NAVIGATION: see page 456.
Use CHS chart #3535 for navigation; for information on obtaining navigational charts see page 456. Soundings are in meters..

1/2 NAUTICAL MILE

NOTES

OLE'S COVE

SHORE DIVE

SKILL
All divers

TIDE TABLE
Point Atkinson:
Add 10 minutes

WHY GO

If you want an old-fashioned reef – no frills, just a good reef – Ole's Cove is it.

From the surface little indicates a reef. Some bull kelp, but it's difficult to see, especially at high tide. You have to go on trust. The easiest way to find the reef is to set your compass and swim under water straight out from shore.

You'll see moon jellies and sea stars in the eelgrass. Shrimp, miniature sea pens and tube-dwelling anemones feathering the sandy shallows. At the rocky reef, 200 to 300 feet (60 to 90 meters) offshore, we saw crabs in the bottom kelp, covered with red anemones, white encrusting sponge, transparent sea squirts and small orange sponges. Striped seaperch and pile perch schooling around the rocks. You might see rockfish, kelp greenlings, painted greenlings, lingcod and dogfish.

A good afternoon dive when the sun has warmed the rocks.

BOTTOM AND DEPTHS

Sand and eelgrass slope gradually from shore to 25 feet (8 meters) deep. Rocky reef starts 200 to 300 feet (60 to 90 meters) offshore and undulates easily down. Some boulders, bottom kelp and bull kelp. Depending on tide height, the reef bottoms out to sand at a depth of 50 to 60 feet (15 to 18 meters).

HAZARDS

Boats and bull kelp, especially in summer. Listen for boats; if you hear one, stay down until it passes. Or better yet – follow your compass back to shore under water.

TELEPHONE

Lord Jim's Resort, inside but available 24 hours. South of the office main entry, go up three stairsteps. Turn left, and immediately right. The telephone is on the right-hand side.

FACILITIES

None at Ole's Cove. Dive shop in Sechelt; air stations in Pender Harbour and Egmont.

ACCESS

Ole's Cove is north of Welcome Passage in Malaspina Strait. It is north of Secret Cove off Sunshine Coast Highway 101. The turnoff is at Mercer Road. Allow 1 hour from Langdale, and 40 minutes from Earls Cove to reach it.

From Highway 101, turn into Mercer Road. From the highway, less than 2/3 mile (1 kilometer) to the dive. Go to Ole's Cove Road. Turn right. Go up the hill, and

Tube-dwelling anemone

94

immediately turn right again into Backhouse Road. Follow Backhouse Road winding through the woods. Drive for ⅓ mile (½ kilometer) to where the road dips down near the water. Space for two or three cars to park at the roadside. Between two homes, you will see a mailbox. Behind it, natural stone steps and a short gravel path to the cove. Since the bottom does not deepen quickly, use your compass and follow it straight out from shore to find the reef.

To get to Mercer Road, north end
• From Sechelt, go north on Highway 101. When 1½ miles (2½ kilometers) past the Buccaneer Bay turnoff, look for Lord Jim's sign at Mercer Road.
• From Pender Harbour, go south on Highway 101. When 5½ miles (9 kilometers) past Francis Peninsula Road, look for Lord Jim's sign at Mercer Road.

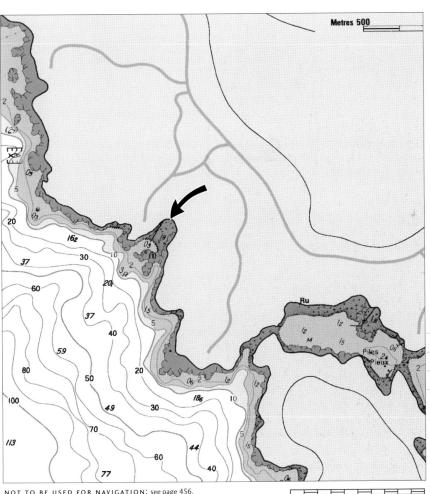

NOTES

NOT TO BE USED FOR NAVIGATION: see page 456.
Use CHS chart #3535 for navigation; for information on obtaining navigational charts see page 456. Soundings are in meters.

1/5 NAUTICAL MILE

MARTIN COVE

SKILL
All divers

TIDE TABLE
Point Atkinson:
Add 10 minutes

WHY GO

If you want a quick uncomplicated dive with a wilderness feeling beneath the water, try this quiet cove south of Pender Harbour.

You'll see flounders. Oregon tritons and sea stars on the sandy sea floor. Look for moon snails as well. Along rocky walls rimming both sides of the cove we found small green anemones contrasting with very red rocks in the shallows; purple crabs scurrying about; and purple stars sticking on the rocks. Millions of almost-transparent blackeye gobies dart all about. Pipefish, pile perch and striped seaperch glint in the sun. Rockfish hang along the wall. Deeper we saw sea peaches, dahlia anemones and lingcod.

Chimney or boot sponges at 60 feet (18 meters) and you're in the wilderness.

BOTTOM AND DEPTHS

The cove is rimmed with rock walls dropping to sandy bottom that slopes to deep water. Some boulders along the wall.

HAZARDS

Wind could blow into the bay. Fatigue, if lured too far by the chimney sponges. Watch your time.

TELEPHONE

In Madeira Park, outside Oak Tree Market. At junction of Francis Peninsula Road and Highway 101, turn left and go to Madeira Park Road. Turn left and go 1/5 mile (1/3 kilometer) to the Oak Tree Market.

FACILITIES

None; use toilet facilities before you arrive. Privately-owned homes rim the cove.

Air fills, camping, accommodations, boat charters, boat rentals and launch ramps at nearby Pender Harbour. Day charters out of Francis Peninsula a short way down the road: you pass it on the way to this dive.

ACCESS

Martin Cove is south of Pender Harbour in Malaspina Strait. Reach it off Highway 101 by way of the southernmost of three access roads to the Pender Harbour area.

Turn onto Francis Peninsula Road and go west for 4 miles (6½ kilometers) to Martin Cove. On the way, cross a small bridge at Bargain Narrows onto Beaver Island. Past this bridge, the road winds all over the place. Keep on the main road to Martin Road. If you reach the end of the road, you have gone 1/3 mile (1/2 kilometer) too far. Park at the roadside, just past Martin Road, and walk 100 paces down a well-worn path through the woods to the beach. Entry is easy.

To get to Francis Peninsula Road
- From Langdale and Sechelt, go north on Sunshine Coast Highway 101. Past Halfmoon Bay and 5½ miles (9 kilometers) past the turnoff to Lord Jim's, turn left into Francis Peninsula Road. It takes an hour.
- From Earls Cove, go south on Highway 101. When 2/3 mile (1 kilometer) past the turnoff to Madeira Park, turn right into Francis Peninsula Road – 25 minutes to it.

Blackeye goby

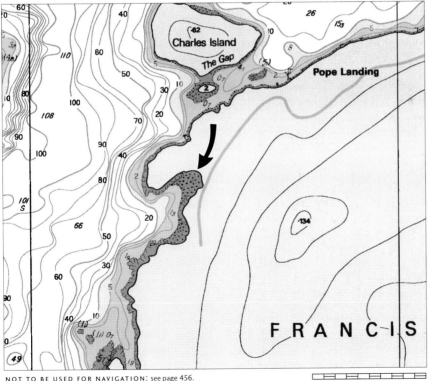

NOT TO BE USED FOR NAVIGATION: see page 456.
Use CHS chart #3535 for navigation; for information on obtaining
navigational charts see page 456. Soundings are in meters.

1/5 NAUTICAL MILE

NOTES

FEARNEY BLUFFS

BOAT DIVE

GPS
49°39.116′ N
124°05.147′ W

SKILL
Expert divers, guided
intermediate divers and
snorkelers

TIDE TABLE
Point Atkinson:
Add 10 minutes

WHY GO

Divers always rave about one thing at
Fearney – the massive cloud sponges!
Fearney is the most fabulous wall, with the
most glorious cloud sponges. Chimney
sponges, too. The granite wall drops
straight down: deep, deep, deep. The
feeling of space is incredible. Back off the
wall to see the whole scene and so you do
not damage the delicate sponges. Come
close, carefully, to look at smaller creatures. We saw flaming red slipper cucumbers. Staghorn bryozoans which look like
hard coral. At 100 feet (30 meters), several small, branching dwarf gorgonian
corals. They were 6 inches (15 centimeters)
tall and bright red. *Paragorgia arborea*,
another species of red gorgonian coral, is
also found at this site. Large fans of these
red gorgonians, some 3 feet (1 meter) high,
live at depths of 165 feet (50 meters) and
deeper in Agamemnon Channel – beyond
sport-diving limits. This gorgonian coral
occurs in few sites in the world, maybe
nowhere else.

We also saw tiny green urchins, red
dahlia anemones, transparent sea squirts,
orange cup corals and yellow ones. Tiger,
quillback and yelloweye rockfish, a couple
of lingcod. Giant barnacles, rock scallops,
feather stars on the wall. Moon jellies in
the open water. A silvery cloud of herring.
Stopping in the shallows is a pleasure,
too, with heaps of purple sea stars, crabs,
seaperch and maroon-and-gray striped
painted greenlings which I love for their
color. For their markings.

It is beautiful all the way. But somehow
nothing really matters at Fearney Bluffs
except the red coral. The white puffs of
cloud sponge. The wall.

BOTTOM AND DEPTHS

A wall. Smooth granite plunges to 280
feet (86 meters) with undercuts in places.
Narrow rocky ledges for safety stops at
10 to 20 feet (3 to 6 meters) close alongside the wall.

HAZARDS

Current, with some swirly water on large
tidal exchanges. Dive on slack.

TELEPHONES

- On the water: VHF radio; if no VHF, try a
cell phone.
- On land at Pender Harbour:
1. Pender Harbour Resort, Garden Bay.
2. Seafarer Millennium Park Ramp,
Madeira Park: top of dock beside parking lot; another across road at Tourist
Infocentre

FACILITIES

Air stations, charters, boat rentals and
launch ramps; hot showers, camping and
accommodations at Pender Harbour and
Egmont. And a water taxi at Egmont.

ACCESS

Fearney Bluffs are located at the south
end of Agamemnon Channel almost in
Malaspina Strait. The site is 2 nautical
miles northwest of Pender Harbour –
when you approach from this direction
you will see the bluffs for a long way. The
dive is 12 nautical miles from Egmont; go
northwest then south through Agamemnon Channel to Fearney Bluffs.

Charter, take a water taxi, rent a boat
or take your own boat. Launch at Pender
Harbour or Egmont and go to Fearney.
The bluff above water mirrors what is below.
Famous last words but I'll risk it – you
can't miss the bluff. Fearney is exposed to
southeast wind; pick a calm day.

At low tides, small boats can pull up
onto a ledge. For larger boats, at all times
it is too deep to anchor and better not to
as you might damage the cloud sponges.
Dive from a "live" boat. Or tie up at the
wall – an arrow within a circle is painted
on the rock wall: it points to an eye-bolt
to tie onto.

Indian paintings on a wall on the
opposite side of Agamemnon, west of the
power lines.

Gearing up at Fearney Bluffs

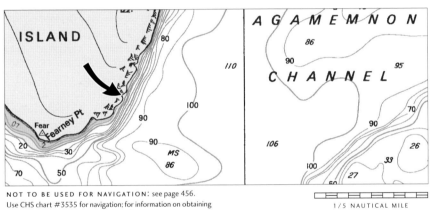

NOT TO BE USED FOR NAVIGATION: see page 456.
Use CHS chart #3535 for navigation; for information on obtaining
navigational charts see page 456. Soundings are in meters.

1/5 NAUTICAL MILE

NOTES

NOT TO BE USED FOR NAVIGATION: see page 456.
Use CHS chart #3512 for navigation; for information on obtaining
navigational charts see page 456. Soundings are in meters.

2 NAUTICAL MILES

BENEATH THE POWER LINES

BOAT DIVE
GPS
49°44.641′ N
124°01.681′ W

SKILL
Expert divers and
guided intermediates
over the wall

All divers and snorkelers
on ledge

TIDE TABLE
Point Atkinson

*Diver descends on
large cloud sponge*

WHY GO

Sponges! Glistening like spun ivory, tentacles of cloud sponges twist from the stark, dark wall beneath the power lines – some as large as 3 feet (1 meter) wide. They reach out and down. Many are shiny yellow. Look for chimney sponges too.

As at Fearney Bluffs, this sponge site is also well known for the large fans of gorgonians up to 3 feet (1 meter) high that live at depths of 165 feet (50 meters) and deeper. I did not see any fans beneath the power lines as I limited my maximum depth to 125 feet (38 meters) – stayed within sport-diving limits. We enjoyed a slow cruise along the wall. And there's another whole dive to enjoy in the shallows.

While I think of Agamemnon as being great for those who "think deep", this site is also excellent for mixed groups because of the life on the ledge. Pile perch and sculpins are everywhere. Look for sea lemons, painted greenlings in the kelp, tube worms, bryozoans, sea peaches and encrusting sponges on the rocks.

BOTTOM AND DEPTHS

Rocky, shallow bottom in the cove. Brown bottom kelp covers the rocks. Bull kelp, especially in summer.

From the cove, the bottom rolls gently down to a sharp ledge or lip at 60 to 70 feet (18 to 21 meters), depending on tide height. From there the bottom disappears into the deep. Accordion-like lines on the chart show the series of ledges in rapid succession – a dramatic plunge into Agamemnon Channel.

HAZARDS

Depth, wind, minimal current and some bull kelp, in summer. If anchoring and it is windy, look at wind direction and consider surface current it will create. Dive near slack. Consider wind when planning the direction of your dive. Do not dive on the ebb if wind is pushing the water in the same direction. Plan for depth as well, and carry it out – these depths are so alluring. Carry a knife for kelp.

TELEPHONES

- On the water: VHF radio; if no VHF, try a cell phone.
- On land: go to Egmont Marina, outside air station behind the Backeddy Pub; it is 4 nautical miles northeast around the corner in Egmont.

FACILITIES

None in Agamemnon Channel. Air stations, charters, launch ramps and accommodations at Egmont and Pender Harbour.

ACCESS

Beneath the Power Lines site is at the northern end of Agamemnon Channel on the eastern shore. It is 4 nautical miles southwest around the corner from the marina at Egmont, and 9 nautical miles northwest of Pender Harbour.

Charter or launch at Egmont or Pender Harbour: go to the power lines and anchor in the cove opposite Caldwell Island. Boats with a tender could do a slow drift along the wall.

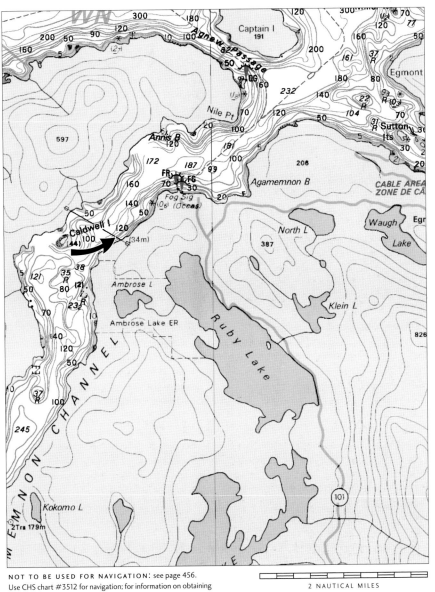

NOT TO BE USED FOR NAVIGATION: see page 456.
Use CHS chart #3512 for navigation; for information on obtaining navigational charts see page 456. Soundings are in meters..

2 NAUTICAL MILES

NOTES

BOAT DIVE or KAYAK DIVE
GPS
49°45.759′ N
123°56.184′ W

SKILL
Intermediate and expert divers

All divers with guide

CURRENT TABLE
Sechelt Rapids:
Subtract 10 minutes

WHY GO

Dive into the famous – or infamous – Skookumchuck Narrows. And you could make it in 10 minutes by dive-kayak from your campsite or cabin at Egmont Marine to this varied, rich site.

Tiger rockfish flash their orange and black stripes beneath the ledges, swimming scallops clap up from the bottom. Lots of them here. We saw heaps of crab shells, leavings of octopuses. And the nooks and crannies down the rocky ledges of the Sutton Islets are perfect places for wolf-eels to lurk. Bright green lettuce kelp, brown bottom kelp and bull kelp provide hiding places for urchins, crabs and pile perch. Sea stars decorate the rocks. At the base of the rocky wall, look for mauve hydrocoral.

More good diving nearby at the northern Sutton Islet, also easily reachable by dive-kayak. Walter, the wolf-eel, used to reside in a den on its western side.

After the dive, there are convenient cold-water taps for washing gear, coin-operated hot showers, food, fireplace and sometimes live music in the Backeddy Pub.

BOTTOM AND DEPTHS

The rocky shore cascades down with easy-to-stop-at ledges. One at 80 to 90 feet (24 to 27 meters), depending on tide height. Bull kelp, especially in summer. Lots of lettuce kelp and brown bottom kelp.

HAZARDS

Current, boats, bull kelp. Dive on slack; the window of time to dive is small. The back eddies are unpredictable. Charter boats often do it as a drift dive. Only expert divers with a great deal of current experience should dive this without a "live" boat. If traveling by dive-kayak, pick a day with a tidal exchange of 5 feet (1½ meters) or less and dive precisely on slack so you can get back to your kayak. Ascending, listen for boats – many speedboats pass through the channel and go

into the marina. Do not ascend through open water: use the kelp as a protected place and hug the contours of the bottom all the way to the surface of the island. Carry a knife for kelp.

TELEPHONES

• On the water: VHF radio; if no VHF, try a cell phone.
• On land: across the channel at Egmont Marina, telephone is outside air station behind the Backeddy Pub.

FACILITIES

None at the Sutton Islets. Dive-kayak rentals at the dive shop in the town of Sechelt.

At the marina on the western shore of the Sutton Islets: charter boats, an air station, launch ramp, restrooms, hot showers, cold-water taps for rinsing gear. Cabins, camping, restaurant and a pub.

In Egmont: boat rentals, water taxi, grocery, tent camping and RV sites; hot showers with restrooms during store hours.

ACCESS

The Sutton Islets are in Skookumchuck Narrows north of Egmont. The dive is less than ½ nautical mile offshore from the Egmont side of the channel.

Go by charter or rental boat, launch your own boat or go by dive-kayak. The closest point to go from by dive-kayak is Egmont Marina. It is less than ½ nautical mile to the channel side of the southernmost of the Sutton Islets, and is a 10-minute paddle. Or you could rent a boat at Egmont or paddle ¾ nautical mile from the public ramp at Egmont to the site. We kayaked out to a small cove on the channel side to gear up. We dived on a high tide at the turn to ebb and worked southward toward the marker for the first half of the dive. Then when almost half our air was gone we drifted back to the cove with the current – there was a small back eddy in the cove which slowed us down when we reached it.

Loading dive gear — then off to Sutton Islets at distant marker

NOTES

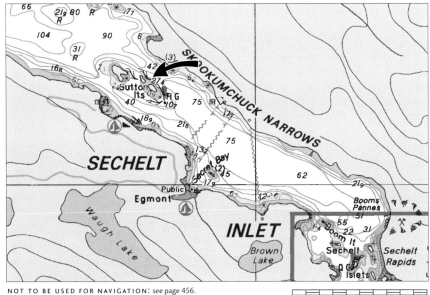

NOT TO BE USED FOR NAVIGATION: see page 456.
Use CHS chart #3514 for navigation; for information on obtaining
navigational charts see page 456. Soundings are in meters.

1 NAUTICAL MILE

—ISLET AT SECRET BAY—

**SHORE DIVE or
KAYAK DIVE**

SKILL
Intermediate and expert
divers

CURRENT TABLE
Sechelt Rapids:
Subtract 10 minutes

WHY GO
Only a few sites where you can dive from
shore and see swimming scallops. Egmont
is one of them.

A circuit of the islet reveals many other
creatures as well. Red tube worms in the
shallows. Gum boot chitons, alabaster
nudibranchs, sea lemons, shrimp and
bright orange branches of dead man's finger
sponges. Deeper in the kelp, greenlings are
all over the place. Sea peaches and transparent sea squirts cling to the wall. Brilliant
red-and-black striped tiger rockfish hide
under ledges. Swimming scallops dot the
bottom, rain up around you when your
shadow passes over them.

BOTTOM AND DEPTHS
Rocky bottom undulates down quickly all
around the islet. Bull kelp and bottom kelp
from 20 to 40 feet (6 to 12 meters).
Some big rocks, crevices and overhangs.
Then the wall drops abruptly, leveling off
to silty sand at 75 to 85 feet (23 to 26
meters). Swimming scallops all over the
bottom on the channel side of the island.

HAZARDS
Current, boats, long swim and bull kelp.
Dive near the slack. Listen for boats and
stay close to the side of the islet all the
way to the surface. Save some energy for
the swim or paddle back, especially if the
current starts up. Carry a knife for kelp.

TELEPHONES
- Bathgate's Store & Marina at Egmont,
  outside; follow the steps uphill from
  the wharf.
- Egmont Marina, outside air station
  behind Backeddy Pub. Go from the
  wharf at Egmont uphill to Maple Road.
  Turn right and go north on Maple for 1
  mile (1½ kilometers); turn right down to
  the marina.

FACILITIES
Boat rentals and water taxi at Bathgate's
Marina in Egmont; also restrooms and hot
showers during store hours. Public launch
ramp at foot of Bradwynne Road off
Maple Road where dive-kayakers can launch.
Air station farther down Maple Road.

Swimming scallops

ACCESS

The Islet at Secret Bay is in the entrance to the bay from Skookumchuck Narrows, top of the Sunshine Coast. The dive is a 15-minute drive off Sunshine Coast Highway 101 at Egmont. The Egmont Road turnoff is immediately south of Earls Cove. From Langdale, 1½ hours to Egmont Road.

At Egmont Road, follow signs toward Skookumchuck Narrows Provincial Park. The road twists and turns. Shortly past the park you reach the wharf at Egmont. Drop your gear beside the wharf and return up the hill to park at the roadside. You need about 15 minutes to swim from the dock to the islet.

Kayak-divers can launch from the public ramp and easily paddle to the islet. The ramp turnoff is just before the wharf. Turn left and go north on Maple Road; then immediately right into Bradwynne Road and right again down the ramp. Wheelchair access at this public ramp; but no level place to park beside the ramp. Space for three or four cars to park at Egmont Road.

To get to Egmont Road
• From Langdale, drive north on Highway 101 to Egmont Road, which is 13 miles (21 kilometers) past the Madeira Park turnoff at Pender Harbour. When you see signs to Skookumchuck Narrows Provincial Park, turn right into Egmont Road.
• From Earls Cove, go ⅔ mile (1 kilometer) and turn left into Egmont Road.

NOTES

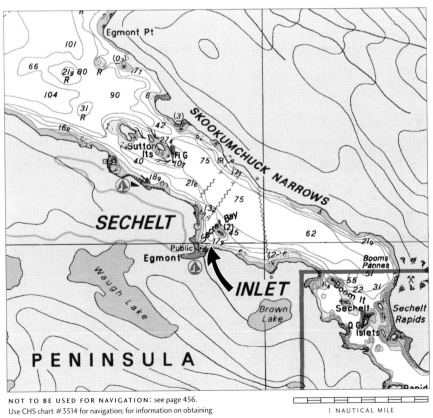

NOT TO BE USED FOR NAVIGATION: see page 456.
Use CHS chart #3514 for navigation; for information on obtaining navigational charts see page 456. Soundings are in meters.

1 NAUTICAL MILE

SECHELT RAPIDS [SKOOKUMCHUCK]

BOAT DIVE

GPS

Entry to dive on flood:
49°44.574' N
123°53.738' W

Entry to dive on ebb:
49°44.293' N
123°53.625' W

SKILL
Expert divers

Intermediate divers with guide

CURRENT TABLE
Sechelt Rapids

WHY GO

Winter and summer, the hottest spot to dive in British Columbia has to be Sechelt tidal rapids. The ocean floor is like a brilliant flower garden of the sea.

At the same time, diving the Skookumchuck is a slow motion flight into a field of wildflowers: pink, powder blue, and mint-green anemones blowing in the wind. Or an informal garden: these delicate flowers of the sea are heaped like blossoms in a flamboyant Renoir painting. Or a formal garden: we see pebble patterns, Japanese style, on the ocean floor. White encrusting sponge covers the rocks, lighting up the depths with reflected sunlight. Yellow encrusting sponge covers the remaining boulders and jagged rocks that are not bright white or pale pastel. Tiny orange cup corals polka dot whatever surface is left to cling to.

On the way up we see two orange-and-black striped tiger rockfish beneath a dark ledge, a brown Irish lord, tube worms, purple urchins, giant barnacles, a school of black rockfish, kelp greenlings flashing past. You might see a Puget Sound king crab. An octopus. Purple sea stars, as always, are heaped in the shallows. While blue sea stars – from deep to shallow – splay their knobby fingers throughout this exotic undersea garden.

It is rich. Potentially dangerous. Worth planning for.

BOTTOM AND DEPTHS

Huge boulders spill in heaps into a gorge to the bright sandy bottom at 100 to 110 feet (30 to 34 meters).

HAZARDS

Current, upwellings and downwellings: sometimes 15- to 16-knot currents race through Skookumchuck. At slack tides, when divers go, a great many boats pass through the narrows, too. One inlet resident coaches boat captains through. Stories of a 50-foot (15-meter) fishing boat flip-ping in the Skookumchuck are rampant at the pub. I've heard that Skookum Island trembles with large tidal exchanges – *not* the day to go.

Dive on a day when it is likely you can dive under control – even then you *must* have a pickup boat. No diver's flag will help you if you pop up unexpectedly beneath a boat – you do not have to fly through these rapids willy-nilly and out of control. Pick your dive time carefully. Winter is best when tidal exchanges are smaller and less boat traffic – visibility is better, too. Your first time, go with a charter operator who knows Skookumchuck, dive with a reliable buddy you know well. And enjoy.

TELEPHONES

- On the water: VHF radio; if no VHF, try a cell phone.
- On land at Egmont, north end:
1. Outside Bathgate's Marina, above the wharf.
2. Outside air station behind Backeddy Pub at Egmont Marina; go 4 nautical miles northeast around corner in Skookumchuck Narrows.
- On land at Sechelt Inlet, south end:
1. Tillicum Marina Resort, east side of Sechelt Inlet and two-thirds of the way back to Porpoise Bay, outside marina office.
2. Lighthouse Pub, outside – top of the wharf at Porpoise Bay.

FACILITIES

None at Skookumchuck. Charters, air fills and launch ramps at town of Sechelt and Egmont.

ACCESS

Sechelt Rapids is at the northern entry to Sechelt Inlet. It is 17 nautical miles north of Porpoise Bay, 1½ nautical miles south of Egmont.

Charter, rent or launch at Porpoise Bay or Egmont. Choose a day when maximum current speed on both sides of slack (ebb or flood) is less than 5 knots. Be ready 30 minutes before predicted slack – it is probably the time to dive. But as always at a high-current site, be there ahead of time ready to go since the currents do not always perform as predicted.

To dive the gorge, sometimes called Glory Hole, on a flood, go to the northwest tip of the islet on the east side of the islets that are north of Sechelt Rapids. To dive the gorge on the ebb, enter at the opposite end of it. (See the map on page 75 and the arrows on the nautical chart on this page.) Watch and wait for the current to slow down; roll off the boat and head down. Leave a boat tender *who is experienced with Sechelt Rapids* ready to pick you up. When the current turns and gathers speed, time to end your dive.

Before diving Sechelt Rapids, you might walk to Roland Point at Skookumchuck Narrows Provincial Park to see the spectacle of the rapids from shore. A footpath heads south from Egmont Road. Allow 45 minutes to walk to Roland Point. Check the current table for Sechelt Rapids and try to arrive at maximum flow.

To get to Sechelt Rapids
- From Porpoise Bay, go north: you will pass Salmon Inlet and Narrows Inlet. You are almost there when you pass Skookum Island and then Rapid Islet on the left-hand side. Speedboat Pass is between two of the northernmost of the Sechelt Islets in Sechelt Rapids. It is between the islet in the center and the islet east of it.
- From Egmont, go south: the first islets you reach are the Sechelt Islets. Speedboat Pass is between the islet in the center and the islet to the east of it.

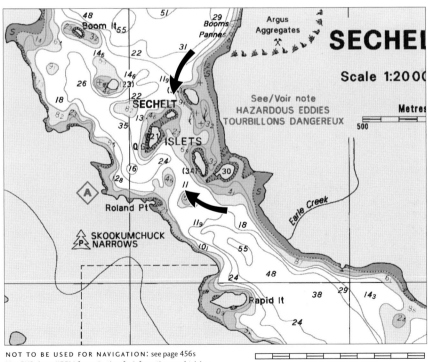

NOTES

NOT TO BE USED FOR NAVIGATION: see page 456s
Use CHS chart #3514 for navigation; for information on obtaining navigational charts see page 456. Soundings are in meters.

1/2 NAUTICAL MILE

Powell River and North

Wood rot and rusty steel "stalagmites" on wreck of Capilano I

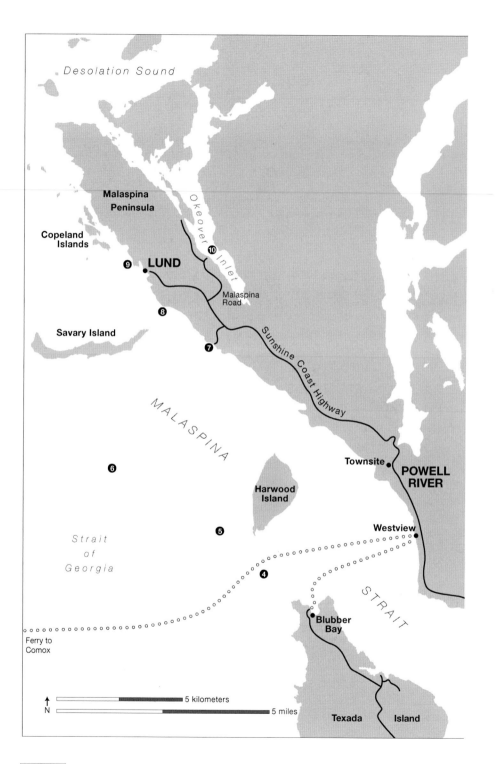

Desolation Sound

Malaspina
Peninsula

Copeland
Islands

Okeover Inlet

⑨ ●LUND

Malaspina
Road

⑩

⑧

Savary Island

⑦

Sunshine Coast Highway

MALASPINA

⑥

Townsite ●

POWELL
RIVER

Harwood
Island

⑤

Westview ●

Strait
of
Georgia

④

STRAIT

Blubber
Bay

Ferry to
Comox

5 kilometers

N

5 miles

Texada   Island

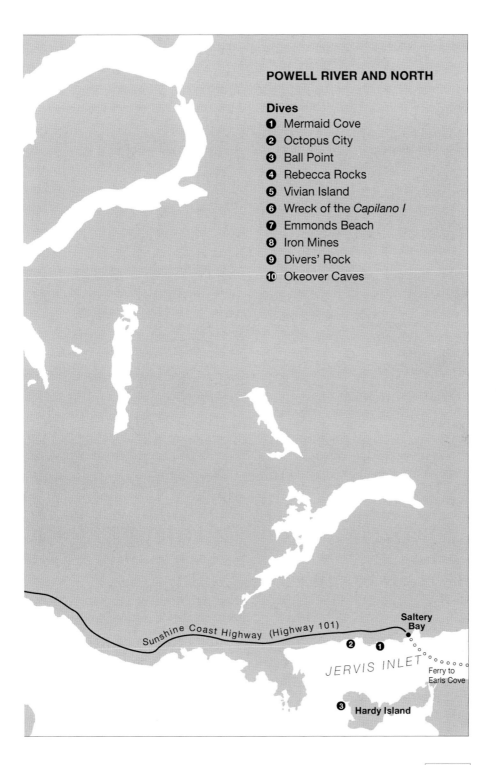

POWELL RIVER AND NORTH

Dives

1. Mermaid Cove
2. Octopus City
3. Ball Point
4. Rebecca Rocks
5. Vivian Island
6. Wreck of the *Capilano I*
7. Emmonds Beach
8. Iron Mines
9. Divers' Rock
10. Okeover Caves

Sunshine Coast Highway (Highway 101)

Saltery Bay

2 **1**

JERVIS INLET

Ferry to Earls Cove

3 Hardy Island

SERVICE INFORMATION

Tide and Current Information
- *Tide and Current Tables, Volume 5: Juan de Fuca Strait and Strait of Georgia,* Canadian Hydrographic Service print annual
- *Current Atlas: Juan de Fuca Strait to Strait of Georgia,* purchase one time. Use with *Murray's Tables* or *Washburne's Tables,* purchase annually; privately produced publications available at marine equipment and supplies stores.
- www.lau.chs-shc.gc.ca: Tide and Current Tables for all of Canada. Go to the web site: click on Pacific; General Information; Tide and Currents, Data Available; then Tide Tables available in PDF form. Select Volume 5 and click on the tide or current table desired – both are on the same list on the pdf.

Weather Information
- Canadian Coast Guard: Speak with a person, 24 hours; telephone Comox (250)339-3613.
- Canadian Coast Guard (Comox Coast Guard Radio): continuous Marine Broadcast (CMB) recorded, 24 hours; listen for weather in the Strait of Georgia, telephone Comox: (250)339-0748.
- Environment Canada: recorded, 24 hours; telephone Vancouver (604)664-9010
    Press 1 for Weather Line
    Press 2 for Marine Weather, press 1 and listen for weather in the Strait of Georgia and Howe Sound.
- www.weatheroffice.ec.gc.ca

Tourist Information
- Toll-free throughout North America: 1-800-435-5622
- From all other locations: (250)387-1642 www.hellobc.com

Diving Emergency Telephone Numbers
On land and water:
- Call 911, request "ambulance" and say, "I have a scuba diving emergency".
- Vancouver General Hospital; for 24-hour, 7-day-a- week response: telephone (604)875-5000 and say, "I want the hyperbaric physician on call".

On the water:
- VHF radio: Call Coast Guard radio, Channel 16 and say, "I have a scuba diving emergency".
- Cell phone: 911, *16 or *311 and say, "I have a scuba diving emergency".

If emergency or medical personnel are unfamiliar with scuba diving emergencies, ask them to telephone DAN (Divers Alert Network) at (919)684-4326. No money for a long distance call? Dial DAN collect at 011-919-684-4326 and say, "I have a scuba diving emergency".

Mark emergency location before leaving scene: other divers might be down.

How to Go
Powell River is located on the mainland of British Columbia but you must take a ferry to get there.
- From Vancouver, go to Horseshoe Bay in West Vancouver and take a 40-minute ferry ride to Langdale on the Sechelt Peninsula. Drive 1 ½ hours to Earls Cove and take a 50-minute ferry ride to Saltery Bay. Drive half an hour to Westview in the center of Powell River.
- From Sechelt go from Earls Cove to Saltery Bay on the ferry – takes 50 minutes, then drive to Westview in Powell River in half an hour.
- From Vancouver Island, go to Courtenay; then follow signs to Little River ferry terminal at Comox. Take a 1 ¼-hour ferry ride to Powell River (Westview).

Ferry Information

British Columbia Ferry Services (BC Ferries)
• Toll-free throughout North America:
  1-888-223-3779
• From all other locations: (250)386-3431
www.bcferries.com
At the time of writing the following information applies – but frequent changes occur; it would be wise to check current requirements on BC Ferries web page before every trip.

Rules Regarding Scuba Tanks on BC Ferries
Persons transporting scuba tanks containing compressed air, full or partially full, are required under Canadian law to declare dangerous goods at the terminal or to a vessel officer. Persons transporting scuba tanks with the valves removed do not need clearance. All pressurized tanks with a UN 3156 sticker, indicating nitrox or mixed gases, are taboo – remove the valve.

Expedite Dangerous Goods clearance at the ferry ticket booth – complete a Dangerous Goods Shipping Document prior to arrival. Obtain it from the web at home or a library: Go to www.bcferries.com: select Travel Planning; click on Carrying Dangerous Goods, then For the General Public. Download Dangerous Goods Shipping Document and complete it: include your name, home address and phone number; Class 2; UN 1002, which indicates compressed air; the number of cylinders you are transporting and quantity in each one: most tanks are 80 cubic feet/2.27 cubic meters.

(To calculate quantity in scuba tanks: 1 cubic foot=0.0283168466 cubic meters.)

Arrive at least 30 minutes prior to intended sailing time or telephone the terminal you will travel through and ask when they suggest you should arrive.
1. Westview-Powell River: (604)485-2943
2. Saltery Bay (604)487-9333

Prearranged Dangerous Goods Clearance Requires 48 Hours
Complete a Dangerous Goods Shipping Document as described above and fax it at least 48 hours before intended sailing time to the terminal manager responsible for the terminal of your departure.
1. Saltery Bay: fax (604)487-9396
2. Westview-Powell River:
   fax (604)485-2949

• DIVE SHOP
Alpha Dive Services
7013 Thunder Bay Street
Powell River BC V8A 4Z5
(604)485-6939
www.divepowellriver.com
(Guiding for shore dives. Also charters.)

• DAY AND MULTIPLE-DAY CHARTERS, BOAT RENTALS AND WATER TAXI
Out of Westview in Powell River
Trailerable 22-foot jet boat
Alpha Dive Services
7013 Thunder Bay Street
Powell River BC V8A 4Z5
(604)485-6939
www.divepowellriver.com
(Day charters for two divers and a guide. The jet boat serves the Strait of Georgia; wreck of the Shamrock at Vivian Island, the Malahat close to Powell River, Rebecca Rocks reefs. It goes out of Saltery Bay to cloud sponges at Texada, Ball Point – wherever you want to dive.)

Gail Warning
Gail Warning Charters
PO Box 92
Powell River BC V8A 4Z5
(604)487-4446; pager (604)483-8780: leave your number
www.gailwarningcharters.com
(Day charters year-round for two to six divers out of North Harbour, Westview; dives range from Vivian Island to Rebecca Rocks to Cyril Rock, north end of Texada Island, to Marshall Rocks and more.)

DAY AND MULTIPLE-DAY CHARTERS, BOAT RENTALS AND WATER TAXI (CONTINUED)

Out of Lund

Trailerable 22-foot jet boat
Alpha Dive Services
7013 Thunder Bay Street
Powell River BC V8A 4Z5
(604)485-6939
www.divepowellriver.com
(The jet boat takes two divers and a guide for day trips that range from Iron Mines to Divers' Rock, Kinghorn Island and more. You name it, they'll go.)

Carousel, Swan Spirit
Pristine Charters
C-25, RR2, Craig Road
Powell River BC V8A 4Z3
(604)483-4541; boat (604)483-1131
www.pristinecharters.com
(One- to three-day charters year-round out of Lund to Desolation Sound and more; all-inclusive packages with food, beverages, diving and accommodation if more than one day.)

Perfidia
Pollen & Company
PO Box 200
Lund BC V0N 2G0
(604)483-4402; cell (604)483-1646
1-800-667-6603: Toll-free throughout
    North America
E-mail: pollen@prcn.org
(Day charters year-round out of Lund to Desolation Sound, Iron Mines, Divers' Rock and more.)

Lund Water Taxi Ltd.
PO Box 196
Lund BC V0N 2G0
(604)483-9749
(Water taxi year-round out of Lund, book in advance.)

Out of Head of Okeover Inlet

Ark
Desolation Resort
2694 Dawson Road, Okeover Inlet
Mailing address: RR2 Malaspina Road, C-36
Powell River BC V8A 4Z3
(604)483-3592
www.desolationresort.com
(Day charters year-round out of Okeover Inlet. Also luxury chalet accommodations. English and German spoken.)
    Turn off Highway 101 onto Malaspina Road and go 2¼ miles (3½ kilometers) to the Leslie Road turnoff, then right onto Dawson Road.

Valiant and a 22-foot trailerable jet boat
Alpha Dive Services
7013 Thunder Bay Street
Powell River BC V8A 4Z5
(604)485-6939
www.divepowellriver.com
(Day charters for small and large groups: the Valiant accommodates up to ten divers and two guides. It goes out of Okeover Inlet to Okeover Caves, all over Desolation Sound and to the Lund area for diving Iron Mines, the wreck of the Adventurer and more.
    The jet boat takes two divers and a guide: it also goes to sites ranging from Okeover Caves in the inlet to Desolation Sound.)

Y-Knot Camp & Charter
2960 D'Angio Road, Okeover Inlet
Mailing address: RR2 Malaspina Road, C-25
Powell River BC V8A 4Z3
(604)483-3243
www.yknot.ca
(Boat rentals year-round. In winter, inquire in advance. Telephone at Okeover Dock. At Y-Knot, a pit toilet; camping and cabins – one rustic, one with running water and hot shower.)
    Turn off Highway 101 onto Malaspina Road: the D'Angio Road turnoff is 2 miles (3¼ kilometers); go to the end of D'Angio.

•LAUNCH RAMPS
At Saltery Bay
For Jervis Inlet
Saltery Bay Picnic Ground Ramp
(Launch free, concrete ramp. Good at medium to high tides; accommodate boats up to 30 feet [9 meters] at high tide. Pit toilets, one is wheelchair-accessible. Telephone at Saltery Bay, north of ferry terminal.)

Off Highway 101, 2 miles (3¼ kilometers) past Saltery Bay ferry terminal, and 19 miles (30 kilometers) southeast of Powell River and Westview.

At Westview and Lund
For Malaspina Strait and Strait of Georgia
Powell River Municipal Marina
North Harbour Ramp
(Concrete ramp on Malaspina Strait; good at all tides. Free launch, parking for a fee. Wheelchair-accessible restrooms and telephone at south end of ferry parking lot in the waiting room, available 6:30 am to 11 pm. Another telephone, available 24 hours, outside Chamber of Commerce building at Wharf Street and Willingdon Avenue. It is immediately behind the ferry terminal building.)

At foot of Courtenay Street, north end of Westview Ferry Terminal parking lot.

Lund Public Ramps
End of Highway 101 North
(Launch for a fee for Thulin Passage and Malaspina Strait: concrete ramps, good at tides of 2 feet [⅔ meter] and greater. At the time of writing, no fee for launch of car-top boats at gravel ramp, south of Harbour Master's building. Telephones outside hotel, shop near hotel, and outside bakery. Wheelchair-accessible shower and toilets in Harbour Master's building next to ramps. Cafés a few steps away.)

At north end of Highway 101: go 19 miles (30 kilometers) north of Powell River to the end of the road at Lund.

All of this Service Information is subject to change.

Dinner Rock Ramp
Dinner Rock Recreation Site
Off Highway 101
(Dirt ramp is free: launch car-top boats for Malaspina Strait. Carry over 30 feet [9 meters] of log-strewn cobble beach to the water. Wheelchair-accessible pit toilet and camping for a fee at launch site. Telephones 5 miles [8 kilometers] north in Lund, outside the hotel, the shops next to the hotel and outside the bakery.)

Dinner Rock Recreation Site is 30 minutes north of Powell River: the turnoff to it is 7½ miles (12 kilometers) north of Sliammon Creek and 2¾ miles (4½ kilometers) south of Lund. From Highway 101, nearly 1 mile (1½ kilometers) to the water. At the time of writing, the road to the recreation site is open annually from May 1 to September 15, closed in winter.

At Head of Okeover Inlet [Okeover Arm]
For Okeover Inlet
Okeover Harbour Authority Ramp
Off Malaspina Road
(Launch for a fee on gravel and concrete ramp: good for boats up to 20 feet [6 meters]. Best at mid-tides of 7 to 8 feet [2 to 2½ meters]; it is difficult to pull forward at high tides. The concrete part of the ramp is exposed at low tides, the gravel part at higher tides. Telephone on dock; pit toilets, one wheelchair-accessible, at nearby Okeover Arm Provincial Park campground.)

Off Highway 101, 30 minutes north of Powell River. When 8½ miles (13½ kilometers) north of Sliammon Creek, or 1¾ miles (3 kilometers) south of Lund, turn north into Malaspina Road. Go 2½ miles (4 kilometers) to the ramp at Okeover Inlet. Okeover Arm was originally named by the British Admiralty in 1860 or 1861 and renamed by the Canadian Hydrographic Service in 1945. At the time of writing, it is commonly known as Okeover Arm.

—MERMAID COVE

SHORE DIVE

SKILL
All divers and snorkelers

TIDE TABLE
Point Atkinson:
Add 10 minutes

WHY GO

To meet a mermaid in the underwater valley at Mermaid Cove. Her hand reaches out. At first sight, it is almost as if to fend you off – then her gesture invites you to the green depths.

When I first saw the mermaid statue, a rockfish was in her hair, like a comb holding it back. We circled cautiously. Her tail rests lightly beside a rock, and she looks startled as if she might swim away. If there were nothing else to see, the timid mermaid would be enough, but look, too, for the nearby resident octopus. Also timid. Other sights at Mermaid Cove include dozens of blackeye gobies in the bottom kelp in the shallows. We saw many kelp crabs, orange dead man's finger sponges, sculpins, rockfish and lingcod; a garden of anemones – dahlia, snakelock and plumose, and you might find bottles.

To dive deep, roll over the edge of the drop-off directly behind the mermaid. Once over the prickly green urchins, you are into the never-never land of big chimney or boot sponges that curve down the steep slope like huge pipes. Ratfish shimmer blue and silver, soar slowly beneath you, lazily ripple their pectoral fins. You may see a red-and-black flash as a tiger rockfish dashes into a crevice. Decorator crabs. And white puffs of cloud sponges below. Deeper, yelloweye rockfish.

The elegant bronze mermaid stands 9 feet (2¾ meters) tall. Beneath the water she looks even larger. The marine life, too, seems bigger than life at Mermaid Cove.

The romantic idea of the underwater mermaid statue was conceived by Jodi Willoughby when her husband, Jim, provided a wet suit for the model of sculptor Elek Imredy. In 1970 Imredy created the "Girl in a Wet Suit" bronze statue that sits on a rock off Stanley Park in Vancouver. From that time, the Willoughbys spearheaded the mermaid project, and many divers pitched in to collect money for it. Nineteen years later Jodi's dream was realized. The "Emerald Princess" was completed by scuba diver/sculptor Simon Morris and ceremoniously sunk at Saltery Bay in 1989.

BOTTOM AND DEPTHS

Rocky bottom covered with lettuce kelp is in the valley leading to where the mermaid is at 50 to 60 feet (15 to 18 meters), depending on the tide height. West of the mermaid, smooth rock undulates to a 150-foot (46-meter) drop-off. Crevices are along the wall. A compass is useful to guide you back over the undulating bottom.

HAZARDS

Boats and poor visibility in summer. Listen for boats: ascend up the marker buoy chain and then snorkel to shore. Or navigate to shore, staying close to the bottom all the way, well out of the way of boats.

TELEPHONE

At Saltery Bay roadside, 300 yards (275 meters) uphill from ferry terminal.

FACILITIES

Changerooms, cold-water showers for divers to wash gear, wheelchair-accessible toilet and picnic table. Campsites, pit toilets and fire rings at Mermaid Cove campground; lots of big trees around each campsite. Boat launch at Saltery Bay picnic site, 1½ miles (2½ kilometers) up Highway 101 toward Powell River.

Emerald Princess

ACCESS

Mermaid Cove is at Saltery Bay Provincial Park on Jervis Inlet near Powell River and is reached by Sunshine Coast Highway 101. Divers arriving by boat should take care not to drop anchor on the mermaid sculpture which is closeby the floating dive flag and inshore from it.

From Highway 101 turn into Saltery Bay campground. Go to the Mermaid Cove sign that says "No Parking Beyond This Point". Drive to the water, where only handicapped persons are allowed to park, and drop gear. Easy entry down the path and zigzag concrete ramp. Because the

ramp stops short of the water at lower tides, wheelchair access only with tides of 10 feet (3 meters) and greater. To see the mermaid, follow the shallow canyon out from shore. Or swim to the dive flag and go down. Dive the left wall face to see anemones and look for old bottles; the right face to see sponges.

To get to Saltery Bay Provincial Park campground
• From Saltery Bay ferry landing, go on Highway 101 for ⅔ mile (1 kilometer).
• From Powell River, drive south on 101 for 30 minutes to the campground.

NOTES

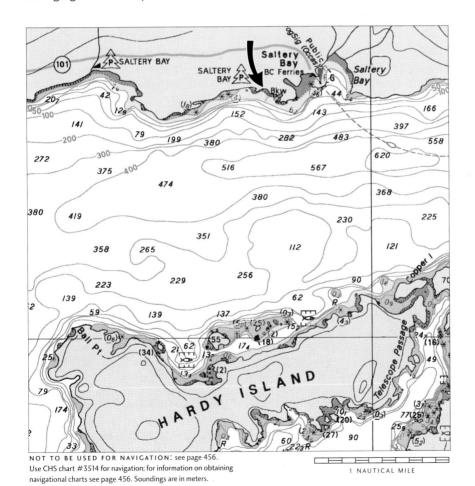

NOT TO BE USED FOR NAVIGATION: see page 456.
Use CHS chart #3514 for navigation; for information on obtaining navigational charts see page 456. Soundings are in meters.

1 NAUTICAL MILE

OCTOPUS CITY

**SHORE DIVE or
KAYAK DIVE**

SKILL
All divers

TIDE TABLE
Point Atkinson:
Add 10 minutes

WHY GO

For easy access, a wreck to look for, to explore the spacey boulder garden called Octopus City. And it's a great night dive with lots of ratfish – hundreds of them.

During the day, we saw two ratfish, flounders rippling over the bottom. A hermit crab tumbling and rolling to escape us. A red rock crab. A purple crab. We saw two octopuses, each hiding beneath a separate boulder, ready to reach out to catch a crab on the sand. Sea pens, dinner-plate-sized sea stars and tube-dwelling anemones are also on the sand. Sparsely scattered orange and white plumose anemones tilt from the tops of the widely spaced boulders. We saw deep purple tube worms, tiny white nudibranchs, peach-colored nudibranchs, delicate alabaster nudibranchs, quillback rockfish and a few lingcod. Seaperch, schools of juvenile rockfish, blackeye gobies and egg cases of moon snails in the eelgrass. At the wreck, many small fish. In winter, watch for Steller sea lions and do not come closer to them than 110 yards (100 meters). Night or day, take a light – to see shy octopuses hiding beneath the boulders.

An uncomplicated dive: Octopus City is a good place to check out new gear, a new diving buddy or simply to enjoy the marine life. But just look and do not take; it is locally honored as a marine life reserve.

BOTTOM AND DEPTHS

Silty sand, then cobble bottom and eelgrass slopes gently from shore to the white sand. Big-leafed, brown bottom kelp is around the large rocks close to shore. Bright white sand surrounds the widely scattered boulders which range from 60 to 80 feet (18 to 24 meters) deep. The wreck is at 50 to 60 feet (15 to 18 meters).

HAZARDS

Boats and poor visibility in summer. Listen for boats and use your compass. If you hear a boat, navigate to shore and then snorkel back to the exit point.

TELEPHONE

Saltery Bay, 300 yards (275 meters) from ferry terminal at roadside.

FACILITIES

Freshwater pump for divers to wash gear, wheelchair-accessible pit toilet, lots of parking space, picnic tables and launch ramp. Air fills in Westview.

ACCESS

Octopus City is on Jervis Inlet near Powell River. It is at Saltery Bay Provincial Park picnic site off Sunshine Coast Highway 101.

At Saltery Bay picnic ground, easy entry down a trail with salmonberries beside it. From the launch ramp, walk 30 feet (9 meters) north in the parking lot to an opening between the trees. Walk 150 paces down the well-worn wooded trail. From the end of the trail, cross the rocks. You can sight on Ball Point, or follow a 190° compass heading to an underwater cable. Then follow the cable out to the boulders. From the boulder at the end of the cable, head southeast to the wreck; then through the eelgrass to the ramp. Or in summer, safer to return to the trail.

In winter, when fewer boats, wheelchair divers could enter at the concrete boat ramp and swim toward the point on the right – it is 300 yards (275 meters). Or go by dive-kayak. When nearing the point, look for the end of the trail, land the kayak, dive and look for the cable.

To get to Saltery Bay picnic site
- From Saltery Bay ferry landing, go on Highway 101 for 2 miles (3¼ kilometers) to the picnic site.
- From Powell River heading south on Highway 101, drive for 30 minutes. Go 19 miles (30 kilometers) to the picnic site. If you reach the campsite, you've gone too far.

Ratfish

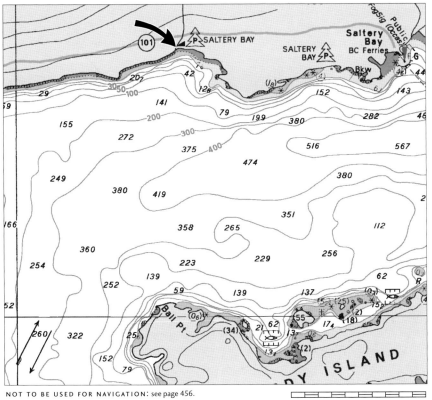

NOT TO BE USED FOR NAVIGATION: see page 456.
Use CHS chart #3514 for navigation; for information on obtaining
navigational charts see page 456. Soundings are in meters.

1 NAUTICAL MILE

NOTES

BALL POINT

BOAT DIVE
GPS
49°44.758' N
124°13.761' W

SKILL
All divers in shallows

Intermediate divers and
advanced divers deeper

TIDE TABLE
Point Atkinson:
Add 10 minutes

WHY GO

Cloud sponges burgeon orange and
yellow and white down the steep slopes of
Ball Point at Hardy Island.

Pale green and golden bottom kelp
decorates the shallows in gossamer folds
veiling tube worms, seaperch, alabaster
nudibranchs, sea lemons, painted greenlings, sea cucumbers, blackeye gobies and
kelp greenlings. We saw seals and rock
scallops. Lots of lingcod, juvenile yelloweye rockfish, dahlia anemones, tiger rockfish, some chimney sponges and great
puffs of cloud sponges like huge rain
clouds in a prairie sunset sky.

Life is in zones. Lots of marine animals
in the kelp to 40 feet (12 meters). From
40 to 60 feet (12 to 18 meters), not
much to see except red-and-pink striped
dahlia anemones. And then sponge,
sponge, sponge . . .

If you like cloud sponges – you'll love
Ball Point!

BOTTOM AND DEPTHS

Rocky bottom covered with kelp falls away
in irregular ledges to a depth of 30 to
40 feet (9 to 12 meters), depending on
tide height. Then a steep rock wall slopes
down.

HAZARDS

Some current, small boats, broken fishing
line and depth. Dive near the slack. Listen
for boats and ascend close to the wall all
the way to shore, well out of the way of
those boats. Carry a knife.

TELEPHONES

• On the water: VHF radio; if no VHF,
  try a cell phone.
• On land: Saltery Bay, 300 yards (275
  meters) uphill from ferry terminal at
  roadside.

FACILITIES

Beautiful place for a picnic at the site.

Giant cloud sponges

Launch ramp, picnic tables and wheelchair-accessible pit toilet at Saltery Bay picnic site. Tenting nearby at Saltery Bay campground. Air fills in Westview.

ACCESS

Ball Point is on the Jervis Inlet side of Hardy Island. From Saltery Bay ramp go 2 nautical miles south to Hardy Island. A small cove just south of Ball Point is convenient for anchoring or beaching your boat.

You might see harbor seals. Before you go diving visit www.pac.dfo-mpo.gc.ca, click on Marine Mammals, select Viewing Guidelines.

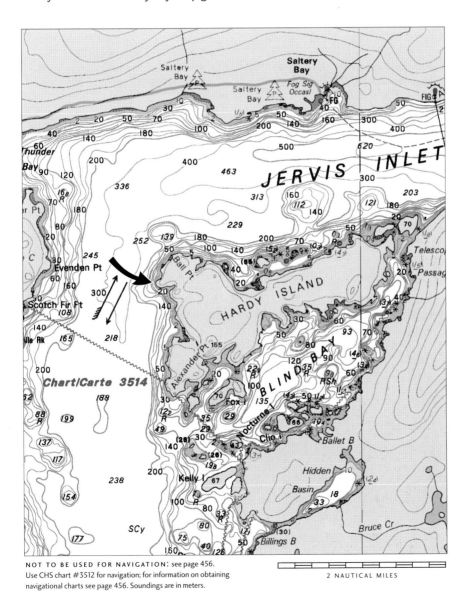

NOT TO BE USED FOR NAVIGATION: see page 456.
Use CHS chart #3512 for navigation; for information on obtaining navigational charts see page 456. Soundings are in meters.

2 NAUTICAL MILES

NOTES

BOAT DIVE
GPS
49°48.927′ N
124°39.625′ W

SKILL
All divers and snorkelers

TIDE TABLE
Point Atkinson:
Add 10 minutes

WHY GO

Even a dark stormy day feels sunny and bright under water at the large reef at Rebecca Rocks.

It's full of all the life a reef should have: lacy white nudibranchs, bright pink limpets, sea lemons, blue and orange sea stars and alabaster nudibranchs. We saw sea cucumbers and rock scallops. Lots of fish, too. Kelp greenlings everywhere. Lingcod, rock greenlings and millions of very small rockfish in the distance. Often harbor seals are present at Rebecca – but do not swim with them, touch them nor offer them food. Just watch.

At the south edge of the reef you can drop into sponge country. Yet to me Rebecca Rocks is most beautiful for the large area of shallow reef swarming with life – thanks to local divers who honor the waters within ¼ nautical mile of the site as a reserve.

All marine life is protected: see viewing guidelines regarding seals at www.pac.dfo-mpo.gc.ca, click on Marine Mammals.

BOTTOM AND DEPTHS

Rocky reef undulates from 30 to 50 feet (9 to 15 meters) deep, depending on tide height. Ledges, overhangs and some bull kelp. Deep on the south side.

HAZARDS

Wind, current, boats, broken fishing line and deceptively undulating bottom. Dive on slack. Listen for boats and ascend cautiously: if you hear one stay down until it passes. Carry a knife. Use a compass and watch the current to determine your position so you do not stray too far from your boat.

TELEPHONES

- On the water: VHF radio; if no VHF, try a cell phone.
- On land: Blubber Bay, Texada Island, uphill from ferry landing beside post office.

FACILITIES

None. Air fills at Westview; charters out of Westview and Lund; also air fills and charters out of Courtenay, Vancouver Island.

Curious harbor seal in shallows

ACCESS

The Rebecca Rocks site is 1 nautical mile northwest of Texada Island in Algerine Passage, Strait of Georgia; it is 5 nautical miles west of Westview in Powell River. It is very exposed to wind from all directions. Pick a calm day.

Charter out of Westview or Lund on the Sunshine Coast or out of Comox on Vancouver Island; or launch at Westview or Texada Island and go to Rebecca Rocks. Anchor, but do not tie onto the marker. It is a federal offense to make fast to a marker or tamper with any aid to navigation. Dive anywhere around Rebecca Rocks; choose your location depending upon direction of wind and current.

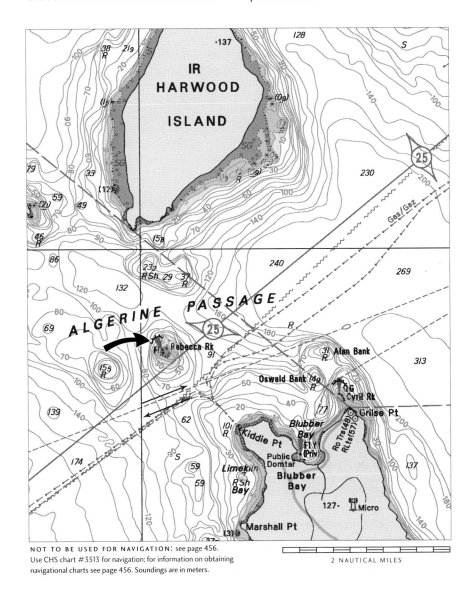

NOTES

NOT TO BE USED FOR NAVIGATION: see page 456.
Use CHS chart #3513 for navigation; for information on obtaining navigational charts see page 456. Soundings are in meters.

2 NAUTICAL MILES

VIVIAN ISLAND

BOAT DIVE
GPS
49°50.431' N
124°41.894' W

SKILL
Intermediate and expert
divers on wall

All divers in shallows and
on the wreck

TIDE TABLE
Point Atkinson:
Add 10 minutes

WHY GO

Vivian Island is an exceptional three-in-one
dive: it includes a sheer sponge-covered
wall; the wreck of the *Shamrock*; huge
limpets, rock scallops and often harbor
seals in the shallows. Do not go closer to
them than 110 yards (100 meters).

Drifting down the wall, the gorgeous
variety of sponges entrances me. Lots of
lemon yellow cloud sponges. Some orange.
Many fluffy white ones. Vase sponges,
too. Snakelock anemone tentacles flow
from the wall. I see the orange-and-white
stripes of a juvenile yelloweye hiding in a
sponge. Another hanging near the wall.
Lots of quillback rockfish.

The *Shamrock*, a 76-foot (23-meter)
tug, is an excellent second dive at this
site, or maybe the only one you'll want to
do. The vessel is a heritage wreck. It was
built in Vancouver in 1887 and had an
active working life before it hit Vivian Island
(then Bare Island) on December 8, 1926.
The next day the tug slowly sank. It was
found by sport divers in 1973, and is scattered down the southeast wall of Vivian
within depths all divers can go to. The
propeller is the deepest part; it is in 40 to
50 feet (12 to 15 meters). Look also for
the unusual steeple steam engine and
more. Details of the wreck are in a book
published by the Underwater Archeological Society of British Columbia (UASBC):
Historic Shipwrecks of the Sunshine Coast.
Read it before you dive. If you see any parts
of the tug referred to, leave them where
they are to be enjoyed by others – it is
protected as all wrecks are. Removal of
artifacts is punishable by stiff fines. If you
see items *not referred to,* you can become
part of the process of documenting the
historic wrecks of British Columbia; make
careful mental notes and inform the UASBC.

Protect the remains of the wreck, the
marine life and the island. Vivian Island is a
sensitive habitat: if you go onto it, do not
walk on the cacti and do not disturb the
bird life – particularly do not land on the

island at nesting time. Avoid approaching
closer than 110 yards (100 meters) to any
marine mammals or birds. Check out the
viewing guidelines at www.pac.dfo-
mpo.gc.ca, click on Marine Mammals. Do
not collect marine life: local divers honor
all waters within ½ nautical mile of Vivian
as a reserve.

It is a rich dive – and in winter, with
100-foot (30-meter) visibility, it is a
photographer's paradise.

BOTTOM AND DEPTHS

Rocky bottom with some boulders at 20 to
30 feet (6 to 9 meters) slopes off quickly
to a depth of 40 to 50 feet (12 to 15
meters) at the edge of the creviced wall.
The sheer rock wall plunges 115 to 125 feet
(35 to 38 meters), depending on tide
height. Clean white sand at its base.

HAZARDS

Wind, current, boats, depth and broken
fishing line. Dive near the slack. Listen for
boats. Carry a knife.

TELEPHONES

• On the water: VHF radio; if no VHF, try a
cell phone.
• On land: Blubber Bay, Texada Island,
uphill from ferry landing beside post office.

FACILITIES

None at this uninhabited island. Air fills
and charters at Westview; charters out of
Lund. Charters also out of Courtenay on
Vancouver Island.

ACCESS

Vivian Island is at the southern end of
Shearwater Passage, 8 nautical miles west
of Westview and 1 nautical mile west of the
southern tip of Harwood Island. Vivian
Island is exposed to winds from all directions. Pick a calm day.

Charter out of Westview in Powell River
or launch your own boat at Texada Island
or Westview. Go to the southeast corner

of the island: a small pebble beach is exposed at low tides. Anchor in 40 to 50 feet (12 to 15 meters) of water just east of dark colored rocks on shore, so you do not disturb remains of the wreck. At the time of writing, a yellow dot painted on the rock face marks the place to go to the *Shamrock,* or anchor near the south side of the island to go over the wall to sponge-land.

Shamrock: steeple steam engine, double height not side by side

NOTES

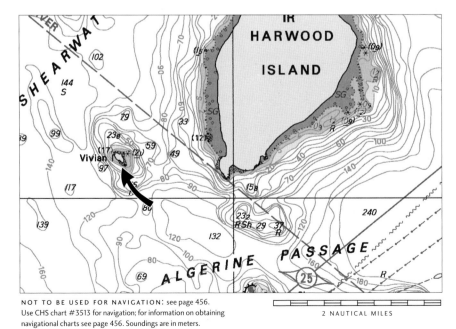

NOT TO BE USED FOR NAVIGATION: see page 456. Use CHS chart #3513 for navigation; for information on obtaining navigational charts see page 456. Soundings are in meters.

2 NAUTICAL MILES

BOAT DIVE
GPS
49°52.126' N
124°48.526 W

SKILL
Expert divers

TIDE TABLE
Mitlenatch Island

Plumose anemones and fish smother the wreck

WHY GO

As we descend the anchor line, a white oval glows below us. The shape looks like a ship. We've found it . . . the *Capilano* . . . our second try. Deeper, the shape is obviously a ship. White plumose anemones smother the rails, outline them: a gray-and-black tartan plaid is in the bed of the oval. And the tartan is moving!

Deeper again I see that the "tartan" is a horde of large lingcod; they swim in all directions between the rails, crisscross the deck, obscure it. Many smaller fish too.

Other divers in our group observe more marine life: a large cloud sponge on the starboard bow rail, an orange plumose anemone, dogfish circling during our safety stop. But the white oval with the tartan plaid is the single stunning image I came away from the *Capilano* with.

The vessel was built for the Union Steamship Line of British Columbia in 1891 and 1892. It carried coal, passengers to Alaska, mail, stone from Nelson Island to Victoria for the Parliament Buildings. On its final voyage October 1, 1915, the vessel was carrying only cargo, no passengers, when it hit a submerged object. It sprang a leak. The crew took to a lifeboat at 3 am; but before rowing to safety at Savary Island, they waited. At 5 am they watched the *Capilano* sink five miles west/southwest of Harwood Island.

The wreck was discovered in 1972 when a fisherman from Lund pulled up a piece of metal railing. The location remained secret for several years. Then, in the early 1980s, charter operations began to take divers to the site. On June 9, 1984, the Underwater Archaeological Society of British Columbia (UASBC) placed a plaque on the stern to encourage divers to respect the wreck. On November 6, 1985, the *Capilano* was designated a Provincial Heritage Site – it is illegal to remove anything from it, and no permanent moorings may be placed on it.

The vessel was built of steel throughout except for the wooden top deck and wheelhouse. At writing, it is intact except for the wooden parts which have deteriorated over time and part of the stern which was probably damaged by an anchor. It is 120 feet (36½ meters) long, 22¼ feet (6¾ meters) wide and 9½ feet (3 meters) high at the waist and amidships; the bow and stern are slightly higher.

The wreck of the *Capilano* is in the middle of nowhere; it is isolated, deep, intact, alive: marine life as well as artifacts and ship's fittings. The rudder and propeller are still in place but nearly hidden by anemones. And on and on. Plan to dive it two or three times. Details of what to look for are included in a book: *Historic Shipwrecks of the Sunshine Coast* published by the UASBC. And, according to the authors: "The *Capilano* is widely considered to be the best wreck dive in B.C."

BOTTOM AND DEPTHS

The wreck sits upright on a featureless, flat sand bottom. It is at a depth of 122 to 130 feet (37 to 40 meters) or more, depending on tide height. It lies on a 184° bearing with the bow pointing south.

HAZARDS

Depth, wind, current and boats. Plan your dive carefully: if windy, don't go. Dive on a tidal exchange no greater than 6 feet (2 meters). Start your dive during slack at the start or end of a rising tide. Do not dive on the ebb. And leave a boat tender for pickup in the event of unexpected current. When ascending, listen and look for boats.

TELEPHONE

On the water: VHF radio; if no VHF, try a cell phone.

FACILITIES

None at Grant Reefs. Charters out of Westview in Powell River, Lund, Comox, Campbell River and Nanaimo.

ACCESS

The wreck of the *Capilano* is in the middle of the northern Strait of Georgia south of Grant Reefs. It is far out – exposed to wind from every direction, especially in the afternoon. And it is difficult to find, even with perfectly calm seas, because of the nearly featureless bottom. Be prepared to try for this dive three or four times.

If you take your own boat: arrive at the site at least an hour before you plan to dive. Go first to the GPS location and place a buoy upcurrent. Then slowly circle the buoy and listen to the depth sounder. The highest point of the wreck is 10 to 15 feet (3 to 4½ meters) high so the sounder paints a very clear picture when you do find it. Note where you pass over it, anchor your vessel upstream from the direction of current and wreck so you do not damage the *Capilano* and so you can descend the anchor line and drift to it.

However, I highly recommend going with a charter operation familiar with the dive: so many factors must be right – even with an experienced charter operation it might take several tries.

NOTES

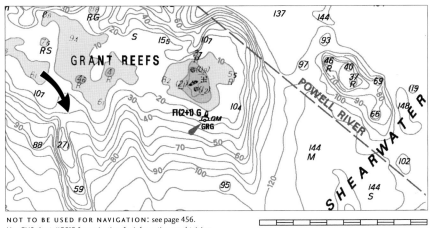

NOT TO BE USED FOR NAVIGATION: see page 456.
Use CHS chart #3513 for navigation; for information on obtaining navigational charts see page 456. Soundings are in meters.

2 NAUTICAL MILES

EMMONDS BEACH

SHORE DIVE

SKILL
All divers

TIDE TABLE
Point Atkinson:
Add 10 minutes

WHY GO

Emmonds Beach is good for a quick, quiet dive anytime, day or night – no crowds at the site. You can see life typically found both on sand and on rock walls. You can dive shallow or deep.

Swimming over the sand we saw wispy tube-dwelling anemones, sculpins, hermit crabs, flounders and shiners. Masses of rockfish hanging around the rock. Over the rock and down the wall, we saw sunflower stars, mustard-yellow trumpet sponges, tiger rockfish, lacy white sea cucumbers and several lingcod.

Land access is easy over a narrow pebble beach. The swim is a moderate one to the place where the bottom drops off quickly. At low tide it is easier: a large rock which dries at 8-foot (2½-meter) tides is 100 yards (90 meters) offshore. The drop-off is just the other side of this rock. When I dived at Emmonds Beach, because the rock was not visible, we set our compasses, swam out over slowly sloping sand till we reached the rock. Then we swam up and over and down the other side where we dropped onto narrow ledges stairstepping steeply down to small cloud sponges at 70 to 80 feet (21 to 24 meters). We also saw the inevitable emerald-eyed ratfish hovering by the wall. Ratfish and cloud sponges – almost always part of the deep Powell River area underwater scene.

BOTTOM AND DEPTHS

Smooth sand slopes to a depth of 30 to 40 feet (9 to 12 meters) at the base of the rock, which dries at 8-foot (2½-meter) tides. Beyond the rock, the creviced wall drops away in steep, narrow ledges.

HAZARDS

Boats and poor visibility, in summer. Small boats might be moored immediately over the dive site. Listen for boats: if the tide is low, ascend up the side of the rock and swim to shore on the surface. If the tide is high, navigate back to shore with a compass.

TELEPHONE

Lund, outside hotel, outside shops next to hotel and outside bakery; at end of Highway 101, it is 4⅓ miles (7 kilometers) north of Emmonds Road and Highway 101 junction.

FACILITIES

Pleasant place for a picnic; a very civilized feeling on this cobbled crescent of beach encircled by homes. Parking space for one car. Air fills at Westview.

ACCESS

Emmonds Beach is on Malaspina Strait near Shearwater Passage. It is north of Powell River near Lund, and is ½ mile (¾ kilometer) off Highway 101 at the end of Emmonds Road.

Go down Emmonds Road which is unpaved. When you see the water straight ahead, do not turn right. Go straight to the end of the road. Walk two or three paces across grass to the pebble beach and swim straight out toward the rock. If it is not visible, set your compass on a 150° heading toward Vivian Island which is 6 nautical miles away or toward the right of the tip of Harwood Island. Swim straight out 100 yards (90 meters) before going down. Descend and continue swimming on a straight line under water. Go over the rock and down the wall.

To get to Emmonds Road
- From Powell River go north following signs to Sliammon and Lund; 25 minutes past Powell River, look for Emmonds Road. It is 5½ miles (9 kilometers) past Sliammon Creek and ½ mile (¾ kilometer) past a large Craig Park sign that is in a sharp curve in the highway. At Emmonds Road turn left.
- From Lund, go 4 miles (7 kilometers) south and turn right; 10 minutes to Emmonds Road.

Trumpet sponges

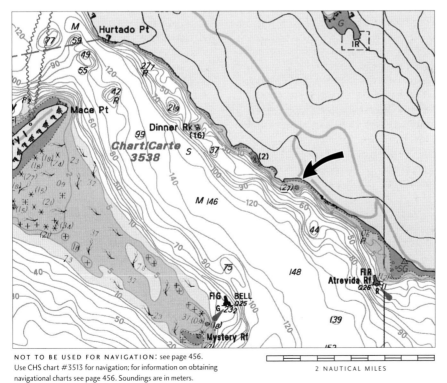

NOT TO BE USED FOR NAVIGATION: see page 456.
Use CHS chart #3513 for navigation; for information on obtaining
navigational charts see page 456. Soundings are in meters.

2 NAUTICAL MILES

NOTES

129

—IRON MINES—

BOAT DIVE or KAYAK DIVE
GPS
49°57.768'N
124°45.065' W

SKILL
Expert divers

Intermediate divers with pickup boat

TIDE TABLE
Point Atkinson:
Add 10 minutes

WHY GO

Dramatic splashes of red and white are down the sheer wall. Did Cézanne paint this dark rock dappled with light, or did Van Gogh throw his paints at it?

Giant cloud sponges plunge in an endless cascade. The cloud sponges at Iron Mines are whiter than any I've seen before – seeming still whiter because of red anemones massed around them. Red snakelocks undulate in the slow flow. We drift past, cruise effortlessly. See a tiny grunt sculpin, acorn barnacles, leather stars, giant red urchins. You might also see galatheid crabs, nudibranchs, brittle stars, tiger rockfish, Puget Sound king crabs, black rockfish at the point. My buddy looks out from the wall, and points as a minuscule squid scoots past. On the wall, we see seamed tennis ball sponges, flabby yellow sponges and hard pink hydrocoral like scrunched up baby's fingers. Gray chimney sponges curve out and upwards like ancient lead pipes. The water is crystal clear. When I look down – it is bottomless. Look up – see coppery red arbutus trees twisting from the cliffs.

Iron Mines is the subject of colorful facts and tales: the caves in the cliff which divers call Iron Mines were never a mine. They were test-tunnels used for samples;

the mine is just south of the holes. This mine was the first Crown-granted mine claim in the area after Lund was settled in 1899. It was operated until 1906 – not for iron but for copper, gold and silver. Stories told after the mine closed are that the tunnels provided a hiding place for pirate treasure: a ship's bell, ship's wheel, portholes, a crystal jug and china taken from the *Cottage City* when it was stranded at Willow Point south of Campbell River in 1911. It is said a spelunker found the treasure at Iron Mines in 1946.

BOTTOM AND DEPTHS

Rock wall sheers to 500 feet (150 meters) on the chart. Rich marine life from the surface to 100 feet (30 meters) and more.

HAZARDS

Depth, some current and boats. Dive the depth you are comfortable at, marine life all the way. If no pickup boat, dive on slack and be aware of current direction – it varies at different levels, especially when windy. *Listen and look for boats* – boat traffic to Desolation Sound is extremely heavy in late summer and sailboats and ocean kayaks move silently. When ascending, spiral and hug the wall all the way to the surface.

Dive-kayakers: overexertion after your dive may increase the risk of bends. Rest before paddling back.

TELEPHONES
• On the water: VHF radio; if no VHF, try a cell phone.
• On land: at Lund outside hotel, outside shops next to hotel and outside bakery.

FACILITIES

None at Iron Mines. Charters, water taxi and launch ramp at Lund; also a grocery store, café, pub, hotel and restaurant – all on the water. Camping and car-top boat launch at nearby Dinner Rock Recreation Site, open seasonally. Air in Westview. Dive-kayak rentals at town of Sechelt.

Off to Iron Mines on Carousel

ACCESS

The Iron Mines dive is beneath the north face of Hurtado Point in Malaspina Strait, 1½ nautical miles southeast of Lund – 5 minutes by water taxi to Iron Mines, and 20 or 30 minutes by dive-kayak to the site. For divers with hand-launchable boats, the dive is 1¾ nautical miles north of Dinner Rock.

Charter, take a water taxi or launch your own boat at Lund and go south. Or launch at Dinner Rock and go north. On the water, look ahead. Past the second point, you will see small depressions and caves in the cliffs with waterfalls spilling over some of them. This is Iron Mines. Remember it. Difficult to see when you reach the site. Take a GPS reading.

Diving from a larger boat you will need a boat tender because it is too deep to anchor. With a pickup boat, part of the pleasure of this dive is doing it as a gentle drift.

If paddling to Iron Mines go with the ebb and return with the flood. At *low tides* you might tie a dive-kayak onto the rocks or secure an inflatable to heaps of rocks beside the wall; expect wash from passing boats. Wheelchair divers who paddle dive-kayaks will find easy access at the ramp and float at Lund.

For less wind on the water, go in the morning. For maximum sunlight, consider the high bluff: dive at noon or after.

NOTES

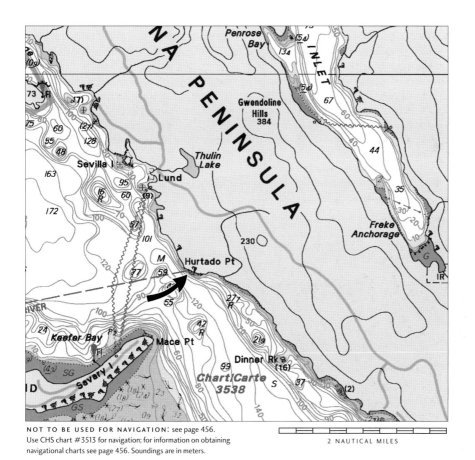

NOT TO BE USED FOR NAVIGATION: see page 456. Use CHS chart #3513 for navigation; for information on obtaining navigational charts see page 456. Soundings are in meters.

2 NAUTICAL MILES

DIVERS' ROCK

BOAT DIVE or
KAYAK DIVE
GPS
49°59.321' N
124°46.555' W

SKILL
All divers at Little Wall

Intermediate and expert
divers at Tim's Wall

TIDE TABLE
Mitlenatch Island

WHY GO

To dive deep at Tim's Wall where you might see tiger rockfish, ratfish, yelloweye rockfish, dogfish and king crabs. And you will see sponges.

To explore marine-life-filled shallows at Little Wall. On the way we saw tube-snouts swimming jerkily through open water; painted greenlings, lingcod, kelp greenlings and clouds of herring cruising in the kelp; sea pens, tube-dwelling anemones and silver nudibranchs in the sand.

The kelp curtain at Little Wall hides sea lemons, alabaster nudibranchs, coils of nudibranch eggs like apple peel, flaming red slipper cucumbers, white crevice-dwelling sea cucumbers, chimney sponges. Sea stars and big fat brown cucumbers are on the bottom beneath the kelp. And, we saw a juvenile wolf-eel in the open – there must be more. Shine your light.

When we dived this site, the fish boat *North Star* was shallow and intact, lying precariously on its side on a steep slope. It looked ready to slide. The *Adventurer* stood upright but was crumbling. The wrecks are probably gone, yet keep an eye open for remains.

Locally honored as a reserve; do not take or disturb any marine life.

Off rocks at the cove, the point behind

BOTTOM AND DEPTHS

Broken rock with bottom kelp slopes quickly to 20 to 30 feet (6 to 9 meters), depending on tide height, to the steep slope where the *North Star* was.

Past it, the *Adventurer* stood upright on a ledge at 60 to 70 feet (18 to 21 meters). Sand is between ledges, some boulders and light silt over all.

The Little Wall is covered with big, broadleaf brown kelp, bottoms out to sand at 50 to 60 feet (15 to 18 meters) with narrow undercut ledges.

Tim's Wall starts at 90 to 100 feet (27 to 30 meters) and drops straight down.

HAZARDS

Boats and depth. Boat traffic to popular cruising sites north of Lund is extremely heavy in summer – many of those boats are ocean kayaks and sailboats that move silently. As you ascend, *listen and look for* boats. Hug the contours of the bottom all the way to the surface well out of the way of those boats. If you find the wrecks, do not penetrate them and stay clear of the steep slope where the *North Star* was.

TELEPHONES

- On the water: VHF radio; if no VHF, try a cell phone.
- On land: at Lund – outside hotel, shops and bakery.

FACILITIES

None at the site. Water taxi, charters and launching at Lund. Charters and air fills at Westview. Dive-kayak rentals at the town of Sechelt.

ACCESS

Divers' Rock is at the south end of Thulin Passage. It is 1 nautical mile northwest of Lund on the Malaspina Peninsula side of the passage. Descending steep steps from Norland Road off Finn Bay Road has been the usual way to reach it, but the land is privately owned. Honor it. Charter or take a water taxi out of Lund or Westview. Launch your own boat or paddle from Lund in a dive-kayak. This site is exposed to southeast winds – thus the many wrecks. Go in calm weather.

To get to Divers' Rock: head northwest out of Lund for 1 nautical mile to the first cove on the right-hand side around the point and past Finn Bay. Two dive flags painted on the wall might be at Divers' Rock.
• Divers with larger boats could anchor north of the rocks to avoid anchoring on the wreck if still there. Beware of wash.
• Kayak-divers can paddle to Divers' Rock from Lund in 15 or 20 minutes. Divers with kayaks or an inflatable could land on the rocks and gear up. Again, beware of wash from Desolation Sound boat traffic.

Enter the water at the south end of the cove at Divers' Rock, but before descending line up on a 210° to 215° bearing from the rocks where the flags were painted to the tip of Savary Island. Start down right away and follow the compass bearing under water. Go out 40 feet (12 meters) to where the *North Star* was poised on a steep wall; then continue on a straight line over a boulder to where the *Adventurer* was.

To dive Little Wall, head north from here. Explore the base of the wall at 50 to 60 feet (15 to 18 meters). Swim back and forth up the wall to the surface.

To get to Tim's Wall, from the boulder where the *Adventurer* was, continue on the line you took from shore. Swim over gently sloping sand and a sandy mound. Keep going. Follow a valley of sand down to the right and then curve left to Tim's Wall.

NOTES

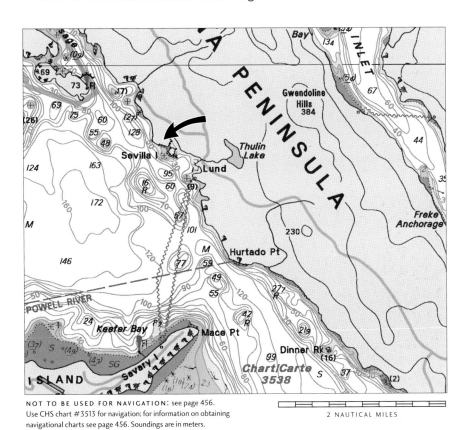

NOT TO BE USED FOR NAVIGATION: see page 456.
Use CHS chart #3513 for navigation; for information on obtaining navigational charts see page 456. Soundings are in meters.

2 NAUTICAL MILES

OKEOVER CAVES

**BOAT DIVE or
KAYAK DIVE**
GPS
45°59.692′ N
123°42.071′ W

SKILL
Intermediate and expert
divers

TIDE TABLE
Point Atkinson:
Add 45 minutes

*Diver at entry of
shallower cave*

WHY GO
You want to see caves or see a feather star swim; winter winds are blowing up in Malaspina Strait, yet it can be calm here; or maybe you just love a fabulous wall. Go to Okeover Inlet.

Orange and white plumose anemones decorate the overhangs and cuts as you plunge to the first cave. We don't see much else until we've gone into the biggest, deepest cave. Then we look around: see a field of feather stars, a single swimming scallop, sea cucumbers and a lingcod that is probably 12 to 15 pounds (5 to 7 kilo-grams). We see crimson snakelock anemones. A rose star. Red and green Christmas anemones. Shallower: moon jellies, hermit crabs, magenta heart tunicates. A small alabaster nudibranch. Sighting a tiny grunt sculpin, our caves dive feels complete.

Brittle stars, long slinky sea worms, orange encrusting sponges and strange mussels also live in the incredibly still waters at Okeover Inlet.

BOTTOM AND DEPTHS
A sheer rock wall drops off. The deeper cave is at 90 to 100 feet (27 to 30 meters), depending on tide height. It is 30 feet (9 meters) wide, 8 feet (2½ meters) high and goes in for 15 feet (5 meters). The second cave is at a depth of 55 to 65 feet (17 to 20 meters). It is 20 feet (6 meters) wide, 8 feet (2½ meters) high and goes in for 8 feet (2½ meters). North of the entry point, beneath the huge bluff, big boulders drop off steeply in huge giant steps. Dive as shallow or deep as you want to.

HAZARDS
Silt year-round, transparent fishing line, boats and, in summer, poor visibility from plankton bloom. Enter the caves carefully and do not kick up silt. Carry a knife. Listen for boats and ascend close to the wall all the way to the surface.

TELEPHONES
• On the water: VHF radio; if no VHF, try a cell phone.
• On land: Okeover Inlet dock.

FACILITIES
Boat charters and boat rentals year-round at Okeover Inlet. Launching at Malaspina Road end – the ramp is good for small boats only. Camping with picnic tables, fire rings and pit toilets, one wheelchair accessible, at Okeover Arm Provincial Park north of ramp. Also nearby, luxury chalets as well as year-round camping; and cabins,

one rustic, one with running water and hot shower. Dive-kayak rentals at the town of Sechelt.

ACCESS

The Okeover Caves site is on the east side of Okeover Inlet, commonly known as Okeover Arm, near Lund. The launch point for it is at Malaspina Peninsula, 30 minutes north of Powell River.

Charter at Okeover Inlet or head across the inlet for ½ nautical mile in your own boat or a rental boat from the ramp at Malaspina Road. A dive-kayak would do it easily. Go toward the smaller black rock bluff on the opposite shore; it is south of a gigantic rock bluff. Look for an indentation in the smaller bluff. The deeper cave is below it and south.

Anchor in the small bay south of the indentation in the bluff. You can land on the flat rock, suit up and swim around to the north side of it. Drop straight away over the wall: at 70 to 80 feet (21 to 24 meters) when you reach a bulge, kick away from the wall and out over it so you don't stir up silt. To find the second cave, work your way up through boulders at the north side of the wall. Imagine where the indentation in the bluff is and go toward it. The second cave is beneath the indentation at 55 to 65 feet (17 to 20 meters).

Wheelchair divers who paddle dive-kayaks will find easy access at Okeover Ramp.

To get to Malaspina Road and Okeover Inlet
• From Powell River head north on Sunshine Coast Highway 101. Go just over 7½ miles (12 kilometers) past Sliammon to Malaspina Road. Watch for signs to Okeover Arm Provincial Park. Turn right and drive 2⅓ miles (3 ¾ kilometers) to the Okeover Harbour Authority Dock.
• From Lund, go south 2 miles (3¼ kilometers) to Malaspina Road; turn left.

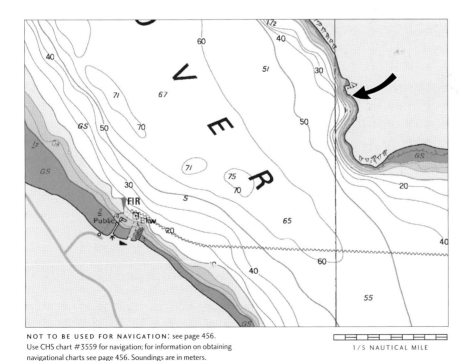

NOT TO BE USED FOR NAVIGATION: see page 456. Use CHS chart #3559 for navigation; for information on obtaining navigational charts see page 456. Soundings are in meters.

1/5 NAUTICAL MILE

Campbell River to Rock Bay

Snorkeling with salmon in the Campbell River

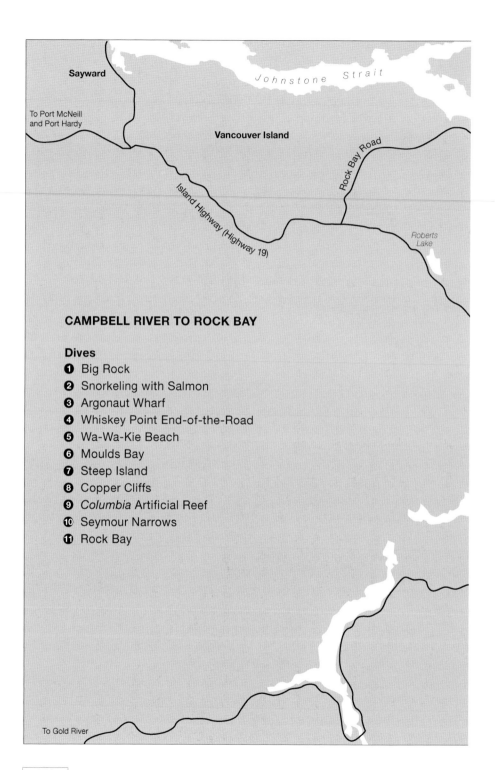

CAMPBELL RIVER TO ROCK BAY

Dives
1. Big Rock
2. Snorkeling with Salmon
3. Argonaut Wharf
4. Whiskey Point End-of-the-Road
5. Wa-Wa-Kie Beach
6. Moulds Bay
7. Steep Island
8. Copper Cliffs
9. *Columbia* Artificial Reef
10. Seymour Narrows
11. Rock Bay

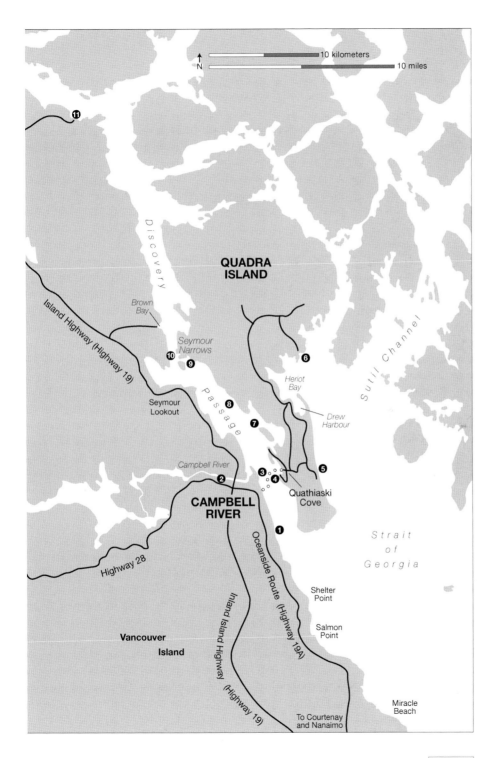

10 kilometers

10 miles

N

QUADRA ISLAND

Discovery

Brown Bay

Seymour Narrows

⑩

❾

Seymour Lookout

Passage

❽

❼

Campbell River

❷

CAMPBELL RIVER

❸

❹

Quathiaski Cove

❺

Heriot Bay

Drew Harbour

❻

Sutil Channel

❶

❶❶

Island Highway (Highway 19)

Highway 28

Vancouver Island

Inland Island Highway (Highway 19)

Oceanside Route (Highway 19A)

To Courtenay and Nanaimo

Shelter Point

Salmon Point

Miracle Beach

Strait of Georgia

SERVICE INFORMATION

Tide and Current Information

- *Tide and Current Tables, Volume 6: Discovery Passage and West Coast of Vancouver Island*, Canadian Hydrographic Service print annual
- www.lau.chs-shc.gc.ca: Tide and Current Tables for all of Canada. Go to the web site: click on Pacific; General Information; Tide and Currents, Data Available; then Tide Tables available in PDF form. Select Volume 6 and click on the tide or current table desired – both are on the same list on the pdf.

Weather Information

- Canadian Coast Guard: Speak with a person, 24 hours; telephone Comox (250)339-3613.
- Canadian Coast Guard (Comox Coast Guard Radio): Continuous Marine Broadcast (CMB) recorded, 24 hours; listen for weather at Cape Mudge, Chatham and in the Strait of Georgia, telephone Comox (250)339-0748.
- Environment Canada: recorded, 24 hours;
1. Marine weather line: listen for weather in Strait of Georgia and Chatham Point, telephone (250)286-3575.
2. Weather line: listen for weather in Campbell River and east Vancouver Island, telephone (250)287-4463.
- www.weatheroffice.ec.gc.ca

Diving Emergency Telephone Numbers

On land and water:

- Call 911, request "ambulance" and say, "I have a scuba diving emergency".
- Vancouver General Hospital; for 24-hour, 7-day-a-week response: telephone (604)875-5000, and say, "I want the hyperbaric physician on call".

On the water:

- VHF radio: Call Coast Guard radio, Channel 16 and say, "I have a scuba diving emergency".
- Cell phone: 911, *16 or *311 and say, "I have a scuba diving emergency".

If emergency or medical personnel are unfamiliar with scuba diving emergencies, ask them to telephone DAN (Divers Alert Network) at (919)684-4326. No money for a long distance call? Dial DAN collect at 011-919-684-4326 and say, "I have a scuba diving emergency".

Mark emergency location before leaving scene: other divers might be down.

How to Go

Campbell River is located on the east side of Vancouver Island at the top of the Strait of Georgia. It is beside Discovery Passage.

- From Nanaimo drive north on Inland Island Highway (Highway 19); it takes 2 hours. Or go on Oceanside Route (Highway 19A) through Parksville, Buckley Bay and Courtenay to Campbell River, 2½ hours.
- From Port Hardy, Port McNeill or Telegraph Cove head south on Island Highway (Highway 19) to Campbell River: from Port Hardy, 4 hours; from Port McNeill, 3¼ hours; from Highway 19 turnoff to Telegraph Cove/Beaver Cove, 3 hours.
- From Powell River, go by British Columbia ferry to Little River ferry terminal at Comox on Vancouver Island. The ferry ride takes 1¼ hours. From the ferry terminal follow signs to Courtenay, 10 minutes: drive 4¾ miles (7¾ kilometers) to a junction: turn right and go north on the Oceanside Route (Highway 19A), 45 minutes to Campbell River.
- From Quadra Island ferry terminal, go by British Columbia ferry to the center of Campbell River: crossing time, 10 minutes.

Tourist Information

Tourism BC

- Toll-free throughout North America: 1-800-435-5622

Ferry Information

British Columbia Ferry Services (BC Ferries)

- Toll-free throughout North America: 1-888-223-3779
- From all other locations: (250)386-3431 www.bcferries.com

At the time of writing the following information applies – but frequent changes occur; it would be wise to check current requirements on BC Ferries web page before every trip.

Rules Regarding Scuba Tanks on BC Ferries
Persons transporting scuba tanks containing compressed air, full or partially full, are required under Canadian law to declare dangerous goods at the terminal or to a vessel officer. Persons transporting scuba tanks with the valves removed do not need clearance. All pressurized tanks with a UN 3156 sticker, indicating nitrox or mixed gases, are taboo – remove the valve.

Expedite Dangerous Goods clearance at the ferry ticket booth – complete a Dangerous Goods Shipping Document prior to arrival. Obtain it from the web at home or a library: Go to www.bcferries.com: select Travel Planning; click on Carrying Dangerous Goods, then For the General Public. Download Dangerous Goods Shipping Document and complete it: include your name, home address and phone number; Class 2; UN 1002, which indicates compressed air; the number of cylinders you are transporting and the quantity in each one: most tanks are 80 cubic feet/2.27 cubic meters.

(To calculate quantity in scuba tanks: 1 cubic foot=0.0283168466 cubic meters.)

Arrive at least 30 minutes prior to intended sailing time at both terminals:
1. Campbell River
2. Quadra Island (west side)

Prearranged Dangerous Goods Clearance Requires 48 Hours
Complete a Dangerous Goods Shipping Document as described above and if departing from Campbell River or Quadra Island (west side) fax it at least 48 hours before intended sailing time to the terminal manager at Campbell River: (250)286-1412; fax (250)286-6899.

CAMPBELL RIVER

• DIVE SHOPS

Beaver Aquatics
760 Island Highway
Campbell River BC V9W 2C3
(250)287-7652
www.connected.bc.ca/~baquatics
(Recreational instruction; nitrox fills.)

Aqua Shack Diving Services
1003A - Island Highway
PO Box 487
Campbell River BC V9W 5C1
(250)287-8944
1-888-467-2822: Toll-free throughout
    North America
www.aquashack.ca
(Recreational instruction; nitrox fills.)

• SNORKEL GUIDING

Paradise Found Adventure Tours
1730 Island Highway, PO Box 487
Campbell River BC V9W 2E7
(250)287-2652
1-866-704-4611: Toll-free throughout
    North America
www.paradisefound.bc.ca
(Snorkel tours, with equipment, on Campbell
River, July 15 through October 31.)

• DAY AND MULTIPLE-DAY CHARTERS

Hang Time
Hang Time Charters
1003 A - Island Highway
PO Box 487
Campbell River BC V9W 5C1
(250)287-8944
1-888-467-2822: Toll-free throughout
    North America
www.aquashack.ca
(Day, multiple-day charters with land-based
accommodation and single-tank dives for
two to ten divers. Dives range from the
Columbia south to Mitlenatch and the
wreck of the Capilano – include Seymour
Narrows, Steep Island, April Point and more.)

• WATER TAXI

Trident, Troika, and Totally Outrageous
Discovery Launch Water Taxi
PO Box 164
Campbell River BC V9W 5A7
(250)287-7577
(Water taxi out of Discovery Harbour, Campbell
River; transportation to and from dive sites.)

• LAUNCH RAMP

Tyee Spit Public Ramp
Campbell River
(Launch free, year-round: concrete ramps,
good at all tides but difficult to load and
launch when the wind blows; also collects
logs and trash. Suitable for wheelchair divers.
Picnic table. No toilets. Telephone across road
outside RV park.)
    Go to Spit Road. Heading north, go
for ¾ mile (1¼ kilometers) past the
Quadra ferry landing turnoff at Tyee Plaza
in Campbell River. From the junction of
highways 19A and 18 in Campbell River,
go east on Highway 19A: 1 mile (1¾ kilometers) to Spit Road.
    From Highway 19A and Spit Road in
Campbell River, go ¾ mile (1¼ kilometers)
on Spit Road to the ramp.

QUADRA ISLAND
• DIVE RESORTS
Abyssal Dive Charters & Lodge
Box 747, 753 Green Road
Quathiaski Cove BC V0P 1N0
(250)285-2420
1-800-499-2297: Toll-free throughout
   North America
www.abyssal.com
*(Dive package on Quadra includes boat
dives on the* Most Outrageous *and the*
Tantalus *– to Steep Island, the* Columbia,
Seymour Narrows, the Capilano *and more.
Hot tub, accommodations, meals, air and
nitrox fills. Wheelchair divers welcome.*

*Dive packages in Campbell River include
boat dives, hotel accommodation and meals.*

*Air and nitrox fills for drop-ins at Quadra
and on Campbell River side – also day charters; pickup at Discovery Harbour Marina in
Campbell River or Quadra side.)*

Dynamike Dive Charters
PO Box 718, Plaza Road
Quathiaski Cove BC V0P 1N0
(250)285-2891
www.dynamike.com
*(Dive packages include hot tub, accommo-
dations and meals, and charters on the
T.N.T – to Steep Island, Seymour Narrows,
the* Columbia, *the* Capilano *wreck and
more. Also day charters. Air fills only available
with charters. Wheelchair divers welcome.)*

• LAUNCH RAMP
Quathiaski Cove Public Ramp
Immediately north of ferry dock
Quathiaski Cove, Quadra Island
*(Launch free for Discovery Passage: concrete
ramp, good at all tides. Restroom and tele-
phone nearby at the ferry landing.)*

All of this Service Information is subject
to change.

NORTH OF CAMPBELL RIVER
• LAUNCH RAMP
Brown's Bay Resort and Marina Ramp
2705 North Island Highway
Campbell River BC V9W 2H4
(250)286-3135
www.brownsbayresort.com
*(Launch for a fee at Brown Bay, north of
Seymour Narrows, for Discovery Passage:
steep concrete ramp, good at all tides.
Restrooms, hot showers and telephones on
shower float behind fuel dock; telephones on
the shore-side of it. At the resort: snacks, a
floating restaurant, an RV park and floating
guest rooms.)*

Located 30 minutes north of Campbell
River: from highway 19 and 18 junctio in
Campbell River, go north 11 miles (18 kilometers) to Brown's Bay Road. Heading
south, from Roberts Lake Resort also on
Highway 19, drive 7 miles (12 kilometers)
to Brown's Bay Road. From Brown's Bay
turnoff, follow signs to Brown's Bay
Resort: go 3 miles (5 kilometers) on this
unpaved road: 10 minutes to Brown Bay.

SOUTH OF CAMPBELL RIVER
• LAUNCH RAMP AND BOAT RENTALS
Salmon Point Resort RV Park & Marina
2176 Salmon Point Road
Campbell River BC V9H 1E5
(250)923-6605
1-866-246-6605: Toll-free throughout
   North America
www.salmonpoint.com
*(All facilities for resort guests only. Launch for
a fee, year-round, for the Strait of Georgia:
concrete ramp, good at 4-foot [1-meter]
tides and greater. Boat rentals. Restrooms;
telephones past reception office and "rec"
hall, northeast corner of the park.)*

Off Oceanside Highway (Highway 19A):
turnoff is 2½ miles (4 kilometers) north of
Miracle Beach connector to Inland Island
Highway (Highway 19), 5½ miles (4 kilometers) south of Jubilee Parkway; follow
marina and resort signs.

BIG ROCK

SHORE DIVE

SKILL
Intermediate and expert
divers

TIDE TABLE
Campbell River

WHY GO
A good mix of fish live on the reef in front of Big Rock and because of the back eddies Big Rock is quite a safe place to dive.

Since the bottom is varied the fish are varied, too, but visibility is usually poor. We could see only 5 to 8 feet (1½ to 2½ meters). The water was murky with silt stirred up by the current and back eddies. Through the silt we saw a great variety of fish. Red Irish lords, small lingcod, flounders and rockfish. An octopus, too. Urchins, giant barnacles and pale orange sponges, nourished by the current, cling tight to the rocks. And lots of purply-red geoduck (pronounced gooey-duck) clams poke up through the silt, with a strand of bull kelp attached to each one. I watched, fascinated, as we drifted slowly downcurrent touching first one then another siphon. As we touched them each geoduck retracted into the sand, pulling the kelp down with it.

BOTTOM AND DEPTHS
The reef at Big Rock parallels the shore. It is 20 to 30 feet (6 to 9 meters) deep. Gently sloping sandy bottom scattered with rocks

Big Rock

and some boulders form it. In summer, bull kelp is attached to the rocks and geoducks.

HAZARDS
Boats, current and bull kelp in summer. Current is not as vicious at Big Rock as at many other Campbell River sites because of that back eddy. However, plan to dive on or near the slack. Salmon-fishing boats are an important consideration at Big Rock as at most Campbell River sites. Fly a floating dive-flag – important at all sites but especially important at this one, and do not count on the dive flag to protect you. Listen for boats; use a compass and navigate back to shore under water. Carry a knife for kelp.

TELEPHONES
• Big Rock Store, 906 South Island Highway.
• Big Rock Motel, 1020 South Island Highway.

FACILITIES
Rotary Park Beach, north of Big Rock, is a large green grassy site with picnic tables and a great deal of parking space. Chemical toilets are at the north end of it. At Ellis Park, immediately south of Big Rock, there is parking space for three or four cars. Air fills in Campbell River and Courtenay.

ACCESS
Big Rock is at the southern entry to Discovery Passage in the town of Campbell River beside South Island Highway with two parks for entry and exit points.

Best to dive on the ebb tide because you can count on the current direction; at flood tide, often a back eddy sets up and the direction of flow is also northward, but you do not know when it will happen.

Some say it is safer to dive Big Rock in summer when kelp is present to grab onto; some say it is safer from October through March – less kelp to tangle your dive-flag float in, good visibility and fewer boats.

Two access points are available:

1. Rotary Beach Park and Seawalk is in the 700 block South Island Highway. It is ½ mile (¾ kilometer) north of Big Rock.

2. Ellis Park, a small green park, is in the 900 block South Island Highway. It is 330 yards (100 meters) south of Big Rock – and it gives access to the most interesting part of the reef which is in the kelp opposite Big Rock Motel. Enter the water at the end of the incoming tide. Swim out, and north to the kelp bed and go down. After your dive, if you have drifted north, you could land at Rotary Park and walk it to Ellis Park. Total distance between parks is just over ½ mile (¾ kilometer).

To get to Ellis Park south of Big Rock

• From Quadra ferry in Campbell River, drive 3¼ miles (5¼ kilometers) south on Island Highway to Ellis Park.

• Heading north on Highway 19A (Oceanside Route): go 3 miles (4¾ kilometers) past Jubilee Parkway junction to Ellis Park.

• Heading south on Highway 19, at the junction of highways 19, 19A and 28 in Campbell River, go east into Campbell River and south. From the junction, 5 miles (8¼ kilometers) to Ellis Park.

NOTES

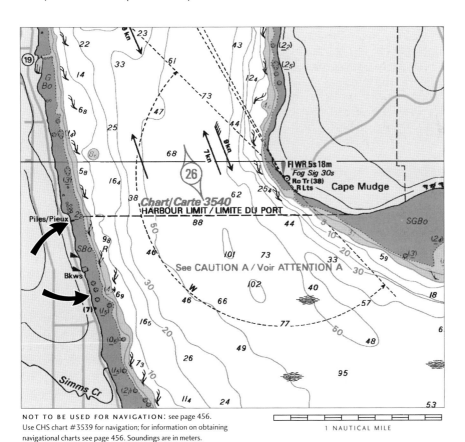

NOT TO BE USED FOR NAVIGATION: see page 456. Use CHS chart #3539 for navigation; for information on obtaining navigational charts see page 456. Soundings are in meters.

1 NAUTICAL MILE

SNORKELING WITH SALMON

SHORE DIVE

SKILL
All snorkelers and divers

TIDE TABLE
None; this is in the non-tidal part of the river

WHY GO

To meet salmon nose-to-nose – cohos, pinks, chinooks, and maybe sockeyes and chums.

We guessed we saw thousands of pinks. They were mostly 24 inches (60 centimeters) long, slim and silvery gray. My buddy saw two chinooks – they are big. Chinooks sometimes weigh in at 60 pounds (27 kilograms) and more. They were just starting upstream for the season when we floated the Campbell, in the river but waiting for rain to make it easier to swim. You see more salmon after rain. Sockeyes are the most colorful, turning brilliant red and green when heading upriver. However, only 200 sockeyes are left to spawn in the Campbell each year. Swimming with salmon is a rare treat – yet in Campbell River, in season, it's a sure thing.

Prime season to go is from early August through mid-October. First you see the silvery pinks – we snorkeled at the end of August, the height of their run. Late August and early September, expect giant chinooks. Early September, cohos start. And maybe you'll see some chums. In October, red and green sockeyes are in the Campbell. Throughout the year you might see steelhead – they are not salmon but are sea-run rainbow trout.

BOTTOM AND DEPTHS

Rocky bottom. Depth ranges from dry rocks to 10 feet (3 meters), averages 3 to 4 feet (1 to 1¼ meters) deep. Most of the time you could stop and stand up if you want to in the quiet shallow parts. But it is easier floating downstream if you follow the deepest channel.

HAZARDS

Current, sudden rises in river level, fallen trees, branches and rubbish. The Campbell looks like a gentle roller-coaster ride but could be dangerous. If you hear a siren, get off the river. And, even with only the slight current usually present, there is potential danger when swimming a river.

When you reach rocky shallow parts, which you can spot because of the white water, roll over on your back and float downstream feet first with your feet held high so they will not become caught between rocks. Harder bumping along on your "bum" than going head first, but safer.

Fallen trees or "sweepers", branches hanging over the river, are also potential hazards. The banks of the Campbell are relatively "clean": the river is dam-controlled providing steady riverflow year-round, with occasional big releases which clean it. Nevertheless, watch the riverbanks and avoid tree branches that hang over the river. When you reach the highway bridge, watch for steel bars – remnants of the old highway bridge that stick up midstream beneath the existing bridge. If you keep to the main channel along the right-hand side, you will probably avoid them. The river is tidal from the highway bridge on, and the current slows down.

TELEPHONES

- Near logging bridge put-in: at entry to Elk Falls Park, Quinsam Campground. From the highway junction, go ⅓ mile (½ kilometer) west on Highway 28 and turn left into the campground.
- Near take-out: west of gas station, southwest corner of Highway 19A and Maple.

FACILITIES

Snorkel guides with rental wet suits, masks and snorkels in Campbell River; also rental equipment at dive shop. Hot showers and restrooms nearby at Discovery Harbour Marina, Island Highway, at shopping center.

ACCESS

Spawning salmon are in the Campbell River from early August to November. To check what life is present, telephone the Quinsam River Hatchery, (250)287-9564.

Float with a buddy. Allow 40 to 50 minutes to snorkel the river. Look for salmon in pools beneath the logging bridge at the start of the run and at the highway bridge near the end of it. In swift parts, watch for salmon in eddies behind rocks as you fly over them. In quiet parts, stop, stand up and look ahead for deep pools, dark sections of river with little or no white water. Look for pools at the outside of each bend; groups of salmon rest in them. Past the highway bridge, move to river-right and drive toward your take-out. The distance from put-in to take-out is 1¼ miles (2 kilometers): use two cars or walk it.

• To the take-out at Maple Street
At the end of the street, space beside the road for six or eight cars to park. Then walk on the right-hand side down an easy path to the water. Look around and leave a large marker so you know where to come off the river.

1. Heading north on Inland Island Highway 19 and approaching Campbell River North: when you reach the Campbell River North exit and see signs toward Downtown and Quadra Island, turn right onto Highway 19A. Go ½ mile (¾ kilometer) to Maple Street. The Quinsam Hotel is on the corner. Turn left into Maple and go to the end of it.

2. Heading north on the Oceanside Route (Highway 19A): go through Campbell River. From the Quadra Island ferry turnoff at Tyee Plaza, continue 1½ miles (2½ kilometers) more on Highway 19A as it curves around to the left and passes Spit Road. At the Quinsam Hotel, turn right into Maple Street and to the river.

3. Heading south on Inland Island Highway 19 and near the town of Campbell River: when you see signs toward Downtown, Gold River and Highway 28, turn left onto Highway 19A. Go ½ mile (¾ kilometer). Just past the Quinsam Hotel, turn left into Maple and go to the end of it.

• To the put-in at the logging road bridge from Maple Street, turn right onto 18th Avenue (Highway 19A), which runs into Highway 28, and go 1¼ miles (2 kilometers). Past the Highway 19 junction, continue straight on Highway 28: follow signs toward Gold River. You will pass the Quinsam River Fish Hatchery turnoff to the left, then the logging road bridge on the right-hand side. Park at the roadside and walk down an easy path to the river. Gear up with wet or dry suit, mask, snorkel and fins, but leave your tank and weight belt behind.

NOTES

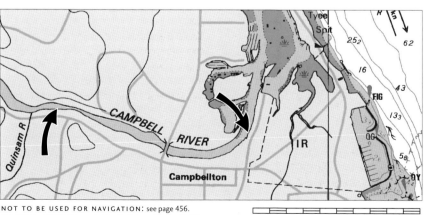

NOT TO BE USED FOR NAVIGATION: see page 456. Use CHS chart #3539 for navigation; for information on obtaining navigational charts see page 456. Soundings are in meters.

1 NAUTICAL MILE

ARGONAUT WHARF

SHORE DIVE

SKILL
Intermediate and
advanced divers

All divers with guide

TIDE TABLE
Campbell River

CURRENT TABLE
Seymour Narrows

*Shy octopus on piling
at Argonaut Wharf*

WHY GO

Night diving under the wharf at Discovery
Terminal – or Argonaut Wharf as it is still
called by most – is a favorite of local divers.

When seeing the spot I realized why
night diving here is so popular. Fishing
lures are more easily seen in the flash of
your light at night. These can be profitable
salvage. But more important, the resident
octopuses come out. I saw four on one
night dive – but just look. Or gently stroke.
Octopuses can be killed by rough handling.

It is safer to dive here at night because
of so many small fishing boats going past,
and so many people fishing from the wharf.

Day or night, there's lots of marine life.
We saw decorator crabs, red and pink
dahlia anemones and white plumose
anemones on the pilings. Flounders all
over the bottom. Some red Irish lords and
a cabezon. And in summer you might see
masses of gray cod on the sand beyond
the pilings.

Enormous skates used to live here. I've
heard of 125-pound (57-kilogram) giant
skates with a 7-foot (2-meter) wingspan
off Tyee Spit, but haven't seen any. They
must have been hunted out. Today all that's
left of them is the legend.

Honor Discovery Passage – no taking
of marine life, all creatures are protected.

BOTTOM AND DEPTHS

The 20- to 30-foot (6- to 9-meter)
sandy bottom gradually deepens as you
move into the channel. Rocks around the
pilings where octopuses hide.

HAZARDS

Current, large ships docked for loading,
small boats, fishermen and broken fishing
line. Dive on slack. Current is unpredictable
and varies at different times of the year: the
tide table is usually most reliable, but use
both tide and current tables. Safest to dive
on exchanges of 3 to 4 feet (1 to 1¼
meters) or less. Arrive at the site ahead of
time and check it out. Do not dive when
large ships are docked for loading. In summer, stay under the wharf. In winter, use a
compass or stay close to the pilings, sometimes called dolphins by the locals. Listen
for boats and ascend up a piling, well out of
the way of boats. Carry a knife.

TELEPHONE

Thunderbird RV Park & Campground,
across road from dive entry point, outside.

FACILITIES

Parking space for five or six cars at the dive entry. North of it, a great deal of parking space and a picnic table beside the launch ramps. Hot showers and restrooms nearby at Discovery Harbour Marina on Island Highway at the Discovery Harbour shopping center.

ACCESS

Argonaut Wharf is located in Discovery Passage. It is at Tyee Spit in the town of Campbell River off Highway 19A. Go out Spit Road for ½ mile (¾ kilometer). Just past the large buildings and wharf on your right is a beach with very easy entry over the sand. Swim to the wharf and go down.

Wheelchair access at the launch ramp for divers who can kayak – or swim, 220 yards (200 meters) from the ramp back to the entry. Then swim to the wharf.

To get to Spit Road
• Heading north on Island Highway 19 toward Campbell River North, when you enter Campbell River you are on Tamarac Street: at Highway 19A (18th Avenue) turn right following signs toward Downtown and Quadra Island. Go nearly 1 mile (1½ kilometers) to Spit Road and turn left.
• Heading south on Highway 19 toward Campbell River, you will see signs toward Downtown, Gold River and Highway 28. Cross a bridge. At the junction of highways 19A and 18, turn left onto Highway 19A. Go 1 mile (1¾ kilometers) and, again, turn left into Spit Road.
• Heading north on Oceanside Route, Highway 19A, go through Campbell River: when ¾ mile (1¼ kilometers) past the Quadra ferry landing turnoff at Tyee Plaza, turn right into Spit Road.

NOTES

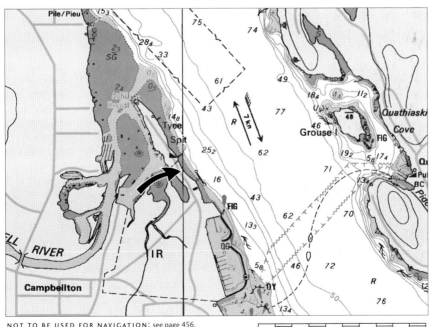

NOT TO BE USED FOR NAVIGATION: see page 456.
Use CHS chart #3539 for navigation; for information on obtaining navigational charts see page 456. Soundings are in meters.

1 NAUTICAL MILE

WHISKEY POINT END-OF-THE-ROAD

SHORE DIVE

SKILL
Expert divers

Intermediate divers
with guide

CURRENT TABLE
Seymour Narrows

WHY GO

The most accessible burst of color and life described in this guidebook is splashed across the bottom at Whiskey Point.

As though created by a painter gone deliriously wild, tiers of rock covered with color cascade in gradual folds from the shores of Quadra Island into Discovery Passage. Swimming under water close to the side, each rock I put my hand on is yet another color – red, yellow or purple. Strawberry anemones so close together that you can write your name in them. I touched some and they closed. Changed from fuzzy multi-tentacled flowers to small bright red berries in a basket. Purple algae are splashed on the rocks. Bright blue sea stars. And sunny yellow encrusting sponge over all the rest.

A mass of life covers the clean-swept rocky bottom. Strange sponges that look like tennis balls. Others like orange bath sponges. Purple-spotted Puget Sound king crabs. Snakelock anemones. Barnacles the size of baseballs, some abalones and some rock scallops. Fish hide under every ledge. Lingcod, red Irish lords and kelp greenlings so tame they'll eat from your hand.

BOTTOM AND DEPTHS

Clean-swept rocks tier down from 30 to 60 to 90 feet (9 to 18 to 27 meters). A lot of bull kelp.

HAZARDS

Currents, upcurrents, downcurrents, whirlpools, small boats, the British Columbia ferry and bull kelp. Dive on slack. And, though you can reach this dive by road, the site is so dangerous that on most days you should have a "live" boat ready in case you are swept away. Strong swimmers can dive here without a pickup boat on slight tidal exchanges. One rule of thumb suggested as safe by a local diver is a change in tide height of 2 feet ($\frac{2}{3}$ meter) or less: refer to Campbell River

tide table for this. Refer to Seymour Narrows current table for slack. Be geared up and ready one hour before slack tide, watching and waiting for the current to slow down.

Best at Whiskey Point on the turn from a flood to an ebbing tide when no back eddies occur, and there is less of a rip. Ascend along the bottom all the way to shore, well out of the way of the many salmon-fishing boats and the British Columbia ferry. Carry a knife for kelp.

TELEPHONES

• Beside shops, top of Quathiaski Cove Road.
• Quathiaski Cove ferry landing.

FACILITIES

Charters and dive packages out of dive resorts on west side of Quadra. Also drop-in air fills at one resort. Day charters and air fills in Campbell River.

ACCESS

Whiskey Point End-of-the-Road dive is on Discovery Passage at Quadra Island. From Campbell River it is a 10-minute ferry ride and 5-minute drive to it.

Take the ferry from downtown Campbell River to Quathiaski Cove on Quadra Island. From the ferry you see Whiskey Point on your right. At Quadra, drive up the hill. Take the first right into Green Road. At Noble Road, turn right again. Continue on it passing Helanton Road. Stay on the pavement and curve around to the right to the end of the paved road. Four or five cars could park. Past the pavement, deep potholes in the road. You might want to walk it.

You are now looking back at Quathiaski Cove. Enter the water and snorkel south toward Whiskey Point. Work your way south under water to a most beautiful wall at 50 feet (15 meters).

Christmas anemone

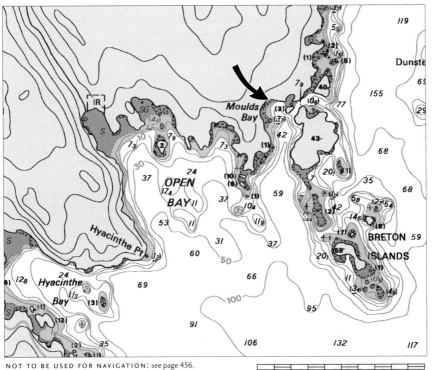

NOTES

NOT TO BE USED FOR NAVIGATION: see page 456.
Use CHS chart #3540 for navigation; for information on obtaining
navigational charts see page 456. Soundings are in meters.

1 NAUTICAL MILE

STEEP ISLAND

BOAT DIVE

GPS
50°04.959' N
125°15.336' W

SKILL
Expert divers

Intermediate divers
with guide

CURRENT TABLE
Seymour Narrows

WHY GO

Purple bouquets of feather duster tube worms cascade down the sheer rock face at Steep Island: a purple waterfall. Purple jungle. A purple profusion too fantastic to describe. Mixed with strawberry anemones. Trumpet sponges. Wolf-eels. Tennis ball sponges. Puget Sound king crabs. Orange cup corals. Octopuses, swimming scallops, rock scallops. Kelp greenlings, lingcod, tiger rockfish, yelloweye rockfish – all can be seen at Steep. But mostly I love Steep for those marvelous giant feather duster bouquets – many of them 3 feet (1 meter) tall. Take a light to see the richness of the purple.

I had dived this site before I wrote the first edition of *141 Dives* yet did not write about it. I had promised not to. But so many divers know of Steep now and Steep is honored as a reserve – as all sites in Discovery Passage are – so it's safe. And happily, I have been released from that promise.

Steep is so splendid I want to chronicle it. Single it out. Shout about it. Steep is one of those dives I label as having "star" quality. Divers who want to visit the most special places in the world will want to go to Steep.

BOTTOM AND DEPTHS

Plummets to a depth of 120 to 130 feet (37 to 40 meters) at the northwest corner. Ledges off gently into Discovery Passage from the middle to the southern end of the island. Bull kelp in summer.

HAZARDS

Current, boats and kelp. On all except the lowest tidal exchanges of less than 1 foot (⅓ meter) per hour, dive with a "live" boat; and dive at the end of an ebbing current. For height, refer to the tide table for Campbell River. For time to dive, refer to the turn at Seymour Narrows. Listen for boats and ascend up the side of the island all the way to the surface. Carry a knife.

TELEPHONES

- On the water: VHF radio; if no VHF, try a cell phone.
- On land:
1. Across Discovery Passage at Tyee Spit: north of Discovery Terminal, north of the launch ramp and across road outside Thunderbird RV Park. It is 2½ nautical miles south of Steep.
2. Quathiaski Cove ferry landing, Quadra Island: 3 nautical miles south of Steep.

FACILITIES

None at Steep Island. Dive resort packages, day charters, air fills and launch ramp on west side of Quadra. Camping year-round and hot showers at Heriot Bay, east side of Quadra. Day charters, water taxi, air fills and launch ramp at Campbell River.

ACCESS

Steep Island is in Discovery Passage near Quadra Island and close to Gowlland Island. It is 3 nautical miles north of Quathiaski Cove, Quadra Island.

Charter or launch at Quathiaski Cove or Campbell River. Go to the northern tip of Steep Island. Best at the end of an ebbing tide. Arrive early and watch the water. When the current slows down, about half an hour before the turn, go in and work your way around the wall on the Discovery Passage side of the island. Follow giant purple tube worms feathering down the northwest corner of Steep, then head south. You can gradually work your way up from ledge to ledge throughout the dive.

*Strawberry anemones
and tiger rockfish*

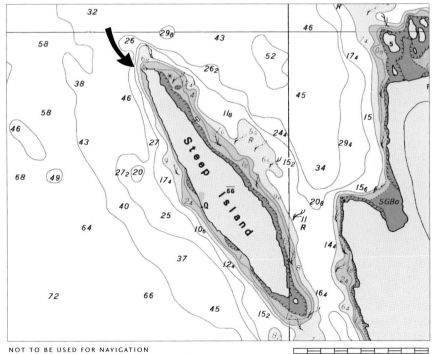

NOT TO BE USED FOR NAVIGATION
Use CHS chart 3540 for navigation; for information on ordering
navigational charts see page 460. Soundings are in meters.

1/5 NAUTICAL MILE

NOTES

COPPER CLIFFS

BOAT DIVE
GPS
50°05.797' N
125°16.187' W

SKILL
Intermediate and expert
divers

All divers with guide

CURRENT TABLE
Seymour Narrows

WHY GO

Copper Cliffs, an immense rock wall rising over 300 feet (90 meters) straight out of Discovery Passage, is almost too big to be true. Under water everything is equally big. Everything from boulders to cloud sponges to lingcod.

Enormous white plumose anemones cluster on the steep rock wall that falls away before you. Giant feather duster tube worms are also on the wall, their stalks covered with brooding anemones. A school of huge black rockfish swims past. Excellent visibility makes everything seem even more oversized. Giant boulders, dotted with thousands of tiny orange cup corals, are scattered on a large ledge below. In only 60 feet (18 meters) of water big clumps of cloud sponges with

small skinny brittle stars oozing out of them, billow between mammoth rocks.

During one dive my buddy and I saw 15 or 20 lingcod, each 3 to 4 feet (1 to 1¼ meters) long, and lots of red-and-black striped tiger rockfish. Peeping under a large boulder covered with strawberry anemones on its north face, we saw a mosshead warbonnet. Even the warbonnet was large for its species, about 4 inches (10 centimeters) long. I looked up while swimming upcurrent and there was a yelloweye rockfish staring at me. Colorful giants fed by giant currents.

Grandiose!

BOTTOM AND DEPTHS

Clean-cut volcanic rock wall sheers to a ledge with large boulders at 50 to 60 feet (15 to 18 meters). Then drops away again to a depth greater than 100 feet (30 meters).

HAZARDS

Current and small boats. Dive precisely on the slack at the end of the ebb. Be geared up and ready one hour before the turn, watching and waiting for the current to slow down. Big currents run through here. On large tidal exchanges leave a pickup person on your boat in case you are swept away. This is a popular salmon-fishing area: in summer, small boats come within inches of the wall. Listen for boats and ascend close to the wall all the way to the surface well out of the way of them.

TELEPHONES

- On the water: VHF radio; if no VHF, try a cell phone.
- On land:
1. Across Discovery Passage at Tyee Spit: north of Discovery Terminal and the launch ramp, and across road outside Thunderbird RV Park. It is 2½ nautical miles south of Steep.
2. Quathiaski Cove ferry landing, Quadra.

*Fishing boat
at Copper Cliffs*

FACILITIES

None at Copper Cliffs. Day charters, dive packages, air fills and launch ramp at Quathiaski Cove, west side of Quadra. Camping and hot showers year-round, east side of Quadra. Camping in summer next to Rebecca Spit Provincial Park.

ACCESS

Copper Cliffs, usually called Copper Bluffs, is in Discovery Passage on the west side of Quadra Island. It is 4 nautical miles north of Campbell River. Charter or launch your own boat and go north to that immense rock wall. You cannot miss it.

NOTES

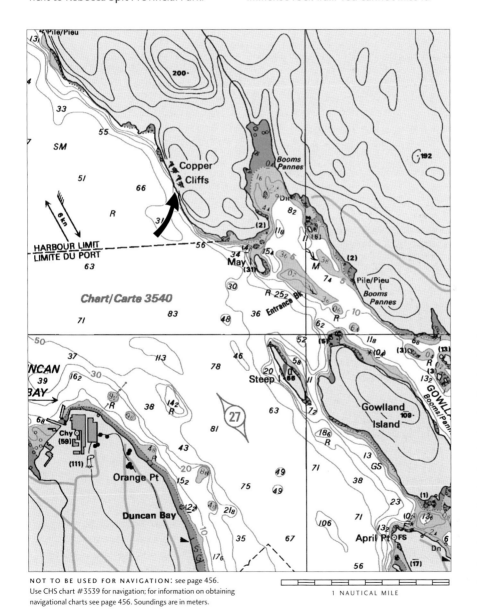

NOT TO BE USED FOR NAVIGATION: see page 456.
Use CHS chart #3539 for navigation; for information on obtaining navigational charts see page 456. Soundings are in meters.

1 NAUTICAL MILE

COLUMBIA ARTIFICIAL REEF

BOAT DIVE
GPS
50°08.005′ N
125°20.204′ W

SKILL
Exterior: all divers

Interior: intermediate and
expert divers experienced
in penetration

CURRENT TABLE
Seymour Narrows

WHY GO

The *Columbia* is a big, easy-to-dive intact vessel. You're sure to find it – just slide down one of the four descent lines marked with a buoy. Minimal current to consider. Great for new divers on the exterior as well as challenging for wreck divers who want to work at penetration skills; the vessel lists to port nearly 350° so is good practice before tackling the *Chaudiére*. Also an excellent site to hone underwater navigation skills.

Dramatic also for divers like me who know little about ships and who need obvious big stuff to look at. Without penetrating, I saw the main guns with two barrels aggressively pointing in front of the flying bridge. These guns give a realistic impression but are replaced by pipe. I also saw the AA (anti-aircraft) gun sitting on the quarterdeck and the anti-submarine Limbo mortars. The main mast. The smoke stack. All at no greater depth, that day, than 84 feet (26 meters).

The 366-foot (112-meter) long destroyer escort HMCS *Columbia* was built in North Vancouver, commissioned on November 7, 1959: first served on the East Coast, and from there, represented Canada at Nigerian independence celebrations. The vessel was decommissioned on February 18, 1974, and served as a stationary training ship. It was sunk by the Artificial Reef Society of British Columbia on June 22, 1996.

Now the *Columbia* is home for marine life: we saw skinny brittle stars scurry all over the deck, the hull, the foc'sle. A giant sunflower star draped over a beam. Moon jellies like tiny balloons. Swimming scallops. Quillback rockfish. Feather stars. Pale orange swimming anemones, bright orange plumose anemones. We watched a huge lion's mane jelly move majestically across the ops (operations) deck, streaming 10-foot (3-meter) long stinging tentacles in its wake. We backed off.

Different marine animals than usually found in the Campbell River area are at this site, mostly mobile critters.

BOTTOM AND DEPTHS

At high tides, the stern of the *Columbia* rests on rock bottom at 100 feet (30 meters) and slopes gradually to the accordioned bow that rests at 120 feet (37 meters) – the bow hit bottom when it went down. It points southeast. The top of the main mast is the shallowest sight to see on the ship at 55 feet (17 meters).

For divers planning to penetrate the vessel, a plasticized Dive Slate Add-on Page provides detail on depths, exits and more on the *Columbia*. It is available from dive shops or contact www.aquatic-realm.com.

HAZARDS

Depth; sometimes current; always the temptation to explore; silt inside the ship. Make a dive plan suitable for your skills and stick with it. Be aware of time. Only divers trained in penetration with full information about the *Columbia* should enter. Ascend at one of the marker-buoy chains, where you can easily make a safety stop.

TELEPHONES

• On the water: VHF radio: if no VHF, try a cell phone.
• On land: fuel dock at Brown Bay, 3½ nautical miles north of the dive site on the Vancouver Island side of channel.

FACILITIES

None at the site.

ACCESS

The *Columbia* is southeast of Seymour Narrows behind Maud Island. Usually little current at the site despite its proximity to Seymour Narrows. Sometimes current on an ebb. We dived on the flood on a day with a tidal exchange of nearly 8 feet (2½ meters) and felt nothing. If diving when current, safest on flood.

Charter out of Quadra Island and Campbell River; or launch north of Campbell River or at Quadra Island. Tie up on one of the four buoys – at the bow, amidships, port side of the vessel or stern. If no buoys are present, use GPS locations and a depth sounder to find the ship. We tied up at the white buoy amidships and descended.

Bow of the Columbia, crumpled when scuttled

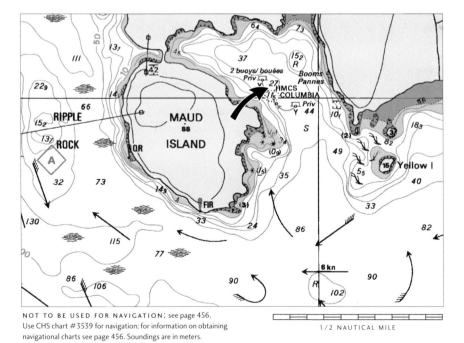

NOT TO BE USED FOR NAVIGATION: see page 456.
Use CHS chart #3539 for navigation; for information on obtaining navigational charts see page 456. Soundings are in meters.

1/2 NAUTICAL MILE

SEYMOUR NARROWS

BOAT DIVE
GPS
50°08.147′ N
125°21.595′ W

This reading is in the center of the bay – choose which end of the bay to start from based on the current direction.

SKILL
Expert divers

Intermediate divers with guide

CURRENT TABLE
Seymour Narrows

Most Outrageous, slack tide at Seymour Narrows

WHY GO

Anemone-land – unbelievably soft, pale pinky-orange anemones with long transparent filaments streaming into the current are massed and tumble loosely over the rocks. We see large white anemones like giant snowflakes. A few tall white plumose anemones tilting into the current. Christmas anemones with flaming red tops and green-and-red bases – their tops look speckled green-black-and-white until you shine a light on them. Red snakelock anemones too. And mixed in, mauve and pink brooding anemones, the size of small cotton balls. Millions of white "stunted" anemones heaped over all like drifted snow. Little guys – have they stayed tiny so they won't be washed away?

We see yellow staghorn bryozoans attached to the rocks. A trumpet sponge. Encrusting sponge coating the rocks with bright yellow. Orange ball sponges. Chitons. Giant red urchins and small green urchins making craters in the rocks. At one depth, miniature white cucumbers cover the ledge – a strange filter feeder I have not seen often and only at very high current sites. Abalones. Swimming scallops. Big fat rock scallops in the crevices. Kelp greenlings. Lingcod – lots of them. A red Irish lord.

Take a light to see the technicolor world of Seymour Narrows.

BOTTOM AND DEPTHS

Rounded ledges start at 20 to 30 feet (6 to 9 meters) and roll gently down into Seymour Narrows deeper than you could go – to 360 feet (110 meters) on the chart. Most life is between 40 and 60 feet (12 and 18 meters). Crevices, nooks and crannies indent the ledges giving places to hide from the current. In summer, the kelp gives a protected place to ascend out of the way of boats.

HAZARDS

Current, tide rips and whirlpools; ships, tugs, barges, fishing boats and small boats. A tremendous "parking lot" of boats waits for slack at Seymour Narrows, particularly at fishing openings and at Alaska supply season. Dive on slack with a "live" boat. While down, watch current direction and be aware when it changes. Do not bob up mid-channel: Seymour Narrows is the main route for large vessels heading up the Island Passage to Prince Rupert and Alaska. When ascending, listen for small boats. Hug the side of the passage: go up crevices, hang onto rocks and surface in the kelp out of the way of boats. Carry a knife for kelp.

Seymour Narrows is big, deep and swift – immense volumes of water move through. It is one of the top three fastest-flowing tidal streams in the world, along with Sechelt Rapids and Nakwakto Rapids for speed. The channel is 3½ nautical miles long with a width of ½ nautical mile. It is powerful – respect that power.

TELEPHONES

- On the water: VHF radio: if no VHF, try a cell phone.
- On land: Brown's Bay Marina, outside on shower float behind fuel dock. This telephone is 1 ½ nautical miles north of Seymour Narrows on the Vancouver Island side of the channel.

FACILITIES

None at Seymour Narrows. Charters out of Quadra Island and Campbell River. Launch ramp, accommodation and RV park at Brown Bay.

ACCESS

Seymour Narrows is halfway up Discovery Passage and close to the Vancouver Island shore. It is 10 nautical miles north of the town of Campbell River and immediately north of Ripple Rock.

Charter or launch out of Quathiaski Cove on Quadra Island or out of Campbell River and head north. After going beneath the power lines, head north 330 yards (300 meters) – go one-third of the way up the west side of Seymour Narrows to a sheltered cove where the depth is only 20 to 30 feet (6 to 9 meters). In summer, you can find this cove by the kelp. But, if you have a depth sounder, take it.

Plan in advance: current can roar through Seymour Narrows up to 16 knots on the flooding tide. Up to 14 knots on the ebb. Even with low exchanges, the water stops only momentarily. Go on a day of the month when the current is no greater than 11 knots at maximum flood or ebb. Any greater current and the back eddies do not stop.

Be geared up and ready to dive an hour before the predicted turn, waiting for slack. The arrow is in the center of the bay; pick the end of the bay for your entry based on current direction. Watch the water, watch the kelp. Current runs almost all the time. When it slows sufficiently to dive, roll off the boat and head down. Go with the current for the first half of your dive – try for a free ride. Watch the kelp while diving, too. When the kelp turns, head back for another free ride. Try for it, but the current might pick up without warning. Dive with a "live" boat; your first time, go with a charter operator experienced at Seymour Narrows.

NOTES

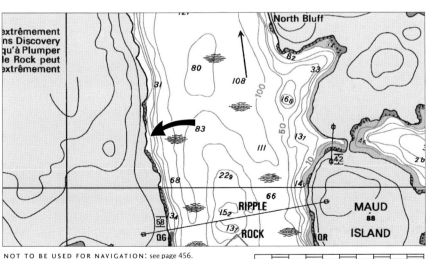

NOT TO BE USED FOR NAVIGATION: see page 456. Use CHS chart #3539 for navigation; for information on obtaining navigational charts see page 456. Soundings are in meters.

1/2 NAUTICAL MILE

ROCK BAY

SHORE DIVE

SKILL
Intermediate and expert
divers

All divers and snorkelers
with guide

TIDE TABLE
Owen Bay:
Subtract 30 minutes

WHY GO

History, shallow diving in the kelp and deep diving to sponge-land are attractions at this relatively current-free site where you can dive almost any time of day. It is excellent for photography, with water that's usually clear and with a good mixture of marine life. Entry is easy. Plus there's the chance of a valuable bottle or china find. Union steamships called here from the early 1900s until at least 1927.

A large logging community was at in the late 1800s. A big hospital was built there in 1905. It burned and another 25-bed one was built in 1911. Though the second hospital was abandoned some years ago when the logging operation closed down, right up until the mid-1950s the hospital plumbing was still connected and you could take a cold shower – the site was made for divers! Then that building burned on Christmas Day in 1971. Today not much remains of the once-large community at Rock Bay: only the hospital ruins and old bottles hidden under the sea and the new seasonal population at the RV campground.

When diving here I saw lots of marine life. Kelp greenlings, delicate nudibranchs, a bright red blenny with blue markings, lingcod, a huge octopus sprawled across a rock as though sunning itself and a cloud sponge so orange it was almost red. One blue swimming scallop clapped right up to my buddy's mask and I almost lost my regulator from laughing.

BOTTOM AND DEPTHS

It's easy to make either a shallow or a deep dive at this site. Rocky bottom scattered with boulders and bull kelp slopes gently to a depth of 30 to 40 feet (9 to 12 meters). Some sand between the boulders. Then a rapid drop to as deep as you want to go.

HAZARDS

Boats, current and bull kelp. Listen for boats and dive with a compass and dive flag: at the end of your dive navigate to shore, staying close to the bottom all the way. In the bay, dive on or near slack and be watchful of swirling currents. If you go around the point on the left, you must

Kelp greenling

dive on slack. Watch for downcurrents on ebb tides at the left-hand side of the bay. Carry a knife for kelp.

TELEPHONES
- Rock Bay Resort manager's office; cell phone, May 1 to September 30.
- Chatham Point Light Station, available 24 hours year-round for emergencies: drive out of Rock Bay, around a corner and pass a small road with a chain across it. Make a sharp left-hand turn up the next road and go 3 miles (5 kilometers). The road is potholed and it takes 15 minutes to reach the light station at the end of it.

FACILITIES
Pit toilets, fresh water. Camping from May 1 to September 30; concrete launch ramp that is good at all tides, plus parking – all for a fee at privately owned Rock Bay.

ACCESS
Rock Bay is near the east end of Johnstone Strait. It is at the end of Rock Bay Forest Service Road off Island Highway (Highway 19). The turnoff is between Port McNeill and Campbell River.

Go down Rock Bay Forest Service Road. Allow 25 to 30 minutes from Island Highway to the dive. There might be logging traffic, too, so drive with your headlights on. You might see moss-covered remnants of railway trestles from steam-engine logging days on the way. Go along this gravel road with potholes for 11 miles (18 kilometers) to Rock Bay where you can drive to the water's edge. Expect to pay a modest parking fee at privately owned Rock Bay. The gently shelving boat ramp is suitable at half-tides for wheelchair divers.

To get to Rock Bay Forest Service Road
- From Campbell River go north on Island Highway for 30 minutes to the Rock Bay turnoff. When almost 6 miles (10 kilometers) past Roberts Lake Resort you will see a narrow forest service road. Turn right.
- From Port McNeill, drive south on Island Highway for 2 hours. When 14 miles (23 kilometers) past the Sayward Road junction, turn left down Rock Bay Forest Service Road.

NOTES

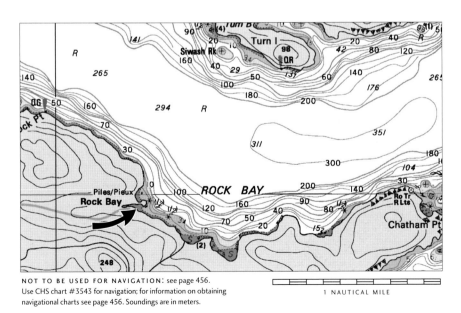

NOT TO BE USED FOR NAVIGATION: see page 456. Use CHS chart #3543 for navigation; for information on obtaining navigational charts see page 456. Soundings are in meters.

1 NAUTICAL MILE

CHAPTER FIVE

Port Hardy, Port McNeill and Telegraph Cove

Pacific white-sided dolphins migrating

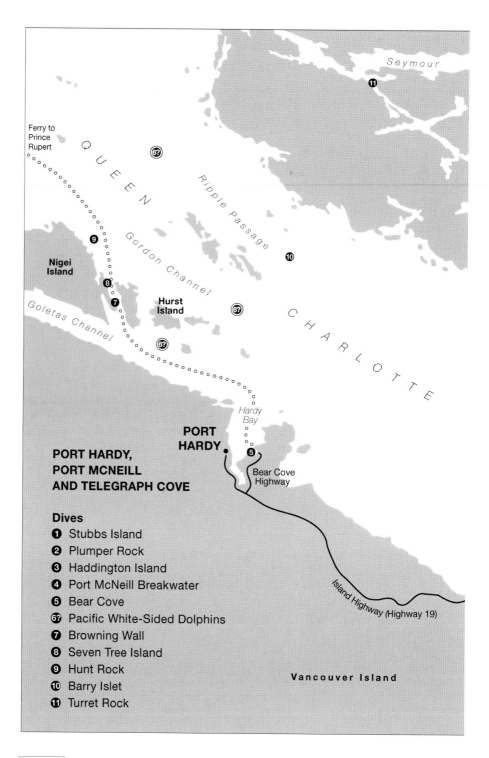

PORT HARDY, PORT MCNEILL AND TELEGRAPH COVE

Dives

- ❶ Stubbs Island
- ❷ Plumper Rock
- ❸ Haddington Island
- ❹ Port McNeill Breakwater
- ❺ Bear Cove
- 6? Pacific White-Sided Dolphins
- ❼ Browning Wall
- ❽ Seven Tree Island
- ❾ Hunt Rock
- ❿ Barry Islet
- ⓫ Turret Rock

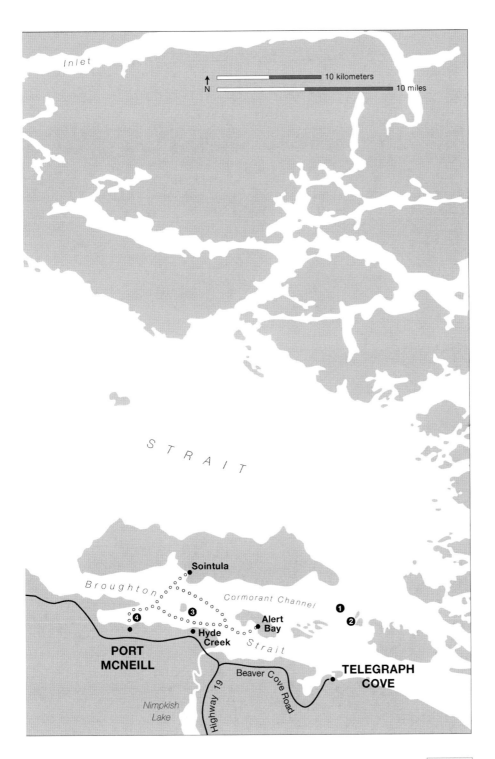

SERVICE INFORMATION

Tide and Current Information
- *Tide and Current Tables, Volume 6: Discovery Passage and West Coast of Vancouver Island,* Canadian Hydrographic Service print annual
- www.lau.chs-shc.gc.ca: Tide and Current Tables for all of Canada. Go to web site: select Pacific; General Information, Tide and Currents; Data Available; then Tide Tables in PDF format. Select Volume 6.

Weather Information
- Canadian Coast Guard: Speak with a person, 24 hours; telephone Comox (250)339-3613.
- Canadian Coast Guard (Comox Coast Guard Radio): Continuous Marine Broadcast (CMB) recorded, 24 hours; listen for weather in Johnstone Strait or Queen Charlotte Sound, in Port McNeill and Alert Bay, telephone (250)974-5305.
- Environment Canada: recorded, 24 hours;
1. Marine weather line: listen to weather for Johnstone Strait, Queen Charlotte Sound, Port Hardy: (250)949-7148.
2. Weather line: listen for weather in north Vancouver Island and Port Hardy, telephone (250)949-7147.
- www.weatheroffice.ec.gc.ca

Tourist Information: Tourism BC
- Toll-free throughout North America: 1-800-435-5622
- From all other locations: (250)387-1642 www.hellobc.com

Diving Emergency Telephone Numbers
On land and water:
- Call 911, request "ambulance" and say, "I have a scuba diving emergency".
- Vancouver General Hospital; for 24-hour, 7-day-a-week response: telephone (604)875-5000 and say, "I want the hyperbaric physician on call".
On the water:
- VHF radio: Call Coast Guard radio, Channel 16 and say, "I have a scuba diving emergency".

- Cell phone: 911, *16 or *311 and say, "I have a scuba diving emergency". *If emergency or medical personnel are unfamiliar with scuba diving emergencies, ask them to telephone DAN (Divers Alert Network) at (919)684-4326. No money for a long distance call? Dial DAN collect at 011-919-684-4326 and say, "I have a scuba diving emergency".*

Mark emergency location before leaving scene: other divers might be down.

Ferry Information
British Columbia Ferry Services (BC Ferries)
- Toll-free throughout North America: 1-888-223-3779
- From all other locations: (250)386-3431

At the time of writing: the following information applies – but frequent changes occur; check current requirements on bcferries.com before every trip.

Rules Regarding Scuba Tanks on BC Ferries
Dangerous Goods Clearance
Persons transporting scuba tanks containing compressed air, full or partially full, are required under Canadian law to declare dangerous goods at the terminal or to a vessel officer. Persons transporting scuba tanks with valves removed do not need clearance. No nitrox or mixed gases (UN 3156) permitted. See page 141: learn how to obtain and complete Dangerous Goods Shipping forms.

Prearranged Clearance is Mandatory
For sailings from Port Hardy to Prince Rupert: clearance must be obtained from Prince Rupert Port Authority, open only Monday through Thursday and closed on weekends – they must receive it at least 48 hours prior to sailing time: fax them at (250)627-8448. They will send clearance papers to Port Hardy – confirm it! Port Hardy telephone: (250)949-6722.

Arrive at Port Hardy terminal 45 minutes prior to departure to pick up clearance.

PORT HARDY

• DIVE SHOP

North Island Diving & Charters
Corner of Market & Hastings
PO Box 1674
Port Hardy BC V0N 2P0
(250)949-2664
www.northislanddiver.com
(Recreational and nitrox instruction. Nitrox fills.)

• DIVE RESORTS

God's Pocket Resort
PO Box 130
Port Hardy BC V0N 2P0
(250)949-1755
1-888-534-8322: Toll-free throughout North America
www.godspocket.com
(Dive packages with boat diving from the Hurst Isle; air and nitrox fills; land-based accommodation and meals at Hurst Island on Christie Passage. Guest pickup in Port Hardy, advance booking required. Waterfront fills for drop-ins. Open March 1 to October 31.)

Browning Pass HideAway Resort
Located north end of Browning Passage, Nigei Island side
PO Box 512, Port Hardy BC V0N 2P0
(250)753-3751
1-877-725-2835: Toll-free throughout North America
www.VancouverIslandDive.com
(Packages include three to four dives a day off Straits Explorer or Wave-hopper to Browning Passage, Deserters and/or Nakwakto areas; cottage accommodation, meals, transport to and from Port Hardy, air and nitrox. Open year-round. Advance booking required. Dillon Rock and more. Also charters out of Port McNeill and Telegraph Cove.)

Malei Island Resort Ltd.
PO Box 5090
Port Hardy BC V0N 2P0
(250)949-8006; cell (250)949-1208
www.malei-island.com
(Resort visits range from three to five days; include land-based accommodation at Malei Island, meals, air fills, and boat diving off the Malei Isle or the Mimir. Guests are picked up in Port Hardy. Maximum seven guests. Air fills for drop-ins. Open May 1 to mid-October.)

BC's Pacific Dreams
Mailing address: #268, 1 - 5765 Turner Road
Nanaimo BC V9T 6M4
(250)816-0455
www.bcspacificdreams.com
(Accommodation at Clam Cove aboard MV Songhee; dives off Eagle XXI from Browning Wall to Seven Tree Island, the Themis and Hunt Rock. April and May, August to mid-October.)

• DAY CHARTERS

Sun Fun
Sun Fun Divers
445 Pioneer Hill Drive, PO Box 1240
Port McNeill BC V0N 2R0
(250)956-2243
www.sunfundivers.com
(Day charters year-round out of Port Hardy and Quatsino, west coast: dives range from Browning Wall to Barry Islet, Robson Reefs.)

Catala
Catala Charters
Box 526, 6170 Hardy Bay Road
Port Hardy BC V0N 2P0
(250)949-7560
1-800-515-5511: Toll-free throughout North America
www.catalacharters.net
(Water taxi transportation to and from dive sites year-round out of Port Hardy.)

PORT HARDY (CONTINUED)
DAY CHARTERS (CONTINUED)
Malei Isle, Mimir
PO Box 5090
Port Hardy BC V0N 2P0
(250)949-2664; cell (250)949-1208
www.northislanddiver.com
(Transportation to and from dive sites year-round. Sites from Browning Wall to Hunt Rock to Barry Islet.)

MV *Straits Explorer* and *Wave-hopper*
HideAway Resort, located north end of
    Browning Passage, Nigei Island side
PO Box 512
Port Hardy BC V0N 2P0
(250)753-3751
1-877-725-2835: Toll-free throughout
    North America
www.VancouverIslandDive.com
(Day charters year-round – advance bookings required: dives range from Browning Passage to Dillon Rock to Nakwakto areas. Water taxi transport to the HideAway. Air and nitrox fills.)

• LIVEABOARD CHARTERS
Mamro
Mamro Adventures
1 - 5765 Turner Road, Suite 203
Nanaimo BC V9T 6M4
(250)756-8872
www.mamro.com
(Out of Port Hardy in spring and fall. Usually range from Browning Passage to Deserters Group to Seymour Inlet. Specialize in small groups – up to seven divers.)

• MULTIPLE-DAY CHARTERS
Viking I
Viking Adventure Tours
#7 - 211 Buttertubs Place
Nanaimo BC V9R 3X8
(250)755-9175; cell (250)616-9336
www.vikingadventuretours.com
(Multiple-day trips out of Port Hardy; also out of Port McNeill.)

• LAUNCH RAMPS
Bear Cove Public Ramps
Bear Cove Road
Port Hardy
(Launch for a fee for Queen Charlotte Strait: steep paved ramps, good at all tides. Picnic tables and pit toilets. Telephones at ferry ticket office, end of road, when ferry terminal open.

Telephones available, 24 hours year-round, at Sunny Sanctuary Campground in the campground and outside the office. Go to Highway 19 [Island Highway] and turn north toward Port Hardy. At the Coal Harbour/Highway 19 junction, look on the right-hand side for Sunny Sanctuary.)

From Port Hardy, go south on Highway 19 for 2¾ miles (4½ kilometers); from Port McNeill go north 22 miles (36 kilometers) to Bear Cove Highway: then, following signs toward the Prince Rupert ferry, go 2¾ miles (4½ kilometers) to the ramps.

Port Hardy Public Ramp
Next to Quarterdeck Marina Resort
6555 Hardy Bay Road
Port Hardy BC V0N 2P0
(250)949-6551
www.quarterdeckresort.net
(Launch for a fee at Hardy Bay for Queen Charlotte Strait: concrete ramp, good at all tides. Pay fee at Harbour Office, 6600 Hardy Bay Road, west of ramp. Parking for a fee. Restrooms, hot showers and accommodation at Quarterdeck Marina Resort. Telephones at top of ramp.)

PORT MCNEILL
• DIVE SHOP
Sun Fun Divers
445 Pioneer Hill Drive, PO Box 1240
Port McNeill BC V0N 2R0
(250)956-2243
www.sunfundivers.com
(Recreational and nitrox instruction. Nitrox fills. Also hostel with kitchen, and charters.)

• DAY CHARTERS
Sun Fun
Sun Fun Divers
445 Pioneer Hill Drive, PO Box 1240
Port McNeill BC V0N 2R0
(250)956-2243
www.sunfundivers.com
(Day charters year-round out of Port McNeill or Telegraph Cove: dives range from Haddington Island to Stubbs Island, Plumper Rock and Booker's Lagoon; also out of Port Hardy and Telegraph Cove.)

Viking Express
Viking West Lodge and Charter
PO Box 113
Port McNeill BC V0N 2R0
(250)956-3431; cell (250)974-8088
E-mail: cachus@telus.net
(Transportation to and from dive sites year-round out of Port McNeill.)

• LIVEABOARD CHARTERS
Viking I
Viking Adventure Tours
#7 - 211 Buttertubs Place
Nanaimo BC V9R 3X8
(250)755-9175; cell (250)616-9336
www.vikingadventuretours.com
(Multiple-day trips out of Port McNeill; also out of Port Hardy.)

• LAUNCH RAMPS
Port McNeill Public Ramps
Off Beach Drive, just west of McNeill Road
Port McNeill
(Launch for a fee for Broughton and Queen Charlotte straits: concrete ramps, good at all tides. Parking for a fee. Restrooms, summer only, Port McNeill Visitor Info Centre: 351 Shelly Crescent. To reach it, go west on Beach Drive which curves, crosses Broughton Boulevard, to the info centre.

Two telephones: one 150 feet [50 meters] west of ramps; a second one at Beach Drive and McNeill Road, one block east of ramps.)

At Port McNeill, follow Campbell Way to Broughton Boulevard and turn right, then left at Beach Drive and to the ramps.

TELEGRAPH COVE
To reach Telegraph Cove: take the Beaver Cove turnoff from Highway 19 (Island Highway). Follow signs to Telegraph Cove; from the turnoff drive 9 miles (15 kilometers) over rough industrial roads to Telegraph Cove. After 6 miles (10 kilometers) you reach a "T" junction; turn left and continue almost 3 miles (5 kilometers) more to Telegraph Cove.

• LAUNCH RAMP
Telegraph Cove Resorts Ramp, head of cove
Telegraph Cove Resorts
PO Box 1
Telegraph Cove BC V0N 3J0
(250)928-3131
1-800-200-4665: Toll-free throughout
    North America
www.telegraphcoveresort.com
(Launch for a fee year-round for Johnstone Strait: concrete ramp, good at all tides. Restrooms and coin-operated hot showers beside ramp. Telephones east of ramp, behind office. Campground and cabins; parking free for resort guests. Open May 1 to October 15.)

All of this Service Information is subject to change.

BOAT DIVE
GPS
50°36.190' N
126°48.900' W

SKILL
Expert divers and
snorkelers

Intermediate divers,
with guide

CURRENT TABLE
Weynton Passage

WHY GO

A carpet of hot-pink brooding anemones and small green pin-cushion anemones covers the rock. I love the big mint-green anemones, large clumps of hard pink hydrocoral, pink soft corals and basket stars like dreadlocks of spun ivory.

We saw giant orange peel nudibranchs, an angry lingcod, blue rockfish, red Irish lords, China rockfish in crevices. Yellow sponges, red knobby sponges. Rock scallops, abalones, giant barnacles and urchins. Huge plumose anemones down deep. And look for Puget Sound king crabs.

In this whale-watching capital of the world, you might meet killer whales on any dive. When we surfaced, the boat tender told us a whale had passed. We followed it to gain information for scientific records of the movements of the whales. The charter operator photographed its rippled dorsal fin with a spot and later identified it certainly as P-1, a transient whale. The resident pods eat fish; the transients eat seals and

similar mammals. You might get in on informal and fascinating whale watching after your dive. In September harbor seals are on the islands; divers sometimes see Dall's porpoises. You can see many of the beauties of the dive snorkeling! But boaters and divers should avoid approaching closer than 110 yards (100 meters) to any marine mammals. See www.pac.dfo-mpo.gc.ca, click on Marine Mammals, select Viewing Guidelines.

Stubbs Island is locally honored as a marine sanctuary.

BOTTOM AND DEPTHS

The steep rocky sides of the island are indented with deep crevices. The northwest corner is the shallowest, the southeast and west sides are deepest, bottoming out to sand at 120 feet (37 meters). Most life for scuba divers to see is at 50 to 60 feet (15 to 18 meters). In summer, some thickets of bull kelp.

HAZARDS

Current, lots of boats, bull kelp and wind. The current floods in through Queen Charlotte Strait and splits at Stubbs Island. It can run up to 6 knots. It helps to have slack but you can almost always find one face of Stubbs that is protected from current. Listen for boats, and ascend up the side of the island. Carry a knife for kelp. When a southeasterly wind blows, you must have a boat tender. With a westerly wind, it is difficult to dive Stubbs. Try Plumper Rock.

TELEPHONES

- On the water: VHF radio; if no VHF, try a cell phone.
- On land:
1. Telegraph Cove, top of launch ramp.
2. Behind Telegraph Cove Resorts office, on left-hand side, top of launch ramp.

*Whale watching
after the dive*

FACILITIES

Launch ramp at Telegraph Cove. Charters out of Telegraph Cove and Port McNeill. Air fills in Port McNeill and Port Hardy.

ACCESS

Stubbs Island is at the east end of Cormorant Channel. It is 3½ nautical miles north of Telegraph Cove; 11 nautical miles from Port McNeill. To dive the most beautiful southeast corner, plan to dive on slack.

Charter out of Port McNeill or Port Hardy or launch your own boat at Telegraph Cove and go to Stubbs Island.

Anchor at the southeast corner if you can – it is the very best location. The current table for Weynton Passage is accurate for the east point of Stubbs where you must dive on slack. Dive the end of the flooding tide, get into a notch and head left. The rest of the island is incredible too. If unable to dive the southeast corner for whatever reason, try someplace else. With current of 5 knots and greater, plan to start your dive 10 or 15 minutes before the turn. With less current, enter 30 minutes before the turn and work the back eddies. On ebbing tides, you can dive the north side on the full ebb except when a westerly wind is blowing. From November through February, wind can blow for several days at a time.

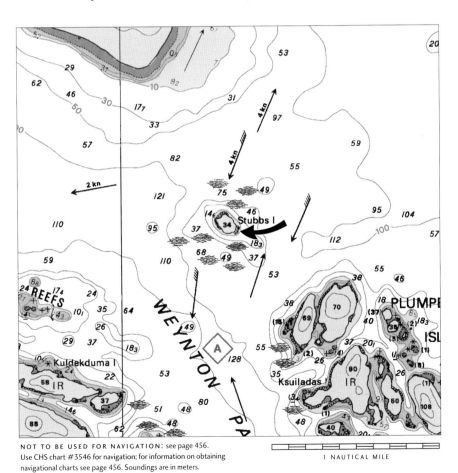

NOTES

NOT TO BE USED FOR NAVIGATION: see page 456.
Use CHS chart #3546 for navigation; for information on obtaining navigational charts see page 456. Soundings are in meters.

1 NAUTICAL MILE

PLUMPER ROCK

BOAT DIVE
GPS
50°35.467' N
126°48.099' W

SKILL
Expert divers

Intermediate divers
with guide

CURRENT TABLE
Weynton Passage:
Subtract 30 minutes

WHY GO

The marine life is a spectacle – not an inch of rock showing except above water at the colorful small seamount called Plumper Rock. And when the wind is blowing elsewhere, you can usually still dive Plumper.

China rockfish – you see them on every dive, but the hard pink hydrocoral and basket stars are still my favorites at this site. Closest thing to wall-to-wall basket stars in the shallows I have seen anyplace.

We saw a beautifully sculpted basket star in only 30 feet (9 meters). Also schools of black rockfish, lots of kelp greenlings, lingcod, red Irish lords and tiger rockfish. Yellow sponges and orange cup corals brighten the scene.

We saw tennis ball sponges, rock scallops, giant barnacles and tube worms waving purple thread-like fingers. Masses of small pink dahlia anemones. A valley of huge white plumose anemones lured us down and down. It looks like the tropics. The color! The underwater visibility! Usually you can see 80 to 100 feet (24 to 30 meters) in winter – when we dived Plumper the last day of February, visibility was down to 75 feet (23 meters). Timing is important; the algae bloom usually comes in April.

After diving when heading home, look for bald eagles – we counted 24 in a glance. And, on shore, the picturesque boardwalk town of Telegraph Cove that was founded in the 1920s is worth a visit.

BOTTOM AND DEPTHS

Plumper Rock dries at 13-foot (4-meter) tides. The valley of plumose-covered rock goes down on the northeast side. It bottoms out to sand at 120 to 130 feet (37 to 40 meters). A scattering of bull kelp streams in the current.

HAZARDS

Current – even downwellings, and boats. You must dive on slack. The current is moving all the time; it just turns around. Listen for boats and hug the rock as you ascend.

TELEPHONES

- On the water: VHF radio; if no VHF, try a cell phone.
- On land:
1. Telegraph Cove, top of launch ramp.
2. Behind Telegraph Cove Resorts office, on left-hand side, top of launch ramp.

FACILITIES

None at Plumper Rock. Charters out of Telegraph Cove and Port McNeill or launch at Telegraph Cove. Air fills in Port McNeill and Port Hardy. In summer, camping at Telegraph Cove.

ACCESS

Plumper Rock is north of Telegraph Cove on the east side of Weynton Passage in the Plumper Islands. It is in the passage between Ksuiladas Island and an island north of it.

Charter out of Port McNeill or Port Hardy, or launch your own boat at Telegraph Cove and go 2¾ nautical miles to Plumper Rock. From Port McNeill, it is 12 nautical miles to Plumper. Best time to start your dive is 45 minutes before high slack when you might get a back eddy around the rock. Arrive at Plumper with gear ready at least an hour before the turn and watch the water and kelp. Best to have a pickup boat.

To find the valley, dive toward the northeast.

China rockfish

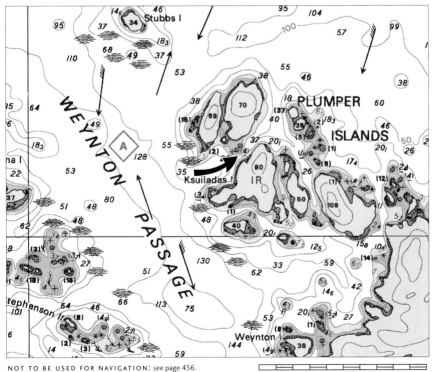

NOT TO BE USED FOR NAVIGATION: see page 456.
Use CHS chart #3546 for navigation; for information on obtaining
navigational charts see page 456. Soundings are in meters.

1 NAUTICAL MILE

NOTES

**BOAT DIVE or
KAYAK DIVE**

GPS
50°35.945′ N
127°00.998′ W

SKILL
Expert divers

Intermediate divers
with guide

TIDE TABLE
Alert Bay:
Add 2 hours

WHY GO

Lingcod, black rockfish, quillback rockfish, kelp greenlings cruise in droves from superb hidey-holes behind giant, squared-off volcanic-rock blocks tumbled down the steep wall at the rock quarry at Haddington Island.

White plumose anemones are huge too – they light the wall, feather the pearly gray rock blocks with glorious white. Many of the blocks are grooved, a different geometric look for an underwater habitat. Painted greenlings hide beneath dark ledges. Crimson slipper cucumbers, orange cup corals and gum boot chitons are on the wall. Green urchins, giant red and purple urchins are heaped in the valleys. Inviting holes to poke your light into where giant lingcod hide are everywhere behind these blocks. They were left behind after the stone was quarried to build the facade of the Parliament Buildings in Victoria, completed in late 1897, and to build the causeway in front of the Empress Hotel in the early 1900s.

The rock quarry dive possesses the same elegance – no, *is the source of elegance* of these two provincial landmarks that originated at Haddington Island.

BOTTOM AND DEPTHS

A slim line of kelp rims the shore and its tumble of giant blocks in the narrow belt of shallows. The wall is steep, the tumbled blocks spill down to gravel, sand and shells at 115 to 125 feet (35 to 38 meters) height. With 13 feet (4 meters) of tide, we saw the most life from 40 to 60 feet (12 to 18 meters).

HAZARDS

Current and depth; possible danger to kayak-divers from overexertion after the dive. Divers with pickup boat could dive throughout the flood. With no pickup boat, dive on high slack. Slack is difficult to predict in Broughton Strait as it is affected by wind. Also the current never stops, it just slows down and then turns. Kayak-divers who have dived deep should take a lunch break and take it easy heading home. The risk of bends may be increased by strenuous paddling after the dive.

TELEPHONES

- On the water: VHF radio; if no VHF, try a cell phone.
- On land:
1. At Hyde Creek, telephone outside the Esso station on the right-hand side of Hyde Creek Road just before junction with Highway 19.
2. At Port McNeill, top of the ramps, turn right; go 64 yards (150 meters) on the water side of Beach Road to the telephone.

FACILITIES

None at Haddington. Air fills, charter boats and launch ramps in Port McNeill.

ACCESS

Haddington Island is in Broughton Strait. It is 3 nautical miles from the launch ramp in Port McNeill, and almost 1 nautical mile across open water from Hyde Creek where kayak-divers might launch.

Charter or launch your own boat at Port McNeill or launch your dive-kayak at Hyde Creek and go to the middle of the rock quarry heap just below a small wooden wreck at the southeast end of Haddington. Plan to dive at the end of the flood on high slack. The flooding current streams around both sides of the island, more or less meeting at the rock quarry. It's better visibility with high tide too. While diving, work your way around the wall toward the Vancouver Island side until you get into current, then head back to the lee side of the island. Lots of rocks

Diver sees quarry rock on shore

to hold onto and use to pull yourself along with. Ascend up one of many valleys protected from current.

Fog and wind can make crossing to Haddington extremely hazardous. Wind blows up quickly in Broughton Strait. Fog can come anytime but usually less fog from May through September. Before you sett off, check weather reports and be sure your craft is properly equipped to get there given the conditions expected.

- Boat divers: launch at Port McNeill Public Ramp and go 3 nautical miles to the rock quarry at the southeastern tip of Haddington Island.
- Kayak-divers: paddle from the foot of the road at Hyde Creek; the turnoff is ¾ mile (1⅓ kilometers) west of the bridge over the Nimpkish River. It is midway between Beaver Cove Road and Port McNeill turnoff. From either, go 2½ miles (4 kilometers) to Hyde Creek Road; then go on Hyde Creek Road for 1 mile (1½ kilometers) to the sea. Roadside parking for one or two cars.

Walk across a narrow stretch of grass, launch and paddle north for almost 1 nautical mile to the rock quarry at the southeastern end of Haddington Island. If diving on the flood, aim for the *western* end of the island to allow for the current drifting you eastward. Approach close to Haddington and paddle close to shore around to the rock quarry. With perfect conditions – flat water, no fog, no wind – the open-water crossing takes 35 to 45 minutes. At the quarry, always some rocks above water where you can land to gear up. Returning to Hyde Creek, again allow for the current. Before leaving, tell someone where you are going so they will check on your return. Advisable to take marine flares – this is wilderness. Also obtain a ferry schedule. At the time of writing, the ferry from Alert Bay to Port McNeill crossed the path we took and while we were paddling the ferry passed us. Its wash was minimal but you never know; beware of potential wash from all passing vessels.

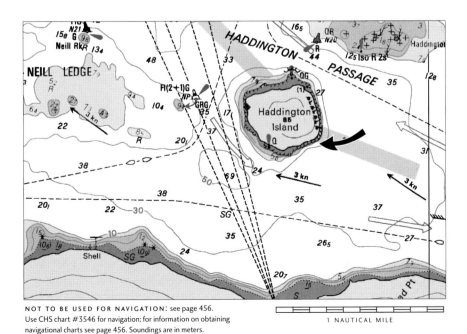

NOT TO BE USED FOR NAVIGATION: see page 456.
Use CHS chart #3546 for navigation; for information on obtaining navigational charts see page 456. Soundings are in meters.

1 NAUTICAL MILE

NOTES

PORT MCNEILL BREAKWATER

SHORE DIVE

SKILL
Intermediate and expert
divers

All divers with guide

TIDE TABLE
Alert Bay

WHY GO
We saw fish galore – quillback, yellowtail
and black rockfish – hordes of them.
China and tiger rockfish. Lingcod, ratfish.
Kelp, spider and red rock crabs. A massive
prawn. Sun stars. Purple urchins. Sea
cucumbers. Abalones. Hooded nudibranchs
beneath the old pilings; a big octopus.
Watch for skates and Puget Sound king
crabs in springtime and summer.

In town, easy access, no current to
consider. A good night dive.

BOTTOM AND DEPTHS
Silty sand bottom with some stringy kelp
slopes gently to ferry dock pilings: 30 to
40 feet (9 to 12 meters) depth at the end
of the breakwater.

HAZARDS
Kelp; carry a knife. Boats and ferries: stay
close to the riprap while snorkeling and
diving; when diving, stay near the bottom
out of the way of boats and ferries. If
turbulent, hold fast to the riprap.

Plan your dive: check the ferry schedule
and plan to dive at least 5 or 10 minutes
before ferries are due to arrive or depart.
Wash from the ferries as they leave the
dock creates turbulence.

When ascending, be aware of boats
inside the breakwater.

TELEPHONES
• Near dive entry: outside Harbour
  Manager's office.
• West of entry: Beach Drive at foot of
  McNeill Road.

FACILITIES
Free parking at roadside near the dive
entry. West of the ferry lineup, a large pay
parking lot near the Steam Donkey in Harbour Park. Restrooms, in summer only, at
Port McNeill Visitor Info Centre, 351
Shelly Crescent. To reach it, go west on
Beach Drive which curves, crosses
Broughton Boulevard and becomes Shelly
Crescent. Hot showers and camping year-
round at Broughton Strait Campsite: go
west on Beach Drive, turn right at
Broughton Boulevard and turn left at a sign
to the campsite – only ⅕ mile (⅓ kilometer)
up the hill.

After the dive, walking
alongside ferry car
ramp to beach

ACCESS

The Port McNeill Breakwater is in the heart of Port McNeill, 5 minutes off Highway 19. Go downhill on Campbell Way almost to the water. At the stop sign, turn right into Broughton Boulevard following signs to the Alert Bay–Sointula ferry.

Go one block on Broughton. Turn left into McNeill Road, then right at Beach Drive. Go 100 meters (109 yards) past the ferry lineup and unload gear at the dive entry stairsteps beside the waterfront park.

Before diving, tell your dive profile to the ticket seller at the ferry to insure you will not be in the path of the ferry.

Gear up, and walk down 18 steps in the seawall and across logs in the shallows to the ferry ramp. Snorkel to pilings beneath the car ferry ramp, hugging the riprap on your left, and descend through stringy kelp. Turn left following the breakwater riprap around the corner.

Also exit close up the riprap that forms the breakwater. Listen for boats and return in the shallows the way you entered, well out of the way of boats.

Access is easier at high tides.

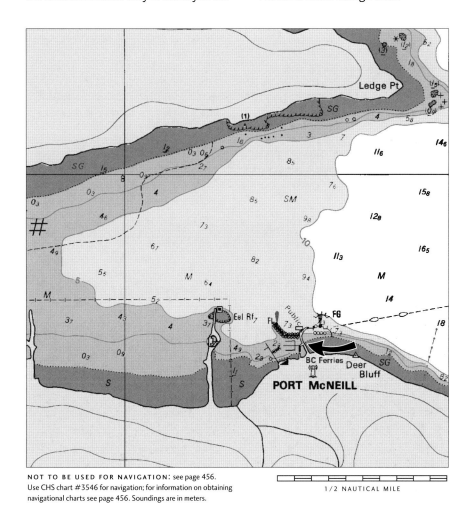

NOT TO BE USED FOR NAVIGATION: see page 456.
Use CHS chart #3546 for navigation; for information on obtaining navigational charts see page 456. Soundings are in meters.

1/2 NAUTICAL MILE

NOTES

BEAR COVE

SHORE DIVE

SKILL
All divers and snorkelers

TIDE TABLE
Alert Bay

WHY GO

Entry is easy, the dive is shallow. A great winter dive when you see miniature "ghosts" on every stringy stalk of kelp at Bear Cove.

The ghosts pulse. They bow. They nod their transparent, shapeless heads in the current. Each one measures 3 to 6 inches (7½ to 15 centimeters) high. Seeing these creatures was a "first" for me. I'll never forget it. These marine ghosts are called hooded nudibranchs, or lion nudibranchs. We saw other nudibranchs too: lemon yellow ones with white tips and white ones with blue tips as well as nudibranch eggs.

At the reef, plumose anemones clump on top of the rocks. We saw lots of kelp greenlings and rockfish, a painted greenling in a clam shell, sea peaches, an abalone. Lots of tube worms and huge snakelock anemones. We saw egg cases of moon snails and sea pens on the sand. Local divers say two octopuses are in residence and we saw leavings of crab – probably at the octopus lair. A pleasant easy site year-round for a quick dive or to try out new gear, and you can almost count on seeing hooded nudibranchs from January into early March.

BOTTOM AND DEPTHS

Two shallow ledges down to a rocky reef at 30 to 40 feet (9 to 12 meters) depending on tide height. Bottoms out to silty sand. Kelp, sparse in winter but still useful to show you where the rocks are.

HAZARDS

Boats, poor visibility, California kelp in summer and lion's mane jellies in the fall. Listen for boats. Stay close to the bottom throughout the dive. Use a compass: navigate back to the breakwater and ascend alongside it. Safer in winter when fewer boats. Best visibility when the ferry is not in, especially in winter. Carry a knife for kelp. If you have seen jellies, check for stinging tentacles before removing masks and gloves.

TELEPHONES

- Inside ferry terminal but available most daylight hours: ⅕ mile (⅓ kilometer) north at end of road.
- At Sunnyside Campground: return to Highway 19, turn north toward Port Hardy. Drive a short way to the Coal Harbour/Highway 19 junction. The campground is on the north side of Highway 19, the telephone outside the office and available 24 hours year-round.

FACILITIES

At Bear Cove, picnic table, pit toilet and parking space. Wheelchair-accessible restrooms at the ferry terminal available most daylight hours. Air fills in Port Hardy and Port McNeill.

ACCESS

Bear Cove is in the southeast corner of Hardy Bay. It is off Highway 19, near the Prince Rupert ferry terminal.

Go on the Bear Cove Highway for 2¾ miles (4½ kilometers) to Bear Cove launch ramp. Drop gear. Park and enter at the ramp: swim out on the right-hand side close beside the riprap breakwater, and head down. Go straight out over two small ledges and turn right around the end of the breakwater to the rocky reef. Safer to stay well north of the green navigational marker throughout the dive – it marks the boat entry. Wheelchair divers with good brakes could launch at this fairly steep ramp.

To get to Bear Cove and Prince Rupert ferry turnoff
- From Port Hardy, go south on Highway 19 for 2¾ miles (4½ kilometers) – takes 5 minutes; turn left, following signs to Bear Cove.
- From Port McNeill, go north on Highway 19 for 22 miles (36 kilometers). It takes 25 minutes. Turn right, following signs to Prince Rupert ferry.

*Hooded nudibranchs,
"ghosts of the sea"*

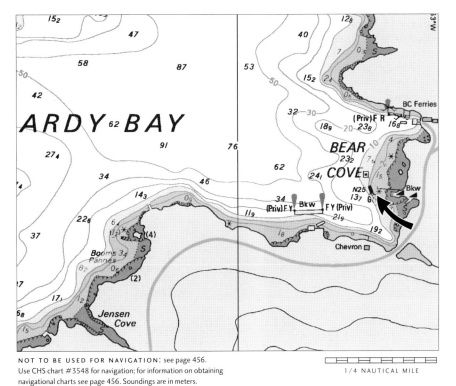

NOTES

NOT TO BE USED FOR NAVIGATION: see page 456.
Use CHS chart #3548 for navigation; for information on obtaining
navigational charts see page 456. Soundings are in meters.

1/4 NAUTICAL MILE

183

PACIFIC WHITE-SIDED DOLPHINS

BOAT DIVE
GPS
Location not applicable,
as dolphins might
appear anywhere.

SKILL
All divers snorkeling

Expert divers, when
descending

TIDE TABLE
Not applicable

WHY GO

Our skipper scans with binoculars. Sees white water.

"Dolphins! – halfway across the channel, leaping and splashing. It's deep. We're over 1,000 feet (300 meters) of water. Gear up for snorkeling – with weight belts", he says, and speeds toward them; slows the boat; stops at the appropriate distance, tells us to stay close together. We drop into the water.

The dolphins scatter and collect as they swim toward us. I am transfixed. Lying on the surface I do not kick or move. The dolphins come to me: one skims past on my left; two on my right. Dolphins crisscross beneath me. I am surrounded by gentle motion like soothing music. I lift my head, look around, see more dolphins approaching from behind. Look into the water again: dolphins, 3 to 5 feet (1 to 1½ meters) long, pass so close I could reach out and touch them. But do not. It feels right for them to choose the contact distance, choose to fly around and beneath me. Beside me.

Afterwards on board the *Hurst Isle*, we are glowing, talking, silent – pondering the experience. One diver tells me a dolphin looked into her eyes. She kicked and

swam in circles to attract them, while I waited. Quiet or in motion, we both had intense feelings of encounter, eye contact but no touching. That evening another dimension presented itself when we heard the chirped underwater conversations of the dolphins as we watched a video in the lounge at God's Pocket. One of our group recorded it that morning. Perhaps we sense those sounds even when we do not hear them through our neoprene hoods. A siren song?

No question – dolphins like people, boats, action. The pod of 100 to 150 dolphins we encountered in Goletas Channel was attracted to our boat and its activity, to us and our activity.

But the ocean is wilderness. Meeting dolphins is a gift, a miracle some lucky persons enjoy. Divers watch. The dolphins are in control, the dolphins choose. They seem to know more than we do.

Why go? To meet kindred spirits from the sea – intelligent, elusive, interested, curious creatures who possess an enviable grace in the water, a grace divers can only dream of. Not match. To spend brief moments with the dolphins in their kingdom. Moments to last a lifetime.

Snorkeling with dolphins off the Hurst Isle

BOTTOM AND DEPTHS
Varies.

TELEPHONE
VHF radio; if no VHF, try a cell phone.

HAZARDS
Snorkeling with the dolphins is a safe thrill.

However, when scuba diving, the dangers are the diver's wish to follow the dolphins spiraling down and disorientation if there are no points of reference. Natural points of reference are a closeby shoreline or a view of the bottom. When in deep water, some charter operators drop a weighted line from a float with a dive flag on it. Divers are to keep the line in sight and are not to go deeper than the weight at 30 to 40 feet (9 to 12 meters). Another diver told me a charter operator tied a dive-flag buoy to him, and he could go no deeper than the length of his tether.

One experienced scuba diver told me he was disoriented by the circling dolphins when diving with them and did not know which was up or down; most divers say the dolphins spiral around them, "pulling" them down – the siren song.

The dolphin experience on scuba is for expert divers.

FACILITIES
None.

ACCESS
The dolphins migrate from the open Pacific into Queen Charlotte Strait usually from mid-August through mid-October; in recent years, also in April and May. In the inner waters, when feeding, they normally do not stop to play. When traveling, they probably will. When the sea is rough and stormy, it is difficult to spot dolphins. So how do you find them?

In season when the water is calm, the day sunny, plan a dive. Charter a boat or launch your own boat, binoculars in hand. On the way, look for killer or humpback whales who often travel with dolphins – or look for the smaller dolphins themselves. From a distance, a pod looks like white water as the dolphins leap and splash.

All of Queen Charlotte Sound diving is excellent but if you see dolphins, it's truly a bonus. Delay or change your dive plan; divers suit up while the skipper moves the boat toward the dolphins, always considering the well-being of the dolphins. Follow official viewing guidelines: go no closer than 110 yards (100 meters) and jump in.

If you are extremely lucky and 10 or more dolphins are bow riding, watch them carefully. If you keep following, you might be getting into their space. If you stop and they come to you, leave a boat tender on board and jump in.

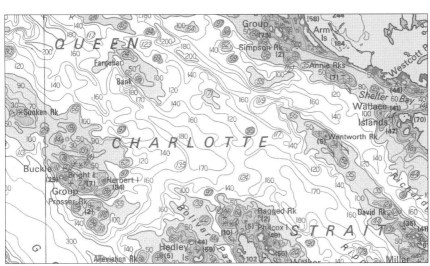

NOT TO BE USED FOR NAVIGATION: see page 456.
Use CHS chart #3605 for navigation; for information on obtaining navigational charts see page 456. Soundings are in meters.

3 NAUTICAL MILES

BROWNING WALL

BOAT DIVE
GPS
Northwest end of wall:
50°50.981' N
127°38.846' W

Northeast end of wall:
50°50.805' N
127°38.619' W

SKILL
Intermediate and expert
divers

All divers with guide

TIDE TABLE
Alert Bay:
Add 1½ to 2 hours

Browning Wall

WHY GO

Pink soft corals and yellow sulphur sponges hide the rock. This sheer dropoff is a living, ever-changing tapestry – yet always recognizable. Once you've been there you know it when you see photographs of Browning Wall.

The intricate curlicue tangles that are basket stars, yellow-and-black China rockfish, kelp greenlings, plumose anemones and sponges galore are more creatures you are sure to see. And look for orange peel nudibranchs – they are a highlight at this site. White encrusting sponge makes everything bright. Fuzzy gray cobalt sponges are along the wall. Look for octopuses too. We saw moon jellies, a decorator crab. Red urchins. Rock scallops – lots of them. Mint green anemones in the shallows. Nudibranch eggs like a string of jewels. Giant barnacles – all are woven into the rich tapestry.

Drift this pink and yellow wall once and you'll want to do it again. But keep it pristine for your return: no taking of marine life at Browning Wall, as at all prime sites in the region.

BOTTOM AND DEPTHS

Sheer drop-off to a ledge at 95 to 105 feet (29 to 32 meters), depending on tide height. The wall feels bottomless, drops to 215 feet (66 meters) on the chart; bottoms out to white sand, I'm told. A great deal of life between 40 and 70 feet (12 and 21 meters) – some stringy kelp.

HAZARDS

Boats, depth, current; lion's mane jellies in late summer and fall. When ascending, listen for boats and stay close to the wall or in the kelp – a great many boats pass immediately alongside. Dive on slack and it will still be a drift. Before you head down, make a dive plan; then stick with your plan. The scene is so beautiful it would be easy to forget to come up. Dive with a "live" boat. If you have seen any lion's mane jellies, check for stinging tentacles before removing masks and gloves.

TELEPHONE

VHF radio; if no VHF, try a cell phone.

FACILITIES

None at Browning Wall. Charters, launch ramp and air fills in Port Hardy and waterfront air fills for drop-ins at two resorts:
1. Browning Pass Hideaway Resort, Clam Cove, Nigei Island, located off Browning Passage. Also dive packages with land-based accommodation and boat dives; day charters with advance notice.
2. God's Pocket Resort, Hurst Island, located across Christie Passage: dive packages with land-based accommodation and boat dives; also hiking trails.

ACCESS

Browning Wall drops to 215 feet (66 meters) on the chart. Look for it on the west side of Browning Passage, at the south end of Nigei Island.

Charter out of Port Hardy or launch your own boat and go to Browning Wall. From Port Hardy go 12 nautical miles northwest across Goletas Channel to Browning Passage and head north. Use GPS to find the general locale: you will see the wall. Depending on current, start at the north or south end of it. And dive with a "live" boat. A superb drift.

Browning Passage is usually protected, even in southeast winds. Boat passage to it is often possible when it is difficult to reach many other sites. Easiest boat access from Port Hardy to Browning is ordinarily in September and October when it is often calm. Fog can come anytime, but normally less fog occurs from May through September.

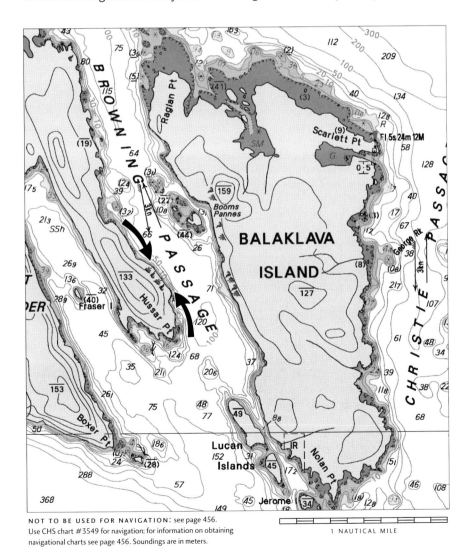

NOT TO BE USED FOR NAVIGATION: see page 456.
Use CHS chart #3549 for navigation; for information on obtaining navigational charts see page 456. Soundings are in meters.

1 NAUTICAL MILE

NOTES

SEVEN TREE ISLAND

BOAT DIVE
GPS
50°51.645' N
127°39.245' W

SKILL
Expert divers

Intermediate divers with guide

TIDE TABLE
Alert Bay:
Add 1½ to 2 hours

WHY GO

The wall plummets into Browning Passage. On the Nigei Island side, small fish swim from the shallow white sand ledges and between the boulders. At the entry, bull kelp streams in the current, makes it easy to haul yourself beneath it so you can swim to the wall without effort – all this variety rolled into one magical dive.

Flagrant color on the wall: pink soft corals, white anemones, yellow sulphur sponges. We see a red Irish lord, dead man's finger sponges, more than I can take in, not an inch of rock to be seen. Each time I've dived here, when heading north along the wall I've seen a bright green anemone at 60 feet (18 meters). It alerts me to the transition from wall to gentle seabed at the northwest corner of Seven Tree. In a rocky crack at 12 to 22 feet (3½ to 7 meters), a docile red and purple rock greenling allows divers to pass it from hand to hand. A perfect place to make a safety stop. I've searched two times: no luck for me yet in finding it.

Rounding the corner to the left, terraces of white sand shelve upward. It's bright. Orange sea pens, alabaster nudibranchs and rose stars are on the sand. In it, oolichans I'm told. Before my first dive at Seven Tree, I was advised to dip a hand in the sand to disturb the oolichans; then watch for kelp greenlings that pounce and eat them. I have not seen the oolichans. But on my third dive at Seven Tree when I stirred up the bottom, a shimmering silver curtain – hundreds of sand lances flashed like a rippling flag toward the surface. Shallower, my safety stop in the feather boa kelp on the Nigei Island side of Seven Tree is alive: swarms of small fish are in the bouldery shallows – painted greenlings and more kelp greenlings. I exit up the rocky inside of the island.

Divers tell of more life they've seen which I have not been conscious of at Seven Tree. In the deep: China rockfish, brown Irish lords, buffalo sculpins, basket stars. In the sandy shallows: look for sole, and sand dabs, like coins rising off the bottom. In the rocky shallows, leather chitons and sunflower stars.

Seven Tree – many reasons to go back.

BOTTOM AND DEPTHS

The wall plunges 130 to 140 feet (40 to 43 meters) into Browning Passage. At the south end of the island, in the bull kelp, the rocky bottom is 30 to 40 feet (9 to 12 meters) deep. West of the bull kelp, north end of the island, starting at 30 to 40 feet (9 to 12 meters), the sandy bottom shelves up in ridges. Inside the island, bouldery rocky bottom slopes gradually to the surface.

HAZARDS

Depth, ever-present current and boats. Be aware of depth throughout the dive. Dive on slack.

TELEPHONE

VHF radio; if no VHF, try a cell phone.

FACILITIES

None at Seven Tree Island. Charters, launch ramp and air fills in Port Hardy. Dive packages and waterfront air fills at God's Pocket Resort. At Browning Pass Hideaway Resort in Clam Cove, waterfront air fills, day charters with advance notice, accommodations and dive packages.

ACCESS

Seven Tree Island, or Snowflake Island as some divers call it, is located on the west side of Browning Passage close to Nigei Island. It is ½ nautical mile north of Browning Wall. Browning Passage is usually protected – even in a southeast wind. Boat passage to Seven Tree is possible when it is difficult to reach many other sites out of Port Hardy.

Charter or launch your own boat and head northwest across Goletas Channel: 12 nautical miles to Browning Passage, then north for 1 nautical mile to Seven Tree. Dive with a "live" boat.

I like to dive Seven Tree at the end of the ebb: haul myself down on the kelp at the south end of the island, and go north along the wall at whatever depth I am comfortable at that day. Gradually work around the corner and up to the sandy shallows behind the island. Many dive boats visit: ascending, listen for boats and stay close to the bottom up the rocky shore or in the kelp.

Seven Tree Island, looking north

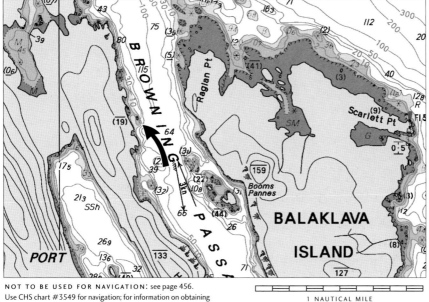

NOT TO BE USED FOR NAVIGATION: see page 456.
Use CHS chart #3549 for navigation; for information on obtaining navigational charts see page 456. Soundings are in meters.

1 NAUTICAL MILE

NOTES

HUNT ROCK

BOAT DIVE
GPS
50°54.325′ N
127°40.792′ W

SKILL
Intermediate and expert
divers

TIDE TABLE
Alert Bay:
Add 2 hours, 20 minutes

WHY GO

Hunt Rock is a wolf-eel haven – or heaven. Gigantic "tame" wolf-eels, Hunter and Huntress, first made Hunt Rock famous. They are no longer there, but a new population of wolf-eels has moved in. Wolf-eels are still a big attraction at Hunt Rock but only one of the highlights.

Incredible beauty is everywhere in the shallows where pastel lavender and pink brooding anemones cover the kelp stalks as well as the rocks. Deeper, we saw basket stars, huge rock scallops, yellow sponges and millions of small white plumose anemones. Look for octopuses. And fish: kelp greenlings, China rockfish, schools of black rockfish, white-spotted greenlings. We saw a 15-pound (7-kilogram) lingcod. And one huge yelloweye weighing 44 pounds (20 kilograms) lived near the wolf-eel dens but deeper.

When we first dropped on the bottom at Hunt Rock, I was horrified to see an enormous – probably 6-foot (2-meter) long – wolf-eel slither from behind our

Huntress and Hunter

guide and up between his legs in front of him. Our guide didn't "miss a beat" – just kept feeding the other wolf-eel in front of him. He was obviously used to it. Six of them came to meet us that day. The alarming thing about it is the potential danger to the wolf-eels should a diver be startled by one. Expect this familiarity from wolf-eels at Hunt Rock.

Remember that Hunt Rock is considered a reserve by local divers and charter operators – do not take any wolf-eels, shellfish or other fish. Probably the best way to prevent the wolf-eels from becoming hurt is for all divers to be informed of the friendly greeting to expect when they dive Hunt Rock. The approach of the wolf-eels is not an attack: spread the word.

BOTTOM AND DEPTHS

Hunt Rock is an open water pinnacle: at high tide, it is 30 feet (9 meters) deep. Wolf-eel dens are at 60 and 75 feet (18 and 23 meters). Bull kelp marks the spot.

HAZARDS

Current, small boats and bull kelp in summer. Dive on slack with a low tidal exchange. Slack is not always as predicted. Go early, watch the water and be prepared to pull out of the dive. Dive with a boat tender. Listen for boats, and ascend up your anchor line or in the bull kelp. Carry a knife for kelp.

TELEPHONE

VHF radio; if no VHF, try a cell phone.

FACILITIES

None at Hunt Rock. Air fills in Port Hardy, and for drop-ins at Clam Cove and God's Pocket. Charters out of Port Hardy.

ACCESS

Hunt Rock is ½ nautical mile offshore from the west end of Nigei Island. It is past the north end of Browning Passage and is 16 nautical miles northwest of Port

Hardy. Far out – Hunt Rock is the most exposed site described in this guidebook.

Charter and go; or launch your own boat at Port Hardy and head out to the green marker buoy at Hunt Rock. At slack water, kelp is visible on the surface. Anchor between two patches of kelp and Hunt Rock. Head down to 60 feet (18 meters) and look for the wolf-eels – if you can find them before they find you.

Leave a boat tender on board. Hunt Rock is too far out and too current-ridden

to take a chance. Safest to dive from a charter boat whose operators know the area and from a boat equipped with GPS and radar equipment. Fog can be a problem and it can come anytime, but usually there is less fog from May through September. The day we dived Hunt Rock radar was absolutely necessary from Browning Passage on. The day before we dived, five boats called for rescue because of the fickle weather.

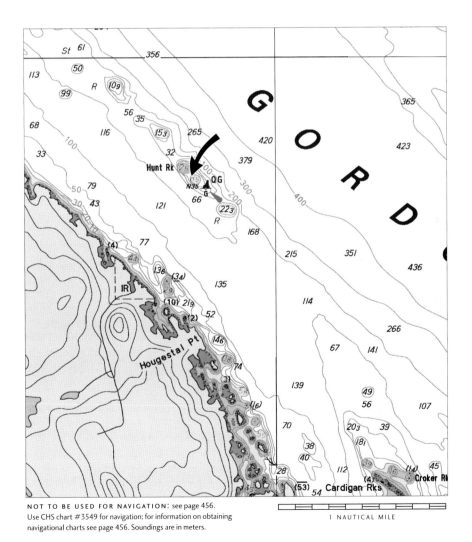

NOTES

NOT TO BE USED FOR NAVIGATION: see page 456.
Use CHS chart #3549 for navigation; for information on obtaining navigational charts see page 456. Soundings are in meters.

1 NAUTICAL MILE

BARRY ISLET

BOAT DIVE
GPS
50°53.224' N
127°25.732' W

SKILL
Intermediate and expert divers

TIDE TABLE
Alert Bay:
Add 20 minutes

WHY GO

A field of bright red gorgonian corals is at the base of the wall – that's what we went for.

Heading down, we saw tall plumose anemones, pink brooding anemones, masses of soft corals, a valley with jillions of flat little white anemones, urchins, leafy hornmouth snails. Deeper still, two Puget Sound king crabs, orange peel nudibranchs, basket stars everywhere, giant barnacles covered with encrusting sponge, and hydrocorals – blue, deep purple and white. Bright yellow sulphur sponges, rock scallops, orange cup corals, a red Irish lord. Two wolf-eels and an octopus beneath the undercuts.

At the base of the wall, we reached the sought-after field of gorgonians at 90 feet (27 meters). As we admired the vivid 6-inch (15-centimeter) high corals, four Steller sea lions came nose-to-nose with a photographer in our group, interrupting her shot. She saw them clearly and photographed them; the rest of us saw the sea lions through the murky silt they kicked up. What a dive!

And it goes on: our end-of-the-dive safety stop was rich too – it became an underwater dance of the seven veils. No rock was visible. First we gently pulled one brown or olive-colored frond of kelp aside, then another. Behind each one was another surprise. We saw a large cabezon at 10 feet (3 meters). Kelp greenlings, purple stars, leather stars, purple urchins.

Gorgonian corals at Barry Islet

BOTTOM AND DEPTHS

Sheer wall with undercuts from 30 to 80 feet (9 to 24 meters). Bottoms out at 110 to 120 feet (34 to 37 meters), depending on tide height, to a broad ledge. Then slopes gently deeper.

HAZARDS

Current, boats and bull kelp; lion's mane jellies in the fall. Go early and wait for slack. Listen for boats and ascend up the wall in the bull kelp. Carry a knife for kelp. If you have seen any jellies, check masks and gloves before removing them.

TELEPHONE

VHF radio; if no VHF, try a cell phone.

FACILITIES

None.

ACCESS

Barry Islet is in Queen Charlotte Strait, south end of Ripple Passage. It is a tiny islet east of the Deserters Group.

Charter or launch at Port Hardy and go north 10 nautical miles to Barry Islet. Choose where to dive depending on the current: you can always dive one side or the other. Start at the top and on the turn to ebb dive the east side; on the turn to flood dive the west side – both sides are equally good!

On the surface avoid coming closer than 110 yards (100 meters) to sea lions. Under water, let them approach you.

NOTES

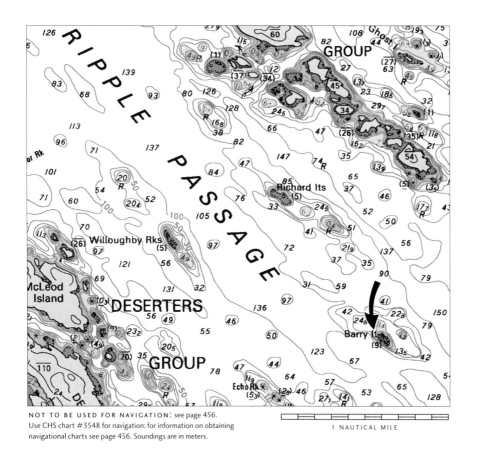

NOT TO BE USED FOR NAVIGATION: see page 456.
Use CHS chart #3548 for navigation; for information on obtaining navigational charts see page 456. Soundings are in meters.

1 NAUTICAL MILE

TURRET ROCK

BOAT DIVE
GPS
51°05.743' N
127°30.210' W

SKILL
Expert divers

Strong intermediates
with guide

CURRENT TABLE
Nakwakto Rapids

TIDE TABLE
Johnson Point

*Remember, the tide tables
do not predict slack water;
refer to them only for
favorable dates to dive.*

WHY GO

The smell of danger, previously considered undivable. Remote, beyond the end of the road – the initial lures. And the hook that holds?

Layers of life – so much it is impossible to see the bottom. A rare site. The top layer is all any diver can take in but you can imagine more. And what you see is more than enough: six-rayed white sea stars – a first for me – stood out. Partly because most sea stars have legs in multiples of five, from five to twenty-five. Partly because of the background. Throughout the dive, the starkly white, slim fingers were splayed across the colorful bottom and walls – on top of bright pink and bright orange encrusting sponges, on top of the rough carpet of brilliant orangey-red-and-pearly-white leaf barnacles, commonly called gooseneck barnacles. Goosenecks are seldom seen subtidally and are the best-known marine highlight of the dive.

Turret Rock is an explosion of color from bottom to top: we saw red sea stars, kelp greenlings, juvenile wolf-eels. In the shallows, pink brooding anemones covering stems of purple plume worms and stalks of kelp.

In the intertidal zone, soft corals.

Visibility is best in summer: excellent in July and August, unlike many sites that are clouded with algae bloom when the sun shines. Winter runoff sometimes clouds the waters. Any time of year wind can make it difficult to reach Seymour Inlet. Because of wind, our group had to wait one day to get out by boat. But, when already in Seymour Inlet, wind does not affect dives.

BOTTOM AND DEPTHS

Just past the the northeast corner of Turret Rock there is a reef, 30 to 35 feet (9 to 11 meters) deep. Beyond the reef it is possible to go deeper than 60 feet (18 meters) but if you do stay close to the rock. On the west side of Turret Rock a notch is in the wall: it starts at 15 to 25 feet (4½ to 8 meters) deep and is a good exit point.

HAZARDS

Current, boats and the desire to stay down longer than recommended. Maximum currents range up to 14½ knots on ebb, and 11½ knots on flood. To avoid boats and to deal with current at the end of your dive, ascend close to the side of Turret Rock all

*Gooseneck barnacles
at Turret Rock*

the way to the surface. Do not succumb to the desire to stay longer than the prescribed maximum dive time.

TELEPHONE
VHF radio; if no VHF, try a cell phone.

FACILITIES
None.

ACCESS
Turret Rock is north of Port Hardy in Seymour Inlet at Nakwakto Rapids, the most northerly dive described in this guidebook.

Charter with an operator who knows the "Tremble Island" site – that's what early charter boat guides called it. Always dive this site with a live boat; it is unsafe to anchor in case of a snag. Timing of exit is crucial and current predictions can be fickle. Local savvy about cautionary measures and currents is absolutely necessary to dive this radical site.

• Entering at the north end of the rock, go in the water on the ebb – 10 minutes before the change to flood. Throughout the dive stay in the lee side of the rock. And get out of the water 20 minutes after the change to flood. Maximum dive time is 30 minutes.

• Entering at the south end, go in the water on the flood – 10 minutes before the change to ebb. And get out of the water 30 minutes after the change. Maximum dive time is 40 minutes.

Our group enjoyed a 25-minute dive. We were put in the water at the northeast corner of Turret Rock before the turn to flood, went immediately down to the reef and, once across it, continued around the north end of the rock in a counter-clockwise direction. In 4 minutes we reached the vivid goosenecks; 10 to 12 minutes more into the dive, we found the notch in the wall and soon reluctantly started to follow it up the side of the rock to the boat through the jungle of brooding anemones, purple plume worms and soft corals.

Plan your trip in advance: check the degree of tidal exchange predicted for the day you hope to dive as bigger exchanges usually mean faster water at floods and ebbs – on the day we dived tidal predictions at Johnson Point ranged from 2½ to 6 feet (¾ to 2 meters); then, you *must* always refer to current tables for *time to dive*.

When planning to dive at Turret Rock, check tides and currents – choose your date.

NOTES

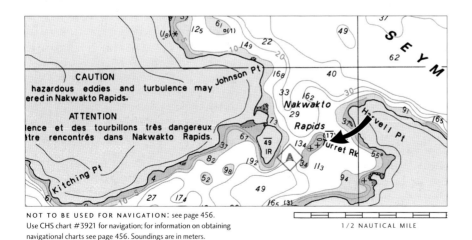

NOT TO BE USED FOR NAVIGATION: see page 456.
Use CHS chart #3921 for navigation; for information on obtaining navigational charts see page 456. Soundings are in meters.

1/2 NAUTICAL MILE

CHAPTER SIX

Nanaimo, Hornby Island and south to Sansum Narrows including Gabriola Island

Diver explores Saskatchewan Artificial Reef

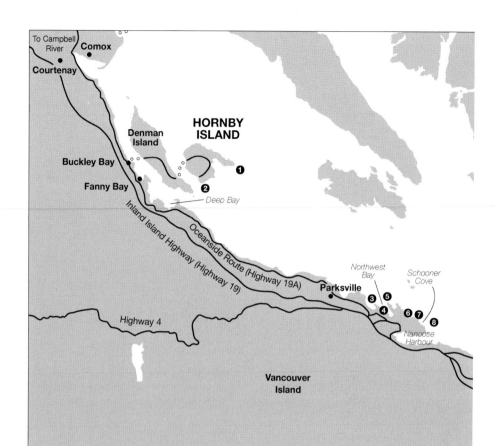

NANAIMO, HORNBY ISLAND
AND SOUTH TO SANSUM NARROWS
including Gabriola Island

Dives

1. Sixgill Sharks
2. Heron Rocks
3. Madrona Point [Arbutus Point]
4. Wall Beach
5. Cottam Point [Beachcomber]
6. Dolphin Beach
7. Seducer's Beach [Tyee Cove]
8. Sea Lions
9. Keel Cove
10. Neck Point
11. Jesse Island
12. Snake Island
13. *Saskatchewan* Artificial Reef
14. *Cape Breton* Artificial Reef
15. Orlebar Point
16. Dodd Narrows
17. Gabriola Passage
18. Evening Cove
19. Maple Bay Underwater Sanctuary
20. Burial Islet

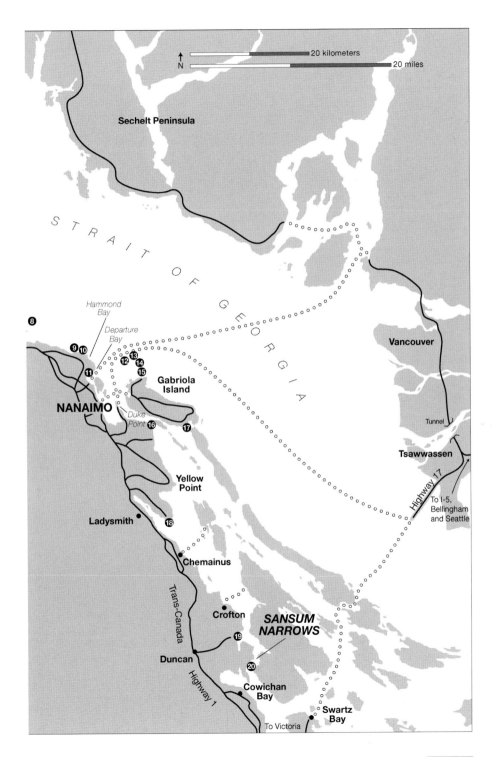

SERVICE INFORMATION

Tide and Current Information
- *Tide and Current Tables, Volume 5: Juan de Fuca Strait and Strait of Georgia,* Canadian Hydrographic Service print annual
- *Current Atlas: Juan de Fuca Strait to Strait of Georgia,* purchase one time. Use with *Murray's Tables* or *Washburne's Tables,* purchase annually; privately produced publications available at marine equipment and supplies stores.
- www.lau.chs-shc.gc.ca: Tide and Current Tables for all of Canada. Go to the web site: click on Pacific; General Information; Tide and Currents, Data Available; then Tide Tables available in PDF form. Select Volume 5 and click on the tide or current table desired – both are on the same list on the pdf.

Weather Information
- Canadian Coast Guard: 1-866-823-1110, speak with a person, 24 hours.
- Canadian Coast Guard (Victoria Coast Guard Radio/Comox Coast Guard Radio): Continuous Marine Broadcast (CMB) recorded, 24 hours.
1. Nanaimo, south of Winchelsea Island; listen for weather at Entrance Island, telephone Victoria (250)363-6492.
2. Nanaimo, north of Winchelsea Island; listen for weather in Strait of Georgia, telephone Comox (250)339-0748.
- Environment Canada: recorded, 24 hours;
1. Marine weather line: listen for weather at Entrance Island and Strait of Georgia, telephone (250)245-8899.
2. Weather line: listen for weather east of Vancouver Island, telephone (250)245-8877.
- Ladysmith: (250)245-8899
- www.weatheroffice.ec.gc.ca

Diving Emergency Telephone Numbers
<u>On land and water:</u>
- Call 911, request "ambulance" and say, "I have a scuba diving emergency".
- Vancouver General Hospital; for 24-hour, 7-day-a-week response: telephone (604)875-5000, and say, "I want the hyperbaric physician on call".
<u>On the water:</u>
- VHF radio: Call Coast Guard radio, Channel 16 and say, "I have a scuba diving emergency".
- Cell phone: 911, *16 or *311 and say, "I have a scuba diving emergency".

If emergency or medical personnel are unfamiliar with scuba diving emergencies, ask them to telephone DAN (Divers Alert Network) at (919)684-4326. No money for a long distance call? Dial DAN collect at 011-919-684-4326 and say, "I have a scuba diving emergency".

Mark emergency location before leaving scene: other divers might be down.

How to Go
Nanaimo is the major gateway city to an immense variety of dive sites on Vancouver Island. Dives in this chapter range from Nanaimo south to Duncan near Victoria; and north of Nanaimo to out-of-the-way Hornby Island; the ferries to Hornby are midway between Nanaimo and Campbell River – 1¼ hours from either one. More excellent diving a 20-minute ferry ride away from downtown Nanaimo at Gabriola Island.

British Columbia car ferries transport visitors from Vancouver to Nanaimo; also from Powell River on the northern mainland to Comox north of Buckley Bay. In addition, ferries go from Buckley Bay to Denman then Hornby Island. An immense number of dive facilities are in the region.

Many sites are easily accessible near the coastal highways: off the Oceanside Route (Highway 19A) north of Nanaimo; off Highway 1, south of Nanaimo.

Tips on Highways and Ferries:
Ferries are easy to sort out but when you land on Vancouver Island it can be complex.

- From Little River terminal follow signs to Courtenay. At a junction, turn left and go on a curvy road following signs toward Nanaimo; at a bridge turn left onto main street. Just past Driftwood Mall turn right: signs direct you to Inland Island Highway (Highway 19) where you can quickly drive south to Nanaimo. Or, go straight and continue south on Oceanside Route (Highway 19), ½ hour to Buckley Bay.
- To go to Hornby Island: first drive to Buckley Bay by way of Inland Island Highway or Highway 19A. Crossing time from Buckley Bay via Denman Island to Hornby Island averages 50 minutes, but varies depending on connections. Plan it.

Tourist Information
- Toll-free throughout North America: 1-800-435-5622
- From all other locations: (250)387-1642
www.hellobc.com

Gabriola Island Visitor Information Centre
#3 - 575 North Road
(250)247-9332
1-888-284-9332: Toll-free throughout
    North America
www.GabriolaIsland.org

Ferry Information
British Columbia Ferry Services (BC Ferries)
- Toll-free throughout North America: 1-888-223-3779
- From all other locations: (250)386-3431
www.bcferries.com
At the time of writing: the following information applies – but frequent changes occur; it would be wise to check current requirements on BC Ferries web page before every trip.

Rules Regarding Scuba Tanks on BC Ferries
Persons transporting scuba tanks containing compressed air, full or partially full, are

Rules Regarding Scuba Tanks on BC Ferries (Continued)
required under Canadian law to declare dangerous goods at the terminal or to a vessel officer. Persons transporting scuba tanks with the valves removed do not need clearance. All pressurized tanks with a UN 3156 sticker, indicating nitrox or mixed gases, are taboo – remove the valve.

Expedite Dangerous Goods clearance at the ferry ticket booth – complete a Dangerous Goods Shipping Document prior to arrival. Obtain it from the web at home or a library: Go to www.bcferries.com: select Travel Planning; click on Carrying Dangerous Goods, then For the General Public. Download Dangerous Goods Shipping Document and complete it: include your name, home address and phone number; Class 2; UN 1002, which indicates compressed air; number of cylinders you are transporting and quantity in each one: most tanks are 80 cubic feet/2.27 cubic meters.

(To calculate quantity in scuba tanks: 1 cubic foot=0.0283168466 cubic meters.)

Arrive at least 45 minutes prior to intended sailing time at Duke Point, and 30 minutes at other terminals listed below.

Prearranged Dangerous Goods Clearance Requires 48 Hours
Complete a Dangerous Goods Shipping Document as described above and fax it at least 48 hours before intended sailing time to the terminal of your departure.
Nanaimo
1. Departure Bay: fax (250)754-3421
2. Duke Point: fax (250)722-3260
3. Nanaimo Harbour and Gabriola Island: fax (250)753-9803
North of Nanaimo
4. Little River (Comox): fax (250)339-1046
5. Buckley Bay (to Denman and Hornby): fax (250)335-0028
South of Nanaimo
6. Chemainus (to Thetis) and Crofton (to Saltspring): fax (250)537-2895

NANAIMO
• DIVE SHOPS
Ocean Explorers Diving
1690 Stewart Avenue
Nanaimo BC V9S 4E1
(250)753-2055
1-800-233-4145: Toll-free throughout
    North America
www.oceanexplorersdiving.com
(Recreational, nitrox, technical and rebreather instruction. Waterfront and roadside air, nitrox and trimix fills. Also daily boat dives; and dive packages.)

Sundown Diving
22 Esplanade, near Harbour Park Mall
Nanaimo BC V9R 4Y7
(250)753-1880
1-888-773-3483: Toll-free throughout
    North America
www.sundowndiving.com
(Recreational, nitrox, technical and rebreather instruction. Nitrox, trimix and soda-lime available. Also day charters.)

The Dive Outfitters
2205 Northfield Road
Nanaimo BC V9S 3C3
(250)756-1863
www.thediveoutfitters.ca
(Recreational and nitrox instruction. Nitrox fills.)

• DAY, MULTIPLE-DAY AND LIVEABOARD CHARTERS
Christie Bay No. 1 and *Seastar*
Ocean Explorers Diving
1690 Stewart Avenue
Nanaimo BC V9S 4E1
(250)753-2055
1-800-233-4145: Toll-free throughout
    North America
www.oceanexplorersdiving.com
(Day charters year-round from dock at the shop: dive Cape Breton, Saskatchewan, Dodd Narrows *and more. Charters to Snake Island to snorkel with seals. Dive packages offered include dives and accommodation.)*

Mamro
Mamro Adventures
1 - 5765 Turner Road, Suite 203
Nanaimo BC V9T 6M4
(250)756-8872
www.mamro.com
(Day charters out of Nanaimo. Specialize in small groups – up to seven divers.)

Neptune's Apprentice
Sundown Diving
22 Esplanade, near Harbour Park Mall
Nanaimo BC V9R 4Y7
(250)753-1880
1-888-773-3483: Toll-free throughout
    North America
www.sundowndiving.com
(Day charters year-round out of Nanaimo Harbour – many destinations as the boat is trailerable. Also a dive shop.)

DAY, MULTIPLE-DAY AND LIVEABOARD CHARTERS (CONTINUED)

Eagle XXI
BC's Pacific Dreams
#268, 1 - 5765 Turner Road
Nanaimo BC V9S 5L6
(250)816-0455
www.bcspacificdreams.com
(Day charters to Saskatchewan, Cape Breton, Riv Tow Lion, Dodd Narrows, Jesse Island and more; out of Nanaimo Harbour June, July and mid-October to end of March. Other seasons multiple-day packages at Port Hardy.)

Shawn Tanis
Divers Choice Charters
#4, 1150 - 132 North Terminal Avenue
Nanaimo BC V9S 5L6
(250)716-8867
1-866-716-8867: Toll-free throughout North America
www.divingbccanada.com
(Day charters year-round out of Nanaimo: dives from Neck Point to Dodd Narrows, the Cape Breton, the Saskatchewan and Orlebar Point, or drift through Gabriola Passage. Custom multiple-day charters with land-based accommodation from Victoria to Campbell River. Rebreather rentals.)

Viking I
Viking Adventure Tours
#7 - 211 Buttertubs Place
Nanaimo BC V9R 3X8
(250)755-9175; cell (250)616-9336
www.vikingadventuretours.com
(Charters year-round out of Nanaimo for Nanaimo and southern Gulf Islands; out of Deep Bay to Hornby and the sixgills – day trips and multiple-day liveaboard trips. Also multiple-day trips out of Port Hardy and Port McNeill.)

• LAUNCH RAMPS

Brechin Civic Ramps
Foot of Brechin Road, at the Public Market
Nanaimo
(Launch for a fee at Departure Bay for Strait of Georgia: concrete ramps, good at all tides. Picnic tables at ramp. Handicapped parking stalls. Restrooms in parking lot; telephone outside, just around the corner on south-facing wall of the market.)

From the ferry terminal at Departure Bay, immediately turn left at the traffic light and right toward the Public Market, then left to the ramps.

Charlaine Public Ramp
Hammond Bay Road
Nanaimo
(Launching is free for the Strait of Georgia on this steep, paved ramp — better at high tides. Chemical toilet. Flush toilets in summer at close-by Piper Lagoon Park, south off Hammond Bay Road. Telephone ¾ mile [1 ⅓ kilometers] north on Hammond Bay Road, outside grocery store. Limited parking.)

To get to Charlaine Public Ramp
• From the ferry at Departure Bay, 15 minutes to the ramp. Follow signs toward Parksville. At the top of the hill, immediately after turning onto Highway 19A turn right into Departure Bay Road and head downhill to the water – if you pass a mall, you have gone too far. Shortly past the beach, at the traffic light, turn right into Hammond Bay Road. Go 2 ¾ miles (4½ kilometers) to Charlaine Ramp.
• From Highway 19 (Nanaimo Parkway) heading north or south, take Aulds Road Exit 28. As you cross Highway 19A, you are into the north end of Hammond Bay Road. Go on Hammond Bay Road for 4 miles (6½ kilometers) to it.

NORTH OF NANAIMO
SCHOONER COVE TO COURTENAY
• DIVE SHOPS AND CHARTERS
Union Bay Dive & Kayak
5559 South Island Highway, PO Box 144
Union Bay BC V0R 3B0
(250)335-3483
1-877-883-3483: Toll-free throughout
    North America
www.seashelldiving.com
*(Recreational and nitrox instruction. A
shore-dive wreck in front of the shop. Day
charters for 2 to 12 divers on MV Skydiver
to see giant octopuses, a boat-dive wreck,
wolf-eels and sixgill sharks at Hornby Island.)*

Pacific Pro Dive
#101 - 2270 Cliffe Avenue
Courtenay BC V9N 2L4
(250)338-6829
1-877-800-3483: Toll-free throughout
    North America
www.scubashark.com
*(Recreational, nitrox, technical and rebreather
instruction. Nitrox, trimix and soda-lime
available.*

   *Day charters on Ata-Tude; also multiple-
day trips (two to five days) with land-based
accommodation and meals to Hornby
Island, wreck of the Capilano, Vivian Island
and Campbell River area.)*

• LAUNCH RAMPS
Snaw-naw-as Marina Ramp
209 Mallard Way, Lantzville BC V0R 2H0
(250)390-3661
*(Launch for a fee at Nanoose Harbour for
Strait of Georgia: concrete ramp, good at all
tides. Wheelchair-accessible marina float.
Chemical toilet at top of wharf. Telephone
outside café/marina office.)*

   Located ⅓ mile (½ kilometer) off
Highway 19. Take Lantzville Road exit off
highway, immediately turn left into Snaw-
naw-as Road and follow signs to marina.

Heading north to Lantzville Road
• From Departure Bay ferry terminal, follow
signs toward Parksville. After Highway 19A
merges into Highway 19, reach Ware Road.
Pass turnoffs to Lantzville at Ware and
Superior roads; when 1 mile (1½ kilometers) past Superior, turn right.
• Heading north, from Duke Point, Duncan or Ladysmith, on Highway 19 follow
signs toward Campbell River. Continue on
Nanaimo Parkway (Highway 19). Shortly
past Aulds Road, exit 28, three exits to
Lantzville. Pass Ware Road and Superior
Road, where there is a traffic light. Go 1
mile (1½ kilometers) more past Superior
and turn right to Lantzville.

Heading south to Lantzville Road
• On Highway 19A: from south end of
Northwest Bay Road, go 3¾ miles (6 kilometers) and turn left into Lantzville Road.
• On Highway 19, take Exit 46 following
signs to "Highway 19A North, Parksville,
Rathtrevor Beach, and Visitor Info". Go
south on Highway 19A for 7½ miles (12
kilometers); turn left into Lantzville Road.

Schooner Cove Resort Hotel & Marina
3521 Dolphin Drive
Nanoose Bay BC V9P 9J7
(250)468-7691
1-800-663-7060: Toll-free throughout
    North America
www.fairwinds.bc.ca
*(Launch for a fee at Schooner Cove for
Ballenas Channel and Strait of Georgia:
concrete ramp, good at all tides 2 feet [⅔
meter] and greater. Restrooms; telephone
outside marina office; hot tub and hot showers.)*

   See map page 213 for turnoffs to Northwest Bay Road, then go to Northwest Bay
Road to Stewart; follow signs to the marina.

Union Bay Public Ramp
Union Bay Community Club
Union Bay BC
(250)335-2500
*(Launch year-round for a fee for Hornby
Island and Strait of Georgia: concrete ramp,
good at high tides. Chemical toilet, telephone.)*

HORNBY ISLAND

• DIVE RESORT AND CHARTERS
Hornby Island Diving
10795 Central Island Road
Ford Cove
Hornby Island BC V0R 1Z0
(250)335-2807
www.hornbyislanddiving.com
(Dive packages include boat dives, lodge accommodation, meals, sauna; non-divers welcomed with groups up to 23 guests. Wheelchair diving groups welcome.

Day charters for individuals and groups up to 12. Dive guiding available with advance notice. Open year-round. Nitrox, trimix and rebreathers with advance notice.)

• LAUNCH RAMPS
AT HORNBY ISLAND
Hornby Public Ramp
Shingle Spit, next to ferry landing
Hornby Island
(Concrete ramp, good at all tides. Telephone outside building on left-hand side at turnoff to the ramp. Flush toilets at ferry waiting room.)

At the first opportunity after leaving the ferry, turn right; just before a sign to Hornby Island Resort, turn right again. Go to the end of the road.

Ford Cove Harbour Authority Wharf
Ford Cove
Hornby Island
(250)335-2141
(Launch dive-kayaks and other car-top boats at beach access beside the wharf. Outhouse. Telephone outside grocery store.)

From Hornby Island ferry landing, head up the hill to your left. Go 5 miles (8 kilometers) along the main road to the Co-op store. Turn right and go 3 miles (4¾ kilometers) on Central Road to Ford Cove.

• LAUNCH RAMPS AT VANCOUVER ISLAND TO GO TO HORNBY
Deep Bay Ramp
Ship & Shore Family Campground & Café
180 Chrome Point Road, Deep Bay
Mailing address: RR1, S-160, C-93
Bowser BC V0R 1G0
(250)757-8399
www.zapbc.com/shipshore
(Launch for a fee year-round: concrete ramp, good at all tides. Restrooms, hot showers and campground. Telephone, top of ramp, outside store and café.)

Pepperland Resort Ramp
8256 South Island Highway (Oceanside Route)
RR1, S-29, C-9
Fanny Bay BC V0R 1W0
(250)335-0920
(Launch for a fee year-round: concrete ramp, good at all except extreme low tides. At high tides, good for wheelchair divers. Restrooms and hot showers; telephones outside restrooms and outside RV park office at Highway 19A.)

SOUTH OF NANAIMO

• DIVE SHOPS

Northwest Technical Diving Services (NTD)
919 Jubilee Street
Duncan BC V9L 1Y2
(250)746-9465; cell (250)246-8773
1-866-987-2822: Toll-free throughout
    North America
www.ntdservices.com
*(Recreational, technical, nitrox and rebreather
instruction. Supply nitrox, trimix and soda-lime.
Operate from July 1 through end of March.)*

Pacific Water Sports
1705 Cowichan Bay Road
Cowichan Bay BC V0R 1N0
(250)746-6669
www.pacificwatersports.ca
*(Recreational dive shop. Guided shore dives
and guided group day-trips: range from Tozier
Rock, Saanich Inlet, north through Burial
Islet to Maple Bay. Waterfront air fills.)*

• DAY AND MULTIPLE-DAY CHARTERS

Themuhwulh and *Cedar Sea*
49th Parallel Dive Charters
PO Box 5-9
Thetis Island BC V0R 2Y0
(250)252-0758
www.divemaster.ca
*(Day charters for groups of two to twelve
range from Gabriola Pass south to Sansum
Narrows and Active Pass; dive sites include the
Boeing 737 artificial reef, Del Norte, Miami,
and Point Grey wrecks. Multiple-day charters
with land-based accommodation. Pick up at
Chemainus, Ladysmith and Gulf Islands.)*

• DIVE RESORT

Cedar Beach Ocean Lodge
120 Clam Bay Road, PO Box 16-2
Thetis Island BC V0R 2Y0
(250)246-9770
www.cedar-beach.com
*(Dive packages include boat dives, air, hot tub
and accommodation for up to eight divers;
marine life expertise every day – also courses.)*

• DIVE-KAYAK RENTALS

Sealegs Kayaking Adventures
579 Hillview Avenue
Ladysmith BC V9G 1W2
(250)245-4096
www.sealegskayaking.com
*(Dive-kayak rentals year-round. Restrooms
in summer only. Telephone, outside wall of
Transfer Beach Concessions.)*

Genoa Bay Marina
#1 - 5100 Genoa Bay Road
Duncan BC V9L 5Y8
(250)746-7621
1-800-572-6481: Toll free throughout
    North America
www.genoabaymarina.com
(Dive-kayak rentals. Also launching.)

• LAUNCH RAMPS

Ladysmith Fisherman's Wharf and
    Boat Ramp
837 Ludlow Road, PO Box 130
Ladysmith BC V9G 1A1
(250)245-7511
www.ladysmithfishermanswharf.com
*(Launch free for northern Trincomali Chan-
nel: concrete ramp, good at all tides.
Restrooms with showers in office building
beside the wharf; telephone outside office
building. Large parking area.)*

At traffic light, north end of Ladysmith,
turn toward the sea into Ludlow Road.
Cross the railway tracks, and curve right
following a sign to a marina. At the stop
sign, do not bear left downhill to the log
sort. Continue straight on Ludlow Road
and downhill to the end of it.

Chemainus Municipal Ramp
Foot of Maple Street, Chemainus
*(Launch for a fee for Gulf Islands: concrete
ramp, good at all tides. Restrooms and picnic tables at park. Telephone ⅓ mile [½ kilo-
meter] away at ferry terminal, foot of Oak
Street at Esplanade Street. From ramp, go
to Oak Street. Turn left and to the ferry.)*

Located 5 minutes off Trans-Canada Highway 1, between Ladysmith and Duncan: go to the south end of Chemainus Road by way of Henry Road. The Highway 1 turnoff onto Henry Road is 7½ miles (12 kilometers) south of the center of Ladysmith and 10 miles (16¼ kilometers) north of the bridge in Duncan. At Henry Road, follow signs for 1 mile (1½ kilometers) to Chemainus Road. Turn left onto Chemainus: go ¾ mile (1¼ kilometers) to Cedar Street; turn right and go to Oak Street; turn right again and go to Maple Street. Turn left into Maple and to the water.

Maple Bay Municipal Ramp
Beaumont Avenue, north of wharf and float
Maple Bay
(Launch for a fee for Sansum Narrows: concrete ramp, good at all tides. Flush toilets at beach park north of wharf, summer only. Telephone outside grocery store beside the wharf.)

Located 10 minutes from Duncan: turn east off Highway 1 at Trunk Road following signs to Maple Bay. Trunk Road runs into Tzouhalem Road, then Maple Bay Road. At the bottom of the hill, turn left and go to the dock at Maple Bay. The launch ramp is just north of it.

Genoa Bay Marina
#1 - 5100 Genoa Bay Road
Duncan BC V9L 5Y8
(250) 746-7621
1-800-572-6481: Toll-free throughout
    North America
www.genoabaymarina.com
(Launch for a fee year-round for Satellite Channel, Sansum Narrows and Saanich Inlet: concrete ramp, good at all tides. Restrooms. Telephones beside road at top of ramp. Dive-kayak rentals.)

Hecate Park Public Ramp
Cowichan Bay Road, Cowichan Bay
(Launch for a fee year-round for Sansum Narrows, Satellite Channel and Saanich Inlet: concrete ramp, good for all boats at 4-foot [1¼-meter] tides and greater. Large parking area. Chemical toilet at south end of sewage treatment plant in the park. Picnic table; telephones ½ mile [¾ kilometer] south in the center of the community of Cowichan Bay, outside shops north of post office; another at hotel at the top of the hill, head of Cowichan Bay, available 24 hours.)

Located south of Duncan on Cowichan Bay Road which loops off Trans-Canada Highway 1. The ramp is midway between the north and south ends of the loop road: from Trans-Canada Highway 1 go 3 miles (5 kilometers) from either north or south end of Cowichan Bay Road to the ramp.

GABRIOLA ISLAND
• AIR STATION, DAY CHARTERS AND DIVE-KAYAK RENTALS
High Test Dive Charters
1780 Stalker Road, corner of Coast Road
Gabriola Island BC V0R 1X7
(250) 247-9753; pager (250) 716-4515
www.hightestdive.com
(Dockside and roadside air fills. Day charters out of Silva Bay on Bottom Time and Thrasher to the Saskatchewan and Cape Breton artificial reefs, Dodd Narrows, Gabriola Passage and Porlier Pass. Hot tubs, two log cabins to accommodate up to 10 persons at a time. A cabin for rinsing and drying gear. Dive-kayak rentals.)

• LAUNCH RAMP
Degnen Bay Public Ramp
Foot of Gray Road, near Gabriola Pass
(Launch at high tides. No toilet, no telephone. Nearest telephone at Degnen Bay Harbour Authority Wharf at the wharf head; space for five or six cars to park.)

From South Road and Degnen Bay Road, head west ⅓ mile (½ kilometer) to Cooper Road; turn left and left again into Gray Road and go to the end of it.

All of this Service Information is subject to change.

SIXGILL SHARKS

BOAT DIVE
GPS
49°30.909' N
124°34.743' W

SKILL
Expert divers

Intermediate divers with guide

TIDE TABLE
Point Atkinson:
Add 30 minutes

WHY GO

Dive Flora Islet to see a sixgill shark, to take videos or photos of it, to count its gills or maybe to swim with one of the ghostly giants.

Flora is one of two locations in the world where divers can plan to see sixgills. Not guaranteed – this is wilderness. The sharks are not baited. But some lucky and alert divers see sixgills on their first dive at Flora. My "guesstimate" is that 30% of searching-for-sixgill dives here are successful. I saw one my fourth try. It swam slowly – cruising. It curved seductively along the base of the wall, close to the sandy bottom of a narrow ledge, slipped along sinuously, then suddenly was gone, back to the void it had come from.

The sixgills are pale gray. They normally range in length from 8 to 12 feet (2½ to 3½ meters); one as long as 18 feet (5½ meters) has been reported. They usually move slowly and dreamily but can turn in a flash. In summer they come up from great depths, perhaps from 800 feet (250 meters), usually to sand-covered shelves at 90 feet (27 meters). They have been seen in water as shallow as 40 feet (12 meters). Little else is known. Reports by divers are scattered and casual, yet dozens of divers have photographed sixgills; many photos include a diver and sixgill in the same shot. "Mug shots" of the sixgills could become a valuable record, as each shark has distinguishing scars and marks. Take photos, but do not disturb

the sharks and do not take, touch or disturb any marine life – just look. For years local divers have honored Flora as a reserve.

Divers first sighted sixgills at Flora in 1977 or 1978. Flora is still the only location in the Strait of Georgia where sixgills are seen often. Another place with frequent sightings is Tyler Rock on the west coast of Vancouver Island and recently a sighting at China Creek. Sporadic sightings have been made in other locations, from Three Tree Point in southern Puget Sound to the Hood Canal and Saanich Inlet.

Best visibility at Flora is September through February – it is great diving year-round. My first dive at Flora was an unforgettable New Year's Eve: after diving and dinner, we celebrated the New Year in the sauna; some divers rolled in the snow – then back to the sauna.

BOTTOM AND DEPTHS

Broadleaf kelp covers the rocky bottom at 30 to 40 feet (9 to 12 meters) where you go off the boat; then the bottom rolls away in a series of rocky ledges. A rock wall sheers off from 80 to 90 feet (24 to 27 meters). From there, the bottom drops to nowhere. At the end of the dive an easy safety stop is in 15 feet (4 meters) beside Flora with lots to see – orange cup corals behind the bottom kelp at 10 feet (3 meters).

HAZARDS

Depth, current, boats; the sharks themselves, and *your desire to stay with them.* If you see sharks at the end of your dive, be careful of narcosis. It is tempting to stay too long – even to follow the sharks down when they head deep. Plan for a safety stop. Dive on slack. Ascending, listen for boats and go up the anchor line. Or follow the contour of the bottom all the way to Flora and then swim to your boat. The sharks may swim close; the temptation to touch them is great. No reports of attacks, but you could be hit by a tail, and the sixgills are meat eaters. They have

Sixgill shark at Hornby

very large mouths and exceedingly sharp teeth. In spite of their sluggish appearance they can react with startling speed when annoyed. It is safer not to touch.

TELEPHONES
• On the water: VHF radio; if no VHF, try a cell phone.
• On land: Ford Cove, outside grocery store.

FACILITIES
Air fills, day charters and packages for groups including accommodation, meals, boat diving and cedar sauna at Ford Cove, Hornby Island – non-divers are welcome with groups. Camping and cabins year-round at Hornby Island Resort, Shingle Spit.

ACCESS
Flora Islet is off the southeastern tip of Hornby Island, near the north end of the Strait of Georgia. The site is exposed to southeast wind. Pick a calm, sunny day. For calmer water, dive early in the morning. Sixgills have been seen only from mid-April through late October – it is a summer

dive. Most likely to see them in July and August.

Charter out of Ford Cove, Hornby Island, Union Bay, Courtenay, Campbell River or Nanaimo. Launch at Hornby Island Public Ramp at Shingle Bay, and go 4 nautical miles southeast around Hornby Island to Flora. Or launch at Union Bay, Fanny Bay or Deep Bay on Vancouver Island and go to Flora Islet. Anchor in 30 to 40 feet (9 to 12 meters) off the southwestern shore of Flora. Swim a short way straight out and go down over a series of ledges. Divers and sixgills usually meet at a depth of 80 to 90 feet (24 to 27 meters).

One method some visitors use to find sixgills is to hit the bottom with a rock or hit their tank to make noise. Sound and light both seem to attract the sharks. Other divers stay shallow and scan the dark void with a powerful light for the flash of a long white tail, then quietly drop to the sixgills. Once you sight sharks, passive behavior – just watching them – will usually keep the sharks with you longer.

NOTES

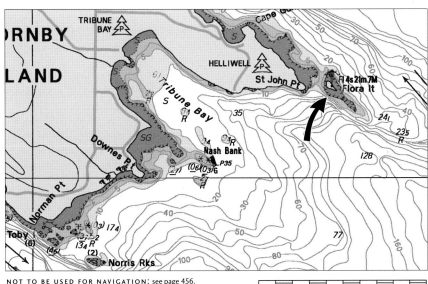

NOT TO BE USED FOR NAVIGATION: see page 456.
Use CHS chart #3513 for navigation; for information on obtaining navigational charts see page 456. Soundings are in meters.

2 NAUTICAL MILES

HERON ROCKS

BOAT DIVE
KAYAK DIVE
or SHORE DIVE
GPS
49°29.369′ N
124°39.946′ W

SKILL
All divers

TIDE TABLE
Point Atkinson:
Add 30 minutes

WHY GO

Heron Rocks is one of the most magnificent of dives. The fish life is fantastic. And masses of invertebrates, too.

Have you ever, on one dive, seen a pair of wolf-eels, lots of little rockfish, schools of young herring, 10 large lingcod, numerous yelloweye rockfish, ratfish, tiger rockfish, pink-and-white giant nudibranchs, red dahlia anemones, orange cup corals, staghorn bryozoans, rock scallops, gum boot chitons, blood stars, rose stars and giant red urchins? That's Heron Rocks at Hornby Island. The bottom is interesting too – even if there were no life. In the shallows, wave-sculpted sandstone drops in shallow ledges. Deeper, beautiful sand-covered corridors through the rocks give an almost lacy feeling to the ocean floor. Deeper still, ledges shelter stacks of life.

BOTTOM AND DEPTHS

Smooth rock shallows with small round rocks graduates to sand at Toby Island. At 15 to 25 feet (5 to 8 meters), eelgrass. Then a steep sand slope to the wall and huge boulders. Ledges and overhangs down to the base of the wall at 65 to 75 feet (20 to 23 meters). Some bottom kelp.

HAZARDS

The Heron Rocks site is exposed to southeast wind; if wind is high. be prepared to dive another day,

Juvenile wolf-eel

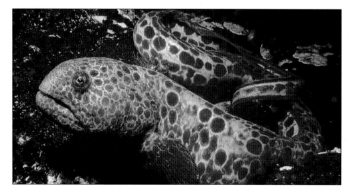

TELEPHONES

• On the water: VHF radio; if no VHF, try a cell phone.
• On land: Ford Cove, outside grocery store.

FACILITIES

At Ford Cove, Hornby Island: air fills, day charters and packages for divers that include accommodation, meals and boat dives; beach access beside the wharf for car-top boats, outhouse nearby. Camping is limited on Hornby: in summer, book in advance. At Shingle Spit, Hornby Island (where ferry lands): accommodation and launch ramp for larger boats.

Ramps on Vancouver Island at Deep Bay, Fanny Bay and Union Bay.

ACCESS

The site is off the southeast side of Norman Point at Hornby, near the south end of Lambert Channel. Southeast wind during winter storms and late afternoon winds from the west during warm weather can make anchoring difficult, so look at the weather before you go.

• Boat Dive

Charter or launch your own boat and go to Heron Rocks. Anchor in 25 to 35 feet (8 to 10 meters) offshore from the first series of rocks you come to that are awash. Smaller boats and dive-kayaks can be anchored in more protected inside waters of Toby Island or pull up on one of the exposed rocks.

Toby Island, immediately west of Norman Point, is the deepest part. For a shallow start enter southeast of Norman Point. At low tides Toby connects to Hornby Island. Toby dries at 7-foot (2-meter) tides – approach cautiously as shoals run from Norman Point to Norris Rocks. Go down and dive east along the submerged rocks and ledges that follow the shape of the shore from Toby Island along the southeast side of Norman Point. They are shown as Heron Rocks on the chart.

• Kayak Dive
Go to Ford Cove on Hornby Island by
ferry and car. The ferry sails from
Buckley Bay, Vancouver Island: it is
midway between Campbell River and
Nanaimo off Island Highway – the
drive is 1 to 1 ¼ hours from each.
Take the ferry to Denman Island: 10
minutes. Drive 7 miles (11 kilometers) across Denman and follow signs
to the Hornby Island ferry. Cross in
10 minutes.

At Hornby Island ferry landing,
head up the hill to your left. Drive
5⅓ miles (8½ kilometers) along the
main road to the Co-op Store. Turn
right and go along Central Road for
3 miles (4¾ kilometers) to Ford Cove.

Launch and paddle 1 ½ nautical
miles southeast to Norman Point and
Heron Rocks. If it's a low-tide day, you
could land on Toby Island to gear up. If
high tide, this dive is for kayak-divers
with advanced skills. Anchor your dive-
kayak and dive from it. Go on a quiet
day before the wind gets up.

Wheelchair divers who paddle
dive-kayaks will find beach access beside
the wharf at Ford Cove.

• Shore Dive
Shore access to the dive site is available
to members of the Heron Rocks Camping Cooperative. The private cooperative offers camping to nonmembers on a
very limited basis, primarily in June. It is
open only in June, July and August. To
reserve: telephone (250) 335-2670
from March 1 through 8 and request a
reservation form. If no luck, in early June
you could telephone to check if any
vacancies.

Access to the campground and beach
is only for members and guest campers
who have booked in advance – absolutely
no drop-ins. Divers who are not registered
would be trespassing if they even entered
the campgrounds to request a site.

*Returning to Vancouver Island, check the
ferry schedule – at the time of writing, the
last ferry leaves Hornby at 6 pm except on
Friday when it leaves at 10 pm.*

NOTES

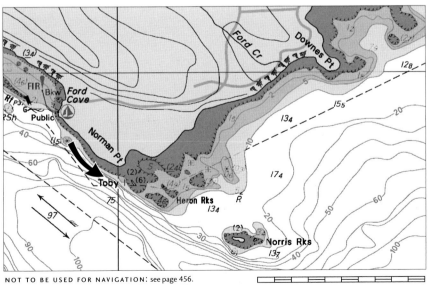

NOT TO BE USED FOR NAVIGATION: see page 456.
Use CHS chart #3527 for navigation; for information on obtaining
navigational charts see page 456. Soundings are in meters.

1 NAUTICAL MILE

NORTHWEST BAY ROAD INFORMATION

Northwest Bay Road dives described in the next ten pages of this book are
• Madrona Point [Arbutus Point]
• Wall Beach
• Cottam Point [Beachcomber]
• Seducer's Beach [Tyee Cove]
• Dolphin Beach

Access to these five dive sites is threatened. The neighborhood is residential and, in the past, some divers have been inconsiderate or perhaps just unaware. Residents have experienced the following problems with divers. They aired their concerns at a neighborhood meeting and their concerns were passed on to me.

If we wish to continue enjoying these excellent shore dives it makes sense to reduce tensions wherever possible by being careful about some of our behaviors. Concerns of residents and some possible answers:

1. Problem: All five dive sites at risk are unsuitable for large groups of divers.
   Solution: Small groups of three or four are best; if a group precedes you, try another close-by dive.
2. Problem: Parking space is limited.
   Solution: Take one small vehicle per group; leave access to driveways, fire hydrants, road traffic. Never park or camp overnight.
3. Problem: No changerooms.
   Solution: Be discreet – do not change at the roadside.
4. Problem: No toilets nearby.
   Solution: Visit a restroom before you reach these sites.
5. Problem: Residents fish, water-ski and boat close to shore and feel restricted by the possibility of hurting divers.
   Solution: Fly your dive flag.
6. Problem: Sounds carry over the water.
   Solution: Day and night be particularly careful to keep voices low; and use judgment: leave compressors and generators at home.
7. Problem: Smoky beach fires sometimes set off fire alarms when the wind blows embers onto privately owned adjacent properties.
   Solution: Do not build fires.
8. Problem: No garbage facilities.
   Solution: Carry out your litter.
9. Problem: Trails to the sites are narrow.
   Solution: Take care not to trample beyond the paths.

HOW TO FIND THE PUBLIC TOILETS SOUTH END

Chemical toilets, open 24 hours at the time of writing, are located near the south end of Northwest Bay Road.

• From highways 19 and 19A and Northwest Bay Road junction, go ¾ mile (1¼ kilometers) east. Turn right into Powder Point Road. Go 100 feet (30 meters) to a chain link fence on the left-hand side: parking space for 30 or more cars. The toilets are at this entry to Jack Bagley Park and ball field near the Nanoose Community Centre.
• If you approach from the north on Northwest Bay Road, you will find the left-hand turnoff shortly past Nanoose Bay Elementary School on the left-hand side, and a shopping mall on the right-hand side. Turn left into Powder Point Road.

HOW TO FIND THE PUBLIC TOILETS NORTH END

Flush toilets are located at the Visitor Info Centre south of Parksville on Highway 19A (Oceanside Route). These restrooms are open only during Visitor Info hours. At the time of writing, in summer the Visitor Info Centre is open Monday through Saturday; in winter, Saturday only. For hours of operation telephone (250) 248-3613
info@chamber.parksville.bc.ca
www.chamber.parksville.bc.ca

HOW TO FIND NORTHWEST BAY ROAD

To get to Northwest Bay Road, north end

- Heading south on the Oceanside Route (Highway 19A), when 1 mile (1⅔ kilometers) past Rathtrevor Beach Provincial Park turnoff, turn left into Franklin's Gull Road, and immediately right into Northwest Bay Road.
- Heading south on Highway 19 (Nanaimo Parkway), take Exit 46 and follow the signs to "Highway 19A North, Parksville, Rathtrevor Beach and Visitor Info". At the first traffic light past Visitor Info, turn right into Franklin's Gull Road. Turn right, again, into Northwest Bay Road.
- Heading north from the ferry at Departure Bay, turn right into the Oceanside Route (Highway 19A): go 13 miles (21 kilometers) to a traffic light and gas station; continue straight for 3½ miles (5¾ kilometers) more and take Exit 46. Curve around and follow signs to Parksville. Pass the Visitor Info Centre sign and, at

the traffic light, turn right into Franklin's Gull Road. Immediately turn right, again, into Northwest Bay Road.
- Heading north on Highway 19 (Nanaimo Parkway), take Exit 46. Curve around and follow signs to Parksville. Shortly past the Tourist Info sign and at the traffic light, turn right into Franklin's Gull Road. Turn right, again, into Northwest Bay Road.

To get to Northwest Bay Road, south end

- Heading north on Highway 19/19A (Nanaimo Parkway or Oceanside Route), at the first traffic light past Lantzville Road you will see a gas station on the right-hand side. Turn right into Northwest Bay Road.
- Heading south on Highway 19 (Nanaimo Parkway), when 4 miles (6¾ kilometers) past Exit 46 to Parksville, turn left at a traffic light next to a gas station into Northwest Bay Road.

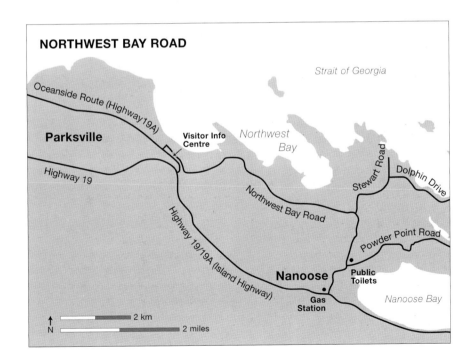

NORTHWEST BAY ROAD

Strait of Georgia

Oceanside Route (Highway 19A)

Parksville

Visitor Info Centre

Northwest Bay

Highway 19

Northwest Bay Road

Stewart Road

Dolphin Drive

Highway 19/19A (Island Highway)

Powder Point Road

Nanoose

Public Toilets

Gas Station

Nanoose Bay

2 km

N

2 miles

—MADRONA POINT [ARBUTUS POINT]—

SHORE DIVE

SKILL
All divers and snorkelers

TIDE TABLE
Point Atkinson

WHY GO
An octopus every five minutes – that's what I saw here! And they are shallow. There are wolf-eels, too, out deeper. But you have to look hard for both.

Madrona Point, commonly called Arbutus Point, is rimmed with rocky ledges and overhangs making all kinds of places for octopuses to hide. Crabs – a ready meal for octopuses – scurry over the sand which comes up to the rock wall rimming the point. You will see a good mixture of anemones, sea stars, some nudibranchs and rockfish as well. In winter, perhaps sea lions. Avoid coming closer to them than 110 yards (100 meters).

A vast plain of ghostly white sea whips stretches north in deep water offshore from the rocky overhangs to the ledge which drops into wolf-eel country and sponge-land.

BOTTOM AND DEPTHS
Rock wall filled with nooks and crannies where octopuses hide. It drops to flat, sandy bottom at 25 to 35 feet (8 to 11 meters). This slopes gradually out a long way. The sea whips are on muddy bottom at 80 to 90 feet (24 to 27 meters). Set your compass and head north across the plain of sea whips. After 100 yards (90 meters) you will come to a ledge that drops off to deeper water where the wolf-eels live.

HAZARDS
Boats. Listen for them; if you hear a boat, stay down until it passes.

TELEPHONES
• Northwest Bay Road (north end), inside Visitor Info; available only when open.
• Corner of Northwest Bay Road (south end) and highway, outside gas station.

FACILITIES
None. See page 212 for toilet locations: stop before you drive to the dive site. Air fills in Courtenay, Union Bay and Nanaimo.

Madrona Point, a good place to see octopuses

ACCESS

Madrona Point is on Northwest Bay near Parksville. It is reached by way of Northwest Bay Road that loops off Highway 19A between Nanaimo and Parksville. The dive is 10 to 15 minutes off the highway. See page 213 for directions to Northwest Bay Road (north and south ends) and then go to Arbutus Drive.

At the junction of Arbutus and Madrona drives, turn north into Arbutus Drive, go to Madrona Drive, turn left and go ½ mile (¾ kilometer) more to the end of Madrona. Space for one or two cars to park. Walk down a short, flat path between tall trees to the layered rock ledges of Madrona Point. Enter and swim around the rocky shore to look for an octopus or snorkel north and go down to look for wolf-eels.

Lots of marine life, but just look and don't take. The following notice is posted: "No harvesting or collecting of seafood by any means at Madrona Point, Marine Life, Research Project underway".

To get to Arbutus Drive
• From the south end of Northwest Bay Road at the gas station, follow signs toward Schooner Cove until you pass Stewart Road – stay on Northwest Bay Road. Continue past Claudet Road and Wall Beach Road: from the turnoff, go 4⅓ miles (7 kilometers) to Arbutus Drive.
• From the north end of Northwest Bay Road, go 1¾ miles (2¾ kilometers) to Arbutus Drive.

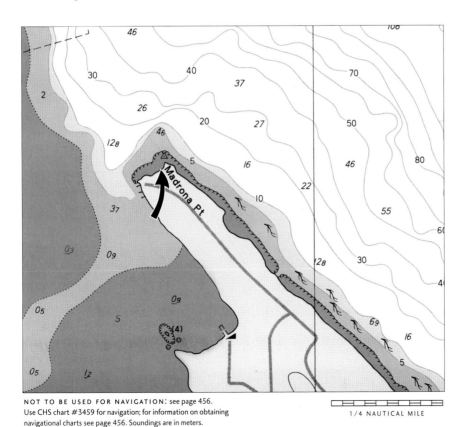

NOT TO BE USED FOR NAVIGATION: see page 456.
Use CHS chart #3459 for navigation; for information on obtaining navigational charts see page 456. Soundings are in meters.

1/4 NAUTICAL MILE

NOTES

WHY GO

Octopuses and wolf-eels are the big lure for most at Wall Beach. But I loved the fish life, the sea stars, the staghorn bryozoans. We saw lots of seaperch, a big fat kelp greenling, lingcod – probably fifty of them. Rockfish galore: two tiger rockfish, quillback rockfish, black rockfish. We were lucky and saw a juvenile yelloweye rockfish, commonly called red snapper. And two ratfish. We saw a painted star, purple stars, striped sun stars, sunflower stars. In the shallows, the egg case of a moon snail, tiny sea pens, sea peaches and a yellow longish creature with vertical ribs that looked like a sea cucumber without its outer knobby rough skin. I'm still looking in the books for that one.

Great at night – one diver saw three octopuses, another diver saw eight wolf-eels on one night dive here. Both creatures hang out around the boulders.

BOTTOM AND DEPTHS

Smooth rock on shore rolls gently down to eelgrass on silty sand bottom. Farther out, lettuce kelp and brown bottom kelp; brown stalks of kelp stand tall. Ten minutes out from shore, a ledge drops 10 to 15 feet (3 to 4½ meters). Depth ranges from 50 to 60 feet (15 to 18 meters). Boulders scattered along it; sand between. Smooth sand bottom slopes gently off beyond the ledge.

HAZARDS

Current, long swim, small boats and wind. Dive near the slack. Listen for boats, use a compass and ascend along the bottom all the way to shore well out of the way of boats. Do not dive at Wall Beach if wind from the southeast – makes entry difficult.

TELEPHONES

- Northwest Bay Road (north end), inside Visitor Info; available only when open.
- Corner of Northwest Bay Road (south end) and highway, outside gas station.

FACILITIES

None. See page 212 for toilet locations: make a stop before you drive to the dive site. Air fills in Courtenay, Union Bay and Nanaimo.

ACCESS

The Wall Beach dive is on Northwest Bay near Parksville. It is reached by way of Northwest Bay Road which loops off highways 19 and 19A (Oceanside Route) between Nanaimo and Parksville. The dive is 10 minutes from the highway (north end), 15 minutes from the highway (south end). See page 213 for directions to Northwest Bay Road (north and south ends) and then go to Wall Beach Road.

At the junction of Wall Beach Road and Northwest Bay Road turn toward the water. Go for ½ mile (¾ kilometer) almost to the water, and turn right onto Seahaven; it becomes a dirt road. Go for ½ mile (¾ kilometer) along Seahaven Road to the end of it. A gate is on your left. Next to it, space for five or six cars to park. Straight ahead, a short trail to the sloping smooth rocks to the water.

Check your compass and swim straight out on the surface for five minutes or until you lose the bottom, then continue under water following your compass.

Wheelchair accessible for groups with a great deal of able-bodied support to help get over the smooth rock that forms the beach, especially at high tide. Expect barnacles at low tide.

To get to Wall Beach Road
- From the south end of Northwest Bay Road at the gas station follow signs toward Schooner Cove. Keep going on Northwest Bay Road past Stewart Road and Claudet Road to Wall Beach Road. From the turnoff, it's 3¾ miles (6 kilometers) to Wall Beach Road.
- From the north end of Northwest Bay Road go 2¼ miles (3½ kilometers) to Wall Beach Road.

Barnacles exposed at low tide, Wall Beach

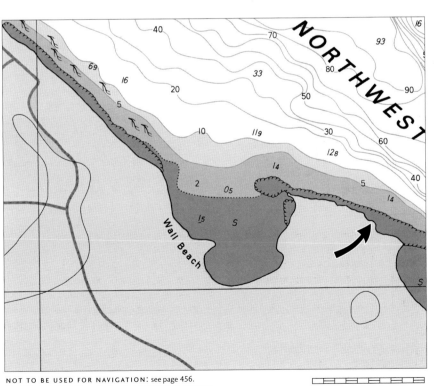

NOT TO BE USED FOR NAVIGATION: see page 456.
Use CHS chart #3459 for navigation; for information on obtaining navigational charts see page 456. Soundings are in meters.

1/4 NAUTICAL MILE

NOTES

COTTAM POINT [BEACHCOMBER]

SHORE DIVE

SKILL
All divers and snorkelers

TIDE TABLE
Point Atkinson

WHY GO

Sightseeing and photography. Good visibility year-round, ranging to 100 feet (30 meters) in winter.

Diving here is like jumping into an aquarium. Cottam Point teems with life. Millions of little rockfish, nudibranchs, sea stars, kelp greenlings and red rock crabs. Painted greenlings. Large white fluffy anemones. Huge boulders, covered with so many small orange fuzzy anemones that you can't see any rock at all, stand immovable between olive-colored bull kelp banners flying in the current. If you look, you may see an octopus or a wolf-eel. Lots of lingcod too. Sea lions, in winter. Abalones are returning, and rock scallops. But just look, don't take. Cottam Point is a sanctuary. A diver's flag sign is beside the steps to the water. Written on it: "Observe but do not touch". In addition, never come closer to sea lions than 110 yards (100 meters). See viewing guidelines at www.pac.dfo-mpo.gc.ca, click on Marine Mammals.

BOTTOM AND DEPTHS

Smooth rocks roll gently down into the water where brown kelp stands tall, lettuce kelp and bull kelp grow luxuriantly over the ledges and reef. Scattered boulders and some sand between. The reef is at a depth of 50 to 60 feet (15 to 18 meters), depending on tide height.

HAZARDS

Small boats, current and wind. In summer, bull kelp. Very heavy boat traffic close to shore. Listen for boats, use a compass and ascend along the bottom all the way to shore. Current up to 2 knots and more. When large tidal exchanges, dive near slack. Carry a knife. Do not dive if wind from the northwest makes entry difficult.

TELEPHONES

- Northwest Bay Road (north end), inside Visitor Info; available only when open.
- Corner of Northwest Bay Road (south end) and highway, outside gas station.
- Beachcomber Marina, inside.

FACILITIES

Parking space is limited. See page 212 for location of toilets: make a stop before going to the dive site. Air fills in Courtenay, Union Bay and Nanaimo.

ACCESS

Cottam Point is on Northwest Bay near Parksville, Vancouver Island. It is reached by way of Northwest Bay Road which loops off highways 19 and 19A (Oceanside Route) between Nanaimo and Parksville. The dive is 10 to 15 minutes from the highway. See page 213 for directions to Northwest Bay Road (north and south ends) and then go to Claudet Road.

At the junction of Claudet and Northwest Bay roads turn into Claudet and go for 1 mile (1½ kilometers) to Dorcas Point Road which goes off to the right. Keep going 1½ miles (2½ kilometers) more to Sea Dog Road. Turn left to the water. Be careful not to block any driveways.

Follow the path beside the cable to 10 concrete steps built between the roots of a tree and down to the rocks. Homes are on both sides. In front of the steps, Cottam Point. The reef goes straight out from the point toward Mistaken Island. An easy entry over smooth rocks.

To get to Claudet Road
- From the south end of Northwest Bay Road at the gas station follow signs toward Schooner Cove, but keep going on Northwest Bay Road past Stewart Road. From the highway junction, it is 2¼ miles (3½ kilometers) to Claudet Road.
- From the north end of Northwest Bay Road go 4 miles (6¼ kilometers) to Claudet Road.

Lingcod, approachable where not hunted

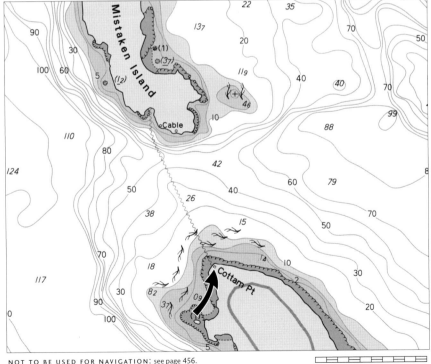

NOT TO BE USED FOR NAVIGATION: see page 456.
Use CHS chart #3459 for navigation; for information on obtaining navigational charts see page 456. Soundings are in meters.

1/4 NAUTICAL MILE

NOTES

DOLPHIN BEACH

WHY GO

Sponge-land is right at hand. I know of no other dive from shore where sponges are so easily accessible as at Dolphin Beach.

Dolphin Beach is good for the deep diver. Good for shallow divers and snorkelers too. We saw seaperch and rockfish swimming in the bull kelp and hiding in crevices. White-petalled alabaster nudibranchs. Moon snails in the eelgrass. Deeper were ratfish, some lingcod and round orange sponges clinging to the wall. Big chimney or boot sponges start at 80 feet (24 meters).

Because this site has been popular for years, food fish have been nearly hunted out in the shallows. But over the wall you might still find some lingcod to photograph.

BOTTOM AND DEPTHS

Rocky beach gives way to eelgrass and sand in the shallows, then tall brown kelp, rocks and bull kelp. Some deep cracks in the rocks. Swim past two valleys to reach the main wall. Beyond the kelp, steeply sloping sand falls away quickly to 80 feet (24 meters) where a stark rock wall drops off to a depth of 110 to 120 feet (34 to 37 meters) in "The Basement".

HAZARDS

Bull kelp, especially in summer, and wind in winter. Carry a knife. If wind makes entry difficult, you can always dive at Seducer's Beach.

TELEPHONE

Schooner Cove Marina, outside marina office: ½ mile (¾ kilometer) to it. Go east and uphill to the right; at the stop sign turn left and follow the road to the marina.

FACILITIES

None at Dolphin Beach. See page 212 for location of toilets: make a stop before you go to the dive site. Hot tub and hot showers nearby at Schooner Cove. Air fills in Courtenay, Union Bay and Nanaimo.

Alabaster nudibranch

ACCESS

Dolphin Beach is on Ballenas Channel near Parksville. It is reached via Northwest Bay Road which loops off highways 19 and 19A (Oceanside Route) between Nanaimo and Parksville. From the highway, 20 minutes to the dive. See page 213 for directions to Northwest Bay Road (north and south ends) and go to Stewart Road.

Go on Stewart to Dolphin Drive to Blueback Drive – Stewart to Blueback is 2½ miles (4 kilometers). Bear left onto Blueback: head down the hill for ⅓ mile (½ kilometer). The road dips and comes near the water. Houses are closeby on either side. This is Dolphin Beach.

Park at the roadside – space for one car – and walk a couple of steps through the brush to the rocky beach. Swim straight out and down. You will pass some underwater valleys before you reach the main wall.

To get to Stewart Road
- From the south end of Northwest Bay Road at the gas station follow signs toward Schooner Cove. Go 2 miles (3¼ kilometers) on Northwest Bay Road to Stewart Road and turn in.
- From north end of Northwest Bay Road go 4 miles (6¾ kilometers) to Stewart Road and turn in.

NOTES

NOT TO BE USED FOR NAVIGATION: see page 456.
Use CHS chart #3512 for navigation; for information on obtaining navigational charts see page 456. Soundings are in meters.

2 NAUTICAL MILES

SEDUCER'S BEACH [TYEE COVE]

SHORE DIVE

SKILL
All divers and snorkelers

TIDE TABLE
Point Atkinson

WHY GO

Easy access, sandy and rocky bottom, marine life shallow and deep; also a "first" for me on this dive. The whole dive feels different. Exotic.

Pink hydrocorals and yellow staghorn bryozoans like hard tropical corals, an extravaganza of giant silver nudibranchs, probably a hundred of them, half a dozen with eggs. We saw leather stars, purple sea stars. Deeper, feather stars. Orange cucumbers. One swimming scallop. Lingcod, a cabezon and a quillback rockfish. Lots of round orange sponges the size of tennis balls with tiny knobs all over them – I call them "puff balls". Then down to the chimney or boot sponges.

Many perch swim about in the sandy shallows. We also enjoyed seeing schools of young tube-snouts, kelp greenlings and black rockfish. Wispy tube-dwelling anemones. Egg cases of moon snails. Blackeye gobies. Swarms of mysids, or opossum shrimp, like millions of tiny ghosts. They are transparent – if the sun is shining you can see their shadow before you see them. The "first" for me this dive was seeing a clinging jelly. We found it beneath a leaf of kelp as we poked around at the end of our dive. This jelly has adhesive pads on its tentacle tips, and is the only jelly that can attach itself to kelp without self-destructing. It is transparent except for the pink cross on its bell.

Seducer's Beach is great for beginners and all divers who want a quick dive close to town.

BOTTOM AND DEPTHS

Sandy bottom with eelgrass soon gives way to rocky bottom 30 to 40 feet (9 to 12 meters) deep. The top of the wall begins at 50 to 60 feet (15 to 18 meters) and bottoms out to sand at a depth of 110 or 120 feet (34 to 37 meters), depending on tide height. Green and brown bottom kelp, with some bull kelp in summer. Staying shallow is easy. But the bottom drops off quickly to sponge-land, so it is also easy to go as deep as you want to – your choice.

HAZARDS

Wind in winter, might be some current but it will not carry you away. Dive near slack.

TELEPHONE

Schooner Cove Marina, outside marina office: ½ mile (¾ kilometer) to it. Go east and uphill to the right; at the stop sign turn left and follow the road to the marina.

FACILITIES

None. See page 212 for toilet locations: make a stop before you drive to the dive site. Hot tub and hot showers nearby at Schooner Cove – all the comforts you wish you had at home for after the dive.

ACCESS

Seducer's Beach is on Ballenas Channel. It is reached by way of Northwest Bay Road between Nanaimo and Parksville. From the Oceanside Route (Highway 19A), 20 minutes to the dive. See page 213 for directions to Northwest Bay Road (north and south ends) and then to Stewart Road.

At Stewart turn right to Dolphin Drive. Go 1½ miles (2½ kilometers) on Dolphin to Blueback Drive. Turn left. Then ½ mile (¾ kilometer) to Tyee Crescent. Turn left. Go 100 feet (30 meters) and park at the roadside – space for one small car. Left of the fire hydrant is a trail between the thimbleberries to a cobbled beach.

To get to Stewart Road
• From south end of Northwest Bay Road at the gas station follow signs toward Schooner Cove for 2 miles (3¼ kilometers) to Stewart Road.
• From north end of Northwest Bay Road go 4 miles (6¾ kilometers) to Stewart Road.

Seducer's Beach

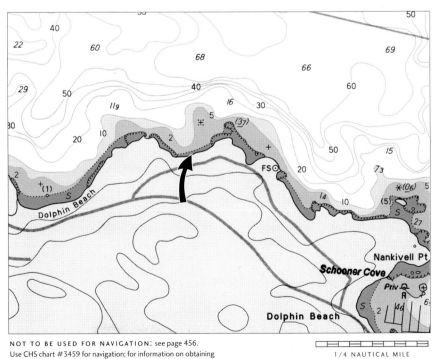

NOTES

NOT TO BE USED FOR NAVIGATION: see page 456.
Use CHS chart #3459 for navigation; for information on obtaining
navigational charts see page 456. Soundings are in meters.

1/4 NAUTICAL MILE

SEA LIONS

BOAT DIVE
GPS
Anchorage near wall:
49°17.047' N
124°05.638' W

Anchor near nature reserve
dock:
49°17.453' N
124°04.794' W

SKILL
Expert divers

TIDE TABLE
Point Atkinson

WHY GO

Go to Ada Rock to look at sea lions – so the sea lions can look at you! At peak time, as many as 500 haul out at Ada Rock. Stellers, also called northern sea lions, are tan colored. California sea lions have darker fur and are smaller – they are the ones that bark.

Big eyes. That's what you see first. And last. The sea lions are curious. They come and go in waves. Dart down, look and shoot away. Before we reach the wall, six Stellers swim to meet us. At the wall, twelve of them – 18,000 pounds (8 tonnes) of wildlife – flip their tails in front of us! The weight of one adult male Steller might be 1,000 to 2,200 pounds (450 to 1,000 kilograms); average length is 10 feet (3 meters). Female Stellers weigh half as much and are up to 8 feet (2½ meters) long. But you are more likely to meet the big ones as there are mostly bulls at haulout sites.

Steller sea lions

The Stellers arrive like a group of friends visiting the zoo, playing and rubbing against one another. One stands on its nose, twirls and stares at us. A thick-necked one shoots down, arches, blows bubbles, then disappears up and away. Bubbles are the first sign of aggression, I'm told. Probably a bull – perhaps the "leader of the pack".

Our leader signals us to leave. We move slowly, stay close to the wall as long as possible. When we reach open water, I look behind me. And, yes, a lone sleek big-eyed sea lion follows. Swoops back and forth behind us, beside us, between us. Gracefully, without menace but with seeming intent, escorts us out of her "yard".

More marine life is at the site, but it is irrelevant: I agree with our guide who said, "Once you see the sea lions, you're not looking for anything else".

BOTTOM AND DEPTHS

The wall is 15 to 25 feet (5 to 8 meters) deep on top, bottoms out to sand at 33 to 43 feet (10 to 13 meters) deep.

HAZARDS

The sea lions themselves – reports of divers injured by playful sea lions have been confirmed: a broken arm, a separated shoulder, severe bruising. Probably accidents. However if you still choose to dive with sea lions, how can you do it as safely as possible? Watch them. Keep your back to the wall. Since blowing bubbles might be a sign of aggression, do not look directly at a sea lion and exhale. The sea lions become less cautious the longer divers are present; do not stay down long. They also become less cautious the greater number of encounters they have with divers.

Throughout our dive the sea lions stayed 3 to 6 feet (1 to 2 meters) away. It was as if they were stopped by a glass wall; were shy or cautious; or respected our space. Divers should respect their space too, because of their sheer size if nothing else. In addition, the *Fisheries Act* forbids disturbing, molesting or killing marine mammals. You may not touch them nor do anything that interferes with whatever the animals are normally doing.

TELEPHONE

- On the water: VHF radio; if no VHF, try a cell phone.

224

• On land: Schooner Cove, outside office. At Nanoose Harbour, telephone outside café/marina office.

FACILITIES
None at Ada Rock. Launch ramp, hot tub and hot showers at Schooner Cove Marina. Chemical toilet at Nanoose Harbour ramp.

ACCESS
The Ada Islands are southeast of Ballenas Channel next to the Winchelsea Islands. Sea lions haul out on Ada Rock or at the nearby nature conservancy from November through March.

Ada Rock is the name used by locals; on the chart it is one of the unnamed Ada Islands. It is white in color and has no shrubs or trees on it. The site is 2 nautical miles east of Schooner Cove on Vancouver Island. You cannot miss it when sea lions are present.

It is a winter dive – timing is vital. Plan to go December through February. To check if sea lions are at Ada or nearby: telephone Schooner Cove Marina at (250)468-5364.

Launch at Schooner Cove or Nanoose Harbour or charter out of Nanaimo. From Schooner Cove, go 1½ nautical miles to Ada Rock. From Nanoose Harbour, just over 2 nautical miles. Approach the Ada Islands slowly. On your boat and in the water with the sea lions, if possible, keep 110 yards (100 meters) between your boat or yourselves and the sea lions.

On the way to observe them, use a depth sounder to find the wall. Do not alarm the sea lions by going too close to Ada Rock, but *do* go close enough to gain an impression of their size and power.

Then return to the sheltered cove on the south side of the largest of the Ada Islands to anchor, or land on the beach. Snorkel three minutes toward the underwater shallow wall. It is halfway to Ada Rock. Go partway on the surface; then descend and swim under water to the wall. Wait with your back to the wall. The sea lions will probably come to meet you before you reach it. If not, bang a rock on the bottom.

NOTES

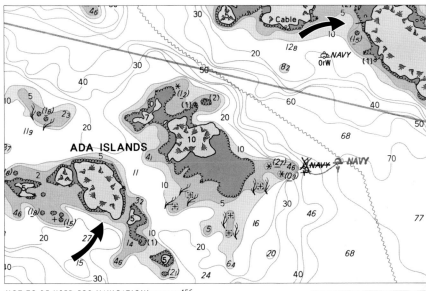

ADA ISLANDS

NOT TO BE USED FOR NAVIGATION: see page 456.
Use CHS chart #3459 for navigation; for information on obtaining navigational charts see page 456. Soundings are in meters.

1/4 NAUTICAL MILE

KEEL COVE

WHY GO

Boulder reef, a tire reef and you will see a few remains of the keel and ribs of the wreck of the *Vance*. Good diving in winter; the site is protected from southeast winds.

On the boulder reef we saw two octopuses. A grunt sculpin. Cabezons, swimming scallops, lots of young lingcod. Kelp crabs, blackeye gobies, red rock crabs, painted greenlings. Feather stars, chitons, decorator crabs, sea squirts, a brittle star. And lots of urchins.

Heading back over the luxuriant forest of big-leafed green and brown bottom kelp and through tall brown kelp, we saw orange cucumbers, a school of young tube-snouts, a moon snail egg case. So much on the boulder reef we didn't make it to the tire reef.

BOTTOM AND DEPTHS

Cobbled beach gives way to sand then rocky bottom smothered in broad-leafed kelp. The bottom slopes gently from shore to boulder reef in 50 to 60 feet (15 to 18 meters). The tire reef is west of it on sand.

HAZARDS

Steep short trail to the beach. You could carry gear down in stages.

TELEPHONE

Outside grocery on Hammond Bay Road: go south 150 yards (138 meters) to it.

FACILITIES

Off Hammond Bay Road, a toilet at Pipers Lagoon Park [Page Lagoon Park]. Air fills in Nanaimo.

ACCESS

Keel Cove is on Horswell Channel north of Nanaimo. It is reached by way of Hammond Bay Road off Departure Bay Road at its south end and off Island Highway at its north end. From the ferry, 15 minutes to the dive.

From Hammond Bay Road, turn into McGuffie and go to the end of it. Turn right down Keel Cove Lane. Space for one or two cars to park. A Public Access sign shows the steep trail to the log-strewn beach. Easier entry with high tides. The bits and pieces of the *Vance* are in a boulder garden on a compass bearing directly north. Turn left off its bow, west to the tire reef.

To get to McGuffie Road, off Hammond Bay Road

- From the ferry at Departure Bay, 15 minutes to Keel Cove. Follow signs toward Parksville. At the top of the hill, immediately after turning onto Highway 19A turn right into Departure Bay Road and head downhill to the water – if you pass a mall, you've missed the turnoff. Go back and head downhill. Shortly past the beach, at the traffic light, turn right into Hammond Bay Road. Go 3¾ miles (6 kilometers) to McGuffie Road.
- Heading north on Trans-Canada Highway 1 from Victoria or from the ferry at Duke Point, continue 3 minutes past the flaming torch at the north end of the city center. Just past the turnoff to Vancouver ferry, turn right into Departure Bay Road. Head downhill to the water. Shortly past the beach, turn right at the traffic light into Hammond Bay Road. Go 3¾ miles (6 kilometers) to McGuffie Road.
- From Highway 19 (Nanaimo Parkway) heading north or south, take Aulds Road Exit 28. As you cross Highway 19A, you are into the north end of Hammond Bay Road. Go 3 miles (5 kilometers) to McGuffie Road.
- From Parksville, heading south on Highway 19A (Oceanside Route), when 7 miles (12½ kilometers) south of Northwest Bay Road (south end), turn left into the north end of Hammond Bay Road. Go 3 miles (5 kilometers) to McGuffie Road. If you reach the pub, you have gone too far.

Feather stars

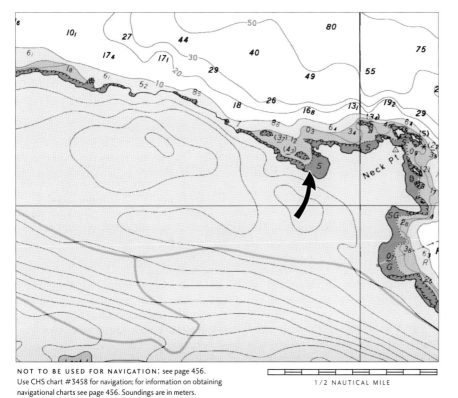

NOTES

NOT TO BE USED FOR NAVIGATION: see page 456.
Use CHS chart #3458 for navigation; for information on obtaining
navigational charts see page 456. Soundings are in meters.

1/2 NAUTICAL MILE

NECK POINT

BOAT DIVE or
KAYAK DIVE
GPS
49°14.225' N
123°57.706' W

SKILL
All divers

TIDE TABLE
Point Atkinson

WHY GO

It's a jungle. In the shallows, tall feathery stalks reach to the surface. Brown, purple and green kelps cover the rocks. Small white sea cucumbers poke between them. We see a tiny silver nudibranch on a kelp leaf. Deeper, tube-dwelling anemones pull slender, pale orange tentacles into the sand as we pass.

It's like swimming in a fish bowl, or an aquarium. So much life. Swarms of herring-spawn flock past, an underwater snowstorm. We see kelp greenlings galore; quillback rockfish; one 2-foot (¾-meter) lingcod and many juveniles; a shy, young cabezon. We are still. The cabezon slips from its hiding place beneath a leaf of purple bottom kelp and peers at us. We stare back. My buddy touches it.

Flocks of orange tube-snouts scoot past with their unique, jerky swimming motion. Moon jellies pulse around us. The bouldery crevices are perfect habitat for wolf-eels and octopuses. Look in all the cracks and beneath narrow ledges. Invertebrates thrive here too. Huge orange sunflower stars; slim red blood stars; fat sun stars; a rose star. Orange plumose anemones. Red-and-green painted anemones. Small urchins. Large sea cucumbers; and my buddy found a 1-inch (2½-centimeter) sea cucumber in a shell – many creatures are small and seem to be new life.

In winter you might see mammoth migrating Steller sea lions pass by.

Unloading gear at beach, south end of reef behind

BOTTOM AND DEPTHS

Rocky bottom at the south end of Neck Point descends gently to a wall that runs from the southern side of Neck Point to the northeast. Easy to follow under water. The wall is broken up with crevices and boulders that provide lots of hiding places. The south end of the wall bottoms out to sand at 20 to 30 feet (6 to 9 meters) and gradually deepens to 40 to 50 feet (12 to 15 meters). On a low-tide day, we found most life in 30 to 40 feet (9 to 12 meters).

A single rock juts from the water at the southern end of Neck Point. A pair of wolf-eels used to live in a crevice in that rock at a depth of 15 to 18 meters (50 to 60 feet). We did not see them. Local divers say they had not been there for months. Yet often wolf-eels either reinhabit their former home or new wolf-eels move in. It's worth looking. Do both. But don't spend too much time deep. The best dive is in shallower water on the wall west of that rock.

Also go to www.pac.dfo-mpo.gc.ca, Marine Mammals, Viewing Guidelines in the event you see sea lions.

HAZARDS

Boats. Listen for them and hug the bottom or wall until you reach the surface.

TELEPHONES

- On the water: VHF radio; if no VHF, try a cell phone.
- On land: outside grocery store on Hammond Bay Road, ⅓ mile (½ kilometer) north of Morningside Drive.

FACILITIES

Pit toilet at Neck Point Park parking lot. Launch ramp at Brechin Point. Charters out of Nanaimo. Dive-kayak rentals at Gabriola Island, Ladysmith and Duncan.

ACCESS

Neck Point is on Horswell Channel north of Nanaimo in Neck Point Park.

Charter out of Nanaimo or launch your own boat at Brechin Point in Nanaimo, and anchor on the north or south side of the point.

Kayak-divers can drive to Neck Point, park at the foot of Morningside Drive. Then paddle. Easiest on a day with no wind or gentle northwest wind. Kayak from Finn Beach beside the Neck Point Park parking lot – 15 minutes to the beach on the south side of Neck Point. Gear up and dive.

To get to Morningside Drive off Hammond Bay Road

• From the ferry at Departure Bay, 15 minutes to Neck Point. Follow signs toward Parksville. At the top of the hill, immediately after turning onto Highway 19A turn right into Departure Bay Road and head downhill to the water – if you pass a mall, you have gone too far. Shortly past the beach, at the traffic light, turn right into Hammond Bay Road. Go 3¼ miles (5⅓ kilometers) to the Neck Point Park sign. Turn right down Morningside Drive and go to the parking lot at the foot of it.

• Heading north on Trans-Canada Highway 1 from Victoria or from Duke Point, continue 3 minutes past the flaming torch at the north end of city center. Just past the turnoff to Vancouver ferry, turn right into Departure Bay Road. Head downhill to the water. Shortly past the beach, turn right at the traffic light into Hammond Bay Road. Go 3¼ miles (5⅓ kilometers) to the Neck Point Park sign. Turn right down Morningside Drive and to the parking lot at the foot of it.

• From Highway 19 (Nanaimo Parkway) heading north or south, take Aulds Road Exit 28. As you cross Highway 19A, you are into the north end of Hammond Bay Road. Go 3½ miles (5¾ kilometers) to the Neck Point Park sign. Turn left to the parking lot.

• From Parksville, heading south on Highway 19A (Oceanside Route), when 7¾ miles (12½ kilometers) south of Northwest Bay Road (south end), turn left into the north end of Hammond Bay Road. Go 3½ miles (5¾ kilometers) to the Neck Point Park sign at Morningside Drive. Turn left and go to the parking lot.

NOTES

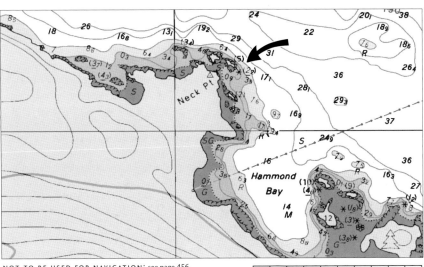

NOT TO BE USED FOR NAVIGATION: see page 456.
Use CHS chart #3548 for navigation; for information on obtaining navigational charts see page 456. Soundings are in meters.

1/2 NAUTICAL MILE

229

JESSE ISLAND

**BOAT DIVE or
KAYAK DIVE**
GPS
49°12.533′N
123°56.776′W

SKILL
All divers

TIDE TABLE
Point Atkinson

WHY GO

Would you believe rock falls and tunnels, walls covered with bright red colonial anemones and old bottles from the 1800s? All at one site?

Jesse Island is safe and easy to dive day or night. It is close to a dive-kayak launch point where you do not have to cross ferry traffic. This popular open-water certification site is picturesque for photographers and sightseers.

At night, it is particularly convenient to get organized for Jesse if you launch at closeby Brechin Civic Ramp. Sorting gear is easy under a bright light by the ramp.

There is so much life to see. Sea pens and sea whips are on the sand. My buddy who was taking photographs pointed out something I'd never seen before. A hermit crab had moved into a small shell, then a yellow sponge had covered the shell, dissolving the hermit crab's adopted home. A nudibranch was eating the sponge!

Locally honored as a reserve. Just take photographs.

BOTTOM AND DEPTHS

Carved sandstone arches and tunnels are along the north side, even above the surface. Depths at the base of the rock wall range from 30 feet (9 meters) at the

*Intricate rock walls
at Jesse Island*

northwest corner to 50 to 60 feet (15 to 18 meters) at the northeast end. Sandy bottom to the base of the wall. Bottles pitched off old Nanaimo coal ships may be found anywhere.

HAZARDS

Small boats, especially in summer. Departure Bay is heavily populated and salmon fishing is popular just outside the bay. Listen for boats and ascend close to the island.

TELEPHONES

• On the water: VHF radio; if no VHF, try a cell phone.
• On land:
1. Brechin Civic Ramp, water side of the Public Market.
2. Departure Bay (north end), at store across Departure Bay Road from beach.

FACILITIES

None on privately owned Jesse Island. Wheelchair-accessible toilets at Kin Park, north end of Departure Bay. Air fills in Nanaimo. Dive-kayak rentals at Gabriola, Ladysmith and Duncan.

Newcastle Provincial Marine Park, an island in Nanaimo Harbour, is nearby: campsite, picnic tables, drinking water and wharfage are at the park year-round. In summer, go to Newcastle from Nanaimo by pedestrian ferry that leaves from Maffeo-Sutton/Swy-a-lana Lagoon Park behind the civic arena. To reach the ferry, go to the foot of Bowen Road that becomes Comox Road as it nears the water. Year-round, go by your own boat to the south end of Newcastle and tie up at the dock. A superb set-up for camping and diving.

ACCESS

Jesse Island is in Departure Bay just north of Nanaimo on Vancouver Island. Charter out of Nanaimo or launch your own boat at Brechin Civic Ramp and go 1 nautical

230

mile north to Jesse Island. Kayak-divers could launch at the park at Departure Bay Beach and paddle just under 1 nautical mile east to Jesse Island. Pull your dive-kayak onto whatever ledge is exposed when you arrive, or anchor in a little bay at the northwest corner and dive along the north side of Jesse Island.

Wheelchair divers who paddle dive-kayaks could launch at Brechin Boat Ramp and paddle to Jesse Island, but watch out for the British Columbia ferries.

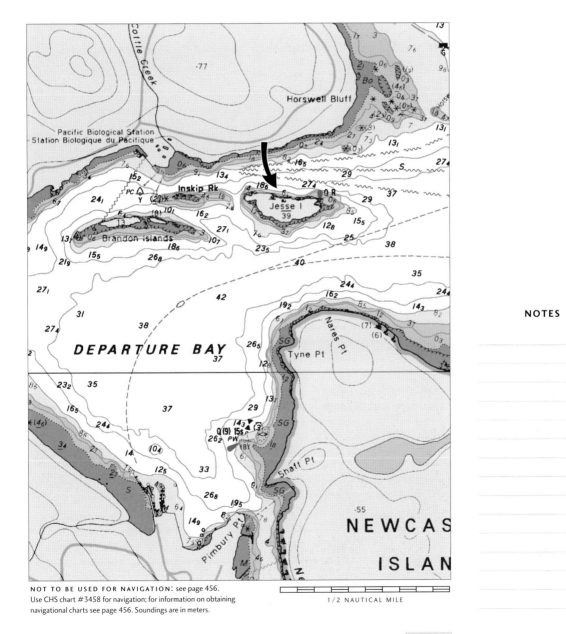

NOTES

NOT TO BE USED FOR NAVIGATION: see page 456.
Use CHS chart #3458 for navigation; for information on obtaining navigational charts see page 456. Soundings are in meters.

1/2 NAUTICAL MILE

231

BOAT DIVE
GPS
49°12.998′ N
123°53.433′ W

SKILL
Intermediate and expert divers and snorkelers

All divers with guide

TIDE TABLE
Point Atkinson

WHY GO

At Snake Island, good sightseeing shallow and deep and on the surface. We saw many invertebrates: kelp crabs, sea stars, nudibranchs. Bright orange dead man's finger sponges poke up through the bottom kelp in the shallows. Some anemones. Bull kelp at 30 feet (9 meters). Deeper, chimney sponges starting at 80 feet (24 meters). And a great many fish: lingcod and rockfish, some yelloweye rockfish, commonly called red snapper. Maybe it's myth, but locals say that the northwest corner of each island in the Nanaimo area is where you are most likely to see fish.

Also a great many harbor seals are in this area. Seals do not migrate – so you might see them year-round. And the chance of encounters is growing: the harbor seal population in the Strait of Georgia has increased from 2,100 in 1973 to 35,000 in 2003. You might meet them on the surface or under water but avoid approach-ing them – if possible, stay at least 110 yards (100 meters) away. At the time of writing Fisheries and Oceans Canada is proposing to amend the exist-ing Marine Mammal Regulations of the *Fisheries Act* to protect all mammals from disturbance because of too much contact with people and boats. In the meantime divers and boaters will want to check out

the viewing guidelines: see www.pac.dfo-mpo.gc.ca, click on Marine Mammals.

BOTTOM AND DEPTHS

Rocky bottom covered with bottom kelp and some bull kelp. Ledges and cliffs fall away fairly quickly all around the island. On the Nanaimo side, caves undercut the island at 140 feet (45 meters). The chart shows a drop to 400 feet (120 meters).

HAZARDS

Boats, bull kelp and wind. Listen for boats and ascend along the bottom all the way to the surface. Carry a knife for kelp.

TELEPHONES

- On the water: VHF radio; if no VHF, try a cell phone.
- On land: Brechin Civic Ramp, water side of the Public Market.

FACILITIES

None. Air fills and charters in Nanaimo. Launching at Brechin Point Civic Ramp.

ACCESS

Snake Island is near Nanaimo on Vancou-ver Island. It is 4 nautical miles northeast of Departure Bay just south of the Horse-shoe Bay–Departure Bay ferry route. Consider wind and tides when planning your dive. Snake Island is exposed to wind from all directions.

Charter out of Nanaimo or Gabriola Island. Or launch at Brechin Civic Ramp and go northeast to Snake Island. Anchor in the bull kelp at the northwest corner of the island or in the bay on the north side. If you leave a boat or other gear on the beach, beware of wash from passing ferries.

Yelloweye rockfish with a dark pigment mark

Seals at Snake Island

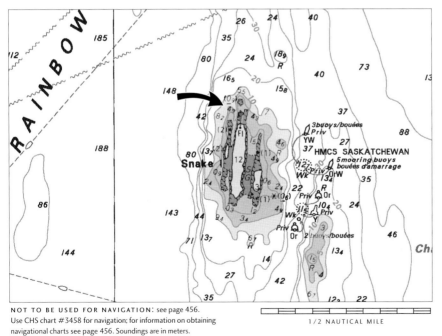

NOT TO BE USED FOR NAVIGATION: see page 456.
Use CHS chart #3458 for navigation; for information on obtaining
navigational charts see page 456. Soundings are in meters.

1/2 NAUTICAL MILE

NOTES

233

BOAT DIVE
GPS
49°12.979′ N
123°53.067′ W

SKILL
On exterior: intermediate and expert divers

On interior: intermediate and expert divers with penetration experience

TIDE TABLE
Point Atkinson

WHY GO

Excellent vessel for divers newly trained in penetration to practice skills on, for recreational divers to tour the outside of a ship and see marine life. The vessel is upright; there is extremely quick access to it on charters year-round and, beneath the surface, current is minimal making the dive easier than other dives with similar attractions.

Feather stars cover the railings around the mortar well. Orange and white plumose anemones, swimming scallops and tube worms cover the back deck where we started our dive. We move on to see more of the ship: pass the anti-aircraft gun and go up to the aft mast and the boiler room air down-takes. On the way we see painted greenlings, sculpins, quillback rockfish, shrimp, decorator crabs, moon jellies. We

Diver waits for gear, then steps off dive grid of Seastar – so easy

swim toward the bow, up the funnel and onto the flag deck; around the forward gun in front of the mast, then to the mast platform amidships. Time to head aft and up the buoy line we used for our descent.

The dive can be simple or complex: a recreational diver's tour was what I went for. I enjoyed the marine life, learned more about ships from my buddies.

More marine life appears all the time, and divers who have penetrated the vessel and gone deep report small cloud sponges in the bridge, a larger one inside the stack; sightings of juvenile yelloweye rockfish and a lingcod on eggs.

Divers trained in wreck penetration will find opportunities to practice skills on the vessel. Because the ship is upright, potential for diver disorientation is decreased. The fuel tanks are cut wide open, and the engine room has been opened for diver access. A great deal of information regarding main dive areas and entry and exit points for penetration is available in the "HMCS *Saskatchewan* Artificial Reef Map" by Bernie Kyle. It can be obtained from dive shops and from www.aquatic-realm.com.

This 366-foot (112-meter) destroyer escort was built in Esquimalt, British Columbia, commissioned February 16, 1963, decommissioned April 1, 1994. Work began to ready the *Saskatchewan* for sinking in 1996. The hull was carefully prepared: holes to provide light and exit points were cut throughout the vessel not only for diver safety and access but also to admit water equally on both sides of the ship when scuttling it. The final holes were cut on June 14, 1997. In less than four minutes, the *Saskatchewan* landed on the bottom upright.

BOTTOM AND DEPTHS

The top of the ship's mast is 60 to 70 feet (18 to 21 meters); the top deck near the mortar well opening is 95 to 105 feet (29 to 32 meters) deep. At high tides, the vessel rests on the muddy ocean floor at 130 feet (40 meters). The bow points south.

HAZARDS

Depth, surface current and the temptation to penetrate the vessel. Choose a low-tidal-exchange day to dive – not on a full moon, and dive near slack. Descend quickly down a marker buoy line to get through any surface current. Remember where it is for your ascent.

Divers not trained in wreck penetration should remain outside the vessel. Make a dive plan suitable for your skill level.

TELEPHONES

- On the water: VHF radio; if no VHF, try a cell phone.
- On land: Brechin Civic Ramp, water side of the Public Market.

FACILITIES

None. Charters daily out of Departure Bay and Nanaimo Harbour; air fills and a variety of accommodations in Nanaimo. Launching at Brechin Civic (Public) Ramp.

ACCESS

The *Saskatchewan* is located between Rainbow and Fairway channels, 1⅔ nautical miles east of Departure Bay, 200 yards (182 meters) east of Snake Island. Access is easy, 10 to 15 minutes from Departure Bay and Nanaimo Harbour.

Charter or launch your own boat and go to the site. The northernmost buoys mark the *Saskatchewan* – the southernmost buoys mark the *Cape Breton*. The vessels are nose-to-nose and 165 yards (150 meters) apart, with a 40-foot (12-meter) ridge between. Find the ship by its buoys, GPS location and a depth sounder.

On the surface the site is exposed: current and southeast wind can make it difficult to reach, especially in winter. Go quickly down the nearest buoy line to the *Saskatchewan*.

NOTES

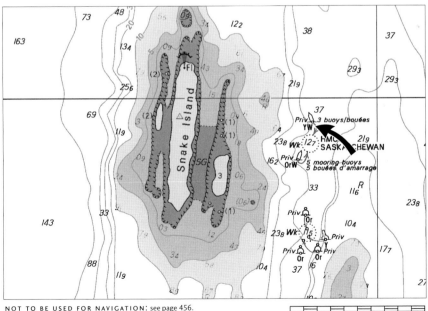

NOT TO BE USED FOR NAVIGATION: see page 456.
Use CHS chart #3447 for navigation; for information on obtaining navigational charts see page 456. Soundings are in meters.

1/5 NAUTICAL MILE

CAPE BRETON ARTIFICIAL REEF

BOAT DIVE
GPS
49°12.827' N
123°53.086' W

SKILL
On exterior: intermediate and expert divers

On interior: expert divers experienced in penetration

TIDE TABLE
Point Atkinson

WHY GO

The *Cape Breton* tempts divers trained in wreck penetration with big-time dares, yet provides safe and awe-inspiring sights for divers who want to scout the exterior. It invites exploration. Time after time after time.

On our recreational dive: easing down the buoy line amidships we saw her bulk slowly loom into view. On the ship, tiny transparent sea squirts were on the rail. And baby anemones – marine life is small, the size of the ship huge. The contrast! – surreal.

We went to the top of the captain's cabin then to the top of the funnel at 55 feet (17 meters). This felt real. Heading up the buoy line fringed with skeleton shrimp, again real. I wonder how many dives I will do on this one before I feel I have seen most of it? How many dives before the size does not take over?

Divers with penetration experience will find opportunities to explore large rooms: swim through the bridge at 75 feet (23 meters) – lots of natural light. Go to the bakery, the sick bay where there are autoclaves, and the officer's ward room – all signposted – none deeper than 110 feet (34 meters) at high tides. Closest access to these rooms is down the buoy line to

Sinking of the Cape Breton, Snake Island behind

the top of the bridge, the white buoy immediately north of the yellow buoy.

I've been told the helicopter deck at the stern is covered in plumose anemones and crinoids, and a large cabezon lives in the shaft that leads from the helicopeter deck to the lower decks.

Challenges for highly experienced experts: access to Burma Road on the *Cape Breton* is excellent. Mid-beam of the ship, safety cuts – or holes – are in both sides of the vessel to provide light and exit points. Openings to the main hatchway topside and to lower decks make movement in all directions possible at this major intersection. At high tides, the Burma Road is at a depth of 120 feet (35 meters). Visiting the engine room could be an epic feat: it is at 152 feet (46 meters) – the deepest room in the ship.

The *Cape Breton* is a former Canadian Victory Ship: length 441 feet (122 meters), beam 57 feet (17 meters), draft 28 feet (9 meters) – the last surviving relic of Canada's merchant navy vessels that served in World War II. It was launched as the HMS *Flamborough Head* in 1944. The Royal Canadian Navy purchased and commissioned it as the HMCS *Cape Breton* in 1953; and decommissioned it in 1964. Before scuttling, 30 feet of the stern was removed to be placed in a maritime museum in North Vancouver. The Artificial Reef Society of British Columbia purchased the ship in 1999. They, in cooperation with the Nanaimo Dive Association, prepared the ship for sinking on October 20, 2001.

Look for environmental monitoring points, numbered small white plastic squares on the main deck, inside and outside the vessel where marine life changes will be noted on a regular basis.

BOTTOM AND DEPTHS

The vessel sits upright on silty bottom. The bow points north. At high tides, the funnel is at 55 feet (17 meters); the bridge at 75 feet (23 meters); the main deck at 110 feet (34 meters). Outside the ship the bottom averages 130 feet (40 meters). The engine room is deeper; the *Cape Breton* dug a trench to rest in when it sank.

HAZARDS

Depth, the temptation to penetrate the vessel, surface current, visibility. Dive on a low tide and near slack. Recreational divers: plan your dive as carefully as those who penetrate the vessel do, and stick with your plan. Upon entering the water, go quickly down the nearest buoy line to escape surface current. Look around: at the end of your dive, ascend the same buoy line you went down and make a safety stop.

Visibility varies. Our group enjoyed exquisite conditions in summer: warm, sun shining, visibility 60 to 80 feet (18 to 24 meters). What a dive it must be in winter!

Before you go, you could check current conditions with a local charter operator.

TELEPHONES

• On the water: VHF radio; if no VHF, try a cell phone.
• On land: Brechin Civic Ramp, water side of the Public Market.

FACILITIES

None at the *Cape Breton*. A variety of services in Nanaimo; charters, launch ramps, dive shops and accommodations.

ACCESS

The *Cape Breton* is located east of Departure Bay; southeast of Snake Island: access is quick. Charter boats and ramp are near the ferry terminal, then 10 to 15 minutes by boat – and, weather permitting, available every day of the year.

Charter out of Departure Bay or Nanaimo, or launch your own boat and go to the ship. The northernmost buoys mark the *Saskatchewan* – southernmost buoys mark the *Cape Breton*. To find it, also use a depth sounder. On the surface the site is exposed: southeast wind can make it difficult to reach, especially in winter. But beneath the waves the scene becomes calm and welcomes divers.

NOTES

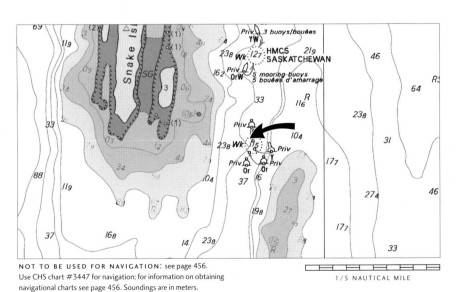

NOT TO BE USED FOR NAVIGATION: see page 456.
Use CHS chart #3447 for navigation; for information on obtaining navigational charts see page 456. Soundings are in meters.

1/5 NAUTICAL MILE

SHORE DIVE

SKILL
Intermediate and expert
divers over the wall

All divers in shallows
with guide

TIDE TABLE
Point Atkinson

WHY GO

It's a wall. Dark gray. Plunging from shore to nowhere-land at Orlebar Point on Gabriola Island.

We follow the dark valley to the edge, then fly out over it. Glide past snakelock anemones – they fling their pink fingers into space. The wall is covered with big scarlet dahlia anemones, pink ones, and fabulous white fluffy plumose anemones cascading out of sight. We see tiny hard pink hydrocorals, transparent sea peaches, orange cup corals, yellow staghorn bryozoans like hard coral. Chimney sponges from 50 feet (15 meters) on down. Small puffs of white cloud sponges. A granddaddy lingcod – 3 feet (1 meter) long. A tiger rockfish beneath a ledge. A yelloweye rockfish, also called red snapper, at 120 feet (37 meters). More fish too. Kelp greenlings, black rockfish, lots of quillback rockfish.

Drama shallow and deep. What is in the shallows? Kelp – more different types than you will probably ever see at another site. Iridescent blue kelp, feathery kelp like red shoestring potatoes. Broad-leafed bottom kelp hiding sea stars, striped red, white and brown. Tall brown trees of kelp, standing upright like ferns. Lots of purple urchins in the rocks. Incredible life. In the sand, tube-dwelling anemones and sea pens. In rocky tidepools, clusters of pink and gray anemones. In the surrounding open water, harbor seals. And we saw sea lions. For viewing guidelines see www.pac.dfo-mpo.gc.ca, click on Marine Mammals.

Going home, if it's low tide, turn right on Malaspina Drive to see the intriguing wind- and wave-carved rock walls of Gabriola – often called Malaspina Galleries.

BOTTOM AND DEPTHS

Rocky and sandy bottom 10 to 20 feet (3 to 6 meters) in the shallows at Orlebar. It's a five-minute swim over these shallows to the sheer wall of sandstone that starts at 45 to 55 feet (13 to 17 meters) and plummets to greater than 120 feet (37 meters).

HAZARDS

Current, bull kelp, wind and depth. Dive near slack. Visibility is best on outgoing tides. Wind from the north can create surf, making swimming through the kelp difficult. Carry a knife; if caught in kelp you can cut your way free. Early morning is best because of less wind and waves. Be aware of how long you are down – it's deep. On your way up, stop and enjoy the shallows.

TELEPHONES

• Surf Lodge, inside front hall and available 24 hours. It is ½ mile (¾ kilometer) back down the road toward the ferry.
• Outside general store at turnoff to mall at Berry Point Road and Ricardo Road junction: 2 miles (3¼ kilometers) back down Berry Point Road toward the ferry.

FACILITIES

Picnic tables near the site. Space for three or four cars to park. Air fills, camping, charters and launch ramp nearby on Gabriola Island and at Nanaimo.

ACCESS

Orlebar Point juts into Forwood Channel at the northeast corner of Gabriola Island. It is a 20-minute ferry ride from Nanaimo; then a 10-minute drive to Orlebar Point.

At Gabriola, drive up the hill to signs toward Gabriola Sands Provincial Park. Turn left. Follow Taylor Bay Road until it goes off to the left. You stay on the main road that is now Berry Point Road. Follow signs toward Surf Lodge. At Norwich Road, turn left. Continue along Berry Point Road, curving around beside the water. From Surf Lodge, go ½ mile (¾ kilometer) more to Orlebar Point. Two picnic tables are on the left. Just beyond the picnic tables, pull off facing the lighthouse. To dive the wall or the shallows, walk down the rocks on the left-hand side and go toward the lighthouse on Entrance Island. Entry is easier at high tides. To reach the wall, follow a compass bearing of 20°. Swim beneath the water for five minutes to an underwater valley or trench.

Then follow the fold in the rock on the left-hand side to the drop-off.

Snakelock anemone

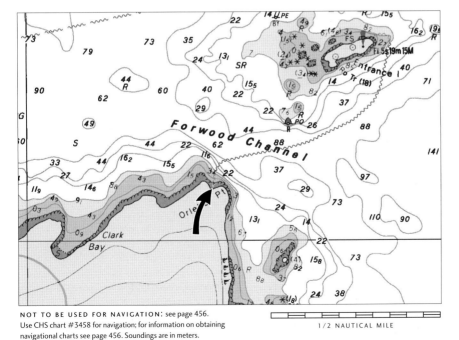

NOT TO BE USED FOR NAVIGATION: see page 456.
Use CHS chart #3458 for navigation; for information on obtaining navigational charts see page 456. Soundings are in meters.

1/2 NAUTICAL MILE

NOTES

—DODD NARROWS—

BOAT DIVE
GPS
49°08.187' N
123°49.158' W

SKILL
Expert divers and
snorkelers

CURRENT TABLE
Dodd Narrows

WHY GO

For a magic carpet ride – in reverse. Visit an inside-out world. Mauve aggregate anemones smother the rocks and you – not the carpet – are moving.

Ride the current up and down and over the gentle indentations in the smooth, smooth rocks near the surface. Heaps of purple sea stars border the tidal stream like big fat flowers. Most life is from the surface down to 60 feet (18 meters). We saw lingcod, large cabezons, a buffalo sculpin, kelp greenlings, schools of striped seaperch. Rock scallops, giant barnacles, swimming scallops, yellow staghorn bryozoans.

Encrusting sponges coat the rocks and millions of small white plumose anemones light up the depths, spill into side-canyons, scatter over the rocks and rocky walls at the edge of the river of sand on the floor of Dodd Narrows.

The deeper you go, the smaller the anemones and the less current there is. At the start of our dive we went deep, then hauled ourselves up the rocks and side-canyons for the magic carpet ride. Before the dive, we cruised past California sea lions at Harmac. After the dive, saw three black orcas, or killer whales, easily slip upstream against the ebbing current in Dodd Narrows. Remember viewing guidelines: www.pac.dfo-mpo.gc.ca, click on Marine Mammals.

BOTTOM AND DEPTHS

At the northern entry to Dodd Narrows, smooth rock ledges cascade down to sand bottom at 85 to 95 feet (25 to 29 meters) depending on tide height. Boulders at the base. South through the narrows, it shallows to a depth of 60 to 70 feet (18 to 21 meters). Narrow canyons cut the sides at intervals, provide shelter from the current. Bull kelp, in summer, in the eddies where you start and stop, at a depth of 25 to 35 feet (8 to 11 meters).

HAZARDS

Current, boats and broken fishing line. Bull kelp in summer. Carry a knife. Dive on slack with a "live" boat. Dive with a low exchange, and know it will still be a drift. Joan Point is like a nozzle: currents shoot through at 8 knots on the ebb; 9 knots on the flood. Throughout the dive find "hiding places" from the current in canyons and behind rocks. Use handholds and stay close to the bottom. Hang on! – to rocks on the bottom, to bull kelp in the shallows, to anything you can find to slow your drift. If you fly to the surface, it's an out-of-control roller-coaster ride and you are exposed to boats in the Narrows.

Safer in winter or weekdays in summer because of fewer small boats. When you surface look for tugboats hauling log booms, fish farms and other freight. Fish-farm pens may have nets trailing.

A charter operator says of Dodd Narrows: "A great drift at slack water".

TELEPHONES

• On the water: VHF radio; if no VHF, try a cell phone.
• On land:
1. Degnen Bay wharfhead, Gabriola Island, 5 nautical miles away.
2. Brechin Civic Ramp, water side of the Public Market, 6 nautical miles northwest to Departure Bay.

FACILITIES

None. Air fills, charters and launch ramps at Gabriola Island, Nanaimo, Departure Bay and Ladysmith.

ACCESS

Dodd Narrows is near Nanaimo on Vancouver Island. It is 11 nautical miles north of Ladysmith and the 49th Parallel; 6 nautical miles southeast of Departure Bay between Mudge and Gabriola Islands and Vancouver Island. You can charter at Degnen Bay on Gabriola and be at the dive in 15 minutes.

Charter or launch at Gabriola Island, Nanaimo, Departure Bay or Ladysmith and go 5 to 11 nautical miles to Dodd Narrows. If diving at the end of flood, you will find a sheltered place to enter in the kelp north of the marker at Joan Point; an exit eddy north of the power line. Dodd Narrows is 250 feet (75 meters) wide at its narrowest point south of Joan Point; it continues at that width for 600 feet (180 meters).

Before diving, check out approaching boats. An entire fish farm – ⅓ mile (½ kilometer) long – was towed through just before we were to begin our dive. We had to wait 15 minutes. No choice, our dive became more of a drift. You can dive on the ebb or flood.

The Mudge Island side of the narrows is favored by many; it drops off quickly. You can go deeper and hug the rock, when ascending, well out of the way of boats.

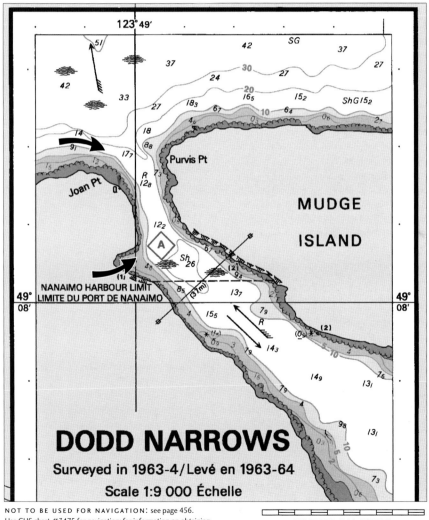

NOTES

NOT TO BE USED FOR NAVIGATION: see page 456.
Use CHS chart #3475 for navigation; for information on obtaining navigational charts see page 456. Soundings are in meters.

437 YARDS (400 METERS)

GABRIOLA PASSAGE

BOAT DIVE
GPS
49°07.637' N
123°42.400' W

SKILL
Expert divers and
snorkelers

CURRENT TABLE
Gabriola Pass

WHY GO

Shallow and packed with life, as only a spot with current can be, Gabriola Passage holds excitement for everyone – photographers, junk collectors and sightseers.

Gabriola Passage is where I made my first dive in a current-swept passage. I couldn't believe that the current never entirely stopped. But in retrospect, the place is not an alarming one for a first big-current experience. Two small points stick out into Gabriola Passage, giving you someplace to swim for in case the current becomes unmanageable.

What's there? To say what isn't in Gabriola Passage is easier. We saw so much that I couldn't pick out anything at first. There were lots of kelp greenlings, some rock scallops; orange sea cucumbers poking up between giant red and small green urchins. Tiger rockfish, huge lingcod, cabezons, yelloweye rockfish and octopuses share the shallow ledges tiering down into the passage. An old anchor, too.

The shallows are also incredibly rich. Large flower-like plumose anemones flourish in 5 feet (1½ meters) of water. Giant sea lemons, bright blue sea stars and little red rock crabs crowd the rocky shores. Even sea pens in small pockets of sand. Marvelous snorkeling.

BOTTOM AND DEPTHS

Rocky ledges tier down to a depth of 30 to 40 feet (9 to 12 meters). There are caves just east starting at Josef Point, where giant octopuses and lingcod live. One hole is 120 to 130 feet (37 to 40 meters) deep. Boulders and bull kelp. Some silt with the constant movement of current. The best visibility you can expect is 50 to 60 feet (15 to 18 meters) in winter.

HAZARDS

Very swift current, boats and bull kelp. Dive precisely on the slack on a small tidal exchange: currents up to 9 knots sometimes run through Gabriola. Be prepared to pull out of the dive if the current starts picking up. Currents do not always run when predicted. A pickup boat is required. Other boat traffic also uses the slack. Throughout your dive, listen for boats and ascend along the bottom all the way to shore well out of the way of those boats. Use a compass and watch the current to find your direction. When you surface, look for tugboats hauling log booms. Carry a knife for kelp.

TELEPHONES

• On the water: VHF radio; if no VHF, try a cell phone.
• On land:
1. Degnen Bay wharfhead, Gabriola Island, ¾ nautical mile away.
2. Brechin Civic Ramp, water side of the Public Market, 6 nautical miles northwest at Departure Bay.

FACILITIES

None at Valdes Island. Air fills, charters and launch ramps, camping and accommodations nearby at Gabriola Island and Nanaimo. Charters out of Thetis Island.

ACCESS

Gabriola Passage is northernmost of the three major passages between the Gulf Islands. Gabriola Island is on the north side and Valdes Island on the south side of Gabriola Passage. The other two major passes are Porlier and Active.

Charter out of Gabriola, Nanaimo, Vancouver or Victoria, and go to Gabriola Passage. Or launch at Degnen Bay on Gabriola Island and go ¾ nautical mile to the south side of the passage. The north side is also a popular dive and more out of the way of boat traffic.

Have a pickup boat follow you. A must.

Cabezon

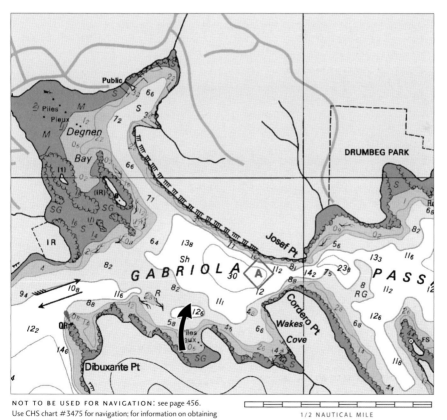

NOT TO BE USED FOR NAVIGATION: see page 456.
Use CHS chart #3475 for navigation; for information on obtaining
navigational charts see page 456. Soundings are in meters.

1/2 NAUTICAL MILE

NOTES

EVENING COVE

SHORE DIVE

SKILL
All divers and snorkelers

TIDE TABLE
Point Atkinson

WHY GO
Acres of sightseeing along this rocky reef reaching a long, thin finger out into Evening Cove.

Hordes of rockfish live around the rocks. Anemones, sea stars, sea peaches, little nudibranchs and sculpins. Octopuses on the reef if you can find them. Once on a night dive I found one too easily. I was poking along the rocks and saw one small white tentacle coiling and uncoiling. I suddenly realized I was almost lying on the mantle of a very large, very red octopus. It must have been 25 pounds (11 kilograms), at least, and in only 15 feet (5 meters) of water. The octopus was just as startled as I was. The shy creature tried to escape under a small ledge much too narrow to shelter it. I backed off and moved on.

Hermit crabs, flounders, pipefish and tube-dwelling anemones live on the sand on either side of the reef. Box crabs in the middle of the cove. A variety of life, easy access and lack of current add up to Evening Cove being a good dive anytime – day or night.

BOTTOM AND DEPTHS
A shallow ridge of rocks reaches out into Evening Cove. Some bottom kelp on the rocks. Sand scattered with small rocks on either side at 15 to 35 feet (5 to 11 meters). A very definite reef and shallow for a very long way out, finally going to 50 feet (15 meters) deep. Then a break, but farther out the reef comes up to 30 feet (9 meters) again.

HAZARDS
Poor visibility, small boats, lion's mane jellies in the fall. Listen for boats, use a compass and navigate back to shore under water. If you have seen jellies, check for stinging tentacles before removing masks and gloves.

Evening Cove

TELEPHONES

- Kumalockasun campground, down Tideview Road.
- Trans-Canada Highway 1, at gas station south of Brenton-Page Road.

FACILITIES

A chemical toilet and two picnic tables at Evening Cove. Camping and hot showers nearby at Kumalockasun campground.

ACCESS

Evening Cove is on Vancouver Island near Ladysmith. It is reached off Trans-Canada Highway 1 between Nanaimo and Ladysmith. Ten minutes off the highway to the dive.

From Highway 1, turn into Brenton-Page Road. When you come to the first "V", bear right following Brenton-Page Road. At the second one, continue straight on Shell Beach Road and go to the end of it; pass Tideview Road on the left. You will see the water. Turn right into Elliott Way and drive to Elliott's Beach Park; 15 or 20 cars can park. To find the reef, face the cove. Look for a small rocky point jutting into the water. The reef goes out from the small point on your right; it is 75 yards (70 meters) west of the road end. Follow the finger of rocks straight out into the cove.

To get to Brenton-Page Road
- From Nanaimo, go south on Highway 1 for 15 minutes. When 1 1/4 miles (2 kilometers) south of Nanaimo airport and just past the Cedar Road traffic light, you will see a sign to Mañana Lodge at Brenton-Page Road.
- From Ladysmith, head north on Highway 1; when 3 1/2 miles (5 3/4 kilometers) past the traffic light – 5 minutes past Ladysmith, look for a sign to Mañana Lodge at Brenton-Page Road.

NOTES

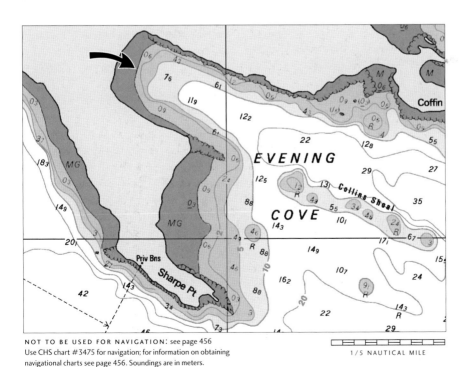

NOT TO BE USED FOR NAVIGATION: see page 456
Use CHS chart #3475 for navigation; for information on obtaining navigational charts see page 456. Soundings are in meters.

1/5 NAUTICAL MILE

245

MAPLE BAY UNDERWATER SANCTUARY

SHORE DIVE

SKILL
All divers

TIDE TABLE
Fulford Harbour

WHY GO

Maple Bay is popular for night diving, and offers a very pleasant afternoon of sightseeing and photography. One of the beauties of Maple Bay is that the rocky reef is shallow, and therefore usually bright enough for available light photography, while the wall is moderately deep. Fish, octopuses and a variety of invertebrates are in the bay.

Diving here we saw many nudibranchs. My buddy was kept busy taking pictures. We saw giant silver nudibranchs – gray with white tips. Several spotted nudibranchs and a sea lemon sitting on the edge of broadleaf kelp. Large orange plumose anemones, small white anemones, shrimp all over the place. And tube-snouts jerkily moving through the shallows. Seaperch hovering around the reef. Some little golden fish I had not seen before. Rockfish hiding in crevices along the wall. Lingcod too. But no taking of marine life: by municipal bylaw, this a marine sanctuary.

In March, April or May, large schools of opalescent squids visit Maple Bay to spawn, to lay eggs in the shallows. Adults can be up to 11 inches (28 centimeters) in length. At that time – I'm told – a night dive with the bioluminescent squids is sensational. But you have to be lucky. Look in the tidal zone near the dock for egg sacs the size of your thumb, check the beach to see if they are there. Timing is all-important and varies from year to year.

BOTTOM AND DEPTHS

The shallow reef is about 100 feet (30 meters) beyond the dock. It runs parallel to the shore, is 30 to 40 feet (9 to 12 meters) deep and is a jumble of rocks and dens – bottom kelp all over the top of it. The deeper rock wall reaches almost straight out into Maple Bay: it starts at 20 to 30 feet (6 to 9 meters) and gradually deepens to 50 to 60 feet (15 to 18 meters), depending on tide height. On the south side of the dock, eelgrass on the sandy bottom out to the reef.

HAZARDS

Small boats and poor visibility in summer. Lion's mane jellies in the fall. When ascending, listen for boats; if you hear one, stay down until it passes. Or better yet, use a compass and navigate all the way back to shore under water. If you and your buddy have seen any stinging jellies, check one another for tentacles on the surface.

TELEPHONE

Outside store at Maple Bay.

FACILITIES

Flush toilets at the beach park north of the government dock, summer only. Air fills and dive guiding for shore dives and boat dives in Duncan.

ACCESS

Maple Bay is near Duncan on Vancouver Island. The dive is 10 minutes off Trans-Canada Highway 1.

Heading north or south on Highway 1, go to Duncan. Turn east at Trunk Road, and follow signs to Maple Bay. Trunk Road becomes Tzouhalem Road then Maple Bay Road and goes to the water. At the bottom of the hill, turn left to the government dock. Space for 10 or 15 cars to park.

To find the reef, at the time of writing, there is an underwater line to follow to the shallow end of the rock wall that goes straight out into Maple Bay. To find this line that is in 30 to 40 feet (9 to 12 meters), depending on tide height, enter at the north end of the dock. Descend and go straight toward the pub dock that is to the right of the launch ramp. When you find the underwater line, turn right and follow it to the wall.

If no line is in place, set your compass toward Paddy Mile Stone, the point on your right, jump off the north arm of the dock and swim out 100 feet (30 meters) under water to the middle of the shallow rocky reef. Turn left to the wall. Right to the end of the shallow reef.

*Opalescent squids mating
on bed of freshly laid eggs*

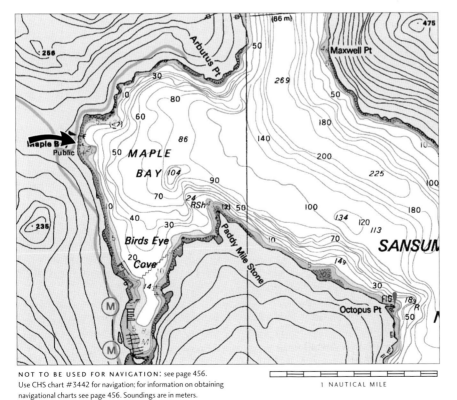

NOT TO BE USED FOR NAVIGATION: see page 456.
Use CHS chart #3442 for navigation; for information on obtaining
navigational charts see page 456. Soundings are in meters.

1 NAUTICAL MILE

NOTES

BURIAL ISLET

BOAT DIVE

GPS
48°46.192' N
123°33.821' W

SKILL
Expert divers

Intermediate divers
with guide

CURRENT TABLE
Active Pass
• Slack before flood:
  Subtract 35 minutes

• Slack before ebb:
  Add 25 minutes

Lion's mane jelly

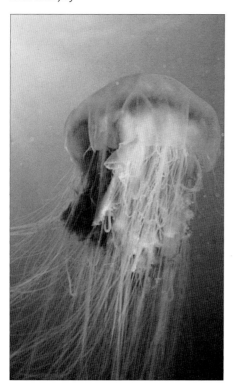

WHY GO

Life upon life encrusts this pyramid of rock beneath the sea. On the surface, it's a barren islet with a marker on top that is like a feather in its rounded skullcap. Around it a "whirlwind" of currents; but almost always a quiet side somewhere.

Makes for a rich dive. We saw a Puget Sound king crab, yellow staghorn bry-ozoans, kelp crabs, lots of quillback rockfish, a buffalo sculpin. Christmas anemones. Plump white anemones. Large orange plumose anemones. Swimming scallops. Alabaster nudibranchs. A sea lemon. Giant barnacles. Purple urchins. Painted greenlings, kelp greenlings, a black rockfish, lingcod, a red Irish lord and lots of pretty little white plumose anemones. Orange cup corals and rock scallops with orange "lips" dot the rocks. We saw three harbor seals on the surface. Take care not to come closer than 110 yards (100 meters) to seals. Look for wolf-eels.

BOTTOM AND DEPTHS

The rock pinnacle called Burial Islet is exposed at all tides. It gradually drops away in stairstep ledges, a pyramid beneath the sea. You can choose your depth. Bull kelp at 20 to 30 feet (6 to 9 meters) and a bright shell bottom scattered with boulders and rocks on the south-west side. Ledges down to a depth of 80 to 90 feet (24 to 27 meters).

HAZARDS

Current, boats and transparent fishing line. Bull kelp in summer, lion's mane jellies in the fall. Dive on slack; plan your dive, date and time carefully. Listen for boats; when ascending, hug the islet all the way to the surface. Carry a knife for fishing line and kelp. If you see any jellies, check one another before removing masks and gloves. At Burial Islet I was stung by one for the first time ever. I swam into an almost transparent tentacle that grazed my upper lip and the stinging sensation lasted nearly 24 hours.

TELEPHONES
• On the water: VHF radio; if no VHF, try a cell phone.
• On land: outside store at Maple Bay.

FACILITIES

None. Charters out of Sidney, Thetis Island and Nanaimo. Air fills at Duncan and Nanaimo. Launch ramps at Maple, Genoa and Cowichan bays and Sidney on Vancou-ver Island; also at Ganges, Saltspring Island.

ACCESS

Burial Islet is on the east side of Sansum Narrows close to Saltspring Island and near Maple Bay on Vancouver Island.

Charter, rent a boat or launch your own boat at Vancouver or Saltspring islands and go to the barren islet with only a marker on it. Anchoring, beware of shallow big rocks at the southwest corner. There is almost always an eddy this side too. Anchor so you are not pushed onto the islet by the current. To Burial Islet:
• From Maple Bay, head east and south through Sansum Narrows. It is 4 nautical miles.
• From Genoa or Cowichan bays, go 3 nautical miles.
• From Sidney, cross Satellite Channel and go north of Moses Point to Burial Islet.
• From Ganges, go south through Captain Passage to Satellite Channel, then north to Burial Islet.

Plan dive date and time as follows. The current is different at Sansum Narrows: choose to dive on a day with a big exchange as slack is more predictable then, probably because wind has a greater effect on current on days when a small exchange follows slack.

1. Look at the Tide Table for Fulford Harbour to see what kind of exchange is happening. Pick a big one. It is best on low slack, but high slack will do.
2. Look at the Current Table for Active Pass, corrections for Sansum Narrows.

a. If diving at low slack, note the time of the turn to flood and add 25 minutes to it.
b. If diving at high slack, note the time of the turn to ebb and subtract 35 minutes from it.
3. In summer, also consider daylight saving time (add 1 hour).
4. Be ready to dive 30 minutes before the corrected time of the turn. Then, at Burial, if you still hit it wrong, look for the side of the islet with the back eddy where you can hide from the current.

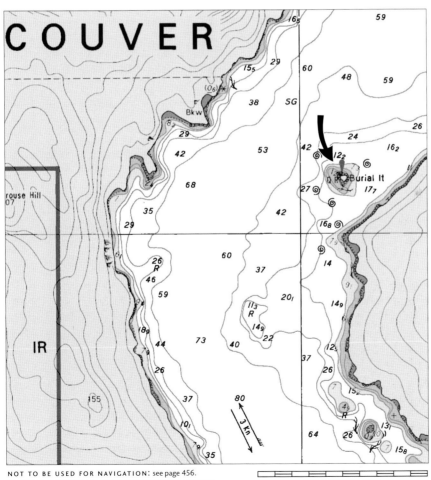

NOT TO BE USED FOR NAVIGATION: see page 456.
Use CHS chart #3478 for navigation; for information on obtaining navigational charts see page 456. Soundings are in meters.

1/2 NAUTICAL MILE

NOTES

Southern Gulf Islands including Galiano, Pender and Saltspring

Lingcod and diver watch octopus on rock

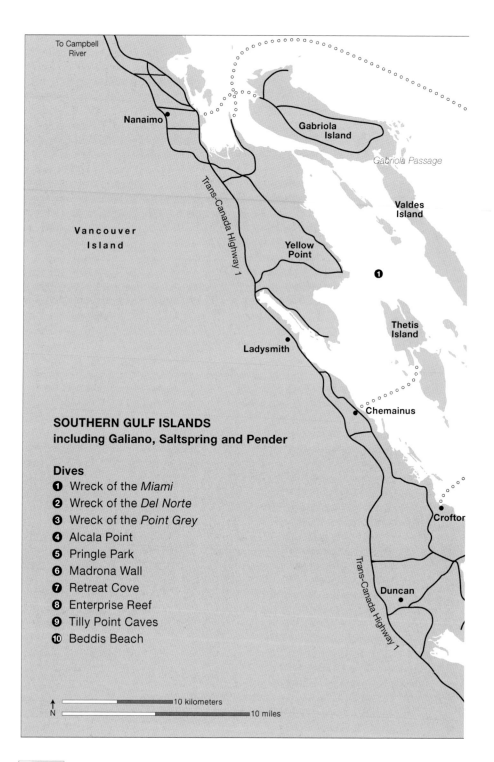

To Campbell
River

Nanaimo

Gabriola
Island

Gabriola Passage

Valdes
Island

Vancouver
Island

Trans-Canada Highway 1

Yellow
Point

Thetis
Island

Ladysmith

Chemainus

SOUTHERN GULF ISLANDS
including Galiano, Saltspring and Pender

Dives
❶ Wreck of the *Miami*
❷ Wreck of the *Del Norte*
❸ Wreck of the *Point Grey*
❹ Alcala Point
❺ Pringle Park
❻ Madrona Wall
❼ Retreat Cove
❽ Enterprise Reef
❾ Tilly Point Caves
❿ Beddis Beach

Croftor

Trans-Canada Highway 1

Duncan

10 kilometers

N

10 miles

STRAIT

OF

GEORGIA

To Vancouver

Highway 99

Fraser River
Delta

To I-5,
Bellingham
and Seattle

Tunnel

Tsawwassen

Highway 17

2

Porlier Pass

3

4 North
Galiano

5

6

**Galiano
Island**

7

*Montague
Harbour*

Sturdies
Bay

Active Pass

Vesuvius

*Long
Harbour*

Mayne

8

Crofton

Ganges

*Ganges
Harbour*

Island

Village
Bay

**Saltspring
Island**

10

*Otter
Bay*

**Pender
Islands**

Saturna
Island

*Thieves
Bay*

*Port
Browning*

*Fulford
Harbour*

*Bedwell
Harbour*

9

To Victoria

To Victoria

**Swartz
Bay**

SERVICE INFORMATION

Tide and Current Information
- *Tide and Current Tables, Volume 5: Juan de Fuca Strait and Strait of Georgia,* Canadian Hydrographic Service print annual
- *Current Atlas: Juan de Fuca Strait to Strait of Georgia,* purchase one time. Use with *Murray's Tables* or *Washburne's Tables,* purchase annually; privately produced publications available at marine equipment and supplies stores.
- www.lau.chs-shc.gc.ca: Tide and Current Tables for all of Canada. Go to the web site: click on Pacific; General Information; Tide and Currents, Data Available; then Tide Tables available in PDF form. Select Volume 5 and click on the tide or current table desired – both are on the same list on the pdf.

Weather Information
- Canadian Coast Guard: 1-866-823-1110, speak with a person, 24 hours.
- Canadian Coast Guard (Victoria): Continuous Marine Broadcast (CMB) recorded, 24 hours; listen for weather in Strait of Georgia or Haro Strait, telephone Victoria (250)363-6492.
- Environment Canada, marine weather line: recorded, 24 hours; listen for weather in Haro Strait, the Strait of Georgia and Saturna Island: telephone Victoria (250)363-6717
- www.weatheroffice.ec.gc.ca

Diving Emergency Telephone Numbers
On land and water:
- Call 911, request "ambulance" and say, "I have a scuba diving emergency".
- Vancouver General Hospital; for 24-hour, 7-day-a-week response: telephone (604)875-5000 and say, "I want the hyperbaric physician on call".

On the water:
- VHF radio: Call Coast Guard radio, Channel 16 and say, "I have a scuba diving emergency".
- Cell phone: 911, *16 or *311 and say, "I have a scuba diving emergency".

If emergency or medical personnel are unfamiliar with scuba diving emergencies, ask them to telephone DAN (Divers Alert Network) at (919)684-4326. No money for a long distance call? Dial DAN collect at 011-919-684-4326 and say, "I have a scuba diving emergency".

Mark emergency location before leaving scene: other divers might be down.

How to Go

To reach Galiano, Mayne, Pender or Salt-spring islands via a British Columbia ferry:

- From Vancouver Island, go by ferry from Swartz Bay, which is at the northern tip of the Saanich Peninsula, 20 miles (30 kilometers) north of Victoria. Sail to Galiano, Mayne or Pender – each of these islands has no choice of harbour. To Salt-spring, sail from Swartz Bay to Fulford Harbour; or sail from Crofton (south of Nanaimo) to Vesuvius Bay on Saltspring.
- From the mainland, go by ferry from Tsawwassen, which is 20 miles (30 kilo-meters) south of Vancouver, to any one of the Gulf Islands. Sailing to Saltspring from the mainland, you go to Long Har-bour. Reservations are recommended, especially on weekends, for cars between the mainland and the Gulf Islands.
- You can sail from Tsawwassen to Swartz Bay and connect to the Gulf Islands at the Tsawwassen/Swartz Bay terminal; ask for a through-fare ticket at Tsawwassen. Likewise, you can sail from Fulford Harbour at Saltspring to Swartz Bay and connect to Tsawwassen at the Swartz Bay/Tsawwassen fare; ask when you buy your ticket at Fulford Harbour.

Tourist Information

Tourism BC
- Toll-free throughout North America: 1-800-435-5622
- From all other locations: (250)387-1642 www.hellobc.com

Ferry Information

British Columbia Ferry Services (BC Ferries)
- Toll-free throughout North America: 1-888-223-3779
- From all other locations: (250)386-3431 www.bcferries.com

At the time of writing the following infor-mation applies – but frequent changes occur; it would be wise to check current requirements on BC Ferries web page before every trip.

Rules Regarding Scuba Tanks on BC Ferries
Persons transporting scuba tanks contain-ing compressed air, full or partially full, are required under Canadian law to declare dangerous goods at the terminal or to a vessel officer. Persons transporting scuba tanks with the valves removed do not need clearance. All pressurized tanks with a UN 3156 sticker, indicating nitrox or mixed gases, are taboo – remove the valve.

Expedite Dangerous Goods clearance at the ferry ticket booth – complete a Dangerous Goods Shipping Document prior to arrival. Obtain it from the web at home or a library: Go to www.bcferries.com: select Travel Planning; click on Carrying Dangerous Goods, then For the General Public. Download Dangerous Goods Shipping Document and complete it: include your name, home address and phone number; Class 2; UN 1002, which indicates compressed air; number of cylinders you are transporting and quantity in each one: most tanks are 80 cubic feet/2.27 cubic meters.

(To calculate quantity in scuba tanks: 1 cubic foot=0.0283168466 cubic meters.)

Arrive at least 30 minutes prior to intended sailing time.

Prearranged Dangerous Goods Clearance Requires 48 Hours
Complete a Dangerous Goods Shipping Document as described above and fax it at least 48 hours in advance of intended sailing time to Long Harbour Terminal: fax (250)537-2895.

GALIANO ISLAND

• CHARTERS AND AIR STATION

Riprunner
Riprunner Recreational Dive Charters
1266 Porlier Pass Road
Site 13, Comp 13
Galiano Island BC V0N 1P0
(250) 539-2551
E-mail: digammon@telus.net
*(Year-round charters range from Active Pass
to Porlier Pass: sites include wrecks of the
Del Norte and the Point Grey, Alcala Point,
Matthews Point – with a swim through! – and
Enterprise Reef. All dives with live boat and
underwater guiding: for experienced buddy
teams – maximum two divers with at least
20 to 60 dives. Dive charters with air fills on
weekends: two weeks' advance notice; nitrox
available if requested when booking dives.
Air fills for drop-ins – also only with two-
week advance notice.)*

• LAUNCH RAMP

Montague Provincial Park
RR 1, south end of island
Galiano Island BC V0N 1P0
(250) 539-2115
*(Launch for a fee for Trincomali Channel:
concrete ramp, good at high tides. Wheelchair-
accessible pit toilets. Telephone in center of
park at park headquarters. From the ramp, go
⅕ mile [⅓ kilometer] straight up the road;
turn right and right again to the telephone.)*

From the ferry landing, follow signs to
Montague Beach. Go 4 miles (7 kilometers)
along Montague Road; you will see the
water. Montague Beach Marina is at the
left. You bear right up Montague Park
Road and go to the end of it.

• TOURIST INFORMATION

Galiano Island Visitor Info Centre
PO Box 73
Galiano Island BC V0N 1P0
(250) 539-2233
1-866-539-2233: Toll-free throughout
   North America
www.galianoisland.com

SALTSPRING ISLAND
• LAUNCH RAMPS
Centennial Boat Launch Ramp
127 Fulford-Ganges Road
Ganges BC V8K 2T9
(250)537-5711
E-mail: ssha@saltspring.com
(Launch for a fee for Captain Passage and Trincomali Channel; or Swanson Channel: concrete ramp, good at all except extreme low tides. Parking for a fee. Flush toilets west side of parking lot. Telephones: one block east and one block north of ramp outside Harbour Building. Outside Visitor Info Centre: at corner of Lower Ganges Road and Hereford Avenue. Go east on Lower Ganges Road.)

Located between Centennial Park and Grace Point Square, the ramp parking lot is on the water side of Fulford-Ganges Road and is marked with a can-buoy. A colorful mural of undersea life is painted around the bottom of it. The structure is 22 feet (7 meters) high.

Saltspring Marina Ramp
Head of Ganges Harbour
124 Upper Ganges Road
Ganges BC V8K 2S2
(250)537-5810
1-800-334-6629: Toll-free throughout
    North America
(Launch for a fee for Captain Passage and Trincomali Channel; or Swanson Channel: concrete ramp, good at all tides. Also wheelchair-accessible toilets; hot showers and at the pub, two fireplaces to warm up in front of. Telephone at top of wharf on outside wall of marina rental office.)

Ramp is east of Moby's Marine Pub in Ganges. Marina office west of Moby's.

Long Harbour Ramp
Long Harbour, east side of Saltspring
(Launch free – good for hand-launchable boats only – for Captain Passage and Trincomali Channel; or Swanson Channel. Roadside parking for one car. Toilet and telephones at Long Harbour ferry terminal.)

Located off Long Harbour Road on Quebec Drive. Go to a "T"; curve right. At the next "T", turn left and go downhill to the water.

Hudson Point Ramp
Northeast side of Saltspring, off North
    Beach Road
(Launch free for northern Trincomali Channel: steep concrete and gravel ramp. Good for hand-launchable small boats. Parking for one car. Toilets and telephones back at Moby's Marine Pub in Ganges.)

From Ganges, follow signs toward Walker's Hook. Head north on Upper Ganges Road, then Robinson Road and Walker's Hook Road to North Beach Road. When ½ mile (¾ kilometer) past Fernwood Road and the wharf, you will find space for one car to park beside the ramp. Heading south, look for it 1 mile (1 ¾ kilometers) past Castillou Way.

• TOURIST INFORMATION
Salt Spring Island Visitor Info Centre
121 Lower Ganges Road
Salt Spring Island BC V8K 2T1
(250)537-5252
1-866-216-2936: Toll-free throughout
    North America
www.saltspringtoday.com

PENDER ISLANDS

• DAY AND MULTIPLE-DAY CHARTERS, AIR FILLS, EQUIPMENT AND BOAT RENTALS

Sound Passage and *Sound Wave*
Sound Passage Adventures
Located at Port Browning Marina Resort
PO Box 4, Pender Island BC V0N 2M0
(250)629-3920
1-877-629-3930: Toll-free throughout
    North America
www.soundpassageadventures.com
*(Charters year-round out of Port Browning
Marina to the Mackenzie, G.B. Church,
Turn Point, Stuart Island and north to
Enterprise Reef. Also pick up dive charter
groups at Mayne and Saltspring islands and
Port Sidney, Vancouver Island.*

*Air fills, dive equipment rentals and high-
speed water taxi from Port Sidney to Pender.
Dive packages with boat dives, accommodation at Poets Cove Resort B&B – or camping
in summer. Additional activities: sailing and
power boating courses; fishing, whale watching and eco-tourism trips. Boat rentals: sailing and power boats.)*

To reach Port Browning Marina: From
Otter Bay follow signs toward South Pender.
Immediately past the shopping center,
turn left down Hamilton Road.

• LAUNCH RAMPS

Otter Bay Marina
RR 1, 2311 MacKinnon Road
Pender Island BC V0N 2M1
(250)629-3579
*(Launch for a fee at Swanson Channel from
North Pender for west side of island. Concrete
ramp, good at medium to high tides. Restrooms
with flush toilets and hot showers. Swimming
pool in summer. Telephone at top of ramp.)*

Located at Otter Bay: 110 yards (100
meters) past the ferry terminal exit, turn
right at Otter Bay Marina sign.

Port Browning [Browning Harbour]
    Public Ramp
Foot of Hamilton Road, North Pender
*(Launch for east or west sides of islands: for
Plumper Sound on the east side or through
the canal between the islands to Bedwell
Harbour and Swanson Channel on the west
side. Concrete ramp covered with gravel, good
at higher tides; the gravel can be difficult for
2-wheel drives. Take chains.*

*Telephone available 24 hours, outside
pub at nearby Browning Harbour Marina
Resort. Also at the resort: hot showers, restrooms, camping, cabins, B&B, café, liquor
store, pub and ample moorage available
year-round – swimming pool in summer only.)*

From Otter Bay follow signs toward
South Pender. Immediately past the shopping center, turn left down Hamilton Road.

Thieves Bay Public Ramp
Foot of Anchor Way, North Pender Island
*(Launch on the west side of island for Swan-
son Channel. Concrete ramp, good at all
except extreme low tides. Picnic tables in
large, grassy park. Lots of parking space. Pit
toilet next to the road just past the ramp
turnaround. Telephone located 35 paces
down the road, left-hand side of the ramp.)*

From the ferry terminal, follow Otter
Bay Road (yellow lines) to the first "T"
junction at the stop sign. Turn right onto
Bedwell Harbour Road; past a shopping
center and Prior Park the road name
changes to Canal Road. Go on Canal
Road to Aldridge Road and bear right.
Aldridge becomes Schooner Way. Follow
Schooner Way for 4¾ miles (7¾ kilometers) through numerous turns, going left
at the fire hall toward Magic Lake. At the
first right-hand turn past the fire hall, turn
right on Privateers Road to Anchor Way
and the ramp.

MAYNE ISLAND
• LAUNCH RAMP
Village Bay Ramp

West side of island, foot of Callaghan
   Crescent

*(Launch free for Active Pass and the south-
east end of Trincomali Channel: concrete ramp,
good at high tides. Toilets and telephone at
ferry landing: telephone is in the covered
foot-passenger walkway to Berth #1, near
the water.)*

   Immediately off ferry, turn right. Go
down Dalton Road, right onto Mariners
Way, then right into Callaghan Crescent to
the water. From ferry, ⅔ mile (1 kilometer)
to Callaghan Crescent.

VANCOUVER ISLAND
• LAUNCH RAMPS FOR GULF ISLANDS
Ladysmith Fisherman's Wharf and
   Boat Ramp

837 Ludlow Road, PO Box 130

Ladysmith BC V9G 1A1

(250)245-7511

www.ladysmithfishermanswharf.com

*(Launch free for northern Trincomali Channel:
concrete ramp, good at all tides. Restrooms
with showers in office building beside wharf;
telephone outside office building. Large
parking area.)*

   At traffic light, north end of Ladysmith,
turn toward the sea onto Ludlow Road.
Cross the railway tracks, and curve right
following a sign to a marina. At the stop
sign, do not bear left downhill to the log
sort. Continue straight on Ludlow Road
and downhill to the end of it.

Chemainus Municipal Ramp

Foot of Maple Street, Chemainus

*(Launch for a fee for Gulf Islands: concrete
ramp, good at all tides. Restrooms at park.
Telephone ⅓ mile [½ kilometer] away at ferry
terminal foot of Oak Street at Esplanade
Street. From ramp, go to Oak Street. Turn
left and to the ferry.)*

   Located 5 minutes off Trans-Canada
Highway 1, between Ladysmith and Duncan:
go to the south end of Chemainus Road
by way of Henry Road. The Highway 1
turnoff onto Henry Road is 7½ miles
(12 kilometers) south of the center of
Ladysmith, 10 miles (16¼ kilometers)
north of the bridge in Duncan. At Henry
Road, follow signs for 1 mile (1½ kilome-
ters) to Chemainus Road. Turn left onto
Chemainus: go ¾ mile (1¼ kilometers) to
Cedar Street; turn right and go to Oak
Street; turn right again and go to Maple
Street. Turn left into Maple and to the water.

All of this Service Information is subject
to change.

259

WRECK OF THE MIAMI

BOAT DIVE
GPS
49°02.407' N
123°42.742' W

SKILL
All divers

TIDE TABLE
Fulford Harbour

WHY GO

The *Miami* is a good safe wreck to dive – it is the skeleton of a ship. It's shallow, easy to find and easy to dive.

The *Miami* was a 320-foot (100-meter) steel freighter that carried coal. On January 25, 1900, it grounded on White Rocks, now named Miami Islet, and went down. Sport divers have been exploring the *Miami* since 1956. In addition to the fun of swimming around and over a skeleton ship, you might see coal and you'll see lots of marine life around the wreck. Rockfish hide under the shadow of the hull. Lingcod use it for shelter in spawning season. Millions of small white plumose anemones dot the dark rounded ribs. In winter, look for hooded nudibranchs, also called lion nudibranchs. We saw giant barnacles, sea peaches and painted greenlings. Giant nudibranchs between the broadleaf bottom kelp. Millions of feathery, tube-dwelling anemones and clams in the silty sand around the *Miami*.

BOTTOM AND DEPTHS

The reef is silt-covered smooth rock and slopes gently down to a depth of 50 to 60 feet (15 to 18 meters). On summer low tides a large portion of the *Miami* used to project above water. The main hull rested on the bottom at 25 to 35 feet (8 to 11 meters). The ship broke its back over the ledge. Some of it slipped down the western slope and some parts were in 50 to 60 feet (15 to 18 meters) of water. Now the hull is almost totally disintegrated, and because of tidal effect it is very widely spread across the reef. It changes all the time, which means you might still see coal.

HAZARDS

Current, wind, poor visibility and the wreck itself. Dive on the slack. Visibility can be poor in summer because of plankton growth, and at any time of year if too many divers stir up the silt. A still, sunny day in winter is the best time to dive. Be careful of sharp metal projections from the wreck.

TELEPHONES

• On the water: VHF radio; if no VHF, try a cell phone.
• On land:
1. Ladysmith government wharf.
2. North Galiano, across road from the wharf and float at Spanish Hills.

FACILITIES

None at Miami Islet. Charters out of Gabriola, Galiano and Pender islands; Sidney, Victoria, Nanaimo and Vancouver. Launch ramps at Ladysmith and Chemainus on Vancouver Island and at Gabriola and Galiano islands.

ACCESS

The *Miami* rests on a reef north of Miami Islet in Trincomali Channel, 1 nautical mile northwest of Pilkey Point on Thetis Island. Wind from any direction can make it difficult to reach the *Miami* which is in an extremely exposed position.

Charter or launch your own boat and go to the red buoy that marks the reef. We launched an inflatable at Yellow Point on Vancouver Island and headed east for 1½ nautical miles to the reef. Do not tie up to the marker. It is a federal offense to make fast to a marker or tamper with any aid to navigation. Do not search for the wreck with side-scan sonar as the hull has disintegrated too much to find it with that. Be careful not to hit the wreck. It dries at 11-foot (3-meter) tides. On a low tide you may spot it from your boat. If not, line up on a direct line between the red marker, Miami Islet and Pilkey Point. Anchor on that line near the bull kelp 100 feet (30 meters) south of the red marker and go down. To find the wreckage, swim south under water along the west side of the reef. Take a light!

From Miami Marker, looking south toward Pilkey Point on Thetis Island

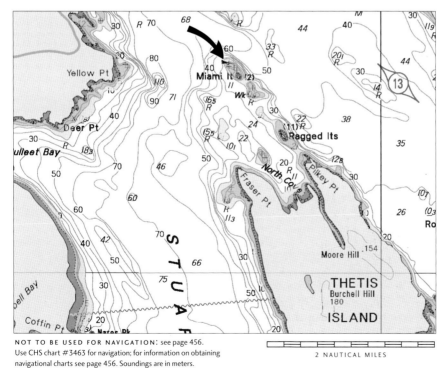

NOT TO BE USED FOR NAVIGATION: see page 456.
Use CHS chart #3463 for navigation; for information on obtaining
navigational charts see page 456. Soundings are in meters.

2 NAUTICAL MILES

NOTES

WRECK OF THE DEL NORTE

BOAT DIVE
GPS
49°01.609' N
123°35.315' W

SKILL
Expert divers

CURRENT TABLE
Porlier Pass

WHY GO

A sturdy steamer on the northern British Columbia run, the *Del Norte* was launched in San Francisco in 1865. It was afloat for less than four years, and went down after hitting the southern Canoe Islet at the northeast entrance to Porlier Pass.

The sunken sidewheeler lay undiscovered, an untouched wreck, until 1971. Even then its location was not generally known. On the first sport diving expedition on this 200-foot (61-meter) vessel in early 1975, one diver came up with an ornate brass deck lamp. Others swam through the boilers. Many artifacts were removed and members of the Underwater Archaeological Society of British Columbia (UASBC) became concerned. In late 1978 they placed a plaque on the wreck, with a brief history of the steamer, and proposed heritage status for it; in the mid-1990s they replaced the first plaque.

The two paddlewheels of this old ship are a reminder of an era that has passed, and the oscillating steam engine is rare in North America. These features made it an important wreck to save.

Even without a wreck, Canoe Islet is an exciting dive. I'll never forget drifting down through a curtain of silvery fish into a rocky field of basket stars. We saw feather stars, orange cup corals and lingcod. Schools of black rockfish parted as we swam off to look for the wreck. Add the excitement of a heritage wreck, and you have a winner!

Diver above starboard paddlewheel of the Del Norte

BOTTOM AND DEPTHS

Rock, rubble, sand and shell bottom. There is almost no hull but the paddlewheels, boilers and engine works are relatively intact, with boilers and engine works sitting in their original location in the center of the wreck. The plaque placed by the UASBC lies at the foot of the *Del Norte* engine works. Big boulders are scattered around and you will see lumps of coal. These too are part of the wreck so just look, don't take. Remains of the wreck run from 40 to 90 feet (12 to 27 meters).

HAZARDS

Very strong current and poor visibility. Dive on slack on a small tidal exchange, no greater than 2 feet (⅔ meter) per hour. The current is most dangerous on an ebbing tide. Plan to dive on a high slack. Leave a pickup person in the boat in case you are swept away by that current. Best visibility in winter when no Fraser River runoff.

TELEPHONES

• On the water: VHF radio; if no VHF, try a cell phone.
• On land: North Galiano, across road from the dock at Spanish Hills.

FACILITIES

Air fills, charters and camping nearby at Galiano and Gabriola islands; charters also out of Nanaimo, Sidney, Victoria and Vancouver. Launch ramps at Galiano and Gabriola islands, and at Ladysmith and Chemainus on Vancouver Island.

ACCESS

The *Del Norte* is 200 yards (185 meters) south of the northern Canoe Islet, the one that is never covered with water. It is near the eastern entrance to Porlier Pass and ½ nautical mile north of Vernaci Point on the Strait of Georgia side of Valdes Island. Galiano Island is on the south side of the pass.

Porlier is the middle of the three major passages between the Gulf Islands. Gabriola Passage lies to the north and Active Pass to the south.

When searching for *Del Norte,* check the GPS location and depth sounder. Anchor upcurrent from the wreck and use the anchor line as a descent line. From the bottom of the anchor line at 80 to 90 feet (24 to 27 meters), depending on tide height, go up the slope to find the *Del Norte.*

No landings allowed at the Canoe islets; it is a provincial ecological reserve, a protected sea bird colony.

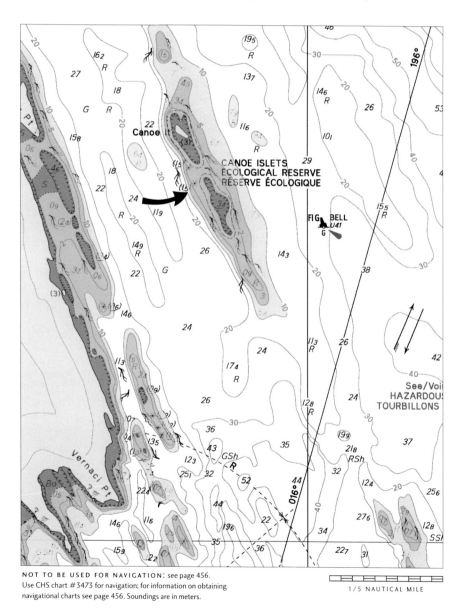

NOT TO BE USED FOR NAVIGATION: see page 456.
Use CHS chart #3473 for navigation; for information on obtaining navigational charts see page 456. Soundings are in meters.

1/5 NAUTICAL MILE

263

NOTES

WRECK OF THE POINT GREY

BOAT DIVE
GPS
49°00.754' N
123°35.589' W

SKILL
Intermediate and expert
divers

All divers with guide

CURRENT TABLE
Porlier Pass

WHY GO

The *Point Grey* is a relatively easy, safe, intact wreck to dive. Although it is upside down, this 105-foot (32-meter) steel-screw steamer tug is photogenic. It is shallow. Visibility is usually good because Fraser River runoff does not reach it.

White plumose anemones cover the drive shaft. More fluffy white plumose anemones are on the ceiling which is really the floor. With a guide, this wreck is within the capabilities of new divers, and, as a wreck that has been singled out and marked with an interpretive plaque, it is of interest to all divers.

The tugboat *Point Grey* was built in 1911 in North Vancouver. In 1949 it was hauling a barge west to Victoria, entered Porlier Pass in dense fog and crashed into Virago Rock. The barge the *Point Grey* was towing hit the tugboat and the tug became stuck on the rock. It sat precariously on Virago Rock until the winter of 1963 when a storm knocked it off and it rolled upside down. Look for the Plexiglas plaque on a concrete slab, placed near the stern of the vessel by the Underwater Archaeological Society of British Columbia.

In 1993 the *Point Grey* suffered new damage. The bow forward of the boiler broke off and turned right side up. This tough steel tug is collapsing. All wrecks are alive, in a state of change, subject to assault by

Diver examines Point Grey propeller damage

natural forces and passing vessels and this one is in a vulnerable location.

Dive it soon.

BOTTOM AND DEPTHS

Virago Rock breaks the surface at the marker. Around it, a thicket of bull kelp. South of Virago, corduroy-like creases in the rock line the bottom running nearly north and south. The *Point Grey* lies in one of these mini-valleys. The wreck rests at 30 to 40 feet (9 to 12 meters), depending on tide height. Beyond the wreck the ridges slope gradually down – we followed one to 90 feet (27 meters).

HAZARDS

Very strong current and boats: currents up to 9 knots sometimes flow through Porlier. Dive on the slack on a small tidal exchange. Leave an experienced pickup person on the boat in case you are swept away by the current. Hug the bottom all the way to the surface well out of the way of boats.

TELEPHONES

• On the water: VHF radio; if no VHF, try a cell phone.
• On land: North Galiano across road from the dock at Spanish Hills.

FACILITIES

Air fills and charters year-round at Galiano Island – arrange two weeks in advance; launch ramp and camping too. Charters and launch ramp at Gabriola Island; ramp at Saltspring Island and at Ladysmith and Chemainus on Vancouver Island.

ACCESS

The *Point Grey* is in the center of Porlier Pass on the south/southwest side of Virago Rock.

Charter or launch your own boat. Virago is 10 nautical miles north of Montague Harbour on Galiano. Go to Virago Rock in Porlier Pass. Drop anchor and

leave a boat tender on board in the event the current picks up before expected. Or dive from a "live" boat. Do not tie up to the marker. It is a federal offense to make fast to a marker or tamper with any aid to navigation. When you roll off the boat, be careful you don't bump your head. It is shallow. Swim to the marker: line up on a 150° compass bearing between the marker on Virago Rock and Alcala Point on Galiano Island and swim under water to it. Or simply eyeball it before heading down and swim

from the marker south/southwest for 50 feet (15 meters) to the wreck.

The *Point Grey* lies on the *west* side of a shallow, narrow underwater valley. The 6-foot (2-meter) high propeller is apparent at the rear of the marker but only two blades remain. You could miss the *Point Grey* altogether if you go over an underwater ridge that is *east* of the marker – I did on my first attempt at Virago. If you do not find the wreck right away, come up and start again.

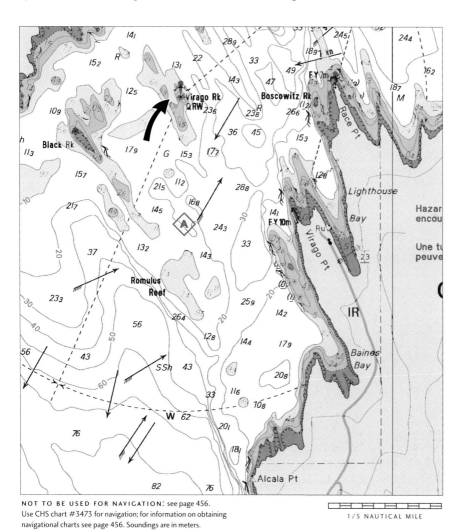

NOT TO BE USED FOR NAVIGATION: see page 456.
Use CHS chart #3473 for navigation; for information on obtaining navigational charts see page 456. Soundings are in meters.

1/5 NAUTICAL MILE

NOTES

BOAT DIVE or
KAYAK DIVE
GPS
49°00.140' N
123°35.376' W

SKILL
Intermediate and expert
divers

All divers with guide

CURRENT TABLE
Porlier Pass

WHY GO

Clusters of white plumose anemones tumble over the rocky cliffs and overhangs like marvelous big underwater bouquets. But the wolf-eels are the most popular feature of this dive – two mated pairs live at Alcala. Much more too.

Immediately off Alcala Point, in summer, you're into bull kelp which streams like olive-colored flags in the current and hides rockfish, urchins and lingcod. We saw trumpet sponges, orange cup corals, yellow hydrocoral and small rock scallops on the walls, swimming scallops and giant barnacles the size of baseballs. Sea pens, kelp green-lings, sea stars, octopuses, tiger rockfish, schools of pile perch, cucumbers and lots of sea lemons. I thought I saw a blue-eyed red brotula slip between the slits in the rocks.

The variety is almost unbelievable, but the wolf-eels are the scene-stealers. The last time I dived Alcala, two wolf-eels were guarding their young. The male did not come out of the den but puffed himself up to fill the opening, rippled his rubbery lips in a comical manner – probably to frighten us away. They are almost tame since they have been visited so often by divers who hand-feed them with urchin roe. Do not be frightened if the wolf-eels find you before you find them.

BOTTOM AND DEPTHS

Rock ledges and overhangs drop to a broad ledge at 60 to 70 feet (18 to 21 meters). Between boulders, there are small pockets of sand. Thick patches of bull kelp, in summer. Particularly beautiful ledges just to the north.

HAZARDS

Current, boats and bull kelp. If inexperienced with the site, dive precisely on slack. Local divers sometimes dive it when the current is ebbing because often a back eddy forms at Alcala. But don't count on it; try this only with a guide. Listen for boats,

and ascend close to the wall all the way to the surface. Carry a knife for kelp.

TELEPHONES

- On the water: VHF radio; if no VHF, try a cell phone.
- On land: North Galiano across road from the Spanish Hills dock.

FACILITIES

At Galiano, air fills and charters year-round with two weeks' advance notice. A launch ramp is at the north side of Montague Provincial Park; and Spanish Hills dock and float at North Galiano is an excellent place to launch dive-kayaks for Alcala Point.

At Gabriola Island, air fills and charters; launch ramps at Saltspring Island.

ACCESS

Alcala Point is at the extreme northwest corner of Galiano Island on Trincomali Channel – it is almost in Porlier Pass. Charter, launch your own boat at Montague Provincial Park or paddle a dive-kayak from Spanish Hills dock to Alcala Point.

- Boaters heading north from Montague Provincial Park should look for the Spanish Hills dock in North Galiano. Soon after passing it, you will reach Alcala Point. Past an oak tree at the point, you come to rocky shore. Boat divers usually anchor just inshore from the bull kelp off the point.
- Kayak divers, allow plenty of time to arrive for slack. Plan on taking 20 minutes for the paddle from the Spanish Hills dock at North Galiano. You can back your vehicle onto the wharf to drop gear, making it a short carry to the float and then park beside the road.

From the float, head north close beside the shoreline. Past an oak tree at Alcala Point, you come to rocky shore. You could land on the rocks just around the point. It is easier at high tide, as there is an abrupt ledge at low tide. At low tides you could anchor but then it becomes an advanced kayak dive.

*Float at Spanish Hills,
Alcala Point behind*

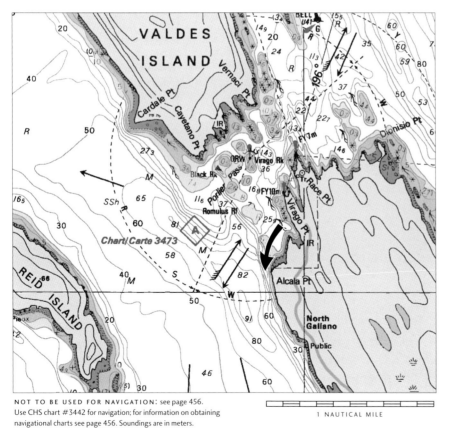

NOT TO BE USED FOR NAVIGATION: see page 456.
Use CHS chart #3442 for navigation; for information on obtaining
navigational charts see page 456. Soundings are in meters.

1 NAUTICAL MILE

NOTES

PRINGLE PARK

SHORE DIVE

SKILL
All divers

CURRENT TABLE
Porlier Pass

WHY GO

Incredible variety at this near-to-current but not-in-it site near Porlier Pass. Fluorescent purple and orange quiver before me. My buddy holds a Puget Sound king crab – it is 1 foot (⅓ meter) across. The exotic giant seems specially designed for this era of hot colors.

We see white plumose anemones beneath a ledge. A blood star. A sunflower star splayed across a rock, nearly 3 feet (1 meter) wide. Purple plume worms decorate a cable down a valley in the rocks. We shine our lights into holes and caverns between tumbled boulders at the base of the wall. See a dark opening. I go in, look up, see an orange-and-red striped tiger rockfish high in the corner.

My buddy signals again. He's holding two barnacled Puget Sound king crabs. They are smaller, their shells the size of a hand with fingers outstretched. We cruise on past two large lingcod, a feather star, gray tennis ball sponges, a sea peach, orange cup corals. See a giant silver nudibranch on the sand, then a giant red one;

an alabaster nudibranch and a sea lemon. Beneath a ledge, the delicate curlicues of a basket star in 25 feet (8 meters) of water. Two swimming scallops clap up in front of us.

BOTTOM AND DEPTHS

A rock wall slopes to a depth of 20 to 30 feet (6 to 9 meters). Becomes deeper around the corner, 50 to 60 feet (15 to 18 meters), depending on tide height. You could go still deeper to 90 feet (27 meters), but most life is shallower beside the wall. Boulders and rocks are heaped at the base of it. Caverns indent it, some large enough to enter. Sand stretches from the base. Bull kelp in summer.

HAZARDS

Boat traffic in and out of Spanish Hills dock in North Galiano, especially in summer. Some current. Dive near slack and work into the current for the first half of your dive. Listen for boats and hug the wall as you ascend.

Puget Sound king crab and red urchins

TELEPHONE

North Galiano, across road from the Spanish Hills dock.

FACILITIES

None at Pringle Park. Before you head up island, stop at the ferry landing restrooms or pit toilets at Montague Provincial Park.

ACCESS

Pringle Park is on Trincomali Channel near the northwest tip of Galiano Island. It is immediately beside Spanish Hills dock, and 1 nautical mile south of Alcala Point.

From Sturdies Bay ferry landing on Galiano follow signs toward Porlier Pass. It is 15 miles (24 kilometers) to Spanish Hills dock and float in North Galiano. First go to a "Y" in the road past the pub, turn right and head north on Porlier Pass Road for 14 miles (22 kilometers). Immediately past the dock at Spanish Hills you will see a sign at Pringle Park. Drop gear and go back toward the dock to park. A gently inclined path in the park leads to the water; dive to the right around the point.

Might be wheelchair accessible if logs were cleared from Pringle Park entry point, but there always seems to be a heap of them.

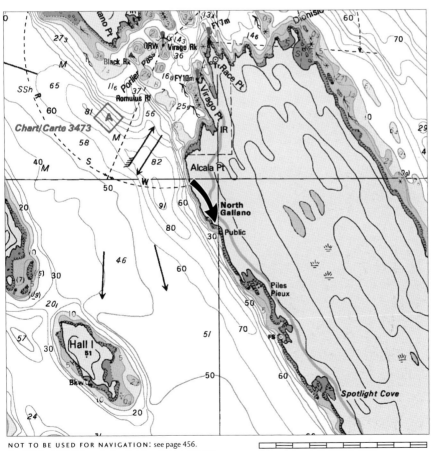

NOTES

NOT TO BE USED FOR NAVIGATION: see page 456.
Use CHS chart #3442 for navigation; for information on obtaining navigational charts see page 456. Soundings are in meters.

1 NAUTICAL MILE

MADRONA WALL

WHY GO

Over the wall with two kicks of your fins from shore. A superb wall for divers who are comfortable to enter where the drop-off is sheer to 60 feet (18 meters).

Immediately over the wall at 25 feet (8 meters) we saw a large intricate basket star clinging to the smooth stark rock. We turned left. Frothy bowers of feather stars were clustered on rocks on the bottom, on the wall and beneath the rocky overhang. Brittle stars ran across the bright white sand. We saw giant purple urchins, a tiny grunt sculpin, a decorator crab, a juvenile Puget Sound king crab, a pale pink dahlia anemone on a ledge. Tube worms that look like caramelized popcorn balls encrusting the wall and leafy hornmouth snails creeping between them. Swimming scallops, rock scallops, a lingcod; an alabaster nudibranch and sea lemons. We saw two sets of nudibranch eggs draped around two rocks like multiple strings of pearls.

Clusters of white plumose anemones were on the rocky part of the wall. My buddy enjoyed seeing leather stars and slime stars.

BOTTOM AND DEPTHS

The wall bottoms out to a broad sandy ledge at 50 to 60 feet (15 to 18 meters), depending on tide height. The clean rock wall is sheer at the entry point, and stretches both to the right and left. At some places it is undercut. At other points the wall turns into heaps of rock and rubble with lots of nooks and crannies for marine life. Beyond the broad ledge, it sheers off to great depths – drops to a depth of 200 to 230 feet (60 to 70 meters) on the chart. Can be slightly cloudy from silt.

HAZARDS

Boats and some current. Listen for boats and do not ascend through the open water. Hug the wall all the way to the surface. When you enter, notice the current direction and dive upcurrent at the start. When half your air is gone, you can turn and cruise back at a shallower depth along the wall.

TELEPHONES

- Top of dive entry: immediately across Porlier Pass Road, outside. The telephone is almost completely hidden in the grape arbor.
- South Galiano: immediately west of junction of Porlier Pass Road and Montague Road near the pub.

FACILITIES

None at Madrona Wall. Before you head up island, stop at the ferry landing restrooms or pit toilets at Montague Provincial Park, southwest end of the island. Air fills and charters year-round at Galiano Island – arrange two weeks in advance.

ACCESS

Madrona Wall is on Trincomali Channel, three-fourths of the way up the west side of Galiano Island.

From Sturdies Bay ferry landing, follow signs toward Porlier Pass. From the ferry it is 13 miles (21 kilometers) to Madrona. At a "Y" in the road past the pub, turn right and go north on Porlier Pass Road for 11 miles (18 kilometers) to Lodge Road on the left-hand side. It looks like a grassy launch ramp, slopes steeply from Porlier Pass Road to the water. About 100 paces, and can be slippery when wet.

Over the wall, turn right or left depending on current direction.

Basket star on wall

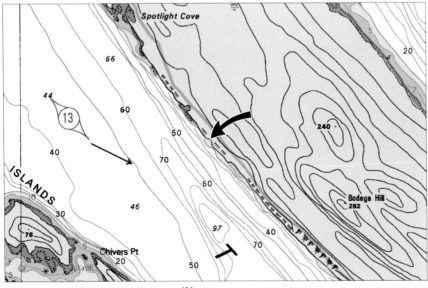

NOT TO BE USED FOR NAVIGATION: see page 456.
Use CHS chart #3442 for navigation; for information on obtaining
navigational charts see page 456. Soundings are in meters.

1 NAUTICAL MILE

RETREAT COVE

SHORE DIVE

SKILL
All divers and snorkelers

TIDE TABLE
Fulford Harbour

WHY GO
"There's so much detail – it's like, where do you start?" my buddy said about Galiano diving as we snorkeled across to the shallow wall at Retreat Cove. Lots of invertebrates here. And it's easy to dive.

Alabaster nudibranchs. Sea lemons. A white nudibranch with maroon tips laying eggs like a string of pearls – we saw all of these sights at Retreat Cove. We also saw nudibranch eggs like a coiled ribbon. Sea stars all over the rocks: leather stars, blood stars, brittle stars, vermilion stars and blue ones. Red rock crabs, deep-purple-colored kelp crabs waving their claws as if attacking. Millions of little creatures like underwater grasshoppers. Rock scallops. Chitons, one that looked like a turquoise gemstone. White plumose anemones beneath the overhangs.

BOTTOM AND DEPTHS
A shallow rock wall with overhangs. Boulders are scattered down it. Bull kelp in summer. The wall starts at 4 to 13 feet (1 to 4 meters), bottoms out to sand at 25 to 35 feet (8 to 11 meters). The white sand reflects the light, giving a bright sunny feeling.

HAZARDS
Bull kelp in summer. Carry a knife; if caught in the kelp you can cut your way free.

TELEPHONES
- South Galiano: immediately west of the junction of Porlier Pass Road and Montague Road – it is outside the pub. Return 8 miles (12¾ kilometers) toward the ferry and turn right into Montague Road. A telephone is outside the shops on both sides of the road.
- On east side of Porlier Pass Road 3½ miles (5⅔ kilometers) north of the Retreat Cove turnoff.

FACILITIES
None at Retreat Cove. No toilets near the site: before you head up the island, stop at the ferry landing restrooms or the pit toilets at Montague Provincial Park; also camping, picnic tables, mooring buoys and concrete launch ramp at the provincial park, southwest end of the island.

Air fills and charters at Galiano Island; arrange it two weeks in advance.

Lined chiton, probably two times life-size

ACCESS

Retreat Cove is on Trincomali Channel halfway up the west side of Galiano Island.

From Sturdies Bay ferry landing go 9½ miles (15 kilometers) to Retreat Cove at North Galiano. From the ferry landing, follow signs toward Porlier Pass Road. Past the pub at a "Y" in the road, turn right and go north on Porlier Pass Road for 8 miles (12½ kilometers) to Retreat Cove Road. Turn left down it. Go ½ mile (¾ kilometer) to the wharf. Roadside parking for three or four cars. Drop off the wharf and snorkel straight across to Retreat Island – it took us 5 minutes. Dive north around the island.

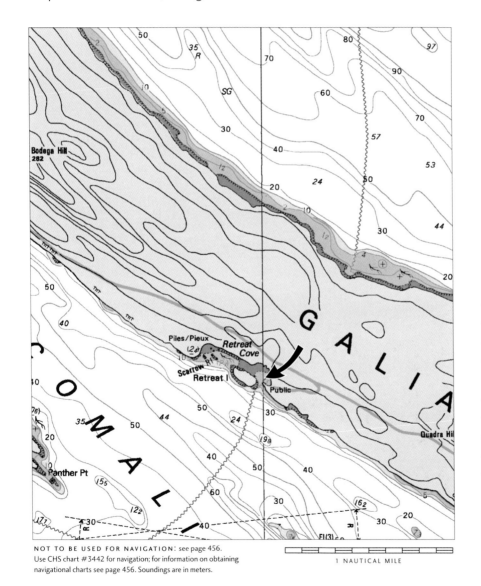

NOTES

NOT TO BE USED FOR NAVIGATION: see page 456.
Use CHS chart #3442 for navigation; for information on obtaining navigational charts see page 456. Soundings are in meters.

1 NAUTICAL MILE

BOAT DIVE
GPS
Start on flood:
48°50.715' N
123°20.925' W

Start on ebb:
48°50.681' N
123°20.863' W

SKILL
Expert divers

CURRENT TABLE
Active Pass

*Cascade of white
plumose anemones*

WHY GO

Enterprise Reef combines rich reef life with one of the best drop-offs in the Gulf Islands. Add the swift currents that flow through Active Pass, and you have the ingredients for one of the most exciting dives around.

You'll probably see Puget Sound king crabs, rock scallops, abalones, large lingcod, rockfish, basket stars and cabezons. Sea lemons in the kelp. We saw masses of giant red urchins and small green urchins. Work your way around the shallow ledges that look like molten rock flowing southward to go to the drop-off at the southern end of the reef. The wall is a "waterfall" of white plumose anemones cascading down the sheer side. White fluffy anemones soften the undercut caves and grottoes sheering down to a depth of 90 to 100 feet (27 to 30 meters). Swimming scallops rain up around you all down the wall.

Divers have been chased from the water at Enterprise Reef by a pod of killer whales. Avoid going closer than 110 yards (100 meters).

BOTTOM AND DEPTHS

On the north side of the marker, smooth rock ledges fall in folds at 20 to 30 feet (6 to 9 meters) deep. Thick bull kelp. Directly south of the marker the rock wall drops off to a depth of 90 to 100 feet (27 to 30 meters).

HAZARDS

Swift currents, boats and bull kelp. Currents up to 7 knots sometimes flow through Active Pass. Dive on slack on a small tidal exchange. Listen for boats and ascend close to the rocks all the way to the surface. Carry a knife for kelp.

TELEPHONES

- On the water: VHF radio; if no VHF, try a cell phone.
- On land:
1. Village Bay ferry landing, Mayne Island.
2. Sturdies Bay ferry landing, Galiano Island.

FACILITIES

Guided charters year-round out of Galiano Island, and air fills – arrange dives and air two weeks in advance. Year-round charters and air fills at Pender Island, Gabriola Island, Nanaimo and Vancouver.

Launch ramp at west side of Village Bay, Mayne Island; at Galiano, Saltspring and Gabriola islands.

ACCESS

Enterprise Reef is at the southern end of Trincomali Channel. It is 1 nautical mile south of the western entry to Active Pass, the way between Galiano and Mayne islands. Active Pass is one of the busiest and most dangerous passes in the Gulf Islands because it is the main shipping and British Columbia ferry route between Vancouver and Victoria.

The reef can be reached by charter. Or launch your own boat at Mayne Island and go 1 nautical mile west – or at Montague Harbour on Galiano Island and go 4 nautical miles southeast to the marker at Enterprise Reef. Anchor in the bull kelp in the shallows on the side of the reef that is sheltered from the current, and go down. On ebb tides, anchor on the south side; on flood tides, anchor on the north side of the reef. Do not tie onto the marker. It is a federal offense to make fast to a marker or tamper with any aid to navigation.

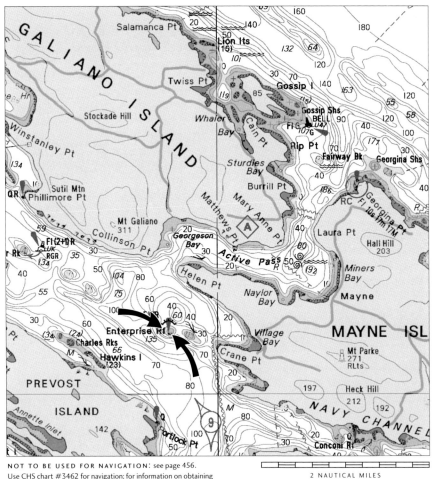

NOT TO BE USED FOR NAVIGATION: see page 456.
Use CHS chart #3462 for navigation; for information on obtaining
navigational charts see page 456. Soundings are in meters.

2 NAUTICAL MILES

NOT TO BE USED FOR NAVIGATION: see page 456.
Use CHS chart #3473 for navigation; for information on obtaining navigational charts see page 456. Soundings are in meters.

1/5 NAUTICAL MILE

NOTES

TILLY POINT CAVES

SHORE DIVE

SKILL
Intermediate and
expert divers

All divers with guide

Snorkelers in bay

TIDE TABLE
Fulford Harbour

WHY GO

Pure magic. It's what you dream diving in a cave should be. You can go in one end and out the other. The oval cave entry is framed with feathery white plumose anemones. Inside, blackness is shot with shafts of sunlight through holes in the rock above. An orange dahlia anemone hangs upside down from the ceiling. We swim through darkness to the end of the room, and then down toward the light through a narrow slot between the rock. Walls framed with more white plumose anemones – we're out of the cave. We glance back, see a Puget Sound king crab shimmering – its purple and orange fluorescent colors glow beneath a rocky ledge. Looking out, we see large orange sea pens arching from the white sand at the base of the island.

The rock wall is bright. It's dark. It's windowed. Large white plumose anemones fill every slot, every seam in the rock. A lingcod swims past, framed by a window of rock. On the surface, we see a harbor seal.

The entire scene is so picturesque I know I will return again and again to confirm I did not imagine it, to reassure myself that the Tilly Point Caves exist.

*Tilly Point Caves
shore access*

BOTTOM AND DEPTHS

The cave entry is at a depth of 5 to 15 feet (1 ½ to 5 meters). The main room is 10 feet (3 meters) wide by 30 feet (9 meters) long, and 10 feet (3 meters) high. The exit slot slopes down from the back of this largest room of the cave on its right-hand side. The narrow channel of rock leads to the sand at a depth of 40 to 50 feet (12 to 15 meters).

Above and below water, the island is a heap of tumbled boulders with small rocks embedded in them. Intricate sandstone and conglomerate. Small undercuts and slots are all along the outside wall, which bottoms out to bright white sand at 60 to 70 feet (18 to 21 meters).

The bay between the island and the shore has a bottom of white shells that is scattered with pastel dahlia anemones from zero to 25 feet (8 meters) deep.

HAZARDS

Current on the outside of the rock, the cave itself and bull kelp. Dive on slack. Weight yourself to be neutrally buoyant at a depth of 5 feet (1 ½ meters) so you will not stir up silt. Carry a knife; if caught in kelp you can cut your way free.

TELEPHONE

At Poet's Cove Resort, foot of Spalding Road. Go to the lower pool area – the telephone is upstairs. Outdoors, available 24 hours.

From Tilly Point, go back along Gowland Point Road for 3 ½ miles (5 ½ kilometers): at Spalding Road continue straight on Spalding to the resort.

FACILITIES

Great beach for a picnic at Tilly Point Caves. Air fills, charters and dive equipment rentals on Pender at Port Browning Marina and at Sidney, Vancouver Island. Camping in summer on Pender Island at Port Browning Resort & Marina and at Prior Centennial Campground.

ACCESS

Tilly Point Caves are at the southern tip of South Pender Island near Boundary Pass, just across the border from the USA. The caves are most easily dived at a high slack tide. Go by way of British Columbia ferry from Tsawwassen or Swartz Bay to Otter Bay at Pender Island. From the ferry landing, it is 11 miles (18 kilometers) to the dive. Takes 35 minutes.

From Otter Bay, use the yellow line indicating the arterial. Go on Otter Bay Road following signs toward South Pender, then Bedwell Harbour. Across the bridge over the canal, turn left and continue on Canal Road for 3 miles (5 kilometers) to Spalding Road. Turn left and continue on Gowlland Point Road for 1¼ miles (2 kilometers) to Craddock Drive. Turn right, and go to the Craddock Beach Access sign. Parking for four or five cars at end of the road, and a great deal of road-side parking along Craddock. From the end of Craddock Drive, walk down 50 shal-low stairsteps to the log-strewn beach. You will see a rock that is an island at high tide. You can walk to it at low tide.

To find the largest cave – the one you can swim through – snorkel out to the right-hand, westernmost side of the rocky island to an indentation on the outside of the rock. The entry is below it. Head down. Look from 5 to 10 feet (3 to 11 meters) deep for the oval entrance framed with white plumose anemones. Enter. Swim slowly straight through the cave. Enjoy everything on your first passage through before the silt is stirred up. At the end of the cave, turn right and go down a narrow slot. You emerge at the base of the wall. Continue exploring around the outside of the island toward its eastern tip. From there, it is a pleasant snorkel to shore.

Weight yourself carefully so you can enter the large cave without touching the anemones – divers following you will appreciate it. Plan to be neutrally buoyant at a depth of 5 feet (1½ meters).

NOTES

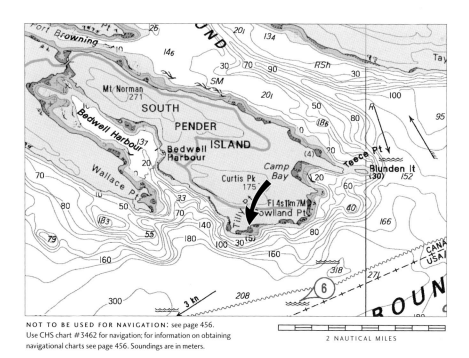

NOT TO BE USED FOR NAVIGATION: see page 456.
Use CHS chart #3462 for navigation; for information on obtaining navigational charts see page 456. Soundings are in meters.

2 NAUTICAL MILES

SHORE DIVE

SKILL
All divers and snorkelers

TIDE TABLE
Fulford Harbour

WHY GO

Low-key easy dive, easy entry, lots to see. White shell beach with a backdrop of the snowy peaks of Mount Baker rising behind the Gulf Islands. Great for a picnic, building sand castles and soaking up summer sun after the dive.

Prickly purple urchins cluster on the rocks in the shallows. Deeper, a purple aura glows around each one – I see "double purple". Then we reach the cool green place. Frothy white plumose anemones hang like a veil beneath an overhang. Kelp greenlings flash past. Oval-shaped chitons are flat on the rocks. They look like black-and-green striped buttons. We see rockfish, painted greenlings, giant barnacles. Red sunflower stars tumble in the current, stick to my arm, stick to the wall. A sea cucumber pokes lacy orange fingers between the rocks. Orange cup corals are sprinkled like confetti. A sea pen rises from the sand like an orange quill pen. A dogfish cruises up from the dark depths to meet us. We are at 50 feet (15 meters).

Shallower, I look under a ledge. Crabs scurry. Swimming back across the bay under water we see red rock crabs galore. The egg case of a moon snail. Several gunnels dart through the eelgrass. Hairy siphons of horse clams suck into the silty sand as we swim over. Bright green lettuce kelp is scattered between like torn tissue.

On the beach, one diver told of trying to tease an octopus out by dangling a crab in front of it, and more tentacles reached out. Two octopuses in the hole.

BOTTOM AND DEPTHS

Gently sloping sand at base of wall at the point. Tumbled boulders. Sandy ledges at 30 feet (9 meters), 50 feet (15 meters) and on down. In the bay, silty sand and eelgrass.

HAZARDS

Current. Dive near slack, especially with large tides and on ebbing tides.

TELEPHONE

Beside Fulford-Ganges Road, immediately after turning right off Beddis Road toward Ganges: the telephone is outside the motel on the right-hand side. From Beddis Beach, 4 miles (6¾ kilometers) to it.

FACILITIES

A chemical toilet beside path to beach. Camping with picnic tables, fire rings and pit toilets at Ruckle Provincial Park near Fulford Harbour; camping in summer at Mouat Provincial Park in Ganges. Air fills off-island only.

ACCESS

Beddis Beach is on Captain Passage at the southeast side of Saltspring Island. It is off Fulford-Ganges Road 5 miles (8 kilometers) out of Ganges. From Ganges to the dive takes 10 to 15 minutes; 30 minutes from Long Harbour; 25 minutes from Vesuvius; 20 minutes from Fulford Harbour.

On Beddis Road, you come to a Beddis Beach sign painted on a concrete road barrier at Lionel Road. Just past it there is a drop-off zone for gear in front of a gated path. Roadside parking for six to ten cars is uphill from it. A path leads from the drop-off zone to the beach. Walk 100 paces on the gravel path to the sandy beach. You could swim to the left and head down at the point. Or walk to the left for 150 yards (140 meters) to the point on the left-hand side and go in.

To get to Beddis Beach public access at Lionel Road
- From Ganges, follow signs toward Fulford Harbour. Go along Fulford-Ganges Road. Just past a motel Beddis Road veers off the main road to the left. Go on Beddis for 4 miles (6¾ kilometers) to the Beddis Beach sign at Lionel Road.
- From Fulford Harbour, drive up the hill. Turn right into Beaver Point Road: go 1½ miles (2½ kilometers) to Stewart Road. Turn left following a sign to Ganges.

Go 2 miles (3¼ kilometers) along Stewart to Cusheon Lake Road. Turn right. Go to Beddis Road and turn right again. Drive along Beddis for 1 mile (1½ kilometers) to the Beddis Beach sign.

• From Long Harbour or Vesuvius follow signs to Ganges. Then follow signs toward Fulford Harbour. Take Fulford-Ganges Road to Beddis Road. Go 4 miles (6¾ kilometers) on Beddis to the public access.

Beddis Beach

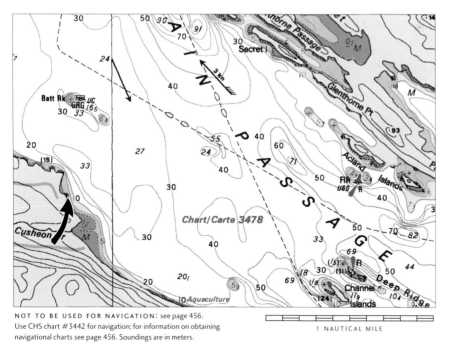

NOT TO BE USED FOR NAVIGATION: see page 456.
Use CHS chart #3442 for navigation; for information on obtaining navigational charts see page 456. Soundings are in meters.

1 NAUTICAL MILE

NOTES

Ferry Information for British Columbia
British Columbia Ferry Services (BC Ferries)
• Toll-free throughout North America:
   1-888-223-3779
• From all other locations: (250)386-3431
www.bcferries.com
At the time of writing: the following information applies – but changes occur; it would be wise to check current requirements on BC Ferries web page before every trip.

Rules Regarding Scuba Tanks on BC Ferries
Persons transporting scuba tanks containing compressed air, full or partially full, are required under Canadian law to declare dangerous goods at the terminal or to a vessel officer. Persons transporting scuba tanks with the valves removed do not need clearance. All pressurized tanks with a UN 3156 sticker, indicating nitrox or mixed gases, are taboo – remove the valve.

Expedite Dangerous Goods clearance at the ferry ticket booth – complete a Dangerous Goods Shipping Document prior to arrival. Obtain it from the web at home or a library: Go to www.bcferries.com: select Travel Planning; click on Carrying Dangerous Goods, then For the General Public. Download Dangerous Goods Shipping Document and complete it: include your name, home address and phone number; Class 2; UN 1002, which indicates compressed air; number of cylinders you are transporting and quantity in each one: most tanks are 80 cubic feet/2.27 cubic meters.

(To calculate quantity in scuba tanks: 1 cubic foot=0.0283168466 cubic meters.)

Swartz Bay: arrive at least 45 minutes prior to intended sailing time. However, it might save you from missing a ferry if you phone the terminal and ask when they suggest you should arrive based on traffic: (250)656-5571.

Mill Bay and Brentwood Bay: arrive at least 30 minutes prior to sailing time.

Prearranged Dangerous Goods Clearance Requires 48 Hours
Complete a Dangerous Goods Shipping Document as described above and fax it at least 48 hours in advance of intended sailing time to the appropriate terminal:
1. Swartz Bay: fax (250)655-3183
2. Brentwood and Mill Bay:
   fax (250)537-2895

Ferry Information for Washington State
Black Ball Transport
• Victoria: (250)386-2202
• Port Angeles: (360)457-4491
• Seattle: (206)622-2222
www.cohoferry.com
(Ferries between Victoria, British Columbia, and Port Angeles, Washington.)

Washington State Ferries
Recorded information 24 hours: between 7 am and 10 pm press "0" to speak with a person.
• 1-888-808-7977: Toll-free throughout North America
www.wsdot.wa.gov/ferries
(Ferries between Sidney, British Columbia, and the San Juan Islands, Washington: Friday Harbor–Anacortes. At the time of writing, vehicle reservations are available both eastbound and westbound, and are strongly advised.)

Victoria Clipper
• Victoria: (250)382-8100
• 1-800-888-2535: Toll-free throughout North America
www.victoriaclipper.com
(Foot-passenger ferry – no cars – between Victoria and Seattle.)

• DIVE SHOPS

Ogden Point Dive Centre
199 Dallas Road
Victoria BC V8V 1A1
(250)380-9119
1-888-701-1177: Toll-free throughout
    North America
www.divevictoria.com
(Recreational, nitrox and technical instruction. Waterfront and roadside air, nitrox and trimix fills. Hot showers, restrooms, lockers. Rinse station available 24 hours. Also charters.)

Frank Whites Dive Stores
2300 Douglas Street
Victoria BC V8T 4L7
(250)385-4713
(Recreational dive shop; dive guiding.)

Wilson Diving
#105 - 1790 Island Highway
Victoria BC V9B 1H8
(250)478-4488
www.wilsondiving.com
(Recreational and nitrox instruction. Nitrox fills. Guided local shore dives. Also guided three-day group trips to Hornby Island, Port Hardy and Barkley Sound.)

Sidney Dive n Surf
#111A - 2506 Beacon Avenue
Sidney BC V8L 1Y2
(250)655-0979
1-866-655-0979: Toll-free throughout
    North America
www.sidneydivensurf.com
(Recreational and nitrox instruction; roadside and waterfront air and nitrox fills. For waterfront fills, tie up at Port Sidney Marina, and cross road to the shop. Also charters.)

BC College of Diving & Undersea Charters
10221 McDonald Park Road West
Sidney BC V8L 5X7
(250)654-0154
1-877-444-3483: Toll-free throughout
    North America
www.bccollegeofdiving.com
(Recreational, nitrox and commercial instruction. Nitrox fills. Also dive charters.)

Frank Whites Dive Stores
2200 Keating Cross Road, Suite D
Victoria (Saanichtown) BC V8M 2A6
(250)652-3375
(Dive guiding. Check winter hours: (250)385-4713.)

• DIVE RESORT

Rockfish Divers at the Marina &
    Eco-Adventure Centre at the
    Brentwood Bay Lodge & Spa
849 Verdier Avenue
Brentwood Bay BC V8M 1C5
(250)889-7282
www.rockfishdivers.com
(Recreational dive shop, dive instruction and resort; all services are available to snorkelers and divers not staying at the resort as well as to resort guests. Air fills for drop-ins. Packages include resort accommodation and diving.)

• DAY, MULTIPLE-DAY AND LIVEABOARD CHARTERS
Out of Victoria and Sidney

Juan de Fuca Warrior and *Cape Able*
Ogden Point Dive Centre
199 Dallas Road
Victoria BC V8V 1A1
(250)380-9119
1-888-701-1177: Toll-free throughout
    North America
www.divevictoria.com
*(Day charters year-round to the Mackenzie
and G.B. Church, Race Rocks and more.
Also weekend and week-long dive vacations
with land-based accommodation; trips
range from Hornby Island to Port Hardy to
Barkley Sound.)*

Queen of Scott and *Barfleurs*
McConnell Marine Services
2406 Central Avenue
Victoria BC V8S 2S6
(250)413-7219
E-mail: mcconnellmarine@shaw.ca
*(Day charters year-round out of Sidney and
Victoria to the Mackenzie and G.B. Church,
Race Rocks and more.)*

Fathom Five, Mystic Quest
Sidney Dive n Surf
#111A - 2506 Beacon Avenue
Sidney BC V8L 1Y2
(250)655-0979
1-866-655-0979: Toll-free throughout
    North America
www.sidneydivensurf.com
*(Daily trips out of Sidney to the artificial reefs,
Saanich Inlet and southern Gulf Islands.
Weekend liveaboard charters to Active Pass:
Aztec Reef, Hole in the Wall caves, Enterprise
Reef; dives range from Sansum Narrows
south to Turn Point, Stuart Island.)*

Leviathan
BC College of Diving & Undersea Charters
10221 McDonald Park Road West
Sidney BC V8L 5X7
(250)654-0154
1-877-444-3483: Toll-free throughout
    North America
www.bccollegeofdiving.com
(Day trips to Mackenzie and G.B. Church.)

Shallon
Shallon Charters
PO Box 20096, E41 - 2320 Harbour Road
Sidney BC V8L 5C9
(250)479-4276
www.shalloncharters.com
*(Day charters out of Tsehum [Shoal] Harbour
for G.B. Church and Mackenzie; Haro Strait,
Saanich Inlet and Sansum Narrows. Also to
Race Rocks. Custom liveaboard charters for
a great many destinations.)*

Out of Brentwood Bay
Loup de Mer
Rockfish Divers at the Marina &
    Eco-Adventure Centre at the
    Brentwood Bay Lodge & Spa
849 Verdier Avenue
Brentwood Bay BC V8M 1C5
(250)889-7282
www.rockfishdivers.com
*(Daily charters in Saanich Inlet for up to
eight divers or snorkelers; the public are
welcome as well as guests of the lodge. Day
trips to the Gulf Islands upon request. Guiding
under water, and warm showers after the dive.)*

Out of Sooke
Sea-Deuce
Go Deep Dive Adventures
#1 Adams Place, Box 12
Victoria BC V9B 6P6
(250)589-3483
www.godeepdive.com
*(Day charters: scuba diving and ocean tours
for two divers or three passengers. Lunch, tanks,
weights; 10 minutes to Race Rocks, 35 minutes
to Victoria. Season: June 1 to September 30.)*

• LAUNCH RAMPS AND BOAT RENTAL

For Juan de Fuca Strait

James Bay Anglers Association Boat Ramps
75 Dallas Road
Victoria BC V8V 1A1
(Launch for a fee year-round in heart of city west of the Breakwater, for a fee. Concrete ramps; good at all tides. Pay nominal membership fee at the ramps office. Also parking for 39 trailers. Telephone at top of ramps at roadside. Restrooms when ramp office is open; also restrooms 1 mile [1½ kilometers] east beside Dallas Road.)

Off Trans-Canada Highway 1: From Mile 0 at foot of Douglas Street go west almost 1½ miles (2½ kilometers) on Dallas Road to James Bay Ramps; a large, green can-buoy is beside entry. Five minutes from the Parliament Buildings.

Pedder Bay Marina Ramps
Box 12, 925 Pedder Bay Drive
Victoria BC V9C 4H1
(250)478-1771
www.pedderbaymarina.com
(Launch for a fee year-round, from Pedder Bay: concrete ramps, good at all tides. Boat rentals for passengers only – not for diving. Restrooms. Telephone outside marina.)

Cheanah Marina Ramp
4901-A East Sooke Road
Sooke BC V0S 1N0
(250)478-4880
(Launch for a fee year-round at Becher Bay: concrete ramp, good at all except extreme low tides. Toilets. Telephone at marina office.)

Pacific Lions Marina & Campground Ramps
241 Becher Bay Road, RR1
Sooke BC V0S 1N0
(250)727-2275
(Launch for a fee, in summer only: concrete ramp, good at all except extreme low tides. Toilets and telephone at top of ramp. Open May to October.)

For Haro Strait

Island View Beach Boat Ramp
Foot of Island View Road
Sidney BC
(Launch at Cordova Channel for Haro Strait; concrete ramp, good at high tides and half-tides. Parking. Restrooms; telephone by office.)

Off Highway 17: the turnoff is at a traffic light 3 miles (4½ kilometers) north of Elk Lake and 6 miles (9½ kilometers) south of the main turnoff to Sidney. Exit at Island View Road, directly opposite Keating Cross Road. Go east on Island View Road to the water – 5 minutes off Highway 17. From downtown Victoria, 30 minutes.

Sidney Public Boat Ramp
Tulista Park, Lochside Drive
Sidney
(Launch for a fee at Sidney Channel; concrete ramp, good at medium and high tides. Restrooms in park. Telephone one block north outside Visitor Info Centre, Ocean Avenue and Lochside.)

Off Highway 17: take Beacon Avenue, turn right. Turn right at the traffic light past Resthaven Drive on the left and a mall on your right, turn right at 5th Street and go four blocks to Ocean Avenue; then straight for ⅕ mile (⅓ kilometer) to Tulista Park. From downtown Victoria, 40 minutes. From Swartz Bay, 5 minutes to Tulista. Ramp entry directly opposite 9560 Lochside Drive.

For Satellite Channel

Van Isle Marina Ramp
2320 Harbour Road, off Resthaven Drive
Sidney BC V8L 2P6
(250)656-1138
www.vanislemarina.com
(Launch for a fee at Tsehum [Shoal] Harbour. Concrete ramp, good at all tides. Restrooms and hot showers. Telephone at end of fuel dock; another one in covered alcove behind café.)

For Saanich Inlet
. . . at Mill Bay
Handy Road Public Ramp
Foot of Handy Road
*(Launch free: concrete ramp. Parking space
for 10 or 12 cars. No toilets. Telephone
south outside restroom at top of privately
owned ramp next door.)*

Off Trans-Canada Highway 1, south of
Cowichan Bay Road and north of Malahat
Drive: many exits to Mill Bay. Take the one
between turnoffs to Shawnigan Lake at the
Deloume Road stoplight. Follow Brentwood
ferry signs, and generic marina and B&B
signs. A large "Mill Bay Shopping Centre"
sign is on the east side of the road at the
turnoff. Go down Deloume Road, pass
shopping centre, turn right at Mill Bay
Road and immediately left into Handy Road.

Mill Bay Marina Ramp
740 Handy Road, PO Box 231
Mill Bay BC V0R 2P0
(250)743-4112
*(Launch for a fee: concrete ramp, good for
larger boats with 3-foot [1-meter] tides and
greater. Restrooms and hot showers available
only to launch, dock and B&B customers.
Telephone top of ramp outside restrooms.)*

. . . at Brentwood Bay
Tsartlip Boat Ramp
800 Stelly's Cross Road
Brentwood Bay BC V8M 1R3
(250)652-3988
*(Launch for a fee year-round: concrete ramp,
good at all tides. Lots of parking. Launch
year-round, camping in summer. No toilets.
Telephone one block south at Peden and
Verdier.)*

. . . at Finlayson Arm
Goldstream Boathouse Marina Ramp
3540 Trans-Canada Highway 1
Victoria BC V9E 1K3
(250)478-4407
*(Launch for a fee; concrete ramp, good at all
tides. Restrooms, parking, telephone on house
opposite marina office.)*

All of this Service Information is subject
to change.

BOAT DIVE
GPS
48°18.648′ N
123°34.990′ W

SKILL
Intermediate and expert
divers

All divers with guide

CURRENT TABLE
Race Rocks

TIDE TABLE
Sooke

WHY GO

To swim through Swordfish Island. White plumose anemones fluff out from the ceiling and walls of the tunnel. Soft pink corals frame its entry and exit. You can swim in one side of Swordfish and out the other.

On the Juan de Fuca side of Swordfish we saw a juvenile wolf-eel, an octopus, a giant mussel, nudibranchs, purple urchins, a red Irish lord that sits in your hand – plus very "west coast" life: China rockfish and surf-washed green anemones.

Heading to Victoria after the dive we saw killer whales recognized by our charter operator. The whales were from a resident pod: a male with a calf, and a female. They crossed over, met, split again. Swam close beside the boat, turned their white bellies up to us. One whale spy-hopped – that was a "first" for me. It leapt straight up out of the water to look around, exposing one-third of its body. Fabulous to see its picturesque black-and-white markings. We kept the appropriate distance from them.

Preparing to enter on
Church Point side
of Swordfish

BOTTOM AND DEPTHS

Swordfish Island is oval shaped and a tunnel runs through it near the eastern end of the island. The tunnel floor is 15 to 25 feet (4½ to 8 meters) deep. On the northern side of Swordfish, the bottom is rocky with some silt and is 25 to 30 feet (8 to 9 meters) deep. It slopes gradually to the southern Juan de Fuca side. The outside wall is indented with crevices. The base of the outside wall of Swordfish bottoms out to sand and rock at 70 to 80 feet (21 to 24 meters). Bull kelp year-round.

HAZARDS

Current and surge caused by wind or passing ships – both destroy visibility in the tunnel. Shallow depth and bull kelp. If a ship is passing in Juan de Fuca, go into the tunnel quickly before surge stirs up silt. Wear enough weight so you can stay down. Carry a knife; if caught in the kelp you can cut your way free.

TELEPHONES
• On the water: VHF radio; if no VHF, try a cell phone.
• On land:
1. Becher Bay at Cheanah Marina, outside office.
2. Pedder Bay Marina, outside office.

FACILITIES

None at Swordfish Island. Charters and air fills in Victoria. Launch ramps at Pedder and Becher bays.

ACCESS

Swordfish Island is in Juan de Fuca Strait. It is 2½ nautical miles southeast of Becher Bay; 6 nautical miles southwest of Pedder Bay. At high tides, Swordfish is 20 yards (18 meters) offshore from Church Point, Vancouver Island. At low tides, it is connected to Church Point.

Charter or launch at Becher Bay or Pedder Bay and go to Swordfish. Early morning is best before the wind gets up.

The easiest way to find the tunnel is to anchor between Swordfish and Vancouver Island near a distinct notch at the east end of the island. The entrance to the tunnel is about 6½ feet (2 meters) to the right of the notch and below the surface. Descend and swim through it to the outside. However, when diving in this direction you stir up silt that follows you. No matter what the current direction, the flow in the tunnel is always southeasterly.

With a guide who knows the way, you can approach from the Juan de Fuca side, dive northwest through the tunnel toward Vancouver Island and the silt is carried away behind you. We did it that way: dropped down the anchor line, swam through bull kelp around the eastern end of the island, cruised the outside of the island. Then followed our guide through a thick kelp curtain into the tunnel and through it to the boat.

Church Point side of island: tunnel right of the notch

NOTES

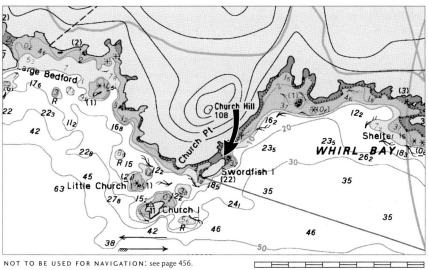

NOT TO BE USED FOR NAVIGATION: see page 456.
Use CHS chart #3410 for navigation; for information on obtaining navigational charts see page 456. Soundings are in meters.

1/2 NAUTICAL MILE

291

BOAT DIVE
GPS
North of Great Race Rock:
48°17.945' N
123°31.887' W

South of Great Race Rock:
48°17.808' N
123°31.974' W

SKILL
Expert divers and
snorkelers

All divers with guide

CURRENT TABLE
Race Passage

TIDE TABLE
Sooke

WHY GO

"Animals!" one diver exclaimed after his first dive at Race Rocks.

The greatest variety of marine creatures I've seen anywhere lives around these current-swept rocks. It's a magnificent mix of protected-waters wildlife and outer-west-coast wildlife – much of it in the shallows. I saw big lacy basket stars in only 30 feet (9 meters); spiny giant red urchins; thick bull kelp; black serpent stars snaking from hot pink hydrocoral more brilliant than tropical coral. In the Great Race, a plush carpet of brooding anemones like pink, pale green and lavender bonbons completely covers the sea floor. Dahlia anemones, Puget Sound king crabs, pale yellow staghorn bryozoans, black rockfish, lingcod, kelp greenlings, sculpins, abalones, orange solitary cup corals, octopuses, cabezons, harbor seals and many more creatures live at Race Rocks.

Steller sea lions and California sea lions haul out here from August until May. We saw sea lions resting on the outermost rocks and scudding down the waves. The last time I was at Race Rocks we saw a gigantic elephant seal lounging on the rocks dangling its long proboscis – my first time to view this marine mammal. It looked bigger than the boat we were in. I'm

told they've been in the area for 10 years and are seen year-round, especially summer.

Divers doing research or looking for special forms of life will find unique hydroids, colonial ascidians and sponges here. See www.racerocks.com/racerock/archives.htm, click on Invertebrates.

Whatever your diving interest – you will love Race Rocks!

BOTTOM AND DEPTHS

At the Great Race north of Great Race Rock the bottom slopes gradually from the dock to a depth of 30 to 40 feet (9 to 12 meters). Some bull kelp. South of Great Race Rock, bright white rocky bottom tiers gradually to a depth of 50 to 60 feet (15 to 18 meters): in summer it's a thicket of bull kelp. I have not dived the northwest corner of West Race Rock, but be warned: it plunges 100 to 110 feet (30 to 34 meters) into Race Passage.

HAZARDS

Current, wind, fog, bull kelp and sea lions. At Race Passage, currents up to 7 knots, more with wind, and downwellings into dropoffs. Dive all locations on slack, and to avoid downwellings, do not go deeper than 50 feet (15 meters) when in current. Dive all locations with a "live" boat. Important for safety too, and advisable to go with a guide who knows the waters and wind. Wear a whistle for fog and wind. Carry a knife for kelp; use in emergency only in this ecological reserve. Sea lions may approach divers; injuries have occurred because of playful animals. They become more aggressive with familiarity. Do not stay long in the water with sea lions.

TELEPHONES
• On the water: VHF radio; if no VHF, try a cell phone.
• On land: Pedder Bay Marina, outside.

FACILITIES
None at Race Rocks. Charters out of Victoria.

*Great Race Rock
light station and dock*

Jelly with red eye-spots

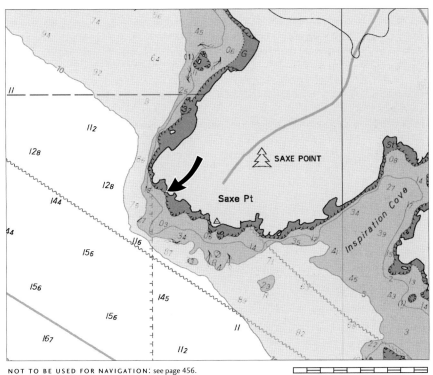

SAXE POINT

Saxe Pt

Inspiration Cove

NOT TO BE USED FOR NAVIGATION: see page 456.
Use CHS chart #3419 for navigation; for information on obtaining
navigational charts see page 456. Soundings are in meters.

1/10 NAUTICAL MILE

NOTES

OGDEN POINT BREAKWATER

SHORE DIVE

SKILL
All divers

TIDE TABLE
Victoria

WHY GO

Going to Ogden Point Breakwater is a "Sunday thing to do": it's a favorite for sightseeing and photography; a popular open-water certification site; excellent for practicing underwater navigation. It's a three-ring circus.

The Breakwater is also a marine sanctuary – rich with life. The marine trail of five underwater plaques is unique in that the plaques are so easy to find: each one is located by a dive flag painted on the Breakwater above the surface. The shallowest plaque features eelgrass animals: we saw leafy hornmouth snailss laying eggs, six lingcod – one huge "ling", kelp greenlings, a swimming scallop, flounders and ghost shrimp on the sand. As we went deeper we saw abalones, gum boot chitons, red urchins. Christmas, dahlia and plumose anemones. China rockfish, seaperch, tiger rockfish, schools of black rockfish. In the riprap, look for penpoint gunnels, octopuses, wolf-eels. At night, look for sailfin sculpins. At the deepest plaque, hordes of swimming scallops.

The first half of the Breakwater is great for new divers to see a variety of marine life and meet other divers. Intermediate and expert divers experienced with current will find the most peaceful diving on the last half of the Breakwater.

BOTTOM AND DEPTHS

Broken rock, or riprap, is heaped along the base of the Breakwater which is 5 feet (1½ meters) deep, sloping to a depth of 80 to 90 feet (24 to 27 meters) at its end. Sand stretches out from the riprap. Thick beds of bull kelp rim the Breakwater which extends ½ mile (¾ kilometer) into the sea. The farther out the Breakwater you go, the more demanding the dive becomes because of increased current and depth. The plaques are from 5 to 50 feet (1½ to 15 meters) deep at low tide.

HAZARDS

Bull kelp, fishing line, wind, and wash from passing boats and current. Carry a knife; if caught in kelp or transparent fishing line you can cut your way free. Southeast wind can blow up surf which makes it difficult to swim through the kelp and climb from the water. On the surface, pay attention to wash from passing boats. Dive the last half of the Breakwater on the slack.

TELEPHONE

At rinse station inside the Ogden Point Dive Centre; available 24 hours.

FACILITIES

Hot showers, restrooms, rinse station, and lockers at the dive centre during dive shop business hours; all divers welcome. Public restrooms available 24 hours in the park 1¼ miles (2 kilometers) southeast of the Breakwater. Eat a bag lunch on the beach or enjoy lunch or dinner at the café, above the dive centre. Air fills and dive charters throughout Victoria and Sidney.

Waves splash on last leg of the Breakwater

ACCESS

The Ogden Point Breakwater is on Juan de Fuca Strait in the heart of Victoria; the Breakwater protects Victoria Harbour.

From the conference center behind the Fairmont Empress Hotel go 1¼ miles (2 kilometers) to it: drive south on Douglas Street to the water. You are now at Mile 0 of Trans-Canada Highway 1. Turn right onto Dallas Road and go ¾ mile (1⅓ kilometers) to the Breakwater. Free parking east of the Breakwater for 20 cars; unlimited parking on Dallas Road; a great deal of pay parking north of the Breakwater.

Look for dive flags painted on the Juan de Fuca side of the Breakwater which locate the plaques. You could start shallow or deep. We started with the plaque that is farthest out, as diving it is dependent on current and we were there at the right time. First we walked to the end of the Breakwater without gear. That took 15 minutes. Next we carried weight belts, fins and masks and dropped them. Then geared up in suits and tanks, walked out and jumped in. We saw what was at flag #5, enjoyed it, surfaced, snorkeled to the next flag. Dived to see what was at #4, surfaced and snorkeled again. We were just skimming and it took us two days to visit the Breakwater. So much information is on each plaque as well as so much marine life below each one, you could take a week over it.

Using the plaques, you could practice underwater navigation skills and go from one plaque to the other, staying under water all the way. The distance and compass bearings are given on each plaque for adjacent plaques.

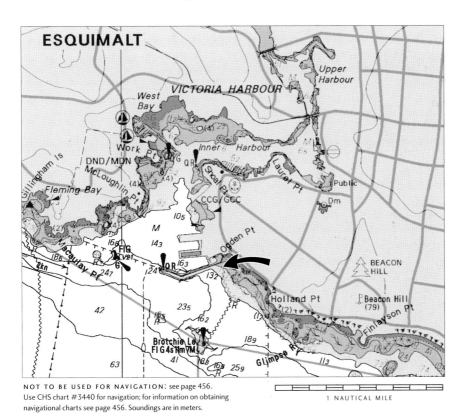

NOT TO BE USED FOR NAVIGATION: see page 456.
Use CHS chart #3440 for navigation; for information on obtaining navigational charts see page 456. Soundings are in meters.

1 NAUTICAL MILE

NOTES

BROTCHIE LEDGE

BOAT DIVE

GPS
48°24.308' N
123°23.427' W

SKILL
Intermediate and expert
divers

All divers with guide

CURRENT TABLE
Race Passage

WHY GO

Brotchie Ledge – part of the Ogden Point area which is closed to spearfishing – is an endless source of gorgeous junk.

Do not take marine life or any artifact that might be connected with a wreck, but look for crockery, old bottles, everyday kind of stuff. Investigate everything you see with a geometric shape, or with giant barnacles on it.

Fifty to one hundred years ago, garbage barges regularly came out of Victoria's Inner Harbour and deposited their load in this area. Search in the silty sand among the swimming scallops, and you will probably find some intriguing relics. On one dive at Brotchie Ledge three of us found two tiger whiskey bottles, two Chinese bean pots, a large flower planter and one crockery marmalade pot. From the size of the barnacles on all of them we guessed they must be at least fifty years old.

We also happened onto something big which might have been a boiler from the 331-foot (100-meter) metal-hulled *San Pedro*. In 1891 the *San Pedro* went down on Brotchie Ledge. Two companies went bankrupt trying to salvage the wreck before it was declared a navigational hazard and blown up. Fragments of the *San Pedro* are flung over Brotchie Ledge. If you find the wreck, look for a plaque on it.

Look but do not disturb any ship wreckage here nor at any other site: at Brotchie there is so much of interest, apart from wrecks, for the treasure hunter to take home. One diver collects nothing here but foot-warmers, sometimes called "pigs".

BOTTOM AND DEPTHS

Silt-covered giant barnacles are attached to everything solid on the mucky bottom slightly beyond the marker where it is as deep as 80 to 90 feet (24 to 27 meters). That's where the finds are.

Close around the marker it is shallow, 5 to 26 feet (1½ to 8 meters) deep.

HAZARDS

Wind, current, poor visibility and sailboats. Currents are not always as predicted. Dive in early morning when the water is calm, on the slack, on a small tidal exchange. If you cannot coordinate all of these factors, dive in the early morning when calm and the pickup person can easily see your bubbles. For best visibility, when delving in the muck try to disturb the bottom as little as possible; wave your hand to expose suspected finds. When you ascend, spiral and look up. Sailboats approach silently.

TELEPHONES

- On the water: VHF radio; if no VHF, try a cell phone.
- On land: At entry to Ogden Point Breakwater, inside Dive Centre rinse station; available 24 hours.

FACILITIES

None.

ACCESS

Brotchie Ledge is just outside Victoria Harbour in Juan de Fuca Strait, less than ½ nautical mile offshore from the Breakwater at Ogden Point.

Charter out of Victoria or Sidney, launch an inflatable at the Breakwater or launch at James Bay. Go to the marker that indicates the ledge. Before diving, look at the water. If there is a back eddy at Brotchie Ledge, do not dive. If the kelp is not on the surface, the current is too great to dive. If all is well, search in the deeper waters beyond the ledge.

The ocean around Brotchie Ledge is too deep and too current-ridden to anchor. And, as at all sites with aids to navigation, do not tie up to the marker. It is a federal offense to make fast to a marker or tamper with it. Leave someone on the boat to follow you and pick you up when you ascend.

Barnacled Chinese
bean pot

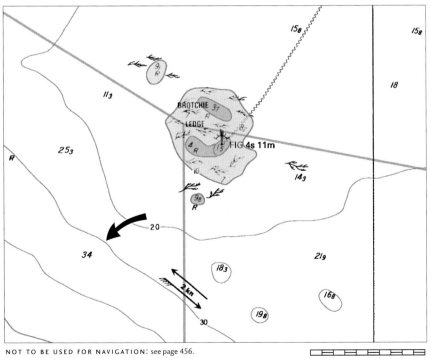

NOTES

NOT TO BE USED FOR NAVIGATION: see page 456.
Use CHS chart #3415 for navigation; for information on obtaining
navigational charts see page 456. Soundings are in meters.

1/10 NAUTICAL MILE

TEN MILE POINT

SKILL
Intermediate and expert divers

All divers with guide

CURRENT TABLE
Race Passage:
Subtract 15 minutes

WHY GO
"Filter-feeder city" is the way one diver describes Ten Mile Point where the current carries food to hungry marine creatures.

Swimming scallops would be enough to lure me to this site. All creatures that feed from the current flourish here. Particularly animals like the many orange and white crevice-dwelling sea cucumbers that put out tentacles to feed. "Suspension-feeder city" is a more accurate description. The wall is a colorful tapestry. Heaps of white sea cucumbers look like organ pipe cacti when their tendrils are retracted. We saw rock scallops, a forest of white plumose anemones, quillback rockfish in the crevices. Small black rockfish swim past in schools. At the base of the wall, abalone shells, giant urchins, massive beds of giant barnacles, thousands of swimming scallops clapping up around us from the sand. You may meet a seal in the kelp.

In 1975 Ten Mile Point was declared a provincial marine ecological reserve for scientific research. Recreational use is permitted as long as it is not damaging.

Giant acorn barnacle feeding from current

It's a photographer's special – no taking of marine life at this reserve.

BOTTOM AND DEPTHS
Rocky bottom, with lettuce kelp, slopes gently to a bed of bull kelp at 30 to 40 feet (9 to 12 meters). The crevice-filled rock wall drops off quickly to a depth of 80 to 90 feet (24 to 27 meters), a sea floor of almost flat sand.

HAZARDS
Current, bull kelp and broken fishing line. Dive on the slack. Current up to 5 to 6 knots can run past this point. Be careful on large tidal exchanges. Carry a knife for kelp or fishing line.

TELEPHONE
Cadboro Bay Village: at gas station, 2 miles (3¼ kilometers) back.

FACILITIES
Space for four cars to park.

ACCESS
Ten Mile Point is on Haro Strait north of Baynes Channel. Reach it via the village of Cadboro Bay, a northern suburb. It is 7½ miles (12 kilometers) from the heart of Victoria.

From the village of Cadboro Bay, go north on Cadboro Bay Road; the road name changes to Telegraph Bay Road. From the village go ½ mile (¾ kilometer) to Seaview Road. Turn right. Then, almost immediately, left into Tudor Avenue. Continue on Tudor for 1 mile (1½ kilometers). Tudor makes a right-angle turn to the left. Shortly past that sharp corner, turn right into Baynes Road. Go almost to the end of Baynes and turn left into White Rock Street to the water. Park by the small turnaround, suit up and climb a few feet down over the rocks to the sea.

If rough water because of wind or if the current is too great at Ten Mile Point, go to nearby Spring Bay.

To get to the village of Cadboro Bay
- From the Fairmont Empress Hotel in Victoria and from the Port Angeles ferry which lands at the Inner Harbour in front of the Empress, 20 minutes to Cadboro Bay. From the Empress, go a few blocks north to Fort Street. Head east on Fort Street which becomes Cadboro Bay Road. When the road dips close to the water you are at the village of Cadboro Bay.
- From Swartz Bay or Sidney, head south on Pat Bay Highway (Highway 17) for 30 minutes to Cadboro Bay. Past Elk Lake take Highway 1–Nanaimo/McKenzie Avenue exit. Stay left on the off-ramp and follow signs to the University of Victoria. Go through a residential section, then past the university. At the Finnerty traffic light, do not turn; continue straight on Sinclair Road into the village of Cadboro Bay.
- From Duncan heading south on Highway 1: past Helmcken Road, exit Highway 1 and follow signs to Ferries, Sidney, 17 North and University of Victoria. From this exit, 15 minutes to Cadboro Bay. Go to Highway 17; cross it and continue on McKenzie Avenue. At Finnerty, continue straight on Sinclair to the village of Cadboro Bay.
- From Duncan heading south on Highway 1: past Helmcken Road, when you reach an overpass, continue straight beneath it and follow signs to the University of Victoria. Go straight on McKenzie Avenue through a residential section, then past the University of Victoria. At Finnerty, continue straight on Sinclair to the village of Cadboro Bay. From the overpass, 15 minutes to Cadboro Bay.
- From the Mill Bay ferry at Brentwood Bay, 25 minutes to Cadboro Bay. Head south on West Saanich Road; when West Saanich Road ends at Highway 17, continue south a short way on Highway 17 to Highway 1–Nanaimo/McKenzie Avenue exit. Stay left on the off-ramp following signs to the University of Victoria. Go through a residential section, and past the university. At the Finnerty traffic light, do not turn. Continue straight on Sinclair Road to the village of Cadboro Bay.

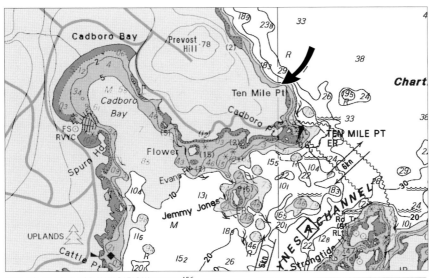

NOT TO BE USED FOR NAVIGATION: see page 456.
Use CHS chart #3440 for navigation; for information on obtaining navigational charts see page 456. Soundings are in meters.

1 NAUTICAL MILE

NOTES

SPRING BAY

SHORE DIVE

SKILL
All divers and snorkelers

TIDE TABLE
Victoria

WHY GO
Easy entry, gentle terraced bottom, in-the-city dive. Excellent for new divers, veterans too. When a southwesterly wind is blowing, come to Spring Bay where it is calm.

Everybody loves an octopus – lots of them here. Hiding in dens in the valleys or rock. A jungle of orange sea cucumbers lights up the brown bottom kelp. Snails scramble all over the place. We saw blood stars, purple stars; kelp greenlings, ling-cod, quillback rockfish; a sea lemon, shrimp, a single swimming scallop, giant barnacles, clam shells and leafy hornmouth snails. A few plumose anemones, gum boot chitons, urchins. Spider crabs. A red-and-transparent striped gunnel with a yellow spot. And three harbor seals. Do not go closer to harbor seals than 110 yards (100 meters).

BOTTOM AND DEPTHS
Gradually sloping rock bottom with mini-canyons covered in leafy brown bottom kelp. Giant purple urchins between. In summer, bull kelp. You will find most of the life in 60 to 65 feet (18 to 20 meters).

HAZARDS
Bull kelp. Carry a knife.

TELEPHONE
Cadboro Bay Village: at gas station, 2 miles (3¼ kilometers) back.

FACILITIES
Crescent of beach with a view of Mount Baker. Great place for a picnic. Air fills in Victoria and Saanichtown. Restrooms at Cadboro-Gyro Park, foot of Sinclair Road. Turn left off Cadboro Bay Road just past gas station in village.

ACCESS
Spring Bay is located on Haro Strait in the village of Cadboro Bay, an elegant northern suburb of Victoria. It is 7½ miles (12 kilometers) from the heart of Victoria.

From the village of Cadboro Bay, go north along Cadboro Bay Road; the road name changes to Telegraph Bay Road. From the village, go ½ mile (¾ kilometer) and turn right at Seaview Road. Then, almost immediately, turn left into Tudor Avenue. Continue on Tudor to the end of it. Space for two or three cars to park. Twelve stairsteps to the gravelly beach, then head around the point on your left and explore along the rocky ledge.

To get to village of Cadboro Bay
- From the Fairmont Empress Hotel in Victoria and from the Port Angeles ferry that lands at the Inner Harbour in front of the Empress, 20 minutes to Cadboro Bay. Head east on Fort Street which becomes Cadboro Bay Road. When the road dips close to the water you are at the village of Cadboro Bay.
- From Swartz Bay or Sidney, head south on Highway 17 (Pat Bay Highway) to Cadboro Bay; it takes 30 minutes. Go past Elk Lake and take Highway 1–Nanaimo, McKenzie Avenue–University of Victoria exit. Stay left on the off-ramp and follow signs to the University of Victoria. Go through a residential section, then past the university. At the Finnerty traffic light, do not turn; continue straight on Sinclair Road into the village of Cadboro Bay.
- From Duncan heading south on Highway 1: past Helmcken Road, when you reach an overpass, continue straight beneath it and follow signs to the University of Victoria. Go straight on McKenzie Avenue through a residential section, then past the University of Victoria. At Finnerty, continue straight on Sinclair to the village of Cadboro Bay. From the overpass, 15 minutes to Cadboro Bay.
- From the Mill Bay ferry at Brentwood Bay, 25 minutes to Cadboro Bay. Head south on West Saanich Road; when West Saanich Road ends at Highway 17, continue south a short way on Highway 17 to Highway 1–Nanaimo, McKenzie Avenue–University of Victoria exit. Stay

left on the off-ramp following signs to the University of Victoria. Go through a residential section, and past the univer-

sity. At the Finnerty traffic light, do not turn. Continue straight on Sinclair Road to the village of Cadboro Bay.

*After dive at Spring Bay,
Ten Mile Point behind*

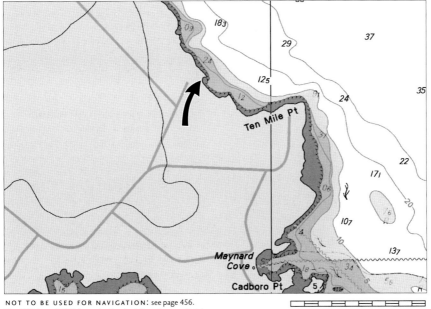

NOT TO BE USED FOR NAVIGATION: see page 456.
Use CHS chart #3424 for navigation; for information on obtaining navigational charts see page 456. Soundings are in meters.

1/5 NAUTICAL MILE

NOTES

MACKENZIE ARTIFICIAL REEF

BOAT DIVE
GPS
48°40.093' N
123°17.161' W

SKILL
On exterior: all divers
with current experience
and guide

On interior: intermediate
and expert divers with
penetration experience

TIDE TABLE
Fulford Harbour

WHY GO

Great ship for recreational divers to explore on the outside, excellent for wreck penetration training. Prolific marine life inside and outside the *Mackenzie*.

We passed the bridge, the radar tower amidships, the huge mortar bay near the stern of this 366-foot (112-meter) long vessel. On the outside of it, we looked into holes cut in the sides to provide light, entry and exit points. In one we saw a row of toilets, the head. In another, a rockfish and a large lion's mane jelly with a 6-inch (15-centimeter) diameter mantle. Outside the ship, many white plumose anemones, lemon peel nudibranchs, a gold dirona nudibranch, a decorator crab. Swimming scallops. A clown shrimp. A cabezon. Copper and quillback rockfish, kelp greenlings and many lingcod. Tube worms in the sand.

Divers in our group training in wreck penetration followed the Burma Road its full length into and out of the vessel – completed it in one dive. An exciting culmination to the ocean training they'd had practicing with reels and flashlights. The Burma Road is at a depth of 90 feet (27 meters) at high tides. The round trip is a distance of more than 700 feet (213 meters) – a long way to go in dark, silty waters in an

*Loading gear onto
Juan de Fuca Warrior,
and off to the Mackenzie*

enclosed-overhead environment. A good vessel to do it on, as it is upright. Next these divers might penetrate the Burma Road on a sunken ship with a list, a longer vessel or a deeper one. The series of artificial reefs throughout British Columbia offers opportunity for this type of gradual growth in wreck-diving skills.

The *Mackenzie* was commissioned on October 6, 1962, operated as an anti-submarine destroyer escort ship for 10 years; a training ship the next 20. In 1973 the *Mackenzie's* crew boarded and seized MV *Marysville*, resulting in a million-dollar drug bust. During 30 years of service, the *Mackenzie* traveled a total of 845,640 nautical miles. It was decommissioned August 3, 1993. The Artificial Reef Society of British Columbia scuttled it September 16, 1995 to provide habitat for marine life and exploration opportunities for divers.

BOTTOM AND DEPTHS

The *Mackenzie* is upright – it settled on silty sand and slopes gently from bow to stern. At high tides, the radar tower is at 70 feet (21 meters); the bow rests at 105 feet (32 meters). The stern is deeper, 115 feet (35 meters). The bow points west/northwest.

HAZARDS

Current and the vessel itself. Avoid diving at this site during ebb tides as currents can be high, unpredictable and erratic. Best to dive on the slack or during minor flood currents.

If the flood at Fulford is greater than 6 feet (2 meters) in 6 hours, do not dive. If the flood at Fulford is more than 4 feet (1¼ meters) in 6 hours, only divers well experienced with current should dive and then with extreme caution. Divers not trained in penetration should not enter. Divers with training in penetration will find it a good wreck to go into, but beware of silt. See the "HMCS *Mackenzie*

Artificial Reef Map" by Bernie Kyle at dive shops or contact www.aquatic-realm.com.

TELEPHONES

- On the water: VHF radio; if no VHF, try a cell phone.
- On land:
1. Canoe Bay [Canoe Cove] southeast of Swartz Bay ferry terminal at Canoe Cove Marina, top of fuel dock at the Coffee Shop.
2. Tsehum [Shoal] Harbour, end of Van Isle Marina fuel dock in Sidney.

FACILITIES

Isle-de-Lis primitive campground at nearby Rum Island Gulf Islands National Park.

ACCESS

The *Mackenzie* is located 3½ nautical miles east of Sidney in Haro Strait. It is 150 yards (140 meters) north of Gooch and Rum islands, just over 1 nautical mile west of the Canada/USA boundary, and well protected from southeast winds.

Charter out of Sidney, Victoria, Pender Island or Friday Harbor, Washington. Or launch your own boat at Sidney and go to Gooch Island. If current, approach the

Mackenzie from downstream in order to avoid divers. Marker buoys are on the bow and stern of the *Mackenzie* and must not be used for mooring – leave them as safe places for divers to ascend.

Mooring buoys are on the Gooch Island side of the vessel that is usually protected from current. Underwater tag lines go from mooring buoy lines to the bow, amidships and near the stern of the *Mackenzie*. Tie up to a mooring buoy: attach a 50-foot (15-meter) drift line to it for divers to hang onto upon entering the water. Leave a boat tender on board.

Divers enter, follow the drift line to the mooring, then descend to tag lines leading to the *Mackenzie*. Follow one. If you descend past the mid-water float the tag lines go from, you will reach a concrete anchor block on the bottom – return up to the float and tag line or lines.

Occasionally one or two buoys are ripped out by weather but all of them going missing is unlikely, and to date has never happened. If it does, use GPS locations and a depth sounder. Anchor in 65 to 75 feet (20 to 23 meters) on the Gooch Island side of the *Mackenzie*, which is usually in the lee of current, and dive.

NOTES

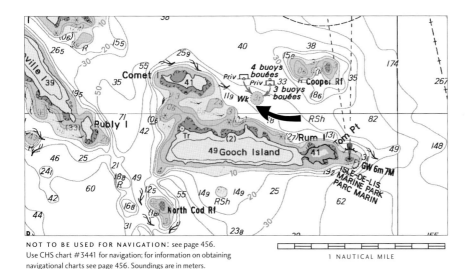

NOT TO BE USED FOR NAVIGATION: see page 456.
Use CHS chart #3441 for navigation; for information on obtaining navigational charts see page 456. Soundings are in meters.

1 NAUTICAL MILE

GRAHAM'S WALL

BOAT DIVE

GPS
48°40.226' N
123°19.380' W

SKILL
Intermediate and expert
divers

All divers with guide

CURRENT TABLE
Race Passage
• Slack before flood:
  Add 1 hour

• Slack before ebb:
  Add 1½ hours

WHY GO

Graham's Wall is covered with life – much of it new to me. It is packed with exotica. As our guide exclaimed after our dive, "You gotta go back to your books after this one!"

Huge plumose anemones billow beneath the undercut wall. Yellow encrusting sponge flames the rock. A few orange cucumbers are in crevices. Pink soft corals too. Staghorn bryozoans twist from the rocks. Pink colonial anemones are beneath the overhangs. We saw tiny sculpins with red markings, large lingcod, giant barnacles, decorator crabs, rock scallops, an octopus den. An orange-spotted clown nudibranch, an alabaster nudibranch, an orange peel nudibranch and nudibranch eggs. Orange cup corals. Crystal clear glass tunicates and a deep red sea peach. We saw heart crabs. A tiny porcelain crab held up its delicate, mauve-colored claws to us, not fearful at all when gently pushed. Stood its ground. This little crab stretched to its full height was 1 inch (2½ centimeters) tall. I don't think any divers could identify every creature they saw on one dive here without looking at several marine identification books.

Just go to the maximum depth you want to dive and weave back and forth up the wall. You do not even have to move – just stay in one place and look. So much to see.

BOTTOM AND DEPTHS

A rocky wall with overhangs but you cannot touch rock nor even see it because of so much life on the wall. The wall does not drop straight down, it undercuts and bottoms out to sand at 90 to 100 feet (27 to 30 meters). East of the wall, rocky bottom with brown bottom kelp and bull kelp, especially in summer, at a depth of 25 to 35 feet (8 to 11 meters). It ledges down gently to the wall.

HAZARDS

Current, small boats, transparent fishing line and bull kelp. The current correction used is for Sidney Channel. Dive on slack or during flood, except for the largest floods; on small ebbs, dive with a pickup boat. If the kelp is on the surface it is divable. Listen for boats and ascend in the bull kelp out of the way of boats. Carry a knife.

TELEPHONES

• On the water: VHF radio; if no VHF, try a cell phone.
• On land:
1. Tsehum Harbour [Shoal Harbour], end of Van Isle Marina fuel dock in Sidney.
2. Wharf at foot of Beacon Avenue where Sidney Spit ferry goes from.

FACILITIES

None at Graham's Wall. Many facilities in Sidney and Victoria, including dive charters as well as waterfront and roadside air fills.

ACCESS

Graham's Wall is in Haro Strait off Domville Island. It is 3 nautical miles east/northeast of Sidney on the east side of Saanich Peninsula.

Charter or launch out of Sidney or Brentwood Bay. Go to the middle of the west side of Domville Island. At low tides look for a rock with bull kelp all around and often harbor seals on it. Avoid approaching closer than 110 yards (100 meters) to the seals. The rock dries at 3-foot (1-meter) tides. If no rock is visible, look for the kelp. In summer, it is a thicket. Anchor between Domville Island and the kelp.

To find the wall: swim west to the kelp, but do not go to the rock. Descend east side of the kelp and head north under water. As you go deeper, stay close to the wall and go left around the corner of the rock to the west-facing wall. The wall is short. Start diving deep and work your way up, zigzagging back and forth. We saw the full length of the wall at three depths going up. Different life each pass we made.

*Off Domville Island, rock
with seals on it*

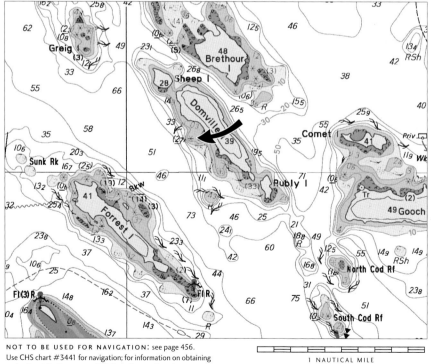

NOT TO BE USED FOR NAVIGATION: see page 456.
Use CHS chart #3441 for navigation; for information on obtaining
navigational charts see page 456. Soundings are in meters.

1 NAUTICAL MILE

NOTES

G.B. CHURCH ARTIFICIAL REEF

BOAT DIVE
GPS
48°43.350′ N
123°21.252′ W

SKILL
Intermediate and expert divers

All divers with guide

CURRENT TABLE
Active Pass

TIDE TABLE
Fulford Harbour

WHY GO

The *G.B. Church* sits upright. This munitions carrier turned herring packer looks ready to sail away. A ghost ship. Burgeoning with new life.

When we first dived it shortly after sinking, frills of nudibranch eggs covered the barnacled hull. We looked for but did not find the giant octopus in the hollowed-out mud beneath the bow – ribbons of brilliant green bull kelp brought by the timid octopus curtained its den. We chuckled. Bull kelp does not grow at this depth. Moving up the side we saw *G.B. Church* painted on the bow. We went into the wheelhouse, saw the control panel and gauges. Swam along the length of the ship, saw a sign saying "Only One Person on the Stairs at a Time", saw a plaque placed on the front of the superstructure by the provincial parks that commemorates the sinking of this ship on August 10, 1991.

Today, the main mast has fallen forward

Exploring wheelhouse shortly after sinking

across the cargo hold but the foremast is okay; marine life is flourishing; a thick growth of plumose anemones blocks the starboard side opening to the wheelhouse so divers now enter on the port side. Large lingcod cruise the ship. Sponges are starting to grow in the hold. And, if you dive early in the morning before others arrive, you will probably also find rockfish crowding the wheelhouse – some quillbacks but mostly copper rockfish.

The *G.B. Church* was the first vessel sunk by the Artificial Reef Society of British Columbia in conjunction with BC Parks. Diver access holes have been cut throughout the ship at a depth of 55 to 65 feet (15 to 20 meters). You can always see light wherever you go. Experienced wreck divers can penetrate the forecastle, engine room and galley.

The vessel was built in 1943: first named *Cerium*, then *G.R. Velie*, then *G.B. Church*. Its steel hull is 175 feet (53 meters) long. Designed as a munitions carrier with a flattish keel and hull, the ship saw action on D-Day in the Second World War, June 6, 1944. A crew member from those days turned up on the day of sinking when the vessel started its new life beneath the sea.

BOTTOM AND DEPTHS

The keel rests on featureless mud bottom at 75 to 85 feet (23 to 26 meters), depending on tide height. The top of the forward mast is the shallowest point of the ship at a depth of 13 to 23 feet (4 to 7 meters). The forepeak of the bow is at 50 to 60 feet (15 to 18 meters).

HAZARDS

Current, small boats and the temptation to penetrate the vessel. On large tidal exchanges, dive near slack. Listen for boats and ascend up one of the marker buoy chains attached to each mast all the way to the surface, well out of the way of boats. Only divers trained in penetration techniques should enter the *G.B. Church*.

TELEPHONES

- On the water: VHF radio; if no VHF, try a cell phone.
- On land:

1. Canoe Bay [Canoe Cove] immediately southeast of Swartz Bay ferry terminal; the phone is at Canoe Cove Marina, top of the fuel dock at the Coffee Shop.
2. Tsehum Harbour [Shoal Harbour], end of Van Isle Marina fuel dock.
3. Pender Island, Bedwell Harbour: at Poet's Cove Resort, go up the dock to the lower pool area – the telephone is upstairs. Outdoors, available 24 hours.

FACILITIES

Backcountry camping at Portland Island in the Gulf Islands National Park Reserve (formerly Princess Margaret Marine Park), accessible only by water.

ACCESS

The *G.B. Church* is beside Moresby Passage in the Gulf Islands National Park Reserve, 550 yards (500 meters) off the southeast corner of Portland Island, 4 nautical miles northeast of Sidney.

Charters out of Sidney and Victoria on Vancouver Island, and out of Pender Island. Or launch your own boat at one of many ramps in Sidney. It's a popular site. You'll probably see more dive boats too – go early for silt-free uncrowded diving. At the time of writing, two buoys were on the vessel, bow and stern; tie onto one of them.

Best to dive at end of the ebb. Look at the water – consider current direction when choosing which buoy to tie up to; then descend on the chain. Work your way around the wreck. When diving, be aware of current direction so you can ascend the chain you descended on or at the buoy that is upcurrent from where your boat is tied up.

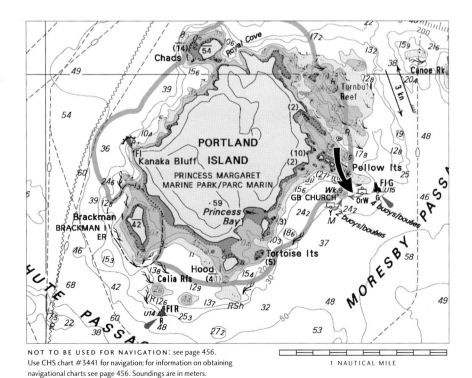

NOTES

NOT TO BE USED FOR NAVIGATION: see page 456.
Use CHS chart #3441 for navigation; for information on obtaining navigational charts see page 456. Soundings are in meters.

1 NAUTICAL MILE

BOAT DIVE
GPS
48°42.361' N
123°26.174' W

SKILL
Intermediate and expert divers

All divers with guide

TIDE TABLE
Fulford Harbour

WHY GO

Arbutus Island is a perfect little gem of an island. Here you can see unusual, brown cemented tube worms that form small reefs or mounds all over the bottom. And in one easy circuit you can see a cross-section of most life seen in the Strait of Georgia.

Sea pens, kelp greenlings, orange spotted nudibranchs, rock scallops, octopuses, small abalones and schools of black rockfish all live at Arbutus Island. Tiger rockfish, sailfin sculpins and decorated warbonnets inhabit crevices in the wall on the west end. Overhangs are thick with white plumose anemones. We also saw small clumps of hard yellow staghorn bryozoans.

Arbutus Island: an easy dive with an outstanding variety of life day or night.

BOTTOM AND DEPTHS

A variety of substrates surrounds this small island. Once thick bull kelp was in 15 to 25 feet (5 to 8 meters) but I saw none when I was last there. It might return in late summer. A vertical rock wall to 45 to 55 feet (12 to 17 meters), caves and arches of rock at 30 to 40 feet (9 to 12 meters), flat sand and large boulders.

HAZARDS

Current and small boats. Watch for abandoned gill nets in the late fall. Dive on the slack or during a rising tide. Many small boats stop at Arbutus Island. Listen for boats and ascend close to the bottom all the way to shore, well out of the way of those boats. Carry a knife.

TELEPHONES

• On the water: VHF radio; if no VHF, try a cell phone.
• On land:
1. Canoe Bay [Canoe Cove] immediately southeast of Swartz Bay ferry terminal: at Canoe Cove Marina, top of fuel dock at Coffee Shop.
2. Tsehum Harbour [Shoal Harbour], end of Van Isle Marina fuel dock in Sidney.

FACILITIES

None at Arbutus Island. Charters out of Sidney, Victoria, Brentwood Bay, Duncan and Pender Island to Arbutus – also air fills. Camping seasonally at McDonald

Sailfin sculpin

Campground – part of the Gulf Islands National Park Reserve. It is near Swartz Bay ferry terminal.

ACCESS

Arbutus Island is in Satellite Channel. It is ½ nautical mile off the northern tip of Saanich Peninsula, ½ nautical mile west of Piers Island. Charter, or launch your own boat at Sidney. Go to the northern tip of Saanich Peninsula, and look for a small uninhabited island with the skeleton of one dead arbutus tree on it. Anchor or land, and dive all around the island. A good place to start is at the caves on the southwest corner.

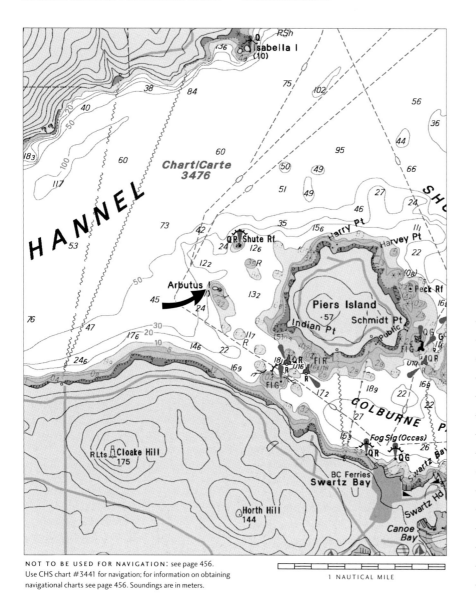

NOT TO BE USED FOR NAVIGATION: see page 456.
Use CHS chart #3441 for navigation; for information on obtaining navigational charts see page 456. Soundings are in meters.

1 NAUTICAL MILE

NOTES

TOZIER ROCK

**BOAT DIVE or
KAYAK DIVE**

GPS
48°37.037′ N
123°30.851′ W

SKILL
All divers

TIDE TABLE
Fulford Harbour:
Add 15 minutes

*Look under ledges
for wolf-eels*

WHY GO

Wolf-eels lurk from their dens when divers bring urchins to them at Tozier Rock – so do not be frightened. "Miss Piggy" lives here. Octopuses too. You can easily go deep, yet ledges cascade down from the marker. There are places to stop all the way to the ridge at 70 to 80 feet (21 to 24 meters). White and orange plumose anemones tilt from the rocks. Lingcod and quillback rockfish swim in and out of the bottom kelp. And, if you find them, those octopuses, those friendly wolf-eels are here.

Look for lead fishing weights to salvage.

BOTTOM AND DEPTHS

Rocky bottom is 25 to 35 feet (8 to 11 meters) deep on the inlet side of the marker and cascades gently to the ridge at 70 to 80 feet (21 to 24 meters). From there, the bottom drops away into the dark fjord. Flat sandy bottom 20 to 30 feet (6 to 9 meters) on the west side of the marker.

HAZARDS

Small boats and broken fishing line. Lion's mane jellies, in the fall. Poor visibility, in summer. Possible danger to kayak-divers by over-exertion after the dive. Listen for boats and ascend at the marker well out of the way of boats. Carry a knife. If you have seen any jellies, check for stinging tentacles before removing masks and gloves. Kayak-divers, especially those who have dived deep, should rest before paddling back.

TELEPHONES

• On the water: VHF radio; if no VHF, try a cell phone.
• On land:
1. Mill Bay: outside restrooms at marina.
2. Brentwood Bay: from Tsartlip Boat Ramp, go one block south toward ferry outside restaurant at Peden Lane and Verdier Avenue.

FACILITIES

None at Tozier Rock. Charters out of Sidney, Brentwood Bay, Victoria, Duncan and Cowichan Bay – also air fills. Air fills also at Saanichtown. Launch ramps at Mill Bay and Brentwood Bay. Dive-kayak rentals at Ladysmith and Genoa Bay.

ACCESS

Tozier Rock is near Mill Bay ferry landing on the west side of Saanich Inlet. It is 2½ nautical miles southeast of Mill Bay, and 3 nautical miles northwest of Brentwood Bay. When it's blowing outside, often little wind in the inlet so usually there's great visibility year-round.

Charter or launch at Mill Bay or Brentwood Bay. Kayak-divers could paddle close to shore from Mill Bay for 2½ nautical miles to the site, anchor near the marker, gear up in shallow water and dive. Beaches to land on all the way, but do not go above high tide line as the property is privately owned. If poor visibility on the surface, do not dismiss the dive – quite often the water clears when you get to 30 feet (9 meters) deep.

Anchor south of the marker in 30 to 40 feet (9 to 12 meters). Do not tie onto the marker. It is a federal offense to tamper with any aid to navigation. Dive southeast of the marker over rocks covered with bottom kelp to the ridge at a depth of 70 to 80 feet (21 to 24 meters). A single chimney sponge reaches out and up from the ledge wall at 65 to 75 feet (20 to 23 meters). One den is above it, another below it.

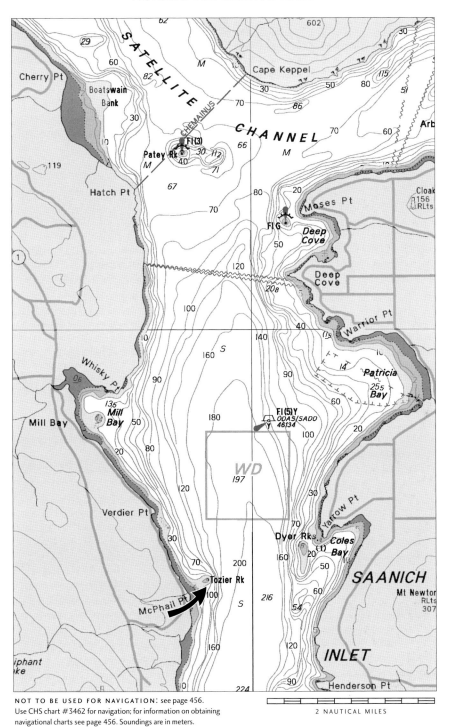

NOT TO BE USED FOR NAVIGATION: see page 456.
Use CHS chart #3462 for navigation; for information on obtaining
navigational charts see page 456. Soundings are in meters.

2 NAUTICAL MILES

NOTES

HENDERSON POINT

WHY GO

Henderson Point is popular with all divers, day and night, because of easy access, few hazards and a variety of underwater life. Excellent for new divers.

Nudibranchs, big and little, decorator crabs, painted greenlings, kelp greenlings, seaperch, lots of little rockfish and moon jellies – you can expect to see them all. We saw one boulder splashed with masses of delicate zoanthids. Look for octopuses, rock scallops and dogfish. They are harder to find, but also present.

BOTTOM AND DEPTHS

Smooth rocks on the shore give way to small rocks scattered with bottom kelp and an occasional boulder. The slope is gentle to smooth sand at 50 to 60 feet (15 to 18 meters) in front of Henderson Point. To the right, a shallow reef. South of the point, deep chasms of rock.

HAZARDS

Small boats and poor visibility, in summer. Lion's mane jellies, in the fall. Listen for boats and ascend along the bottom all the way to shore, well out of the way of them. If you have seen any jellies, you and your buddy should check one another for stinging tentacles before removing your masks and gloves.

TELEPHONES

• Mount Newton Cross Road and East Saanich Road, 2 miles (3¼ kilometers) east of dive: outside building, southwest corner of junction.
• Pioneer Village Shopping Centre, northwest corner of junction; beside sidewalk entry to mall.

FACILITIES

None. Limited parking space and the site is very close to private homes. Make a toilet stop before you go; be quiet, when there; and clean up before you leave. In summer, camping at Tsartlip Land of Maples Campground at Brentwood Bay and McDonald Campground – part of the Gulf Islands National Park Reserve. It is near Swartz Bay.

ACCESS

Henderson Point is on Saanich Inlet at the north end of Brentwood Bay. It is 10 minutes off Patricia Bay Highway (Highway 17).

From Highway 17 and Mount Newton Cross Road junction, go west 3½ miles (5½ kilometers) on Mount Newton Cross Road. Cross East Saanich Road, then West Saanich Road. Continue west on Senanus Drive another ½ mile (¾ kilometer) to the end of the road. A paved turnaround gives room for 8 to 10 cars to park. If too many divers, come back another day. If not overcrowded, walk 80 paces down the path through the woods to the easy rocky entry.

To get to Mount Newton Cross Road and Highway 17
• From the Parliament Buildings in Victoria and from the Port Angeles ferry which lands in front of the Parliament Buildings, 35 minutes to Henderson Point. Head north to Blanshard Street (Highway 17) toward Swartz Bay ferry terminal; go 8 miles (13 kilometers) to Mount Newton Cross Road.
• From Swartz Bay and from Sidney ferry terminals to Henderson Point takes 15 minutes. Head south on Highway 17 and follow signs toward Brentwood Bay to Mount Newton Cross Road.
• From Duncan heading south on Highway 1: past Helmcken Road, turn left following signs to Ferries, Sidney, 17 North and University of Victoria. From this turnoff, 30 minutes to Henderson Point. Go to Highway 17 and then north to Mount Newton Cross Road.
• From Mill Bay ferry at Brentwood Bay, it takes 10 minutes to reach Henderson Point. From the ferry landing, go to West Saanich Road and turn left. Go north on West Saanich Road to Senanus Drive and Mount Newton Cross Road junction.

Zoanthids at
Henderson Point

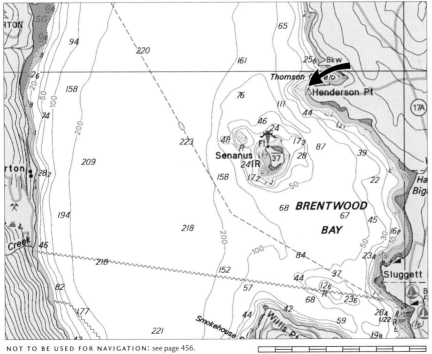

NOT TO BE USED FOR NAVIGATION: see page 456.
Use CHS chart #3441 for navigation; for information on obtaining
navigational charts see page 456. Soundings are in meters.

1 NAUTICAL MILE

NOTES

SENANUS ISLAND REEFS

BOAT DIVE
GPS
At anchorage:
48°35.526' N
123°29.433' W

SKILL
Expert divers

TIDE TABLE
Fulford Harbour

Shallon anchored at dive entry, Senanus Island behind

WHY GO

To see cloud sponges – big ones. White and yellow. Sparsely spaced. Shown off against an amphitheater of black rock. A most unusual view of cloud sponges.

We approached at depth – the cloud sponges were straight ahead. We swam slowly in dark, clear water across the big underwater valley toward the sponges on the far wall. I saw only cloud sponges. Our dive plan was to spend eight minutes at depth with the sponges, then turn back, and I was using those precious minutes to burn this sight on my brain. When my buddy flashed his light, I paid no attention. Later he told me he was pointing out one mature and one juvenile yelloweye rockfish nearby.

After we left cloud-sponge-land, my spirit was freed up to observe the myriad more creatures at Senanus – so much. While returning up the bright white, broken-shell-covered crevice, we saw chimney sponges, large orange plumose anemones, a few swimming scallops, an opalescent nudibranch.

Hordes of coonstripe and sidestripe shrimp scrambled over the broken shells; tube-dwelling anemones spread their transparent arms up between them. On the rocky reef we saw helmet, spider and red rock crabs; calcareous tube worms and small barnacles. Copper and quillback rockfish.

As we ascended the anchor line through open water, we saw red lion's mane jellies with grooved mantles, yellow fried-egg jellies with smooth mantles.

Why go? For the magical sponges. I will return again and again – maybe never physically; I will not need to. The image of the Senanus amphitheater will be with me always. The largest sponge was a mixture of yellow and white: 12 feet (4 meters) wide from side to side, 3 feet (1 meter) high and 4 feet (1¼ meters) deep from front to back. Other smaller ones were scattered across the dark wall. Previously I had always dived down a wall and viewed cloud sponges from the top. I could see these cloud sponges better than any I've dived to before because we approached them head on.

BOTTOM AND DEPTHS

Two reefs reach out from Senanus Island:
- The south reef bottoms out at 110 to 120 feet (34 to 37 meters).
- The north reef bottoms out at 131 to 164 feet (40 to 50 meters).
- The anchorage is in a rock crevice in 50 to 60 feet (15 to 18 meters).

HAZARDS

Depth, darkness, stinging jellies in summer and fall. Dive on a low tide, and be aware: excellent buoyancy control is required. Take a light. If you see jellies, avoid them, and on the surface, check for tentacles before removing masks and gloves.

TELEPHONES
- On the water: VHF radio; if no VHF, try a cell phone.
- On land: Brentwood Bay, Tsartlip Ramp: walk one block south of ramp toward the ferry. Telephone is outside a restaurant at Peden Lane and Verdier Avenue.

FACILITIES
None at Senanus Island.

ACCESS
Senanus Island Reefs are located in Saanich Inlet near Brentwood Bay. Charter out of Brentwood Bay, Sidney or Victoria. Or, launch your boat at Brentwood Bay, Mill Bay, the head of Saanich Inlet or Sidney.

Anchor on a reef west of Senanus Island. The problem: two underwater reefs are west of Senanus; one north, one south.

Before anchoring, locate both of them. The north reef is deeper: it is 60 feet (18 meters) on top, but not a good anchorage. Go to the *south* reef: it is 45 feet (14 meters) on top, and find a rock crevice on its northwest corner that is 50 to 60 feet (15 to 18 meters) deep.

Be careful: do not rely only on GPS; if any error you might anchor in the sponges and destroy what you are looking for. Do use the GPS location; then – most importantly – a depth sounder. Compass bearings could be useful too to find the crevice: the tall silo at Bamberton on the west shore of the inlet is on a 65° bearing; Senanus Island light, a 230° bearing. Once anchored in crevice, accesss is easy.

We descended the anchor line to the anchor at 55 feet (17 meters); attached a wreck-diving reel line to it and descended to 100 feet (30 meters). Attached a light stick to the reel line to guide us back.

Established neutral buoyancy and swam north/northwest across the dark valley. Our eyes adjusted to the darkness and pristine cloud sponges gradually appeared – at first, like ghosts. When closer, like elegantly twisted wax or ivory. Cloud sponges take thousands of years to become large and they are fragile. When near them, be aware that positive buoyancy is better than negative; finning to stay down is not as potentially destructive to the sponges as finning to stay up.

Two mooring buoys, maintained by local divers, might be present. They are on both ends of the north reef and mark the best parts of the cloud sponge wall.

Caution: do not attempt to anchor on top of the shallower north reef. It is smooth, rounded rock that does not hold an anchor. The anchor will slide off and damage the cloud sponges. If the buoys are present, you could tie up to one and descend. But the way we dived the site as described above was special – and safer for the cloud sponges.

NOTES

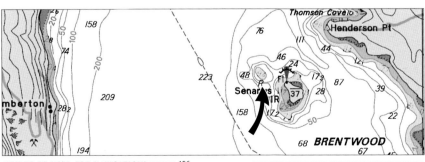

NOT TO BE USED FOR NAVIGATION: see page 456.
Use CHS chart #3441 for navigation; for information on obtaining navigational charts see page 456. Soundings are in meters.

1 NAUTICAL MILE

WILLIS POINT

SHORE DIVE

SKILL
All divers

TIDE TABLE
Fulford Harbour

WHY GO

Willis Point must be what off-the-wall is. You can fly out over the dark fjord into space, dive deep, then on the way up stop at a perfectly placed ledge with lettuce kelp and shimmering blue kelp. We saw orange plumose anemones and white ones, as well as wispy tube-dwelling anemones; nudibranch eggs, alabaster and dorid nudibranchs and a pale pink giant nudibranch – it was 1 foot (⅓ meter) long. We saw red slipper cucumbers and crevice-dwelling white sea cucumbers. Blackeye gobies, quillback rockfish, blennies, silvery perch; sunflower stars, a big white sea star, a blood star. Red rock crabs, shrimp, rock scallops and large boot or chimney sponges.

Willis Point is a protected inlet wall dive, place-to-go when the wind is blowing outside. And no currents to consider.

BOTTOM AND DEPTHS

The wall starts past the rocky ledge covered with bottom kelp at 15 feet (5 meters). It drops to a ledge at a depth of 80 feet (24

Silver nudibranch

meters) or so; then to a depth of 100 to 110 feet (30 to 34 meters). Overhangs scattered throughout. Take a light to look into crevices.

HAZARDS

Boats and poor visibility in summer; lion's mane jellies in the fall. Listen for boats and ascend close to the wall all the way to the surface. If you saw any jellies, check for stinging tentacles before you remove masks and gloves.

TELEPHONE

West Saanich Road and Prospect Lake Road, outside gas station. Go south from Wallace Drive and Willis Point Road, 1¼ miles (2 kilometers) to it.

FACILITIES

None at Willis Point. Air fills at Brentwood Bay and Saanichtown. Camping near Trans-Canada Highway 1 at the head of the inlet at Goldstream, and across the inlet at Bamberton Provincial Park.

ACCESS

Willis Point is south of Brentwood Bay on the east side of Saanich Inlet. It is 15 minutes from the junction of Wallace Drive and Willis Point Road to the dive.

From Wallace Drive (5600 block) and Willis Point Road, go west along a wide curving road through the woods for 5¼ miles (8½ kilometers) to Mark Lane. Turn right. From there, ⅓ mile (½ kilometer) more to the dive. The road is twisting and narrow. Go down a steep hill. When coming close to a curve to the right, look for a gravel road on your left-hand side. It is an unmarked fire access road to the sea. You could back down it to drop gear, but park at the roadside in Mark Lane. Swim straight out and down to the ledges and wall.

To get to Wallace Drive and Willis Point Road from the north

- From Swartz Bay and Sidney ferry terminals to the dive takes 40 minutes. Head south on Highway 17 toward the Mill Bay ferry. Turn right into McTavish Road and go to West Saanich Road. Turn left. Go on West Saanich Road past the shops of Brentwood Bay. Shortly past the turnoff to the Mill Bay ferry, do not turn right into Wallace Drive. Continue on West Saanich Road past the turnoff to Butchart Gardens: from Keating Cross Road, go 2⅓ miles (3¾ kilometers) to Wallace Drive. Turn right and go ⅓ mile (½ kilometer) to Willis Point Road.
- From Mill Bay ferry at Brentwood Bay, 20 minutes to Willis Point. From the ferry, go uphill on Vernier Avenue and turn right onto West Saanich Road. After going ⅓ mile (½ kilometer) do not turn right into Wallace Drive. From Vernier Avenue and West Saanich Road go 3½ miles (5½ kilometers) south to Wallace Road. Turn right and go ⅓ mile (½ kilometer) to Willis Point Road.

To get to Wallace Drive and Willis Point Road from the south

- From the Fairmont Empress Hotel in Victoria and from the Port Angeles ferry at the Inner Harbour, 40 minutes to the dive. Head north on Blanshard Street toward Swartz Bay ferry terminal. Go on Highway 17. Go to Royal Oak Drive. Head west on Royal Oak to West Saanich Road (Highway 17A); turn right. From Royal Oak, 3½ miles (5¾ kilometers) to Wallace Drive. Turn left and go ⅓ mile (½ kilometer) to Willis Point Road.
- From Duncan heading south on Highway 1: when just past Helmcken Road, follow signs to Ferries, Sidney, 17 North and University of Victoria – from this turnoff, 30 minutes to the dive. Go to Highway 17; head north to Royal Oak Drive then West Saanich Road (Highway 17A). From Royal Oak, 3½ miles (5¾ kilometers) to Wallace Drive. Turn left and go ⅓ mile (½ kilometer) to Willis Point Road.

NOTES

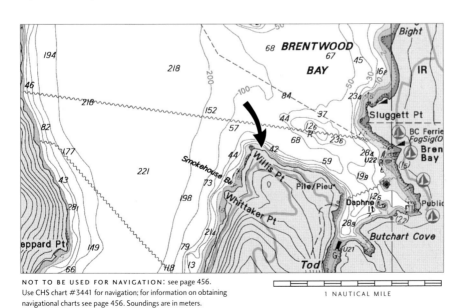

NOT TO BE USED FOR NAVIGATION: see page 456.
Use CHS chart #3441 for navigation; for information on obtaining navigational charts see page 456. Soundings are in meters.

1 NAUTICAL MILE

CHRISTMAS POINT

WHY GO

Christmas Point is bright, it's dark, it's spooky. Interesting shallow and deep. Sea stars on the rocks near shore look like purple and red ornaments on a Christmas tree. Moon jellies pulse in the open water like transparent baubles.

As we paddled our dive-kayaks up the inlet, one seal followed us. When we landed at the point to gear up, an audience of 30 seals came close to watch, flip their tails, splash and play. We felt on stage for the amusement of the seals. But when we went down they slipped away. I saw only one seal under water, my buddy saw two. Avoid going closer to seals than 110 yards (100 meters).

Kelp greenlings were in the shallows, but very few fish – probably frightened away by the seals. At the edge of the drop-off, we peered into dark nothingness; shallower we saw blackeye gobies, large prawns hiding in the kelp, an orange crab with white dots, piles of empty clam shells and crab shells in the rocks, but no octopus. The octopus was probably prowling about – it was night. Shallower still, we saw coon-stripe shrimp, and schools of tiny fish that looked like goldfish darting between plumose anemones on wooden wreckage. Though the seals "made" this dive for me, there is much more to see and imagine.

On the surface, without anything else, it was spooky paddling back in total dark-ness. Then my buddy told me about the Cadborosaurus, the legendary – or maybe not so legendary – gentle dragon-like creatures that most people refer to as "Caddy" and that some biologists now believe to be real. The cryptozoologists say that Saanich Inlet is the major breed-ing ground of these serpentine sea-dwellers that are said to be as long as 60 feet (18 meters). The Caddies have thin coils on their long necks, and heads like a horse or camel. They are shy deep-water animals that come up to feed on ducks at night. Numerous Caddy sightings from Oregon to Alaska have been reported during the past century – many in the Victoria region, with two reported sightings at Saanich Inlet in 1993.

BOTTOM AND DEPTHS

Broken rock covered with brown bottom kelp and iridescent blue kelp drops to a ledge of 35 to 45 feet (11 to 14 meters); another ledge at 75 to 85 feet (23 to 26 meters), depending on tide height. Then plunges. The depth on the chart is 400 feet (120 meters).

HAZARDS

Small boats, poor visibility; lion's mane jellies, in the fall. Possible danger to kayak-divers by overexertion after the dive. Listen for boats, and ascend close to the contours of the bottom all the way to the surface. If you saw jellies, check one another for stinging tentacles before removing masks and gloves. Kayak-divers who have dived deep should rest before paddling back. The risk of bends may increase with strenuous exercise after diving.

TELEPHONES

• On the water: VHF radio; if no VHF, try a cell phone.
• On land:
1. Goldstream Marina on house opposite marina office, head of Saanich Inlet.
2. Brentwood Bay: from ferry, go one block; telephone outside restaurant at Peden Lane and Verdier Avenue.

FACILITIES

None at Christmas Point. Dive-kayak rentals in Ladysmith and Genoa Bay.

ACCESS

Christmas Point is on the west side of Finlayson Arm just over 1 nautical mile north of Saanich Inlet head.

Charter, or launch your own boat or dive-kayak and go north from the ramp at the head of Saanich Inlet – just over 1 nautical mile to the giant checkerboard marker on the left-hand side of the inlet. It is beneath the power line. If going by dive-kayak, easiest to paddle on an ebbing tide, dive at slack and paddle back with the flood tide.

Or go south by boat for 8 to 12 nautical miles from Brentwood Bay or Mill Bay to Christmas Point.

Coonstripe shrimp

NOTES

NOT TO BE USED FOR NAVIGATION: see page 456.
Use CHS chart #3441 for navigation; for information on obtaining navigational charts see page 456. Soundings are in meters.

1 NAUTICAL MILE

CHAPTER NINE

San Juan Islands
including
San Juan, Orcas and Lopez

Three southern-resident orcas hunting for salmon in Haro Strait

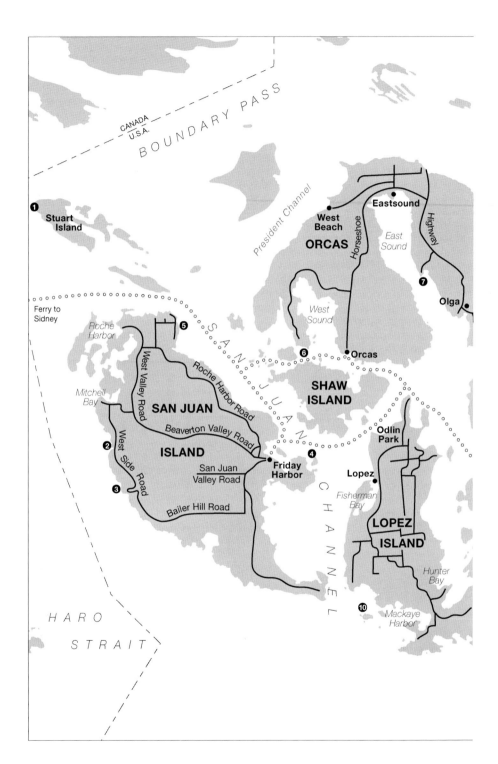

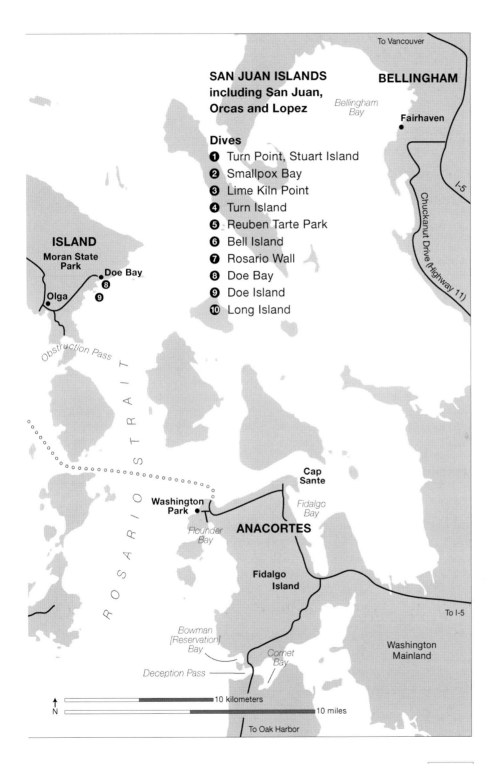

**SAN JUAN ISLANDS
including San Juan,
Orcas and Lopez**

*Bellingham
Bay*

BELLINGHAM

Fairhaven

Dives

❶ Turn Point, Stuart Island
❷ Smallpox Bay
❸ Lime Kiln Point
❹ Turn Island
❺ Reuben Tarte Park
❻ Bell Island
❼ Rosario Wall
❽ Doe Bay
❾ Doe Island
❿ Long Island

To Vancouver

Chuckanut Drive (Highway 11)

I-5

ISLAND

**Moran State
Park**

Doe Bay
❽

Olga
❾

Obstruction Pass

R O S A R I O   S T R A I T

**Cap
Sante**

*Fidalgo
Bay*

**Washington
Park**

*Flounder
Bay*

ANACORTES

**Fidalgo
Island**

To I-5

**Washington
Mainland**

*Bowman
[Reservation]
Bay*

*Cornet
Bay*

Deception Pass

↑
N

10 kilometers

10 miles

To Oak Harbor

SERVICE INFORMATION

Tide Information
- National Oceanic Atmospheric Administration (NOAA) print annual: *Tide Tables, High and Low Water Predictions – West Coast of North and South America*
- www.tidesandcurrents.noaa.gov/tides07
- www.mobilegeographics.com/pugetsoundtides.html

Current Information
- National Oceanic Atmospheric Administration (NOAA) print annual: *Tidal Current Tables – Pacific Coast of North America and Asia*
- *Current Atlas: Juan de Fuca Strait to Strait of Georgia,* purchase one time. Use with *Murray's Tables* or *Washburne's Tables,* purchase annually; privately produced publications available at marine equipment and supplies stores.
- www.tidesandcurrents.noaa.gov/currents07
- www.mobilegeographics.com/pugetsoundcurrents.html

Weather Information
- US Coast Guard Radio: Coastal Marine Forecast, recorded 24 hours. Telephone Bellingham (360)645-2301.
- www.atmos.washington.edu/weather.html For up-to-date information click "Weather" at bottom center of page and select your location.
- www.nws.noaa.gov/om/marine/zone/west/sewmz.html

Diving Emergency Telephone Numbers
On land and water:
- Call 911 and say, "I have a scuba diving emergency".
- Cell phone: Dial *24 and say, "I have a scuba diving emergency".
- Virginia Mason Hospital: telephone the hyperbaric unit, (206)624-1144, ask for Emergency Room and say, "I have a scuba diving emergency".

On the water:
- VHF radio: Call Coast Guard radio, Channel 16 and say, "I have a scuba diving emergency".
- Cell phone: Dial *24 and say, "I have a scuba diving emergency".

If emergency or medical personnel are unfamiliar with scuba diving emergencies, ask them to telephone DAN (Divers Alert Network) at (919)684-4326. No money for a long distance call? Dial DAN collect at 011-919-684-4326 and say, "I have a scuba diving emergency".

Mark emergency location before leaving scene: other divers might be down.

How to Go

Go to the San Juan Islands via Washington State Ferries from Anacortes, Washington, on the mainland, or from Sidney, British Columbia, on Vancouver Island. At the time of writing, reservations are available only on international travel between Sidney and Friday Harbor, and between Sidney and Orcas Island: reservations are strongly advised.

Take a Ferry on the Anacortes–Sidney Ferry Route

- To San Juan Island, westernmost island stop on the route: from Anacortes to Friday Harbor at San Juan takes 1 to 2 hours, depending on island stops; from Sidney to Friday Harbor, 2 hours.
- To Orcas Island, midway on the Anacortes–Sidney ferry route: from Anacortes to Orcas takes 1 to 1¼ hours, depending on ferry stops. From Sidney to Orcas, almost 3 hours: sail to Friday Harbor at San Juan Island and tranfer to an Orcas-bound ferry.
- To Lopez Island, easternmost stop on the route: from Anacortes to Lopez takes 40 minutes. From Sidney to Lopez, nearly 4 hours: sail to Friday Harbor at San Juan Island and transfer to a Lopez-bound ferry.

Ferry Terminal Access at Anacortes, Washington

The ferry terminal is accessed off I-5 (Interstate Highway 5): take Exit 230 and go west on Highway 20 for 30 minutes to Anacortes. Continue through Anacortes to the San Juan ferry terminal.

- Heading north from Seattle, 1¾ hours to the Anacortes turnoff. From Everett, 35 minutes to it.
- Heading south from Vancouver, 1½ hours to the turnoff. From Bellingham, 30 minutes to it.

Ferry Terminal Access at Sidney, British Columbia

The ferry terminal is north of Victoria and is accessed by way of Highway 17 (Pat Bay Highway). From Highway 17, take the Beacon Avenue turnoff to Sidney: go east on Beacon Avenue; turn right at the first traffic light past Resthaven Street on the left and a mall on your right-hand side and go 4 blocks to Ocean Avenue. Turn left to the ferry terminal.

- Heading north from Victoria on Highway 17, from McKenzie Avenue it is 13 miles (21 kilometers) to the Beacon Avenue turnoff to Sidney.
- Heading south from Swartz Bay ferry terminal, 5 miles (8 kilometers) to the Beacon Avenue turnoff.

Ferry Information

Washington State Ferries
Recorded schedules, 24 hours, with touch-tone menu choices. To speak with a person during working hours 7 days a week, just wait – do not push any buttons.
(206)464-6400
1-888-808-7977: Toll-free throughout North America
www.wsdot.wa.gov/ferries

Tourist Information

San Juan Islands Visitors Bureau
(360)378-3277
1-888-468-3701: Toll-free throughout North America
www.guidetosanjuans.com

San Juan County Park Board
#8 - 350 Court Street
Friday Harbor WA 98250
(360)378-8420
www.co.san-juan.wa.us/parks

Washington State Tourism
1-800-544-1800: Toll-free throughout North America, Hawaii and Alaska
www.experiencewashington.com

SAN JUAN ISLAND

• DIVE SHOP, DAY AND MULTIPLE-DAY CHARTERS

San Juan Diver, Chewy, Sea Horse and
Island Diver Too
Island Dive & Water Sports
2A Spring Street Landing, PO Box 476
Friday Harbor WA 98250
(360)378-2772
1-800-303-8386: Toll-free throughout
North America
www.divesanjuan.com
*(Recreational, nitrox and technical instruction,
and instruction for divers with special needs.
Nitrox and trimix available. Waterfront and
roadside gas fills – land at the marina dock
and walk up to the shop; cold-water rinse at
shop. Divers' cottage for rent to divers – up
to eight in a group. Restrooms at dive shop;
coin-operated hot showers at nearby Port of
Friday Harbor building, north end of Front
Street.*

*Day and multiple-day charters with
land-based accommodation for up to
14 divers out of Friday Harbor: destinations
throughout the San Juan Islands and, in
Canada, to the Mackenzie, G.B. Church
and Nanaimo sites. Dive packages available
include boat diving and accommodations.
Pickup at Orcas Island, and group pickup at
Anacortes.)*

• LAUNCH RAMPS AND BOAT RENTALS

Snug Harbor Marina Resort
1997 Mitchell Bay Road
Friday Harbor WA 98250
(360)378-4762
www.snugresort.com
*(Launch for a fee at Mitchell Bay for Haro
Strait: concrete ramp, good at high tides.
Also boat rentals. Restrooms. Telephone at
head of pier.)*

Roche Harbor Resort
248 Reuben Memorial Drive,
PO Box 4001
Roche Harbor WA 98250
(360)378-2155
1-800-451-8910: Toll-free throughout
North America
www.rocheharbor.com
*(Launch for a fee at Roche Harbor for Haro
Strait: concrete ramp, good at high tides,
small boats only. Coin-operated hot showers
and restrooms on north side of marina. Telephones outside, under a shelter on south
side of grocery store. Also accommodations,
from rustic cabins to luxurious suites at this
historic site.)*

ORCAS ISLAND
• DAY AND MULTIPLE-DAY CHARTERS
San Juan Diver, Chewy, Sea Horse and *Island Diver Too*
Island Dive & Water Sports
2A Spring Street Landing, PO Box 476
Friday Harbor WA 98250
(360)378-2772
1-800-303-8386: Toll-free throughout
    North America
www.divesanjuan.com
(Day and multiple-day charters with land-based accommodation; dives range through-out the San Juan Islands and, in Canada, to the Mackenzie *and* G.B. Church: *out of Orcas Island or Friday Harbor, San Juan Island; and out of Anacortes for groups up to 14 divers. Divers with special needs welcome. Also recreational, nitrox and technical instruction; nitrox and trimix available at dive shop in Friday Harbor.*

• LAUNCH RAMPS
Bartwood Lodge
178 Fossil Bay Drive
Eastsound WA 98245
(360)376-2242
1-888-817-2242
www.bartwoodlodge.com
(Launch from Orcas north shore for President Channel and northern islands. Concrete ramp, good at all except extreme low tides. Launching is free for guests, a nominal fee for drop-ins. At Bartwood, telephone outside the lodge; no toilets and no gasoline available. Chemical toilets at Buck Park. It is on the south side of Mount Baker Road, ⅓ mile [½ kilometer] east of North Beach Road. You could go there on the way to Bartwood.)

Obstruction Pass Public Ramp
Orcas Island, southeast side
(Launch at Obstruction Pass for Rosario Strait. Concrete and sand ramp, good at all tides. No toilet. Telephone outside Obstruction Pass Store at Lieber Haven Marina Resort.)

From Orcas ferry landing, 35 minutes to Obstruction Pass. Follow the main road past the turnoff to Eastsound and past the airport. Continue on it following signs toward Olga and Mount Constitution. Go through Moran State Park. After crossing a one-lane bridge, go 1½ miles (2½ kilometers to a café at Olga. Turn left. Continue ½ mile (¾ kilometer) and turn right following sign for 2 miles (3¼ kilometers) more to Obstruction Pass. Pass a turnoff onto Trailhead Drive then go 1 mile (1½ kilometers) to a junction of three roads; keep right to go to the ramp beside Lieber Haven Resort.

West Beach Resort
190 Waterfront Way
Eastsound WA 98245
(360)376-2240
1-877-937-8224: Toll-free throughout
    USA
www.westbeachresort.com
(Ramp for resort guests only: launch for President Channel. Concrete ramp: good for large boats only at high tides; for small boats, good at all except extreme low tides. Telephone at head of dock, another beside store. Cabins, RV and camping.)

Located on President Channel, west side of Orcas Island — not in town. From the ferry landing, follow the main road for 9 miles (14 kilometers) to Enchanted Forest Road. Turn left and go to where West Beach Road turns left. You go straight into the resort.

LOPEZ ISLAND

• LAUNCH RAMPS

Odlin County Park Public Ramp
Lopez Island, north end
1480 Odlin Road
Lopez Island WA 98261
(360)468-2496
(Launch for a fee at Upright Channel for San Juan Channel. Concrete and sand ramp, good at medium and high tides. Camping year-round; wheelchair-accessible pit toilets; telephone beside road near park office, another telephone outside ferry ticket office.)

From the ferry landing, go 1¼ miles (2 kilometers). Turn right to Odlin Park.

Islands Marine Center (IMC) Ramp
Lopez Island, west side
PO Box 88
2793 Fisherman Bay Road
(360)468-3377
www.islandsmarinecenter.com
(Launch for a fee at Fisherman Bay, for San Juan Channel: concrete ramp, good for small boats at high tides of 6 feet [2 meters] and greater. Restrooms and hot showers. Telephone outside ferry ticket office.)

Hunter Bay Public Ramp
Lopez Island, southeast side
End of Islandale Road
(Launch free for Lopez Sound: concrete ramp, good at all except extreme low tides. No toilets, telephone available 24 hours outside ferry ticket office.)

Located 11 miles (18 kilometers) from the ferry: drive to a "T" junction. Take the left fork and go south for 7 miles (11 kilometers) on Center Road. At another "T", go left into Islandale Road and to the end of it.

Mackaye Harbor Public Ramp
Lopez Island, south end
(Launching for Middle Channel and San Juan Channel is free at Mackaye Harbor: steep, grooved concrete ramp, good at all except extreme low tides. Wheelchair-accessible float close to ramp. Large parking space. Telephone and toilets: from the ramp, go uphill past the parking area. At Norman Road turn left to Mud Bay Road. Then turn right onto Mud Bay Road; immediately past the Mackaye Harbor Road turnoff, a telephone and restroom are inside a grocery/gas station, available during working hours only. From ramp to grocery is nearly ½ mile [¾ kilometer]. Toilet, available 24 hours: from Mackaye Harbor Road and Mud Road, go south on Mackaye Harbor Road for 1¾ miles [2¾ kilometers] to a pit toilet at Agate Beach. Telephone 24 hours, outside ferry ticket office.)

Located at the south end of Lopez, 11 miles (18 kilometers) from the ferry landing. From the ferry go to a "T" junction. Turn left and twist and turn down the island for 7 miles (11 kilometers) on Center Road. At the "T", turn left and go 2¾ miles (4½ kilometers) on Mud Bay Road to the Mackaye Harbor turnoff. Turn right and right, again, following signs to the ramp.

MAINLAND SERVICES FOR SAN JUAN ISLANDS

• DIVE SHOPS

Whidbey Island Dive Center
#1 - 1020 NE 7th Avenue
    (at Highway 20)
Oak Harbor WA 98277
(360)675-1112
www.whidbeydive.com
(Recreational and nitrox instruction. Nitrox fills.)

Anacortes Diving & Supply
2502 Commercial Avenue
Anacortes WA 98221
(360)293-2070
www.anacortesdiving.com
(Recreational and nitrox instruction. Nitrox fills.)

Adventures Down Under
701 East Holly Street
Bellingham WA 98225
(360)676-4177
www.adventuresdownunder.com
(Recreational, nitrox, technical and rebreather instruction. Nitrox, trimix and soda-lime.)

Washington Divers
903 North State Street
Bellingham WA 98225
(360)676-8029
(Recreational dive shop.)

• DAY AND MULTIPLE-DAY CHARTERS

Out of Anacortes

Dash
Porthole Dive Charters
PO Box 109
Milton WA 98354
(253)564-5335; cell phones (253)405-3462, (253)405-9029
www.portholedivecharters.com
(Personalized day and multiple-day charters with land-based accommodation for groups of six divers. Boat is trailerable; can pick up divers in any location depending on dives.)

Deep Sea
Deep Sea Charters
Cap Sante Boat Haven
"B" Dock, Slip 22
Anacortes WA 98271
(360)661-6101, (360)658-5024
www.deepseacruise.com
(Day and multiple-day charters with land-based accommodation out of Anacortes throughout the San Juan Islands.)

Lu-Jac's Quest
Diver's Dream Charters
Skyline Marina, Slip TD-22
558 Klamath Drive
La Conner WA 98257
(360)202-0076
www.lujacsquest.com
(Charters out of Anacortes for 8 to 14 divers. Day charters; also 1- to 3-day packages with land-based accommodation. Destinations throughout the San Juan Islands and to the Mackenzie and G.B. Church in Canada.)

San Juan Diver, Chewy, Sea Horse and *Island Diver Too*
Island Dive & Water Sports
2A Spring Street Landing, PO Box 476
Friday Harbor WA 98250
(360)378-2772
1-800-303-8386: Toll-free throughout
    North America
www.divesanjuan.com
(Day and multiple-day charters with land-based accommodation throughout the San Juan Islands and, in Canada, to the Mackenzie and G.B. Church; out of Friday Harbor or Orcas Island or group pickups at Anacortes.)

Sampan, Naknek and *Ocean Quest*
Bandito Charters
PO Box 9456
Tacoma WA 98409
(253)973-0370
www.banditocharters.com
(Occasional day and multiple-day charters with land-based accommodation out of Anacortes [or Seattle] for San Juan Islands.)

MAINLAND SERVICES FOR SAN JUAN ISLANDS (CONTINUED)

• LAUNCH RAMPS AND SLING

For Rosario Strait

. . . at Whidbey Island

Cornet Bay Public Ramps
Deception Pass State Park
Whidbey Island, north end
(Launch for a fee at Cornet Bay: concrete ramps, good at all except extreme low tides. Restrooms and hot showers. Telephone at top of float at privately owned Deception Pass Marina. It is opposite Canyon Road and ⅓ mile [½ kilometer] west of the public ramps.)

From Highway 20, when 1 mile (1½ kilometers) south of Deception Pass Bridge, go east on Cornet Bay Road for 1½ miles (2½ kilometers) to Cornet Bay Ramps.

. . . at Fidalgo Island including Anacortes

Bowman [Reservation] Bay Public Ramp
Fidalgo Island, south end
(Launch for a fee: concrete ramp good only at high tides. Limited parking space. Restrooms, year-round camping and telephone south of bridge at Deception Pass State Park.)

Off Highway 20: immediately north of Deception Pass Bridge and south of Pass Lake, turn west. Immediately turn left into Bowman Bay Road and follow signs to Bowman Bay and the ramp.

Washington Park Ramps
Fidalgo Island, north end
(Launch for a fee at Fidalgo Head, near Anacortes ferry terminal: steep concrete ramp, good at all tides for small boats – can be difficult for larger boats; coin-operated gate to it. Restrooms and coin-operated hot showers. Telephone in front of park superintendent's home beside curve of drive out.)

Washington Park is 4 miles (6 kilometers) west of Anacortes off Highway 20. Follow signs through Anacortes toward San Juan ferry. From Commercial Avenue and 12th, go 3 miles (5 kilometers) toward the ferry. You will see a sign to a marina: Bear left through the stop sign and go on Sunset Avenue for ¾ mile (1¼ kilometers) to Washington Park at the end of the road.

Cap Sante Marine
Cap Sante Boat Haven, PO Box 607
Anacortes WA 98221
(360)293-3145
1-800-422-5794: Toll-free throughout North America
www.capsante.com
(Sling launch at Fidalgo Bay. Restrooms and coin-operated hot showers 150 paces north next to Cap Sante Harbor office, Port of Anacortes. Telephones across road from Cap Sante Marine near sling launch. In winter, check if open.)

. . . at Bellingham

Squalicum Harbor Public Ramps
Foot of Bellwether Way
Bellingham Bay, north end
(Launch for a fee: concrete ramps, good at all tides. Large parking space, freshwater taps in parking area to wash gear. Wheelchair-accessible restrooms and showers; telephones beside restrooms at north end of Harbor Center. Top of the ramp, turn left and walk 80 yards [75 meters] through Harbor Center to these facilities at the Port of Bellingham.)

In Bellingham, 5 to 10 minutes off I-5 (Interstate Highway 5), at north end of Bellingham Bay. Turn off Harbor Loop Route into Bellwether Way and turn right at Boat Launch Parking sign to the ramps.

- Heading souhth on I-5, take Exit 256. Turn right at Meridian Street and go to traffic light at Squalicum Way. Turn right and follow the Squalicum Harbor sign toward the water; the road curves left into Roeder Avenue. Go on Roeder for just over ½ mile (¾ kilometer) passing various harbor facilities. Go to the south end of Squalicum Harbor and turn right into Bellwether.
- Heading north on I-5, take Exit 253 to Lakeway Drive and go back under I-5. Go along Lakeway following Squalicum Harbor signs; continue on Holly Street through the city center; turn left onto "F" Street. Turn right at Roeder Avenue, then left at Bellwether Way.

Fairhaven Public Ramp
Harris Avenue, just past 6th Street
Bellingham Bay, south end
(Launch for a fee at south end of Bellingham Bay: concrete ramp, good at all except extreme low tides. Wheelchair-accessible restrooms; telephone outside of restrooms.)

In Bellingham, Fairhaven district, just east of the Alaska ferry dock and Amtrak railway station. Heading north or south on I-5 (Interstate Highway 5), take Exit 250: follow signs to the Alaska ferry. The ramp is 2 miles (3¼ kilometers) off the highway. Go on Old Fairhaven Parkway (Highway 11) toward Chuckanut Drive. At junction with Chuckanut, do not turn left. Turn right into 12th Street; then left onto Harris Avenue. Go to 6th Street and turn right to launch. The ramp parking is on the right.

All of this Service Information is subject to change.

TURN POINT, STUART ISLAND

BOAT DIVE

GPS
48°32.162′ N
122°58.214′ W

SKILL
Intermediate and
expert divers

CURRENT TABLE
Admiralty Inlet
• Slack before flood:
  Add 26 minutes

• Slack before ebb:
  Add 1 hour, 18 minutes

WHY GO

A wall is a wall is a wall: the wall south of Turn Point plunges. Sheers off. It is the blackest, most bottomless wall I have dived. White plumose anemones brighten the black rock as far as we can see. You might find fossils. And a large undercut cave is the third special thing about this dive. Four of us go in and shine our lights. The roof and walls are brilliant with encrusting sponges, red and orange.

Outside the cave, giant barnacles. A blood star. A beige-and-blue striped sun star. A couple of lingcod. One rockfish, yellow staghorn bryozoans like miniature tropical coral. Chitons. Metallic blue kelp. Orange fish in crevices that look like tropical squirrel fish. White dahlia anemones, a Christmas anemone, snakelock anemones. Purple tube worms. Decorator crabs. Painted greenlings. Shrimp. Sea cucumbers. "Dusty" looking cloud sponges. Orange cup corals in 15 feet (5 meters). Brown kelp. Mauve coralline algae in the shallows. Green and purple urchins. The

massive wall at Turn Point is a conglomerate formation of the Upper Cretaceous age – about 65 to 85 million years old. It has sandstone lenses that weather into caverns, the cave. The rock walls are folded and that is where you might find fossils. The entire dive is stunning.

But the dark wall and the white plumose never-never land is what I will never ever forget.

BOTTOM AND DEPTHS

The chart puts the wall at 900 feet (270 meters) deep. The cave is undercut into the wall for 25 feet (8 meters). Its floor is at 75 to 85 feet (23 to 26 meters), depending on tide height. Its ceiling is 10 feet (3 meters) high. Bull kelp marks the shallows close beside the wall.

HAZARDS

Current, big ships and bull kelp. Dive on high slack, on the turn to ebb. Maximum ebb current at Turn Point is almost 3 knots. If a smaller ebb – up to 2 knots. You could dive with a "live" boat almost throughout the ebb. But do not dive on the turn to flood.

If diving from an anchored boat or if a medium or large tidal range, dive on high slack at the start of the ebb. Again, do not dive on the turn to flood.

Always stay south of the point, then you will not be swept into the shipping lanes where enormous ships pass. I heard one. Those on the surface told us two Japanese freighters and one Seaspan tug hauling railway cars passed while we were down. If caught in the rip current off the point, you could be pulled out into the shipping lanes. Carry a knife for kelp.

At Turn Point

TELEPHONE
VHF radio; if no VHF, try a cell phone.

FACILITIES
None.

ACCESS
Turn Point is at the northwest tip of Stuart Island on Haro Strait – almost at the United States/Canada border – the border is shown on the chart below. Turn Point is 2½ nautical miles north of the top of San Juan Island. Far out.

Charter or launch at San Juan Island, Anacortes or Bellingham and go to the northwest tip of Stuart Island. From Roche Harbor, Mitchell Bay, Smallpox Bay or Friday Harbor at San Juan Island the distance to Turn Point is from 6 to 14 nautical miles. Fog in spring or fall could make it impossible to reach this site, but boaters find protection from wind at Turn Point except strong winds from the south.

With all except the slightest tidal exchanges dive with a "live" boat. With a very low tidal exchange you could anchor an inflatable or other small boat in the bight just south of the wall. Plan to dive on the turn to ebb and stay south of the point.

The wall dive is south of Turn Point Lighthouse and north of the small bight. The wall you see on the surface is a hint of what is below water – but only a hint. At the site: roll off the boat, swim immediately to the wall and then go down. If you do not reach the wall, you might never orient yourself to find the cave!

To find the cave: dive deep at the start, then gradually work your way up while drifting slowly south. You will find the dark hole at 75 to 85 feet (23 to 26 meters).

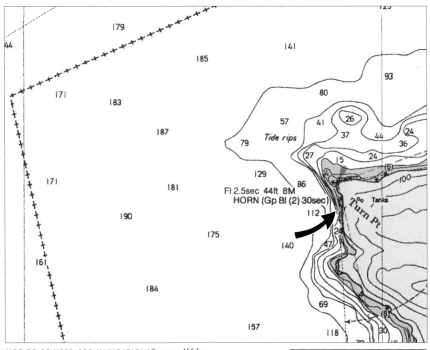

1/2 NAUTICAL MILE

NOTES

SMALLPOX BAY

SHORE DIVE

SKILL
All divers and snorkelers

TIDE TABLE
Port Townsend:
Add 30 minutes

WHY GO

Varied seascape – fish and shellfish – plus clean, clear water. Since divers have flocked to Smallpox Bay for years, I can't imagine how this is all still here, feeling unspoilt and wild. But it is. And so accessible. You can walk from your tent to the water.

New divers and snorkelers can enjoy easy diving in the bay with its shallow sandy bottom rimmed with rock. Even the tidepools hold lots of life. Small pastel green and pink anemones burgeon like flowers. Tufts of orange cucumbers soften the bright white rocks. Blue sea stars, little green urchins, gum boot chitons, kelp greenlings and giant red urchins decorate the rocky shallows.

Beyond the bay and south around the point you swim into bull kelp and rocky bottom that falls away quickly into big-boulder country and rocky overhangs. Shrimp, black rockfish, lingcod, white plumose anemones, bright yellow encrusting sponge, abalones and swimming scallops are some of the animals we saw. Look for octopuses too.

Do not go north to nearby Low Island. It is a National Wildlife Refuge – divers and boaters must not come closer to it than 200 yards (180 meters). This restriction is to protect the young birds, bald eagles and seal pups.

When smallpox was rampant many First Nations persons who lived in the San Juans jumped into the bay, believing the saltwater plunge would cure them. Thus the bay got its name.

BOTTOM AND DEPTHS

In the bay the shallow sandy bottom is scattered with eelgrass. Rock rims the bay. Beyond the southern point of the bay where the bull kelp begins, the rocky bottom is 10 to 20 feet (3 to 6 meters) deep. From here it falls away fairly quickly in ledges and folds to a depth of 40 to 50 feet (12 to 15 meters) to big boulders, small caves and overhangs. Then into very deep water.

HAZARDS

Current. Bull kelp, in summer. Beyond the bay, dive on slack. Carry a knife for kelp.

TELEPHONE

San Juan County Park, outside office.

FACILITIES

Campsites, flush toilets, picnic tables and launch ramp at San Juan County Park; in summer, campsite reservations strongly recommended. At Friday Harbor: air fills, charters and dive packages including accommodation; hot showers at the Port of Friday Harbor.

ACCESS

Smallpox Bay is on Haro Strait, west side of San Juan Island at San Juan County Park.

From Friday Harbor ferry landing, go 10 miles (16 kilometers) to the dive. Drive up the hill on Spring Street to Second Street. Turn right. Head out of town on Second which becomes Guard Street, later Beaverton Valley Road. At the Friday Harbor junction of Guard and Tucker, do not turn right to Roche Harbor but continue straight, following signs toward Mitchell Bay. From this junction, go 6½ miles (10 kilometers) along Guard and Beaverton Valley roads to Mitchell Bay Road. Turn left. Go on Mitchell Bay Road for 1¼ miles (2 kilometers). When you see signs pointing straight ahead to Snug Harbor, turn left. Go north on West Side Road to San Juan County Park.

If coming from Lime Kiln, go 2½ miles (4 kilometers) north on West Side Road to San Juan County Park.

For diving in the bay or beyond the southern point, enter over sandy beach in front of the campground office. Wheelchair access might be possible at the ridged concrete ramp with lots of sand on it – not for sure, but it could work. At high tides, a wheelchair diver would need able-bodied help to get over about 6 feet (2 meters) of sand.

*Open-water certification
site at Smallpox Bay*

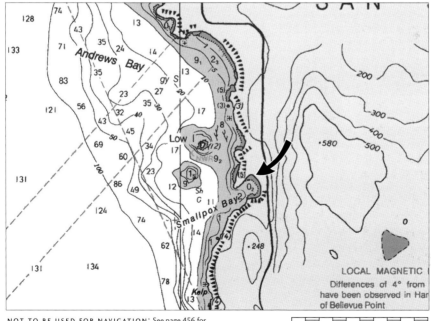

NOT TO BE USED FOR NAVIGATION: See page 456 for
information on obtaining navigational charts; use NOAA chart #18433.
Soundings are in fathoms and feet to 11 fathoms.

1/2 NAUTICAL MILE

LIME KILN POINT

WHY GO

Bright dive in the afternoon – the white shells reflect the sunlight. Abalones, gum boot chitons, lined chitons cling to the rocks. Mauve coralline algae feather the bottom from the bright white shallows to the olive-green world beneath the kelp.

Deeper, we see a glass tunicate like a miniature crystal vase. Pink hydrocorals and yellow staghorn, bryozoans on the rocks. Giant red and purple urchins, rock scallops, dahlia anemones, white plumose anemones, feather stars, giant barnacles. We swim over a smooth roll of rock down to a ledge. Swimming scallops clap up around us from 30 feet (9 meters) and deeper. A few scallops are still present at 100 feet (30 meters). We see a lingcod, quillback rockfish, kelp greenlings. A giant octopus jets away.

The current is picking up: we crawl along holding onto rocks, cannot afford to let go, are glad when we reach the bull kelp – it is something strong to hold onto.

Rocky crevice dive entry beside lighthouse

We have been lured deep, must stop on the way up. Lots to see in the shallows too: alabaster nudibranchs, sculpins, a Christmas anemone at 10 feet (3 meters). Brilliant red knobby sponge is on the rocks behind big fat leaves of brown bottom kelp.

Acorn barnacles – a giant's bed-of-nails on the flat rocks near shore as we coast with the current to Lime Kiln Lighthouse.

It was built around 1880; became a whale research station in 1983, the first whale-watching park in the country in 1984. Southern resident killer whales swim past from June to September hunting salmon in Haro Strait; the whale-watching lecturer who goes to the site every Sunday in summer says he sees them more than 50% of the times he is there. Divers sometimes meet whales under water at Lime Kiln. If you see whales, come no closer to them than 100 yards (90 meters).

BOTTOM AND DEPTHS

Rocky bottom with brown bottom kelp slopes to a bull kelp forest at 20 to 30 feet (6 to 9 meters). From there, rock rolls gently but quickly in a series of smooth ledges, folds and smooth walls to 110 to 120 feet (34 to 37 meters), depending on tide height. Scattered boulders.

HAZARDS

Currents up to 4 knots in Haro Strait; bull kelp, in summer; and a long walk to the water. Dive on slack, on the turn to ebb. Current at Lime Kiln runs parallel to shore and never stops, it just turns around. Carry a knife for kelp.

TELEPHONE

At lower parking lot, beside map of park.

FACILITIES

Whale-watching site, picnic tables and wheelchair-accessible restrooms at Lime Kiln. Air fills and charters at Friday Harbor. Camping at nearby San Juan County Park.

ACCESS

Lime Kiln Point is on Haro Strait, southwest side of San Juan Island. It is in Lime Kiln Point State Park also referred to as Whale Watch Park. From Friday Harbor ferry landing, go 9 miles (14½ kilometers) to it: drive uphill and out of town on Spring Street that runs into San Juan Valley Road. From the ferry, nearly 2 miles (3¼ kilometers) to Douglas Road. Turn left. At Bailer Hill Road, turn right. Bailer Hill Road runs into West Side Road and you follow it to Lime Kiln Point State Park. If starting from Smallpox Bay at San Juan County Park, go 2½ miles (4 kilometers) south on West Side Road to Lime Kiln.

At Lime Kiln Point State Park, go to the lower parking lot to unload gear, and to park if space. A map of the park, a telephone beside it; wheelchair-accessible restrooms, and the start of the lighthouse trail are here. Go to one of two entry points: for the easiest and safest entry, follow signs toward the lighthouse. Before

reaching it, you will see service buildings; turn right and follow a well-graduated path for 100 paces to a viewing platform: the restored lime kiln is in this bay. An easy water-entry is to the left of the platform. Another entry: go to the lighthouse but do not turn right. Pass the service buildings and keep going to the lighthouse. Climb down a rocky crevice on the left-hand side of it to the water.

Surge from wind and passing freighters sometimes makes entry impossible at Lime Kiln. Haro Strait often becomes rough in the afternoons. Dive on a calm day. Safer to dive on the turn to ebb; watch the current direction and work your way north of the lighthouse for half the dive. On the way back, if you accidentally surface you have a short way in which to swim across the current to the cove south of the lighthouse before being swept into Juan de Fuca. If you hit the current right, you can coast home.

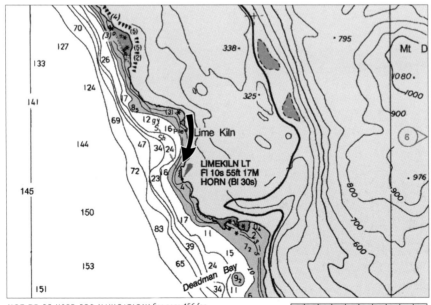

NOT TO BE USED FOR NAVIGATION: See page 456 for information on obtaining navigational charts; use NOAA chart #18433. Soundings are in fathoms and feet to 11 fathoms.

1/2 NAUTICAL MILE

NOTES

TURN ISLAND

BOAT DIVE or KAYAK DIVE
GPS
48°32.110′ N
122°58.376′ W

SKILL
Intermediate and expert divers

CURRENT TABLE
San Juan Channel
• Slack before flood:
Add 1 hour

• Slack before ebb:
Add 5 minutes

Blood star with ring-top snails and fluted bryozoans

WHY GO

Rich marine life; camping on Turn Island. An easy first kayak-dive. The paddle is short and you can land and gear up on the beach. You could turn it into a week of paddling, camping, bird watching and diving.

Christmas anemones, orange cup corals, flaming red slipper cucumbers and white plumose anemones are on the wall, between the rocks, in crevices. The color! Orange cucumbers and white ones, yellow staghorn bryozoans, gray sponges with knobs and pink encrusting sponge covers the rocks. Red urchins, purple ones too. Black, copper and quillback rockfish. Lingcod. Swimming scallops. Blood stars. White anemones. Swimming back through the bull kelp and tall brown stalks of kelp, we saw schools of juvenile rockfish. Kelp greenlings. Kelp crabs. Snorkeling we saw moon jellies, lots of them, pulsing through the shallows.

My buddy and I started the dive with another couple and, when we met later on the beach, we learned he had proposed under water. She nodded yes and pulled off her neoprene mitt. He slid the diamond on her finger. A second surprise for the bride-to-be was that champagne and a dozen red roses were waiting on the sunny beach, delivered by inflatable.

BOTTOM AND DEPTHS

Cobble and sandy beach give way to gravel and rocky bottom with bull kelp at 23 to 33 feet (7 to 10 meters). Around the point, ledges drop in gentle stairsteps. Rock walls indented with crevices, cracks and overhangs spill from ledge to ledge. We reached 70 feet (21 meters) before heading back. It goes deeper. You could also enjoy an entire dive in the shallows.

HAZARDS

Current, bull kelp and transparent fishing line as well as fishing lures. Dive on slack. Carry a knife.

TELEPHONES

• On the water: VHF radio; if no VHF, try a cell phone.
• On land:
1. Port of Friday Harbor, top of pier.
2. Outside waiting rooms, top of ferry landing.

FACILITIES

Turn Island visitors may land, moor their boats, picnic, camp, build fires, hike and dive from beaches. Before you go, telephone (360)902-8844 during the week to check if a burn ban is in effect. Primitive camping for a fee, pay at the "Iron Ranger". Take drinking water. Air fills and charters at Friday Harbor. Coin-operated hot showers at the Port of Friday Harbor.

Turn Island is a National Wildlife Refuge. On the water and on land, stay 200 feet (61 meters) away from any bird life.

ACCESS

Turn Island is in San Juan Channel near Friday Harbor. It is less than ½ nautical mile offshore from a public beach on San Juan Island where you can hand-launch a kayak and paddle to it, or charter.

At Turn Island, go north past the mooring buoys at the state park to the northern end of the island. Go to a tiny beach that is around the corner and close to San Juan Channel. Land, gear up and dive from the small beach or dive from your boat. Swim a short way to the bull kelp and go down. Dive around the point on the right.

- Charter out of Friday Harbor or Anacortes. Or launch your own boat at Lopez and go to Turn Island. From Friday Harbor, 4 nautical miles; from Lopez, 6 nautical miles to Turn Island.

- Kayak-divers: Drive to the public beach to launch and paddle to Turn Island in 10 minutes. Head uphill on Spring Street to First Street. Turn left and go 2 miles (3¼ kilometers) to Turn Point Beach access. Go past the ferry lineup; First Street becomes Harrison Street then Turn Point Road; continue straight on this main route. Past Sutherland Road, you will see the water and the main road curves to the right. Go straight past the yellow "No Overnight Camping" sign and turn right into the parking area; space for 12 to 15 vehicles to park. Walk 8 paces to the beach – wild blackberries are beside the path. From this log-strewn beach on San Juan Island, paddle to the left-hand side of Turn Island. Wheelchair divers, who paddle dive-kayaks and who can cross a small stretch of sand with some logs, could dive at Turn Island.

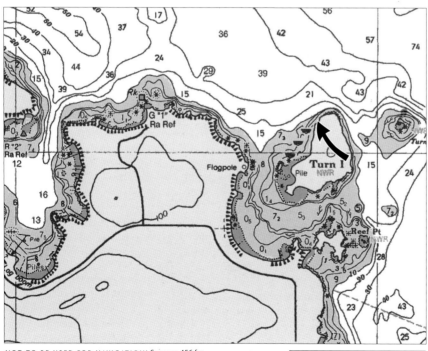

NOTES

NOT TO BE USED FOR NAVIGATION: See page 456 for information on obtaining navigational charts; use NOAA chart #18434. Soundings are in fathoms and feet to 11 fathoms.

1/2 NAUTICAL MILE

—REUBEN TARTE PARK—

SHORE DIVE

SKILL
Intermediate and
expert divers and
snorkelers

CURRENT TABLE
San Juan Channel
• Slack before flood:
  Add 23 minutes

• Slack before ebb:
  Subtract 1 hour

WHY GO

A beautiful reef! The sort of reef you usually have to struggle over lots of water to reach. But here – when the road is open – it's within a few steps from the rocky beach.

The cove has the clean-swept look of a spot with current and much of the life that goes with it. Bright orange crevice-dwelling sea cucumbers, giant barnacles all over the bottom, rock scallops, a scattering of swimming scallops, rockfish, big California sea cucumbers, lingcod, trumpet sponges and strange orange and white encrusting sponges. When diving here I held a red Irish lord. I saw a scarlet blenny with vertical stripes. Spider crabs, hermit crabs and kelp greenlings flashing through the bull kelp. Lots of blue-and-yellow striped seaperch shimmering in the shallows. Chitons, limpets, bright blue sea stars and giant red urchins stuck to the rocks. It's a good place for available light photography.

BOTTOM AND DEPTHS

White rocky wall with overhangs and crevices drops to a depth of 25 to 35 feet (8 to 11 meters), then undulates slowly to a depth of 50 to 60 feet (15 to 18 meters) and levels off. Big white boulders are scattered around. Bottom kelp and bull kelp are attached to the bright white rocks. Take a light for looking into holes.

HAZARDS

Current and bull kelp. Dive on the slack. Carry a knife.

TELEPHONES

• Roche Harbor, 6 miles (9½ kilometers) away. Go via Rouleau and Roche Harbor Roads, turn right and go to the end.
• Friday Harbor ferry landing, 11 miles (17½ kilometers) away.

FACILITIES

Parking space for four or five cars at Reuben Tarte Park, and a pit toilet. At Friday Harbor, air fills and charters; and hot showers at Port of Friday Harbor.

A wide choice of accommodations nearby at Roche Harbor: stay in a vintage hotel, cottage, modern condominium or an executive suite. Camping at San Juan County Park – reservations strongly recommended in summer.

ACCESS

Reuben Tarte Park is on San Juan Channel at the southeast end of Spieden Channel. It is at the northeast side of San Juan Island.

From Friday Harbor go 11 miles (17½ kilometers to Reuben Tarte County Park. The drive takes 20 minutes. From the ferry landing, head uphill on Spring Street to Second Street. Turn right. Go to Tucker Avenue and turn right following signs toward Roche Harbor and Lonesome Cove. Drive 7 miles (12 kilometers) along Roche Harbor Road, then turn right into Rouleau Road. Go along it to Limestone Point Road and turn right. At San Juan Drive, turn right again. Go ⅓ mile (½ kilometer) to the Reuben Tarte parking area.

From time to time the road from the parking lot to the beach is closed. Then you must walk 300 paces down the steep hill to the water – an extremely difficult hike with dive gear. I do not recommend this dive unless the road is open. But when the road is open it is a shore dive with very easy access. Then you can turn left down the steep hill, drop your gear and return up the hill to park. Once down the hill again, walk a few steps across the beach to the water. Dive around the point on your right.

The situation might change; at the time of writing the road is open for daytime loading and unloading only. Parking is permitted at the bottom of the hill for handicapped persons.

If you are at San Juan Island, access to the site is worth checking out.

344

Hermit crab in Oregon triton shell

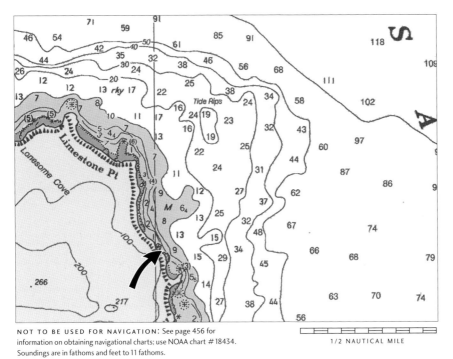

NOT TO BE USED FOR NAVIGATION: See page 456 for information on obtaining navigational charts; use NOAA chart #18434. Soundings are in fathoms and feet to 11 fathoms.

1/2 NAUTICAL MILE

NOTES

BELL ISLAND

BOAT DIVE
GPS
West side of island:
48·35.743′ N
122·58.886′ W

East side of island:
48·35.771′ N
122·58.808′ W

SKILL
Intermediate and expert
divers

All divers and
snorkelers with guide

CURRENT TABLE
San Juan Channel
• Slack before flood:
  Add 19 minutes

• Slack before ebb:
  Add 15 minutes

*Crevice-dwelling
sea cucumbers*

WHY GO

Bell Island is divable at all times, because you can always hide on the side of the island where the current is not. Drop from ledge to ledge and stop at whatever depth you are comfortable at. Or drop to the bottom and work your way up.

Prowl through the red and yellow encrusting sponge finding life, big and small. The largest octopuses in the world live in the Pacific Northwest but it is often difficult to find them. Slow down. Look in impossible places. Octopuses squeeze into narrow slits, make themselves small, hide beneath ledges, change color as chameleons do. Wolf-eels in the region too; they also hide beneath ledges. Take a light.

And the little guys? Also difficult to find. Decorated warbonnets camouflage themselves with whatever local marine life they find; their maximum recorded length is 16½ inches (42 centimeters). We saw more life at Bell Island: blue sun stars, orange and blue sea stars, a clown nudibranch, one white crevice-dwelling sea cucumber and lots of orange ones. Look for kelp greenlings and lingcod.

BOTTOM AND DEPTHS

Ledges with big, brown leafy bottom kelp down all sides of Bell Island. Bottoms out to white sand at 80 to 90 feet (24 to 27 meters), depending on tide height.

HAZARDS

Current, depth and small boats. Strong current, if you dive the wrong side of the island on the change. It never feels like a drop-off, but notice your depth; plan your dive. Stay close to the wall when you ascend.

TELEPHONES

• On the water: VHF radio; if no VHF, try a cell phone.
• On land: Deer Harbor Marina, two outdoor telephones, top of wharf in West Sound.

FACILITIES

None.

ACCESS

Bell Island is located in Wasp Passage, west of Crane Island, north of Shaw Island, east of Harney Channel and southwest of West Sound on Orcas.

Charter out of San Juan or Orcas islands, Anacortes or Bellingham. Or launch your own boat and come to Bell Island. Strong currents are all around. Plan to arrive before the current turns and dive on the east or west side of the island, depending on the current direction. When you arrive, scout the periphery of the island. Observe the direction of current: check out how the bull kelp lies.

*San Juan Diver
at Bell Island*

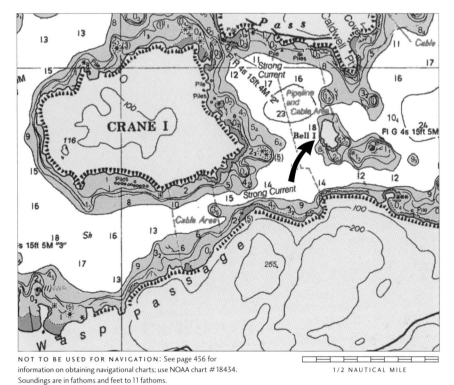

NOT TO BE USED FOR NAVIGATION: See page 456 for
information on obtaining navigational charts; use NOAA chart #18434.
Soundings are in fathoms and feet to 11 fathoms.

1/2 NAUTICAL MILE

NOTES

ROSARIO WALL

BOAT DIVE
GPS
48°38.628' N
122°52.345' W

SKILL
All divers with guide

TIDE TABLE
Port Townsend

WHY GO

Lots of critters in the underwater wilderness. Easy access – 5 minutes by boat, or paddle your own dive-kayak to the wall. On land, your choice of amenities: the Moran Mansion, an elegant Victorian hotel, overlooks the site; a campground is minutes away.

Dive anytime, no current disturbs the scene. Descent is gentle down stairstep-like ledges. One ledge rolls over to the next level. And another. On one dive we pass four active octopus dens with abundant litter of dead crabs and clams outside. But nobody home. Red urchins. Rock crabs. A horny lithode crab sidesteps and scurries around us. My buddy points out a big-scaled crab – a first for me. Copper and quillback rockfish swim past. Sea cucumbers lounge on the rocks. On the bottom, sunflower stars dig for clams. Look for crescent gunnels, C-O sole and sculpins: longfin, great and sailfins are here. The rock crevices are alive with krill.

BOTTOM AND DEPTHS

Gentle rocky ledges stairstep from the top of Rosario Wall at 55 to 65 feet (17 to 20 meters), depending on tide height, to its base. The wall is indented with crevices. The octopus dens we saw were between 40 and 60 feet (12 and 18 meters) deep. Take a light. The wall bottoms out to silty sand at 90 to 100 feet (27 to 30 meters), depending on tide height. Broadleaf red-brown kelp is on the ridge, top of the wall.

HAZARDS

Boats, silt and depth. Be aware of depth throughout the dive. Maintain good buoyancy control and stay off the bottom; silt could be stirred up and be disorienting.

Visibility varies: we enjoyed 15- to 30-foot (4½- to 9-meter) visibility on a sunny midsummer day. Visibility ranges up to 50 feet (15 meters) in winter.

When ascending, spiral up: listen and look for boats.

Passing Moran Mansion on way to Rosario Wall

TELEPHONES

- On the water: VHF radio; if no VHF, try a cell phone.
- On land: on fuel dock at Rosario Resort, outside the Harbor Master's office.

FACILITIES

Day charters and air fills at Friday Harbor, San Juan Island and at Anacortes. Air fills at Oak Harbor and Bellingham.

Luxurious accommodation overlooking the site at the Moran Mansion. Five minutes away from the dive; camping with picnic tables, fire rings and coin-operated hot showers, in summer, at Moran State Park: reservations in summer.

ACCESS

Rosario Wall is located in Cascade Bay, East Sound, Orcas Island: the wall starts just offshore straight out from the point closeby, west of the Moran Mansion.

Charter out of San Juan Island or Anacortes; charters also out of Tacoma. Or launch your own boat and come to Cascade Bay. Find the site with GPS locations and a depth sounder. Descend your anchor line to the top of the wall. Keep the wall on your left-hand side as you cruise south and down.

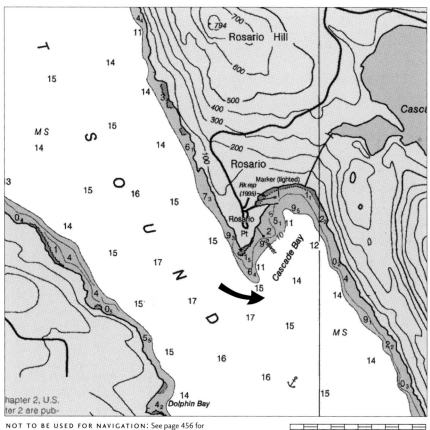

NOT TO BE USED FOR NAVIGATION: See page 456 for information on obtaining navigational charts; use NOAA chart #18430. Soundings are in fathoms and feet to 11 fathoms.

1/2 NAUTICAL MILE

SHORE DIVE

SKILL
All divers

TIDE TABLE
Port Townsend:
Add 25 minutes

WHY GO
Super-easy entry, hot showers after the dive, stacks of marine life.

Kelp greenlings and white-spotted greenlings flash past. Behind curtains of brown bottom kelp we see blackeye gobies. Dungeness crabs. A blood star. Purple sea stars plastered in heaps on the rocks. Two giant sunflower stars which I measure with my arm. They are 3 feet (1 meter) across. Pale blue. We see acorn barnacles on shallow rocks. Clown nudibranchs, alabaster nudibranchs, periwinkles. Around some boulders, the classic signs of octopus: a mess of shells and crab parts scattered on the sand. I look in the nearest hole between the rocks straight at a string of big suckers – 2 inches (5 centimeters) in diameter. This giant's den is in only 20 to 30 feet (6 to 9 meters) of water. Near it, beneath a ledge, we see a tiny grunt sculpin with precise markings like a tropical fish.

We see decorator crabs, gum boot chitons, giant purple urchins. Purple encrusting sponge. A few "dusty" looking sponges that look like they were hurled there after cleaning the car. Brilliant red knobby encrusting sponge beneath an overhang.

Sea butterfly

A few frilly white plumose anemones. A mass of leafy hornmouth snails filling a slot. A large quillback rockfish, a fat sea cucumber, a rock scallop.

Moon jellies as we snorkel across the bay. A large white anemone in shallow water. And a "first" for me: two sea butterflies. They are swimming along upright, waving semicircular pink wings together. Each butterfly is ¼ inch (½ centimeter) across; maximum wingspread of this little creature is 2 inches (5 centimeters). The movement the butterflies make is like a slow-motion clapping of hands to propel themselves forward through the open water.

BOTTOM AND DEPTHS
Eelgrass in the bay. Rock walls at both sides of the bay. On the left-hand side, the rock wall at the first point bottoms out at 10 to 20 feet (3 to 6 meters). Along the wall, periodic rock outcroppings ledge down to silty sand. At the second point on the left-hand side, rocks and boulders are scattered down to a 10-foot (3-meter) high ledge bottoming out to mud at 38 to 48 feet (12 to 15 meters). Brown bottom kelp covers the rocks. Some sand between. Very thick silt over all.

HAZARDS
Silt, shallow depth, some current and small boats – many ocean kayaks and sailboats come and go silently in the bay. Do not bob up unexpectedly in the bay; stay near the wall. Try not to stir up silt; weight yourself so you can stay down and yet stay off the bottom. Dive near slack. When ascending, stay close to the rocks and wall all the way to the surface, well out of the way of boats.

TELEPHONE
Doe Bay Resort and Retreat, outside store.

FACILITIES
Parking space, restrooms, clothing-optional hot tubs, sauna and hot showers for a

small day-use fee at Doe Bay Resort. Wheelchair-accessible toilets and showers. Also camping, cabins and trails to walk on year-round; a café in summer. This funky resort has a gentle feeling, is a slow-you-down type of place: www.doebay.com.

ACCESS

Doe Bay is next to Rosario Strait, east shore of Orcas Island.

Orcas is midway on the Anacortes–Sidney ferry route. From Orcas ferry landing, 35 minutes to Doe Bay. Follow the main road past the turnoff to Eastsound and the airport. Continue on it following signs toward Olga and Mount Constitution. Go through Moran State Park. After crossing a one-lane bridge and leaving the park, curve left, head down a hill and you will see the water. The Olga café is on a corner. Turn left past it, into Point Lawrence Road. Continue 3 ¾ miles (5⅓ kilometers) to Doe Bay Road and the resort.

From the beach at Doe Bay Resort and Retreat swim across the small bay with buildings facing onto it. It takes about 10 minutes to reach the second point on the left-hand side.

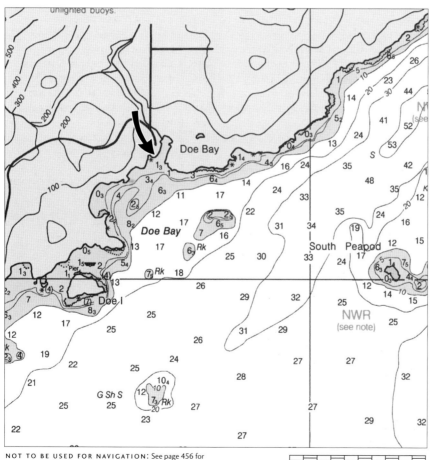

NOTES

NOT TO BE USED FOR NAVIGATION: See page 456 for information on obtaining navigational charts; use NOAA chart #18430. Soundings are in fathoms and feet to 11 fathoms.

1/2 NAUTICAL MILE

DOE ISLAND

**BOAT DIVE or
KAYAK DIVE**

GPS
48°37.972' N
122°47.133' W

SKILL
Intermediate and expert
divers and snorkelers

CURRENT TABLE
Rosario Strait
• Slack before flood:
  Add 8 minutes

• Slack before ebb:
  Add 49 minutes

WHY GO

Swimming scallops, rock scallops and yellow staghorn bryozoans – lots of them. And it's an easy first kayak dive: a short paddle and you can gear up on the beach. With hot showers after the dive.

The moment I put my face in the water periwinkles tumbled about rolling all over the rocks. We saw hermit crabs. Purple sea stars. A tiny decorator crab with tufts of kelp streaming. Schools of seaperch, schools of young black rockfish and kelp greenlings. Giant purple urchins at the base of the kelp. Under a ledge, glass tunicates, orange sea peaches, a gum boot chiton. Leafy horn-mouth snails. Bright red knobby sponge. Orange cup corals on the rocks. Giant barnacles. A small sea lemon. Two gunnels dart past us – I never get to look at them as long as I want to. Some white plumose anemones. Shrimp all over the place. Swimming scallops are thick from 50 to 70 feet (15 to 21 meters). We cannot put a hand down without touching one. Their bright eyes around the edges of their shells are shining. Some clap up around us.

BOTTOM AND DEPTHS

Rocky bottom covered with bottom kelp rolls gently down. White sand between the rocks. Light silt over all. Go as deep or as shallow as you want to – all good diving. But kelp at 20 to 30 feet (6 to 9 meters), depending on tide height. In summer the bull kelp is thick.

HAZARDS

Current, small boats, bull kelp and fishing line. Dive on slack. The current never stops, it just turns around. Stay close to the bottom throughout the dive; use rocks and bull kelp to pull yourself along. This marine park invites small boats: do not surface unexpectedly beneath one. Ascend in the bull kelp out of the way of boats. Carry a knife for kelp and fishing line.

*From Doe Bay, off
to Doe Island*

TELEPHONES

- On the water: VHF radio; if no VHF, try a cell phone.
- On land: Doe Bay Resort, outside store.

FACILITIES

Primitive camping beneath Douglas firs on Doe Island with picnic table, pit toilet and fire rings. Pay your fee at the "Iron Ranger". Take drinking water. Before you go, telephone (360)902-8844 during the week to check if a burn ban is in effect. On the north side of the island, a dock and small anchorage. But do not use the mooring buoys. They are privately owned.

Air fills at Friday Harbor, San Juan Island, Anacortes, Bellingham and Oak Harbor. Launch ramps at Orcas Island, Anacortes and Bellingham. Also a sling at Anacortes.

ACCESS

Doe Island is on the western side of Rosario Strait just offshore from east side of Orcas Island.

- Charter out of Anacortes or San Juan Island; or, launch your own boat and go to Doe Island. Anchor on the outside of the island – the Rosario Strait side – and head down.
- Kayak-divers: Doe Island is ½ nautical mile from Doe Bay Resort. See directions to it on page 351. Launch at Doe Bay and paddle for 15 minutes to Doe Island. The entire island is a marine park. You can land where you wish. Two beaches. We landed at a crescent of beach on the northeast side of the island to gear up, swam to the point, dived down through the bull kelp and south around the outside of the island.

NOTES

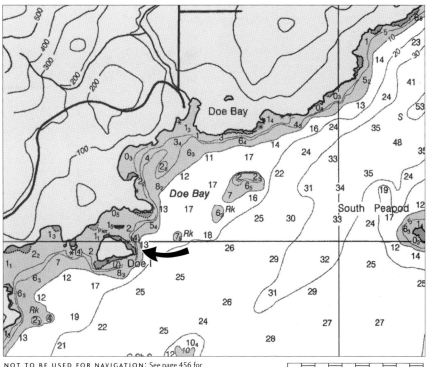

NOT TO BE USED FOR NAVIGATION: See page 456 for information on obtaining navigational charts; use NOAA chart #18430. Soundings are in fathoms and feet to 11 fathoms.

1/2 NAUTICAL MILE

LONG ISLAND

BOAT DIVE
GPS
48°26.588' N
122°55.732' W

SKILL
Intermediate and expert
divers and snorkelers

CURRENT TABLE
San Juan Channel

*Down through the
bull kelp*

WHY GO
Long Island has a couple of good drop-offs
as well as shallow diving. And it's protected
from the southeast wind.

The bright white wall covered with
abalones rolls in rounded mounds down
the cliff. The rock wall looks melted and
poured. Chitons cling to it. Small white
plumose anemones cluster under the
overhangs. You can easily snorkel and see
abalones here. I saw some as shallow as 5
feet (1½ meters).

The dark wall drops off from clean-swept,
kelp-covered white rocks dotted with lacy
bright orange tentacles of crevice-dwelling
sea cucumbers. It falls from 30 feet (9
meters) down to nowhere. You plummet
over the edge. Huge white plumose
anemones blanket the wall in froth, cascade
down the cliff. The free-fall of white is broken
only by a few narrow ledges where giant
barnacles cling in the cracks. Some barnacles are so encrusted with sponge that
you can't see them – only their pink feeding fans. Crimson slipper cucumbers, also
called creeping pedal cucumbers, splash
the wall with red. A few small rockfish swim
out over the bottomless black. There are
very few fish and the abalones have been
over-harvested, but if you like drop-offs,
this is a good one. Strawberry anemones
on the west side of Long Island.

BOTTOM AND DEPTHS
Rocky bottom with bull kelp at 25 to 35 feet
(8 to 11 meters), drops off to a depth of
90 to 100 feet (27 to 30 meters), depending on tide height.

HAZARDS
Boats, lots of current and bull kelp. Listen
for boats and ascend close to the wall all
the way to the surface, well out of the way
of those boats. Dive on the slack as there
is a great deal of current. Carry a knife for
kelp.

TELEPHONES
• On the water: VHF radio; if no VHF, try a
  cell phone.
• On land:
1. Mackaye Harbor Road and Mud Bay
   Road; from Mackaye Ramp, go up the
   road, ⅓ mile (½ kilometer) to the telephone on the other side of the fire hall
   beside Mud Bay Road.
2. Fisherman Bay dock.

FACILITIES
None at privately owned Long Island. On
Lopez, camping at Odlin County Park;
accommodations at Fisherman Bay.
Launch ramps at Mackaye Harbor, Fisher-
man Bay and Odlin County Park.

ACCESS

Long Island is next to Middle Channel, south of San Juan Channel. It is southwest of Lopez Island just offshore.

Charter out of Friday Harbor, San Juan Island; Anacortes or Bellingham. Or take your own boat: launch at Mackaye Harbor and go west 2¼ nautical miles to Long Island, or launch at Fisherman Bay, Odlin County Park or Hunter Bay and go to Long Island. Anchor in the small bay on the north side of Long Island, leave a boat

tender on board and dive from your boat. East to the white wall. West to the dark drop-off.

When you approach Long Island, be careful not to come close to Mummy Rocks; it is a National Wildlife Refuge. To protect the young sea birds and seals, visitors must stay 200 yards (180 meters) offshore at the wildlife refuge and avoid approaching closer than 100 yards (90 meters) to the seals.

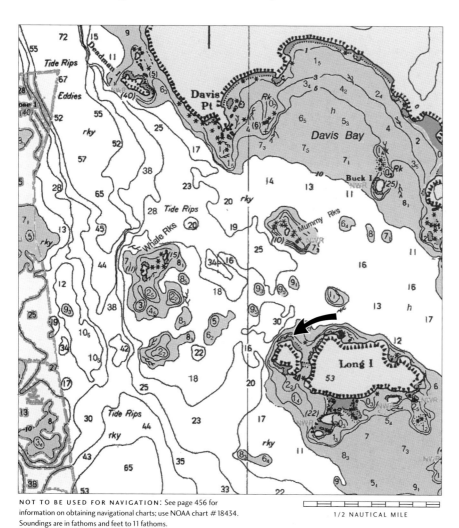

NOTES

NOT TO BE USED FOR NAVIGATION: See page 456 for information on obtaining navigational charts; use NOAA chart #18434. Soundings are in fathoms and feet to 11 fathoms.

1/2 NAUTICAL MILE

CHAPTER TEN

Seattle, Tacoma and Puget Sound including Fidalgo and Whidbey Islands

Divers at Keystone Jetty, Port Townsend across water

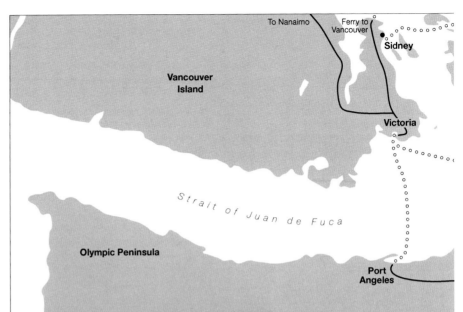

SEATTLE, TACOMA AND PUGET SOUND
including Fidalgo and Whidbey Islands

Dives

❶ Sares Head
❷ Rosario Beach
❸ Deception Pass
❹ Fort Casey Underwater
  Natural Area [Keystone]
❺ Bracketts Landing
  [Edmonds Underwater Park]
❻ Agate Passage
❼ Point White Dock
  [Crystal Springs Pier]
❽ Rockaway Beach
❾ Metridium Wall
❿ Seacrest Park
⓫ Alki Pipeline
⓬ Harper Fishing Pier
⓭ Tramp Harbor Dock

⓮ Dalco Wall
⓯ Sunrise Beach Park
⓰ Z's Reef
⓱ Fox Island, East Wall
⓲ Tacoma Narrows Bridge
⓳ Titlow Beach
⓴ Sunnyside Park
㉑ Sund Rock
㉒ Octopus Hole
㉓ Pinnacle [Brinnon Pinnacle]
㉔ Hood Canal Bridge
㉕ Sisters
㉖ Fort Flagler Fishing Pier
㉗ Fort Worden Science
  Center Wharf
㉘ Point Wilson Reef

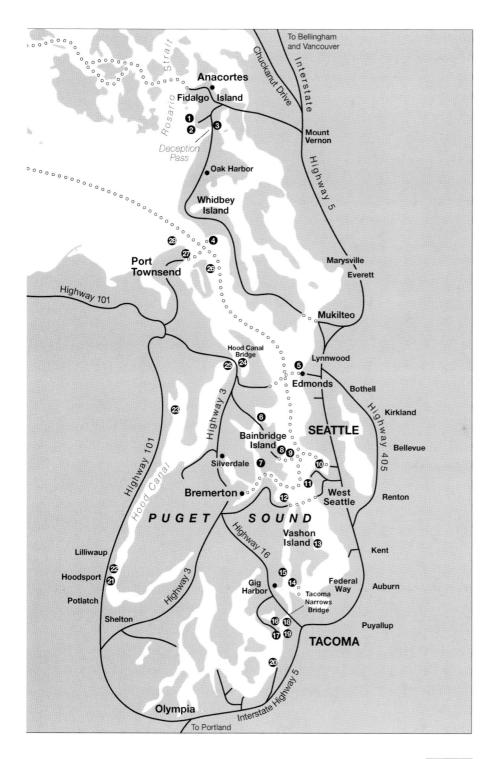

To Bellingham
and Vancouver

Anacortes

Rosario Strait

Chuckanut Drive

Interstate

Fidalgo Island

❶
❷ ❸

Deception
Pass

Mount
Vernon

Oak Harbor

Whidbey
Island

Highway 5

㉘ ❹
㉗
㉖

Port
Townsend

Marysville

Everett

Highway 101

Mukilteo

Hood Canal
Bridge

㉕ ㉔

❺

Lynnwood

Edmonds

Bothell

Kirkland

㉓

Highway 405

Highway 3

Highway 101

Hood Canal

❻

Bainbridge
Island

SEATTLE

Bellevue

❽ ❾

Silverdale

❼

❿

Bremerton

⓫

West
Seattle

Renton

⓬

PUGET   SOUND

Highway 16

Vashon
Island ⓭

Kent

Lilliwaup

Hoodsport

㉒
㉑

Highway 3

⓯

Gig
Harbor

⓮

Tacoma
Narrows
Bridge

Federal
Way

Auburn

Potlatch

Shelton

⓰ ⓲
⓱ ⓳

TACOMA

Puyallup

⓴

Olympia

Interstate Highway 5

To Portland

SERVICE INFORMATION

Tide Information

- National Oceanic Atmospheric Administration (NOAA) print annual: *Tide Tables, High and Low Water Predictions – West Coast of North and South America*
- www.tidesandcurrents.noaa.gov/tides07
- www.mobilegeographics.com/pugetsoundtides.html

Current Information

- National Oceanic Atmospheric Administration (NOAA) print annual: *Tidal Current Tables – Pacific Coast of North America and Asia*
- *Current Atlas: Juan de Fuca Strait to Strait of Georgia,* purchase one time. Use with *Murray's Tables* or *Washburne's Tables,* purchase annually; privately produced publications available at marine equipment and supplies stores.
- www.tidesandcurrents.noaa.gov/currents07
- www.mobilegeographics.com/pugetsoundcurrents.html

Weather Information

- US Coast Guard Radio: Coastal Marine Forecast, recorded 24 hours. Telephone Bellingham (360) 645-2301.
- www.atmos.washington.edu/weather.html For up-to-date information click "Weather" at bottom center of page and select your location.
- www.nws.noaa.gov/om/marine/zone/west/sewmz.html

Diving Emergency Telephone Numbers

<u>On land and water:</u>
- Call 911 and say, "I have a scuba diving emergency".
- Cell phone: Dial *24 and say, "I have a scuba diving emergency".
- Virginia Mason Hospital: telephone the hyperbaric unit, (206) 624-1144, ask for Emergency Room and say, "I have a scuba diving emergency".

<u>On the water:</u>
- VHF radio: Call Coast Guard radio, Channel 16 and say, "I have a scuba diving emergency".
- Cell phone: Dial *24 and say, "I have a scuba diving emergency".

If emergency or medical personnel are unfamiliar with scuba diving emergencies, ask them to telephone DAN (Divers Alert Network) at (919) 684-4326. No money for a long distance call? Dial DAN collect at 011-919-684-4326 and say, "I have a scuba diving emergency".

Mark emergency location before leaving scene: other divers might be down.

How to Go

Landmarks used for directions are the large cities, bridges and ferry landings. Today, as well as in historic Puget Sound days, boats are an important part of the transportation system – car ferries connect many communities within Puget Sound in addition to connecting Seattle with Vancouver Island.

Time to travel from place to place is included in access directions for divers unfamiliar with Washington State; but these times are approximate. Time varies depending on traffic and ferry lineups – travel at uncongested times to meet the times given.

- Seattle is the hub: distances measured from it are from I-5 (Interstate Highway 5) at Stewart Street and Denny Way near the city center, Exit 166.
- Tacoma and Olympia are at the southern end of I-5. Distances from these locales are usually from Exit 132 in Tacoma and Exit 104 in Olympia.
- West of Seattle, Bainbridge Island and Bremerton are important centers: car ferries and roads lead to these points from all directions. Road distances given are from Highway 3 or 303. The Hood Canal and Agate Passage bridges are locator points.
- Port Townsend and the Hood Canal are the westernmost locales in this chapter – Port Townsend is the actual hub of the entire chapter. Car ferries and roads converge on Port Townsend. You can drive north from Tacoma and Bremerton via the Hood Canal on Highways 3, 104 and 20 to Port Townsend. Drive from Olympia and Shelton on Highways 101 and 20.

Ferries ply from Keystone, Whidbey Island to Port Townsend; Victoria, British Columbia to Port Angeles, then drive to Port Townsend; Edmonds to Kingston and Seattle to Bainbridge Island.
- Bellingham is the northernmost location in Washington State from which directions are given for this chapter.

Ferry Information

Washington State Ferries
Recorded schedules, 24 hours, with touch-tone menu choices. To speak with a person during working hours 7 days a week, just wait – do not push any buttons.
- (206) 464-6400
- 1-888-808-7977: Toll-free throughout North America
www.wsdot.wa.gov/ferries

Black Ball Transport
- Seattle: (206) 622-2222
- Port Angeles: (360) 457-4491
- Victoria: (250) 386-2202
www.cohoferry.com
(Ferries between Port Angeles, Washington and Victoria, British Columbia.)

Victoria Clipper
- Seattle: (206) 448-5000
- 1-800-888-2535: Toll-free throughout North America
www.victoriaclipper.com
(Foot-passenger ferry – no cars – between Seattle, Washington and Victoria, British Columbia.)

Tourist Information

Washington State Tourism
(360) 725-5050
1-800-544-1800: Toll-free throughout North America, Hawaii and Alaska
www.experiencewashington.com

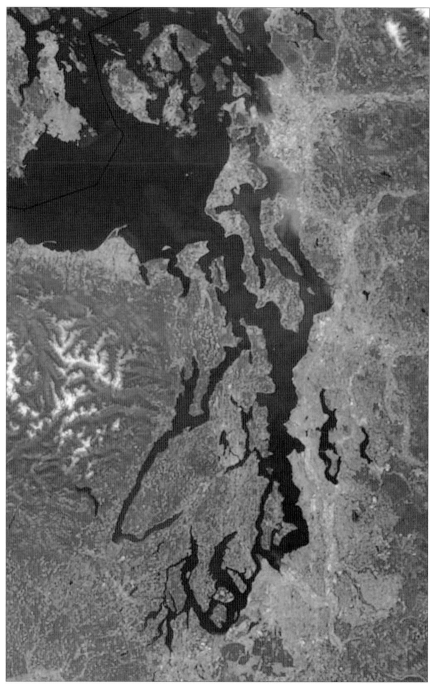

Puget Sound, Hood Canal, Strait of Juan de Fuca – water, dive shops, dive resorts, charter boats and launch ramps on all sides. What surroundings for divers!

• DIVE SHOPS AND INSTRUCTION

SEATTLE

Discount Divers Supply
2710 Westlake Avenue N
Seattle WA 98109
(206)298-6998
1-877-728-2238: Toll-free in continental
    USA
www.discountdivers.com
(Recreational dive shop.)

Lighthouse Diving Center
8215 Lake City Way NE
Seattle WA 98115
(206)524-1633
1-800-777-3483: Toll-free throughout
    North America
www.lighthousediving.com
(Recreational and nitrox instruction.
Nitrox fills.)

Underwater Sports
10545 Aurora Avenue N
Seattle WA 98133
(206)362-3310-8811
1-800-252-7177: Toll-free in USA
www.underwatersports.com
(Recreational, nitrox, technical and rebreather
instruction. Nitrox station.)

SOUTH OF SEATTLE

Underwater Sports
34428 Pacific Highway S
Federal Way WA 98003-7325
(253)874-9387
www.underwatersports.com
(Recreational dive shop.)

NORTH OF SEATTLE

Underwater Sports
264 Railroad Avenue
Edmonds WA 98020-4133
(425)771-6322
www.underwatersports.com
(Recreational dive shop.)

Edmonds Technical Diving Service
PO Box 531
Edmonds WA 98020
(206)618-3096
1-888-254-1550: Toll-free throughout
    North America
www.etds.org
(Technical and recreational instruction only.
Vacation rental for groups of divers at the
Yellow House in Hoodsport.)

Lighthouse Diving Center
#6, 5421 - 196th Street SW
Lynnwood WA 98036
(425)771-2679
1-800-777-3483: Toll-free throughout
    North America
www.lighthousediving.com
(Recreational dive shop.)

Jerome Ryan Diving Instruction
Independent instructor
Lynnwood WA
(206)769-4332
E-mail: jryan@engravingsbyjerome.com
(Technical instruction only: advanced nitrox
through trimix.)

Underwater Sports
Casino Square
#4 - 205 East Casino Road
Everett WA 98208-2830
(425)355-3338
www.underwatersports.com
(Recreational, technical and rebreather
training.)

• DIVE SHOPS AND INSTRUCTION

EAST OF SEATTLE

Underwater Sports
#59 Brierwood Center
12003 - NE 12th Street
Bellevue WA 98005-2455
(425)454-5168
www.underwatersports.com
(Recreational dive shop.)

Silent World Diving Systems
13600 - 20th Street NE
Bellevue WA 98005
(425)747-8842
1-800-841-3483: Toll-free throughout
    North America
www.silent-world.com
*(Recreational, nitrox, technical and
rebreather instruction. Nitrox, trimix and
soda-lime are available.)*

Northwest Sports Divers
8030 NE Bothel Way
Kenmore WA 98028
(425)487-0624
www.nwsportsdivers.com
*(Recreational, nitrox, technical and
rebreather instruction. Nitrox, trimix and
soda-lime are available.)*

Underwater Sports
11743 - 124th Avenue NE
Kirkland WA 98034
(425)821-7200
www.underwatersports.com
(Recreational dive shop. Nitrox station.)

Bubbles Below
17315 - 140th Avenue NE
Woodinville WA 98072
(425)424-3483
www.bubblesbelow.com
*(Recreational, nitrox, technical and
rebreather instruction. Nitrox fills.)*

WEST OF SEATTLE – BAINBRIDGE ISLAND TO BREMERTON

Exotic Aquatics Scuba & Kayaking
146 Winslow Way West
Bainbridge Island WA 98110
(206)842-1980
1-866-842-1980: Toll-free throughout US
www.exoticaquaticsscuba.com
*(Recreational dive shop, guiding for shore
and boat dives. Rent nitrox tanks to out-of-
towners.)*

Sound Dive Center
5000 Burwell Street
Bremerton WA 98312-3302
(360)373-6141
1-800-392-3483: Toll-free throughout
    North America
www.sounddive.com
*(Recreational, nitrox, technical, and
rebreather instruction. Nitrox fills.
Dive guiding.)*

Tagert's Extreme Ocean Sports Center
1230 Bay Street
Port Orchard WA 98336
(360)895-7860
www.oceanmom.com
(Recreational dive shop.)

TACOMA

Lighthouse Diving Center
2502 Pacific Avenue
Tacoma WA 98402
(253)627-7617
1-800-777-3483: Toll-free throughout
    North America
www.lighthousediving.com
(Recreational dive shop.)

Underwater Sports
9608 - 40th Avenue SW
Tacoma WA 98499-4302
(253)588-6634
www.underwatersports.com
*(Recreational, nitrox, technical and rebreather
instruction. Nitrox station.)*

Fort Lewis Scuba
NCO Beach Road, Building 8050
Fort Lewis WA 98433
(253)967-3405
E-mail: lfred.James.Johnson1@us.army.mil
and casey.specht@us.army.mil
*(Full service dive shop – only for government
I.D. card holders: open daily except Tuesday
and Wednesday. Recreational and nitrox
instruction; rebreather training and soda-
lime when instructor in the country.)*

• BOAT RENTALS

Point Defiance Boathouse Marina
Point Defiance Park, foot of Pearl Street
5912 North Waterfront Drive
Tacoma WA 98407
(253)591-5325
www.metroparkstacoma.org: Click on
Parks & Facilities, select Beaches & Boats,
then Boathouse Marina.
*(Boat rentals. No reservations, easier to obtain
on weekdays or in winter out of fishing season.
The boats work for diving. Wheel your gear
by handcart, available at marina, from curb
to boat. Then diver and gear are lowered to
the water. Telephones outside marina store
and office next to restrooms.)*

OLYMPIA AND SOUTH

Underwater Sports
1943 Fourth Avenue East
Olympia WA 98501
(360)493-0322
www.underwatersports.com
(Recreational dive shop.)

Capital Divers & Aquatics
110 Delphi Road NW
Olympia WA 98502
(360)866-3684
www.capitaldivers.com
*(Recreational, nitrox, technical and rebreather
instruction. Nitrox and trimix fills.)*

Beneath the Waves
6403 East Mill Plain Boulevard
Vancouver WA 98661
(360)546-1494
www.beneaththewaves.com
*(Recreational, nitrox and rebreather
instruction. Nitrox fills.)*

Thunder Reef Divers
12104 NE Highway 99
Vancouver WA 98686
(360)573-8507 or (503)228-3767
www.thunderreef.com
*(Recreational and nitrox instruction.
Nitrox fills.)*

HOOD CANAL TO PORT TOWNSEND

• DIVE SHOPS AND INSTRUCTION

Mike's Diving Center
22270 North Highway 101
Potlatch WA
Mailing address: 22270 North
Highway 101, Shelton WA 98584
(360)877-9568
*(Recreational dive shop; also heritage house
rental. It is a complete house with kitchen, rec
room and four bedrooms – for eight divers.)*

Edmonds Technical Diving Service
Yellow House Divers' Inn
23891 North Highway 101
Hoodsport WA
(206)618-3096
1-888-254-1550: Toll-free throughout
    North America
www.etds.org
*(Technical and recreational instruction only.
Vacation rental for larger groups of divers at
the Yellow House in Hoodsport. Nitrox, trimix
and air fills for students and divers at the Yellow
House; for drop-ins by pre-arrangement.)*

Hood Sport 'n Dive
27001 North Highway 101
PO Box 1445
Hoodsport WA 98548
(360)877-6818
www.hoodsportndive.com
*(Recreational, nitrox and technical instruction.
Nitrox, trimix and soda-lime available. Fee
for diving at Sund Rock includes a hot shower
afterwards. Dive package for groups includes
accommodation and air fills.)*

Townsend Bay Dive Shop
2205 Sims Way
Port Townsend WA 98368
(360)379-3635
www.townsendbaydive.net
*(Recreational, nitrox and technical instruc-
tion; nitrox and trimix available.)*

• RESORT AIR STATIONS

Mike's Beach Resort
38470 North Highway 101
Lilliwaup WA 98555
(360)877-5324
1-800-231-5324: Toll-free throughout
    North America, Hawaii and Alaska
www.mikesbeachresort.com
*(Resort air station: waterfront cabins, tent
and RV camping; dive-kayak rentals and hot
tubs for resort guests only. Concrete launch
ramp, good except at extremely low tides.
Telephone outside office. Restrooms with hot
showers. Day-use fee for divers and boat
launch drop-ins.)*

Sunrise Motel & Dive Resort
24520 North Highway 101
PO Box 554
Hoodsport WA 98548
(360)877-5301
www.hctc.com/~sunrise
*(Resort air station; also boat rentals, and
dive packages including accommodation.)*

• BOAT RENTALS

Pleasant Harbor Marina
308913 Highway 101
Brinnon WA 98320-9758
(360)796-4611
1-800-547-3479: Toll-free throughout
    North America
www.pleasantharbormarina.com
*(Boat rentals include a hot shower after
diving.)*

WHIDBEY ISLAND, ANACORTES AND BELLINGHAM
• DIVE SHOPS AND INSTRUCTION

Whidbey Island Dive Center
#1, 1020 - 7th Avenue NE
   (at Highway 20)
Oak Harbor WA 98277
(360)675-1112
www.whidbeydive.com
(Recreational and nitrox instruction. Nitrox fills. Guiding for shore dives.)

Anacortes Diving & Supply
2502 Commercial Avenue
Anacortes WA 98221
(360)293-2070
www.anacortesdiving.com
(Recreational and nitrox instruction. Nitrox fills.)

Adventures Down Under
701 East Holly Street
Bellingham WA 98225
(360)676-4177
www.adventuresdownunder.com
(Recreational, nitrox, technical and rebreather instruction. Nitrox, trimix and soda-lime available.)

Washington Divers
903 North State Street
Bellingham WA 98225
(360)676-8029
(Recreational dive shop.)

• DAY AND MULTIPLE-DAY CHARTERS
Out of Seattle, Tacoma, Hood Canal and Bainbridge Island

Sampan, Naknek and *Ocean Quest*
Bandito Charters
PO Box 9456
Tacoma WA 98409
(253)973-0370
www.banditocharters.com
(Day and weekend multiple-day charters with land-based accommodation out of Tacoma and Seattle ranging to the San Juans; usually out of Tacoma – also sometimes out of Anacortes for the San Juans.)

Dash
Porthole Dive Charters
PO Box 109
Milton WA 98354
(253)405-3462
www.portholedivecharters.com
(Personalized day and multiple-day charters with land-based accommodation for groups of six diving Puget Sound, Hood Canal, Neah Bay and the San Juans. Boat is trailerable; can pick up divers at any location depending on dives – mainly out of Tacoma, either Day Island Marina or Point Defiance Public Boat Launch.)

Deep Insight
Teal Water Charters
5407 - 99th Avenue NW
Gig Harbor WA 98335
(253)377-9194
www.tealwater.com
(Day charters range from Seattle and Bainbridge Island south to Olympia; out of Gig Harbor and public docks at Desmoines, Point Defiance, Manchester and Allyn.)

Mija
Zero Gravity Dive Charters
7505 NE Airport Way
Portland OR 97218
(503)341-6271
E-mail: danaomeara1@msn.com
(Custom day charters for groups of four to six divers out of Hoodsport, Trident Cove and anywhere in Hood Canal – you name it. The boat is trailerable.)

Down Time
Pacific Adventure
PO Box 550
308913 Highway 101
Brinnon WA 98320
(206)714-1482
www.pacadventure.com
(Day charters out of Pleasant Harbor Marina, Highway 101 on the west side of the Hood Canal for diving in the Hood Canal. Hot freshwater shower on deck.)

Spirit
Spirit Diver
Home Port, Bainbridge Island
Contact Exotic Aquatics: (206)842-1980
(Day and weekend multiple-day charters with land-based accommodation out of Eagle Harbor, Bainbridge Island for diving around Blake and Bainbridge islands.)

Out of Anacortes and Everett

Dash
Porthole Dive Charters
PO Box 109
Milton WA 98354
(253)405-3462
www.portholedivecharters.com
*(Personalized day and multiple-day charters
with land-based accommodation for groups
of six diving the San Juans. Boat is trailerable,
can pick up divers at any location depending
on dives.)*

Deep Sea
Deep Sea Charters
Cap Sante Boat Haven
"B" Dock, Slip 22
Anacortes WA 98271
(360)661-6101, (360)658-5024
www.deepseacruise.com
*(Day and multiple-day charters with land-
based accommodation throughout northern
Puget Sound and the San Juan Islands; out
of Everett or Anacortes.)*

Lu-Jac's Quest
Diver's Dream Charters
Skyline Marina, Slip TD-22
558 Klamath Drive
La Conner WA 98257
(360)202-0076
www.lujacsquest.com
*(Day charters for 8 to 14 divers; also 1- to
3-day charter packages with land-based
accommodation. Destinations throughout
the San Juan Islands and to the Mackenzie
and G.B. Church in Canada.)*

Sampan, Naknek and *Ocean Quest*
Bandito Charters
PO Box 9456
Tacoma WA 98409
(253)973-0370
www.banditocharters.com
*(Occasional day and multiple-day charters
with land-based accommodation to the San
Juan Islands out of Anacortes [or Seattle].)*

San Juan Diver, Chewy, Sea Horse and *Island
Diver Too*
Island Dive & Water Sports
2A Spring Street Landing, PO Box 476
Friday Harbor WA 98250
(360)378-2772
1-800-303-8386: Toll-free throughout
    North America
www.divesanjuan.com
*(Day and multiple-day charters with land-
based accommodation ranging throughout
the San Juan Islands and, in Canada, to the
Mackenzie and G.B. Church: out of Anacortes
for groups up to 14 divers. Divers with special
needs welcome.)*

369

• **LAUNCH RAMPS**
For Puget Sound
Don Armeni Public Ramps
1200 Block Harbor Avenue SW
West Seattle
(Concrete ramps, good at all except minus tides. Launch for a fee on Elliot Bay. Plenty of space to park. Wheelchair-accessible flush toilets; telephones ⅓ mile [½ kilometer] east of ramp entry, outside cafe at Seacrest Park.)

From I-5 (Interstate Highway 5), drive 5 minutes to the ramps
• Heading south on I-5, take Exit 163A onto West Seattle Bridge, then Harbor Avenue Exit. Turn right and go 1½ miles (2½ kilometers) around the waterfront to Don Armeni ramps entry at Seacrest Park.
• Heading north on I-5, take Exit 163 to West Seattle Bridge, and Harbor Avenue Exit. Turn right and go 1½ miles (2½ kilometers) around the waterfront to Don Armeni ramps entry at Seacrest Park.

Eagle Harbor Waterfront Park Ramp
Foot of Shannon Drive, Winslow
Bainbridge Island
(Concrete ramp, launch for a fee: good except at extreme low tides. Severely limited parking space. Chemical toilets top of dock.

Telephone is visible from small, launch-ramp parking lot. Walk a short way uphill on a paved path to the edge of the park; the telephone is at the roadside, immediately across from Bainbridge Island Commons on Brien Drive.)

Immediately off ferry from Seattle or heading south on Highway 305, follow signs to Winslow city center. Go west on Winslow Way to the stop sign at Madison Avenue and turn left. Take first left at Bjune Drive, then right on Shannon Drive and to the water.

Fort Ward State Park Ramp
Bainbridge Island, south end
(Concrete ramp: launch for a fee, good at all tides. Parking space; wheelchair-accessible pit toilets. Telephone at Lynnwood Center in front of theater; this telephone is 1½ miles [2½ kilometers] from ramp.)

(Fort Ward State Park Ramp continued)
On Highway 305 heading north off ferry from Seattle, or south from Agate Passage, watch for a sign to Fort Ward State Park at High School Road: follow it through a residential district, up Bucklin Hill Road curving between the trees; past shops in Lynnwood; and along Pleasant Beach Drive, past the "Dead End" sign to the ramp.

Port of Manchester Public Ramp
Foot of Main Street
Manchester
(Concrete ramp: good for small boats at all tides; for boats 14 feet [4 meters] and more at tides greater than 5 feet [1½ meters]. Lots of parking space; picninc tables Wheelchair-accessible restroom, limited hours, at parking area. Telephones outside grocery on Main Street.)

Located off Colchester Drive between Port Orchard and Southworth
• From Southworth ferry landing follow Southworth Drive and Colchester Drive: go 6 miles (10 kilometers) to Manchester; turn right on Main Street to the ramp.
• From Tacoma, go north on Highway 16 to Highway 106 (Sedgewick Drive): turn right and continue east on Sedgewick to Southworth ferry terminal. Go north on Southworth and Colchester drives to Manchester. Turn right onto Main to the ramp.
• From Bremerton: follow signs southeast around the bay to Port Orchard. Continue through the center of town to traffic lights on the east side of Port Orchard. A junction: two ways to Manchester.

For a leisurely scenic drive, bear left along Bay Drive that becomes Beach Drive – about 6 miles (10 kilometers) to Manchester State Park, then 2 miles (3¼ kilometers) more to Manchester. Turn left into Main Street and to the foot of it.

For a shorter route, bear right up the hill on Highway 166. At the traffic circle, stay left; Highway 166 becomes Mile Hill Road: 5¾ miles (9⅓ kilometers) to Manchester.

For Tacoma and Gig Harbor

Point Defiance Park Public Ramps
Foot of Pearl Street, Tacoma
5912 North Waterfront Drive
Tacoma WA 98407
(253) 591-5325
www.metroparkstacoma.org: Click on
Parks & Facilities, select Beaches &
Boats, then Boathouse Marina.
*(Concrete ramps, good at all tides. Launch
for a fee. A great deal of parking space.
Restrooms across road at ferry landing; tele-
phone outside restrooms. Convenient for
Dalco Wall, Tacoma Narrows Bridge, Z's
Reef and Sunrise Beach dives.)*

Gig Harbor Public Ramp
Foot of Randall Road
Gig Harbor
*(Concrete ramp, good at all tides: launch is
free. Roadside parking. Wheelchair-accessible
flush toilets, open year-round at City Park,
across from start of Randall Road. Telephone
outside shop on North Harborview Drive;
return up Randall, turn left, and follow the
arterial for ⅔ mile [1 kilometer] to shop on
east side of the road. If you reach the flashing
light, you have gone too far. Convenient for
Dalco Wall, Tacoma Narrows Bridge, Z's Reef
and Sunrise Beach dives.)*

In Gig Harbor city center, head downhill
to foot of Pioneer Road and turn left.
Curve around Harborview Drive to the
flashing light and turn right into North
Harborview Drive. Follow the arterial road
nearly 2 miles (3¼ kilometers) to Randall
Drive NW. Turn right. A short way to the
foot of Randall and the ramp.

Narrows Marina
9011 South 19th Street
Tacoma WA 98466
(253) 564-3032
www.narrowsmarina.com
*(Concrete ramps, good at all except extreme
minus tides. Launch for a fee. A great deal of
parking space. Restrooms; and telephone
beside bait shop. Convenient for Tacoma
Narrows Bridge, Z's Reef, Dalco Wall and
Sunrise Beach dives.)*

Wollochet County Public Ramp
Foot of 10th Street NW
Wollochet Bay
*(Concrete ramp, good at all tides: launch
free for Hale Passage. Roadside parking for
four or five cars. No toilet. No telephone.
Convenient for Z's Reef and Tacoma Narrows
Bridge dives.)*

Located off Highway 16: the turnoff is
just north of Tacoma Narrows Bridge
• Heading north on Highway 16: when
  immediately north of the bridge take
  the Wollochet–Point Fosdick exit. From
  the bridge, 2½ miles (4 kilometers) to
  the ramp. Follow the road under the bridge
  and continue west on Stone Drive NW,
  passing Tacoma Narrows Airport, to
  Point Fosdick Drive. At Point Fosdick
  Drive, turn left and go nearly ⅔ mile
  (1 kilometer) to 10th Street NW. Turn
  right. Go on 10th to the water.
• Heading south on Highway 16: take
  Olympic Drive exit and go south on
  Point Fosdick Drive for 2¾ miles
  (4½ kilometers) to 10th Street NW.
  Turn right and go on 10th to the water.

• LAUNCH RAMPS

For Agate Passage

Charles Lawrence Memorial Ramp
Foot of Suquamish Way
Suquamish
(Steep concrete ramp; good at mid-tides to high tides. Lots of parking space, a tiny beach for picnics and a dock where people fish. Telephones are straight up the road from the launch ramp in the next block: one at the roadside in front of a shop; the second, outside the post office. No toilets. But pit toilets are closeby at Old Man House [Chief Seattle Park]; go back up Suquamish Way to Division Avenue, turn left and follow signs to Old Man House at foot of McKinistry Street.)

Ramp is located on Port Madison, 5 minutes off Highway 305: immediately west of Agate Pass Bridge at traffic light, go north 1½ miles (2½ kilometers) to end of Suquamish Way.

Port of Poulsbo Public Ramp
Foot of Hostmark Street
Poulsbo
(Concrete ramp, good at all tides. Limited parking space. Telephone at top of "D" dock, Port of Poulsbo, immediately west of ramp parking lot. Wheelchair-accessible flush toilets at Poulsbo Waterfront Park, a block away and past the Port of Poulsbo restrooms.)

The ramp is in Poulsbo off Highway 305; it is a short way east off Highway 3. At a traffic light in Poulsbo, head downhill; follow signs to "City Center" and "Marine Science Center". Go to the foot of Hostmark Street. Where Hostmark curves right, turn sharply left following signs down a one-way slot into a parking lot and to the Marine Science Center. Half-circle the parking lot to the narrow ramp. It is immediately beside the riprap shoring up the science center.

For Hood Canal, Dabob Bay

Quilcene Boat Haven
PO Box 98
1731 Linger Longer Road
Quilcene WA 98376
(360)765-3131
www.portofpt.com: click on Marine Information then Quilcene Marina.
(Launch year-round for a fee, for Dabob Bay and the Hood Canal: clean concrete ramp, good at all tides, except for large boats at minus tides. Plenty of parking space.

Restrooms and hot showers. Emergency telephone for 911 only outside fuel shack near the water. Also RV and tent camping.)

For Hood Canal, near Hood Canal Bridge, north side
Salsbury Point County Park Ramps
Foot of Whitford Road NE
North of Hood Canal Bridge (east end)
(Concrete ramps, good at all tides. Huge parking area. Flush toilet and hot shower – both wheelchair accessible. Playground, picnic pavilion. Telephone at Port Gamble General Store, outside; go to highway and then north 1 mile [1½ kilometers] to Visitor Info and Museum signs. Turn left to the General Store.)

Located off Highway 104: it is north of the east end of Hood Canal Bridge. From junction of Highways 3 and 104, head north toward Port Gamble. Go ½ mile (¾ kilometer) to Wheeler Street with signs to Salsbury Point County Park. Turn left down Wheeler that curves back toward the bridge. Go to Whitford Road NE. Turn right to the water.

Termination Point [Shine Tidelands] Ramp
North of Hood Canal Bridge (west end)
(Concrete ramp, good at all tides. Extremely limited roadside parking. No toilets.

Telephone outside Port Gamble General Store: drive east across Hood Canal Bridge, turn left and go 1¼ miles [2 kilometers] to Port Gamble; at Visitor Info and Museum signs, turn left to it. Another telephone 5 miles [8 kilometers] west of Hood Canal Bridge, north of Junction of Highways 104 and 19 between the Visitor Center and chemical toilets.)

The ramp is at the west end of the Hood Canal Bridge. Heading west on Highway 104, immediately across the bridge turn right into Paradise Bay Road, then immediately right again and downhill to the ramp.

For Hood Canal, near Hood Canal Bridge, south side
William Hicks County Park Ramp
Shine Road loops off Highway 104,
South of Hood Canal Bridge (west end).
(Concrete ramp, good at medium and high tides. Limited parking, wheelchair-accessible pit toilet and picnic table in this park. Telephone outside Port Gamble General Store. Go by road to the east side of Hood Canal Bridge, turn left and go 1¼ miles [2 kilometers] to Port Gamble. At Visitor Info and Museum signs, turn left to the General Store. Another telephone at Visitor Center, Junction of Highways 104 and 19; go west from Hood Canal Bridge for 5 miles [8 kilometers], turn right and immediately left into the Visitor Center. Telephone outside between Visitor Center and chemical toilets.)

Off Highway 104 on Squamish Harbor; south of the west end of the Hood Canal Bridge. Turn south into Shine Road, the first road at the west end of the bridge off Highway 104; go 1¼ miles (2 kilometers) and turn left into the park. Or, approaching from the west, turn right off Highway 104 into Shine Road when just over 2½ miles (4 kilometers) east of Highway 19 junction. Go on Shine 1 mile (1¾ kilometers) to the park.

For Admiralty Inlet
Fort Worden State Park Ramps
200 Battery Way
Port Townsend WA 98368
(360)344-4400
www.fortworden.org
(Launch for a fee: concrete ramps, good at all tides. Lots of parking space. Telephone across road, outside refreshment stand. Wheelchair-accessible flush toilet, behind refreshment stand. Camping with hot showers year-round; advance registration is required.)

• LAUNCH RAMPS
For Rosario Strait
. . . at Fidalgo Island and Anacortes
Bowman [Reservation] Bay Public Ramp
Deception Pass State Park
Fidalgo Island, south end
(Launch for a fee: concrete ramp, good only at high tides. Limited parking space and picnic tables. Restrooms and year-round camping nearby: return to Bowman Bay Road and turn left to the interpretive center. Telephone off Highway 20, south side of Deception Pass Bridge; turn right into Deception Pass State Park. Telephone is near the entry.)

Off Highway 20: immediately north of Deception Pass Bridge and south of Pass Lake, turn west. Immediately turn left into Bowman Bay Road and follow signs to Bowman Bay and the ramp.

Washington Park Ramps
Fidalgo Island, north end
Anacortes
(Launch for a fee at Fidalgo Head, near Anacortes ferry terminal: steep concrete ramp, good at all tides for small boats – can be difficult for larger boats; coin-operated gate to it. Restrooms and coin-operated hot showers. Telephone in front of park superintendent's home beside curve of drive out.)

Washington Park is 4 miles (6 kilometers) west of Anacortes off Highway 20. Follow signs through Anacortes toward San Juan ferry. From Commercial Avenue and 12th, go 3 miles (5 kilometers) toward the ferry. You will see a sign to a marina: bear left through the stop sign and go on Sunset Avenue for ¾ mile (1¼ kilometers) to Washington Park at the end of the road.

• SLING LAUNCHES
For Rosario Strait
. . . at Anacortes
Cap Sante Marine
Cap Sante Boat Haven
PO Box 607
Anacortes WA 98221
(360)293-3145
1-800-422-5794: Toll-free throughout
   North America
www.capsante.com
(Sling launch at Fidalgo Bay. Restrooms and coin-operated hot showers 150 paces north next to Cap Sante Harbor office, Port of Anacortes. Telephones across road from Cap Sante Marine near the sling launch. In winter, check if open.)

Skyline Marina (Penmar Marine)
2011 Skyline Way
Anacortes WA 98221
(360)293-5134
(Sling launch on Burrows Bay for Flounder Bay and Rosario Strait, south of Fidalgo Head near Anacortes ferry terminal. Flush toilets; ask for combination at marina. Telephone beside marina office.)

• LAUNCH RAMPS
For Rosario Strait
. . . at Bellingham

Squalicum Harbor Public Ramps
Foot of Bellwether Way
Bellingham Bay, north end
(Launch for a fee: concrete ramps, good at all tides. Large parking space, freshwater taps in parking area to wash gear. Wheelchair-accessible restrooms and showers; telephones beside restrooms, north end of Harbor Center. At the top of the ramp, turn left and walk 80 yards [75 meters] through Harbor Center to these facilities at the Port of Bellingham.)

Located in Bellingham, 5 to 10 minutes off I-5 (Interstate Highway 5) at north end of Bellingham Bay. Turn off Harbor Loop Route into Bellwether Way and turn right at "Boat Launch Parking" sign to the ramps.

To get to Bellingham from I-5
• Heading south on I-5, take Exit 256. Turn right at Meridian Street and go to traffic light at Squalicum Way. Turn right and follow the Squalicum Harbor sign toward the water; the road curves left into Roeder Avenue. Go on Roeder for just over ½ mile (¾ kilometer) passing various harbor facilities. Then go to the south end of Squalicum Harbor and turn right into Bellwether.
• Heading north on I-5, take Exit 253 to Lakeway Drive and go back under I-5. Go along Lakeway following Squalicum Harbor signs; continue on Holly Street through the city center; turn left onto "F" Street. Turn right at Roeder Avenue, then left at Bellwether Way.

Fairhaven Public Ramp
Harris Avenue, just past 6th Street
Bellingham Bay, south end
(Launch for a fee at south end of Bellingham Bay: concrete ramp, good at all except extreme low tides. Wheelchair-accessible restrooms; telephone outside of restrooms.)

In Bellingham, Fairhaven district, just east of the Alaska ferry dock and Amtrak railway station. Heading north or south on I-5 (Interstate Highway 5), take Exit 250: follow signs to the Alaska ferry. The ramp is 2 miles (3¼ kilometers) off the highway. Go on Old Fairhaven Parkway (Highway 11) junction with Chuckanut; do not turn left. Turn right into 12th Street; then left onto Harris Avenue. Go to 6th Street, turn right to the ramp; parking is on the right.

For Deception Pass
. . . at Whidbey Island

Cornet Bay Public Ramps
Deception Pass State Park
Whidbey Island, north end
(Launch for a fee at Cornet Bay: concrete ramps, good at all except extreme low tides. Restrooms and hot showers. Telephone at top of float at privately owned Deception Pass Marina. It is opposite Canyon Road and ⅓ mile [½ kilometer] west of the public ramps.)

From Highway 20, when 1 mile (1½ kilometers) south of Deception Pass Bridge, go east on Cornet Bay Road for 1½ miles (2½ kilometers) to Cornet Bay Ramps.

All of this Service Information is subject to change.

**BOAT DIVE or
KAYAK DIVE**

GPS
48°25.503′ N
122°40.347′ W

SKILL
Intermediate and expert
divers

All divers with guide

Advanced kayak-divers

CURRENT TABLE
Rosario Strait
• Slack before flood:
  Add 3 minutes

• Slack before ebb:
  Add 17 minutes

WHY GO

A cascade of white plumose anemones spills over Sares Head like a gigantic waterfall. A dark cavern is beneath it. Basket stars are scattered like giant snowflakes at its entrance. Swimming scallops, too – some clap up around us. Inside the cave, basket stars in shadowy corners.

We look up beneath another overhang, a small one. In the darkest corner, see creeping pedal sea cucumbers like red lace. Swim away from the wall, lie back and look up: white froth of plumose anemones burgeons from the black bulge of rock. Sares Head appears like the prow of a ship breaking waves. A black rockfish swims past. Yellowtail rockfish. A lingcod. You might see tiger rockfish. On the way up we see lined chitons dotting the rocks. Giant purple urchins between boulders. A rock scallop. We see broken shells on the bottom – must be an octopus. We look for it in the crevice above the shells. We are rewarded by finding a decorated warbonnet, nearby a painted anemone on a rock, and a 1½-foot (½-meter) lingcod cruises past in the thicket of kelp.

So much! But basket stars, shallow and deep, are the best things to me about Sares Head. They're extravagant.

BOTTOM AND DEPTHS

The rock wall at Sares Head bulges like a gigantic monolith and drops to sand at 90 to 100 feet (27 to 30 meters). A cavern at its base. Rocky ledges stairstep up from the cave to the narrow ledge south of Sares Head that is at 30 to 40 feet (9 to 12 meters). Boulders scattered from deep to shallow. Basket stars start at 30 to 40 feet (9 to 12 meters).

HAZARDS

Current, thick curtains of bull kelp and boats, especially in summer. Dive on slack. Carry a knife. Listen for boats. Ascend close to the wall all the way to the surface.

TELEPHONES

• On the water: VHF radio; if no VHF, try a cell phone.
• On land: Cornet Bay Marina, top of the dock.

FACILITIES

None at Sares Head. Air fills in Oak Harbor, Anacortes and Port Townsend.

Launch ramps in Deception Pass State Park: one at Cornet Bay with restrooms and hot showers; another ramp at Bowman Bay with restrooms and hot showers in the campground nearby. At Rosario Beach, dive-kayak launching across the beach, parking and picnic tables year-round; restrooms, in summer. Hot showers and camping year-round in one part or another of Deception Pass State Park.

ACCESS

Sares Head is on Rosario Strait at Fidalgo Island. It is 1½ nautical miles north of Deception Pass. At the time of writing, you know you are there by the dead tree snag on the point at Sares Head.

Charter out of Anacortes; or launch at Bowman [Reservation] Bay, Cornet Bay or Anacortes. Kayak-divers can hand-launch at Rosario Beach (see road directions to it on page 379): walk 22 yards (20 meters) down a trail to the water and paddle to Sares Head in 15 minutes. Easier to paddle with the flooding current and dive on high slack; then coast back with the ebb. At Sares Head: divers with inflatables and kayak-divers can anchor in a cove immediately south of Sares Head where there is a narrow ledge at 30 to 40 feet (9 to 12 meters). In summer, a forest of bull kelp marks it. In winter, thin wisps of kelp. Larger boats cannot anchor at Sares Head because of depth, and must leave a boat tender on board.

Cornet Bay, Bowman Bay and Rosario Beach are all in State Park and are open year-round.

Basket star at Sares Head

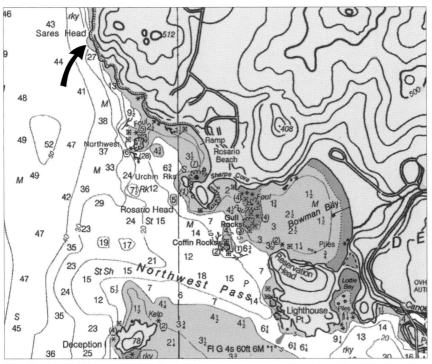

NOTES

NOT TO BE USED FOR NAVIGATION: See page 456 for information on obtaining navigational charts; use NOAA chart #18427. Soundings are in fathoms.

1/2 NAUTICAL MILE

—ROSARIO BEACH

SHORE DIVE

SKILL
All divers

TIDE TABLE
Port Townsend

WHY GO

The underwater setting is wild, the surface civilized, the dive within the capability of all divers. This wilderness feeling is the unique offering of Rosario.

Unlike many nearby sites, Rosario is a totally natural underwater scene. No man-made pilings to attract marine animals. No jetty. Just bottom kelp, bull kelp, red and green seaweed feathering up in the water. Many animals too: big frothy white plumose anemones, kelp greenlings, grunt sculpins, octopuses, gum boot chitons, decorator crabs and thousands of spider crabs. Millions of transparent shrimp hop and skitter about – the bottom is like a field of grasshoppers in July. Look for juvenile wolf-eels and umbrella crabs.

If you've ever wanted to stroke a fish, Rosario is the place you can probably do so. There are some red Irish lords here. And although I wouldn't say they *like* back scratching, they tolerate it. The waters are within Deception Pass State Park, an under-water reserve. Do not take any marine life.

Rosario is good for underwater sight-seeing with a civilized setting on the surface – both the good and bad of it. Huge evergreens are on shore. Jet aircraft whistle and roar overhead – the sound is ever-present, even under water. Then after the dive, off for a hot shower nearby in Deception Pass State Park.

BOTTOM AND DEPTHS

Shallow and sandy in the bay; around Urchin Rocks, undulating rocky bottom covered with bull kelp to a depth of 40 to 50 feet (12 to 15 meters). Sand beyond.

HAZARDS

Current, bull kelp and poor visibility. Dive near slack; carry a knife. The water is usually silty with debris stirred up by currents through nearby Deception Pass. It is particularly turbid in spring because of Skagit River runoff. Visibility is best at high slack tide in very early spring and late fall.

Red Irish lord

TELEPHONE

On the south side of Deception Pass Bridge near the entry to Deception Pass State Park.

FACILITIES

At Rosario, parking and picnic tables year-round; in summer, also restrooms.

Hot showers and camping year-round at one part or another of Deception Pass State Park.

ACCESS

Rosario Beach is on Rosario Strait *north* of Deception Pass. It is at the south end of Fidalgo Island in Deception Pass State Park off Highway 20. You can go all the way to Rosario by road – no ferries.

In Deception Pass State Park, just south of Pass Lake, turn toward the sea and follow signs to Rosario Beach and the marine center. Immediately past the marine center, you reach Rosario. Walk 240 yards (220 meters) down a groomed path past the pavilion to the beach where the entry is very easy over the sand. Walk up the beach to your left and snorkel out to Urchin Rocks.

To get to the turnoff to Rosario Beach

- From Seattle, go north on I-5 (Interstate Highway 5) and take Exit 230. Go west on Highway 20 and follow signs to Whidbey Island and Deception Pass. Then turn left, still on Highway 20, and go 5 miles (8 kilometers) south to the Rosario turnoff. From Seattle, 2¼ hours to the dive.
- From Bellingham, go south on I-5 (Inter-state Highway 5) and take Exit 230. Go west on Highway 20 and follow signs to Whidbey Island and Deception Pass. Turn left, still on Highway 20, and go 5 miles (8 kilometers) south to the Rosario turnoff. From Bellingham, 50 minutes to the dive.
- From Anacortes, go east on Highway 20 for 2½ miles (4 kilometers) to the turnoff to Oak Harbor and Port Townsend ferry. Turn right. Still on Highway 20, go for 5 miles (8 kilometers) south to the Rosario turnoff. From Anacortes, 15 minutes to the dive; from San Juan ferry, 25 minutes.
- From Oak Harbor, go north on Highway 20. Drive 11 miles (18 kilometers) to the Rosario turnoff. It is just across the bridge at Deception Pass. Takes 20 minutes.

NOTES

NOT TO BE USED FOR NAVIGATION: See page 456 for information on obtaining navigational charts; use NOAA chart #18427. Soundings are in fathoms.

1/2 NAUTICAL MILE

DECEPTION PASS

BOAT DIVE
GPS
48°24.410' N
122°38.538' W

SKILL
Expert divers

CURRENT TABLE
Deception Pass

WHY GO

An extravaganza of suspension feeders and fish looks like a surrealistic underwater painting down the steep rock walls of Pass Island.

Purple plume worms burst out along the entire wall in flamboyant bouquets, their purple tufts not even disturbed by divers. Masses of 2-inch (5-centimeter) red, pink and green dahlia anemones carpet the space between. Confetti-like bright red anemones and hot pink brooding anemones are scattered side-by-side in a splash of color. The brooding anemones spill over onto the parchment-like plume worm tubes. Other feather duster tubes are completely encased in yellow sponges. Not enough room for all the life on the rocks!

Strange finger sponges poke out from the most current-washed parts of the wall like flabby pale yellow rubber gloves. We saw urchins, chitons and white plumose anemones which soften the deep crevices. Large lingcod, cabezons and huge kelp

Beneath Deception Pass Bridge, approaching Pass Island

greenlings sweep out of the dark and back again.

In 1792 Captain Vancouver named this waterway Port Gardner. When he discovered it was not an inlet but a pass between two islands – he renamed it Deception Pass.

BOTTOM AND DEPTHS

A steep rock wall drops from the island to a depth of 100 to 110 feet (30 to 34 meters) in the pass, depending on tide height. Deep crevices and overhangs. Some bull kelp by Pass Island.

HAZARDS

Current, downcurrents, whirlpools, boats and poor visibility. Very swift currents. Dive on a day with a small tidal exchange – best at the turn before ebb and precisely on slack. Arrive at the site 45 minutes before the predicted turn at the end of the flood. As with all current predictions, slack may not happen as scheduled. Watch the water and when it slows down, go in. Have a "live" boat ready to pick you up if you are swept away. Listen for boats and ascend close to the steep sides of the island well out of the way of those boats.

Visibility can be poor, particularly when the Skagit River is in flood in springtime or after heavy rain. Also, Deception Pass is different from most places. The ebbing tide carries flotsam and jetsam out of the bay into the pass. For best visibility, dive on the tail end of a flooding current.

TELEPHONES

- On the water: VHF radio; if no VHF, try a cell phone.
- On land:
1. Bowman Bay, beside road.
2. Cornet Bay Marina, top of the dock.

FACILITIES

Launch ramps in the park at Cornet Bay where there are flush toilets and coin-operated hot showers, and ramps at Bowman [Reservation] Bay.

ACCESS

Deception Pass is between Fidalgo and Whidbey islands in Deception Pass State Park. Charter out of Anacortes; or launch at Cornet Bay south side of Deception Pass or Bowman [Reservation] Bay northwest of it. Then go by boat to Pass Island which is under the bridge. Leave someone in your boat as a pickup while you dive.

Before diving, try to see Deception Pass in action. Go when the 5- to 8-knot current is running: see the impressive whirlpools, the wild current whipping through. Park at the scenic overlook at the north end of the northernmost bridge over the pass. Pass Island is below. To reach Deception Pass by road: from I-5 (Interstate Highway 5), take Exit 230. Go west on Highway 20 to signs pointing south to Deception Pass State Park. From Anacortes, go east on Highway 20 to signs pointing to it; turn right. Drive south for 10 minutes to the park.

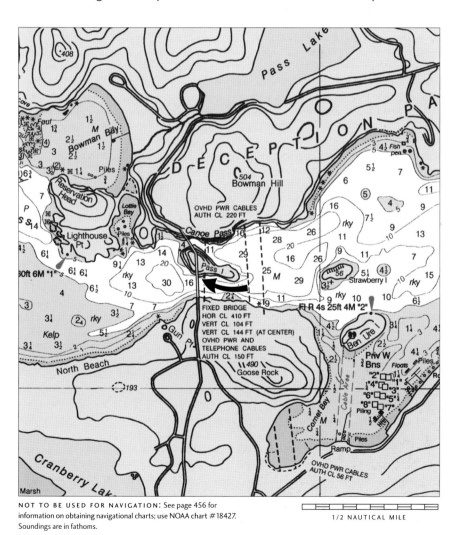

NOT TO BE USED FOR NAVIGATION: See page 456 for information on obtaining navigational charts; use NOAA chart #18427. Soundings are in fathoms.

1/2 NAUTICAL MILE

NOTES

—FORT CASEY UNDERWATER NATURAL AREA [KEYSTONE]—

SHORE DIVE

SKILL
All divers and snorkelers
first half of jetty

All divers with guide to
end of jetty and to wharf

CURRENT TABLE
Admiralty Inlet
• Slack before flood:
 Subtract 31 minutes

• Slack before ebb:
 Add 1 minute

*On beach at Fort Casey,
campground other
side of ferry landing*

WHY GO

Fort Casey Underwater Natural Area,
formerly known as Fort Casey Underwater
Park and better known as Keystone, is a
"must" for anyone who wants to dive all
the best sites in the northwest. Especially
popular with photographers.

Keystone Jetty concentrates life. The
fish are fat in this current-washed area.
And very tame, too. The fish seem to
know that Keystone has been a wildlife
sanctuary for years. Many divers actually
hand-feed kelp greenlings that live beside
the jetty. One photographer says the
painted greenlings are tame to the point
of being a nuisance. "They get in the way
when you're taking pictures!"

White plumose anemones are heaped
on the riprap at the base of the jetty like
dollops of whipped cream. Other colorful
invertebrates, too. Countless rockfish in
crevices. An octopus in a dark hole. Wolf-
eels. Life stacked on life. Even divers are
accepted as part of this underwater scene.
On weekends, expect to meet lots of them.

The abandoned wharf at the left of the
jetty provides more shelter for marine life,
but watch the current. Dive here on slack.
I love drifting with schools of seaperch
between these pilings covered with purple
plume worms.

After diving, walk uphill to Fort Casey;
see the fortifications that guarded the
entry to Puget Sound in the 1890s.

BOTTOM AND DEPTHS

The jetty, made of heaps of rock or riprap,
is 75 yards (70 meters) long. It is a solid
breakwater structure and you could not
slip beneath it into the path of the ferry.
Maximum depth at the tip of the jetty, 50
to 60 feet (15 to 18 meters). The abandoned wharf (east of the jetty) harbors
much life on its 30- to 40-foot (9- to
12-meter) deep pilings. Smooth sand and
pebble bottom between the wharf and jetty.

HAZARDS

Current, southeast wind, ferry, small
boats, broken fishing line and bull kelp.
Look for people fishing before you go in.
Dive on slack, especially at the wharf and
when current is ebbing. Be careful not to
be swept around the end of the jetty into
the path of the ferry. Stay down, hold
onto rocks and pull yourself along the
jetty back toward shore. Do not dive when
southeast wind blows surf onto the
exposed beach. Carry a knife; if caught in
kelp or fishing line you can cut your way
free.

TELEPHONE

Outside ferry building.

FACILITIES

Picnic tables, a great deal of parking space,
cold water for rinsing gear, restrooms with
wheelchair-accessible flush toilets and hot
 showers; and launching ramp at Fort
 Casey Underwater Natural Area. Camping other side of Keystone Harbor at Fort
 Casey Historical Park, also with hot
 showers. Dive guiding and air fills in Oak
 Harbor; air fills in Port Townsend and
 Anacortes.

ACCESS

Fort Casey Underwater Natural Area is at
Keystone Harbor on Admiralty Bay,
Whidbey Island. It is 20 minutes south of
Oak Harbor at the end of Highway 20;
follow signs to Port Townsend Ferry and

Fort Casey State Park.

Take Keystone turnoff from Highway 20 and Highway 25 junction, and go 3 miles (5 kilometers) along Keystone Spit. Turn left into the parking area for the underwater park. The Port Townsend ferry landing is just past the parking area. If you reach it, you have gone too far. Enter the water at the left of the jetty.

Wheelchair access is possible for divers who also paddle dive-kayaks. From the launching ramp in the parking area: paddle around the jetty and back to the beach on the other side. Total distance is 220 yards (200 meters). Not far to paddle, but do not try to swim it. Too much current and you are exposed to ferry traffic. Leave your dive-kayak on the beach and enter the water on the left-hand side of the jetty.

To get to turnoff for Keystone
• From Seattle, a choice of two routes:
1. Drive all the way: go north on I-5 (Highway 5) and take Exit 230. Go west on Highway 20. When signs point to Deception Pass and Whidbey Island, turn left. Head south through Oak Harbor; follow the signs to Port Townsend ferry.

2. Driving and ferry: go north on I-5; take Exit 182. Go to Mukilteo-Clinton ferry on Highway 525; sail to Columbia Beach at Whidbey Island in 20 minutes; then drive north on Highway 525. From Clinton, it is 22 miles (35 kilometers) to the Keystone turnoff: then follow signs to Port Townsend ferry. Both routes take 2 hours or more, depending on traffic and ferry lineups.
• From Bellingham, drive south on I-5 (Interstate Highway 5) and take Exit 230. Go west on Highway 20 to signs pointing to Deception Pass and Oak Harbor. Turn left. Still on Highway 20, follow signs through Oak Harbor to Port Townsend ferry: from Oak Harbor, 15 miles (24 kilometers) to Keystone turnoff. From Bellingham, 1½ hours.
• From San Juan ferry at Anacortes, go east on Highway 20. When 2½ miles (4 kilometers) past Anacortes, turn right. Still on Highway 20, follow signs to Whidbey Island, Port Townsend ferry and Keystone turnoff. Takes 1 hour.
• From Oak Harbor, go south on Highway 20: follow signs to Port Townsend ferry; go 15 miles (24 kilometers) to Keystone turnoff. Takes 20 minutes.

NOTES

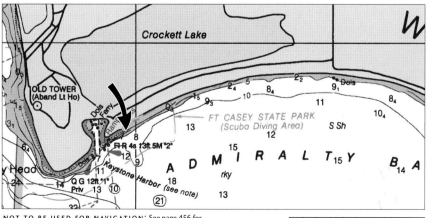

NOT TO BE USED FOR NAVIGATION: See page 456 for information on obtaining navigational charts; use NOAA chart #18471. Soundings are in fathoms and feet to 11 fathoms.

1/2 NAUTICAL MILE

BRACKETTS LANDING [EDMONDS UNDERWATER PARK]

SHORE DIVE

SKILL
Intermediate and expert
divers

All divers with guide

CURRENT TABLE
Admiralty Inlet
• Slack before flood:
  Add 44 minutes

• Slack before ebb:
  Add 19 minutes

WHY GO

An underwater Disneyland-type park with heaps of marine life, sunken vessels and more easy-to-find attractions. To see them, follow underwater paths, trails of rope held in place with pipes, rocks and yellow road cones. Probably the most-dived site in the Pacific Northwest, Edmonds is a mecca for photographers, a great place to meet new divers.

The park began in 1935 – before modern scuba gear was invented – with the sinking of the 300-foot (90-meter) DeLion Dry Dock. It was the first dry dock on the west coast with a concrete keelson and you can still see the keelson today. In 1970 it was officially designated an underwater park, the first on the west coast. In 1972 the 94-foot (29-meter) tug *Alitak* was scuttled. The two ships have sheltered so much life – and still do.

On my first visit I saw rockfish, red Irish lords, painted greenlings and decorated warbonnets ranging the vessels. A wolf-eel in the open. An octopus too. Archways of fluff rose around us as we swam through plumose-covered ribs of the *Alitak*, past the sunken dry dock. In 1982 the 76-foot (23-meter) *Fossil* was added to the park; in 1992, the 28-foot (9-meter) *Sky Hi*. The

most recent large additions are the *Molly Brown* in 1996 and the 70-foot (64-meter) *Triumph* in 1999. Sunken vessels and marine life abound. During a recent dive my buddy and I met a huge lingcod guarding eggs. We saw at least 20 giant cabezons cruising the sunken ships. Copper rockfish. Pipefish. Clown nudibranchs. Purple tube worms. Hermit, kelp and Dungeness crabs – too much to name!

Photographers will find best visibility on weekdays in early- to mid-August, then again in winter when plankton levels are low and fewer divers stir the silt. Remember, taking of marine life and parts of the vessels is prohibited.

For up-to-date information go to www.ci.edmonds.wa.us: click on City Departments and under Recreation choose Discovery Programs, then scroll down to Edmonds Underwater Park.

BOTTOM AND DEPTHS

The dry dock rests on silty sand at 25 to 35 feet (8 to 11 meters), depending on tide height. It is northwest of the ferry pier. The deepest part of the park is 45 feet (18 meters) at high tide; it is on the south end near the ferry. In summer, some bull kelp is attached to the dry dock showing where it is. Boundary buoys mark the 32 acres (13 hectares) of park where boats are prohibited. Between the underwater enhancements and shore you will find eelgrass, moon snails, flounders and all the other life associated with a sandy bottom.

HAZARDS

Long swim (long walk, if tide is out), some crosscurrent and close proximity to the ferry dock. Poor visibility especially in summer and fall, and the underwater trails themselves. Some bull kelp, some lion's mane jellies. Current is created by wind, tides and the ferry propeller-wash. Watch current direction and notice whether you are being swept sideways. Unless you are very familiar with the dive, stay on the

Diver with plumose anemones at Edmonds Underwater Park

underwater trail and use your compass. Since the mid-1970s, all new features have been placed away from the dry dock to avoid proximity to the ferry slip. However, do not go near the ferry slip; the underwater park boundary is marked by a row of tires. The trail lured me far out to sea; remember to turn around and come back. Watch your air, avoid a long surface swim and save some sights for a second dive. On the surface, look for buoys with tails that show current direction. Carry a knife. If you have seen jellies, check for tentacles before removing masks and gloves.

TELEPHONES
• Beside north side of Main Street, across railway tracks from anchor.
• Inside Edmonds ferry terminal.

FACILITIES
Wheelchair-accessible toilets and change-rooms, open year-round; cold-water showers for gear. Limited parking space, including handicapped parking, and a gear drop-off zone. Extensive interpretive displays. Air fills just down Railroad Avenue in Edmonds.

ACCESS
Bracketts Landing is on Puget Sound at Edmonds. The dive is 15 minutes west of I-5 (Interstate 5). From Seattle, go north 15 minutes to Exit 177 onto Highway 105; from Bellingham, go south 2 hours to it.

Follow signs to the city center. Stay left – out of the ferry line-up. Go on 5th Avenue South to a traffic circle. Turn left into Main Street and continue to the end of it. Cross the railway tracks, where you will see a big anchor; turn right into Bracketts Landing.

For easier entry across the beach and for the most silt-free water, dive at high slack. In the water, follow the submerged system of ropes. It starts at the base of the piling closest to the ferry pier. You will swim past the *Alitak* on your way to the dry dock and the many attractions. To learn where highlights of the park are, and for information about new additions, see the map outside the changerooms.

Night diving is by permit only. To apply for it, and to obtain a brochure about the park, contact Edmonds Parks & Recreation, 700 Main Street, Edmonds WA 98020, telephone (425) 771-0230.

NOTES

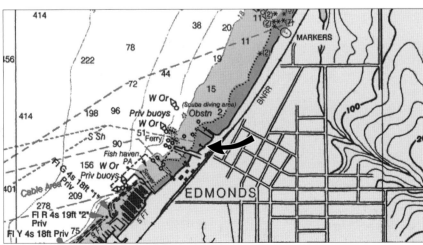

NOT TO BE USED FOR NAVIGATION: See page 456 for information on obtaining navigational charts; use NOAA chart #18446. Soundings are in feet.

1/2 NAUTICAL MILE

AGATE PASSAGE

SKILL
Expert divers

Intermediate divers with pickup boat

CURRENT TABLE
Admiralty Inlet
• Beginning of ebb:
  Subtract 47 minutes

• Maximum speed on ebb, 3.6 knots

WHY GO

Tumbling and flying through a fantasy-land of fish and rocks, travel ⅔ mile (1 kilometer) through current-swept Agate Passage without kicking a fin.

Starting the rollercoaster ride you fly through giant pile perch schooling around the piers of the bridge. Sweeping on, you hurtle toward a bright white hedge of horse clams. A gentle push of your hand and you're over it; slowing down, you pick up a red Irish lord in your palm. Then off again. Past large rocks encrusted with bright yellow sponges and millions of miniature white anemones. A big rock. You're going to hit it! The current carries you up and over. You look behind boulders in the lee of the current, large lingcod stare back at you. A cabezon on eggs. There's no way to stop. You somersault for the sheer joy of it, float upside down to see where you've been.

BOTTOM AND DEPTHS

The bottom is 25 to 35 feet (8 to 11 meters) through Agate Passage. Mostly sand and gravel. Rocks and boulders north of the bridge. Bull kelp around the bridge piers.

Divers surfacing north of Agate Passage Bridge

HAZARDS

Currents and boats. Currents run up to 7½ knots. Current is greater at the southern end of the passage and on flooding tides. Safest to dive on an ebbing tide.

Plan a "drift" dive carefully according to current predictions. Listen for boats and ascend with a reserve of air. If you hear a boat you can stay down until it passes. When drifting do not take a camera, spear gun or goodie bag; extra gear will be in the way. Hold hands with your buddy, and tow a dive flag to show the pickup boat, and other boats, where you are. After drifting for 20 minutes, surface and check where you are. Do not miss the take-out.

TELEPHONES: Suquamish, in a shopping center at the southeast corner of Division Avenue and Suquamish Way.

FACILITIES

At north end of Agate Passage: launch ramp at end of Suquamish Way at the water's edge. Picnic tables, fire ring, drinking water, a pit toilet and interpretive display at Old Man House historic site where Chief Sealth lived for years. Some house posts remain from about 1800. A ramp at Suquamish.

No facilities at the south end of Agate Passage on the Bainbridge Island side of the bridge.

ACCESS

Agate Passage is between Bainbridge Island and the Kitsap Peninsula. The dive is reached off Highway 305. From Seattle by ferry and car, 50 minutes. By road from Bremerton, 35 minutes. From Hood Canal Bridge, 25 minutes.

Go first to the *north* end of the passage at the west side of Agate Pass Bridge on the Kitsap Peninsula. At the signal light, west end of the bridge, turn north onto Suquamish Way and go 1 mile (1½ kilometers) following signs to Old Man House and Chief Sealth's grave. At a sign

pointing to Old Man House Park, turn right into Division Avenue. When you reach McKinistry Street, turn left to a parking space for two cars at the road end at Old Man House. Walk a few steps to the water and look at the take-out.

Then cross the bridge on Highway 305 to the put-in at the *south end* (Bainbridge Island side) of Agate Pass Bridge. Immediately east of the bridge, turn north down Reitan Road, then bear left to park under the large power pole – space for one or two cars at the most. Stairsteps go 100 feet (30 meters) down to the shore just north of the bridge. Three of us were diving: we launched our inflatable beneath the bridge where you start and took turns drifting with a partner and the third diver following in the pickup boat. We just kept going

throughout the ebb.

A buoy marks the northern end of Agate Passage. If you have a pickup boat that requires a launch ramp, go to Suquamish to put-in and take-out.

If you have no pickup boat, set up a shuttle: leave vehicles at the north and south ends of Agate Passage.

To get to Agate Pass Bridge
• From downtown Seattle, take the Seattle–Bainbridge Island ferry to Winslow and drive north on Highway 305 to Agate Pass Bridge.
• From Bremerton, drive north on Highway 3 to Highway 305. Turn right to the bridge.
• From Hood Canal Bridge, drive south on Highway 3 to Highway 305; turn left and go to Agate Pass Bridge.

NOTES

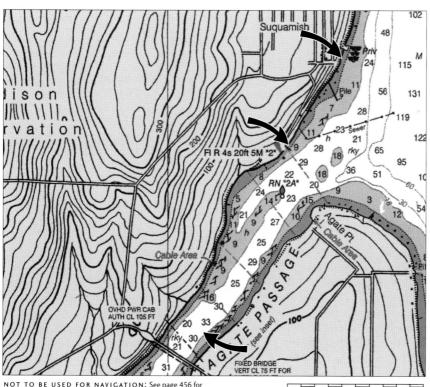

NOT TO BE USED FOR NAVIGATION: See page 456 for information on obtaining navigational charts; use NOAA chart #18446. Soundings are in feet.

1/2 NAUTICAL MILE

POINT WHITE DOCK [CRYSTAL SPRINGS PIER]

SHORE DIVE

SKILL
All divers and snorkelers

CURRENT TABLE
Admiralty Inlet
• Slack before flood:
  Subtract 44 minutes

• Slack before ebb:
  Subtract 46 minutes

WHY GO

Sand dollars – only the second dive where I've seen live ones. Point White has the advantage of current. That's what makes it different from most sandy beach sites. And access is extremely easy; climb across two or three logs to the sand.

The collection of creatures I saw on one dive at Point White was varied, including a "first" for me – always special, a pink scoop-shovel nudibranch. It was the size of my hand, but frilly and delicate. Orange and white plumose anemones decorate an old cartwheel that is past the end of the dock. You will see blue striped seaperch, tube-snouts, gunnels, flounders. Hermit and Dungeness crabs and lots of red rock crabs. More everyday stuff, too: tiny pink and purple tube worms. Giant barnacles, Mussels. Lots of razor clams. Big smooth moon snails, lumpy sea cucumbers, wispy tube-dwelling anemones. Sea lettuce. Coonstripe shrimp. Metallic ribbon kelp, shimmering blue. Moon jellies. Geoducks. Leafy hornmouth snails. Sunflower stars, leather stars, mottled stars, purple stars heaped on the pilings. We saw many juvenile sea pens that looked like frayed rubber. And many brown-striped nudibranchs – they go with sea pens like bacon and eggs as they feed on them.

The Mosquito Fleet used to call here, so there might be old bottles. Also look for skates, sometimes here I'm told. I've still never seen one in the wild, but I keep hoping.

BOTTOM AND DEPTHS

Sandy bottom slopes gently from the beach to a depth of 10 to 20 feet (3 to 6 meters) at the end of the dock, depending on tide height. Dock pilings provide attachment for barnacles, shelter for fish. Most life is around the dock and down to 30 feet (9 meters). We reached 50 feet (15 meters) maximum. You could go deeper.

HAZARDS

Current and shallow depth. Dive on slack. But be aware that predictions are unreliable at Point White. Go to the site and look at the water. You might have to wait or even give up on the dive. If diving with slight current, start your dive west of the pilings. Weight yourself well so you can stay down at shallow depths. That is where the life is.

TELEPHONE

Lynnwood Center, in front of theater. Go 2 miles (3¼ kilometers) back to the junction and turn right.

FACILITIES

Parking for 9 or 10 cars at Crystal Springs Park, Point White; in summer, camping at Faye Bainbridge State Park, north end of island. Air fills and dive guide in Winslow.

ACCESS

Point White Dock juts into Port Orchard Narrows just north of Point White. It is on Bainbridge Island, 15 minutes from Winslow.

From Bremerton via Highways 3 and 305 to Winslow on Bainbridge, it takes 50 minutes; from Hood Canal Bridge (also via Highways 3 and 305) to Winslow takes 50 minutes; by ferry from downtown Seattle to Bainbridge Island, 35 minutes.

At Winslow, off the ferry from Seattle (or heading south into town on Highway 305), follow signs to the city center. From Winslow Way and Highway 305 it is 5½ miles (9 kilometers) to the dive. Go west on Winslow Way to the stop sign at Madison Avenue. Turn right. At Wyatt Street, turn left. Go straight to the end of Wyatt and the road curves left. At the "Y" turn right and follow signs up Bucklin Hill Road toward Ford Ward State Park. At Lynnwood Center turn right into Point White Drive which becomes Crystal Springs Drive. Wind your way past waterfront homes – from Lynnwood Center, 5 minutes to Crystal Springs Pier north of Point White.

Enter at the left-hand side of the dock; if current is ebbing, enter at the right-hand side of the dock. Access is especially easy at high tide because the walk is so short. And there is *no* swim. When you've got your boots wet, you're there. If entering at low tide be careful not to walk on live sand dollars. The gray ones are dead, the dark purple ones alive.

Red rock crab

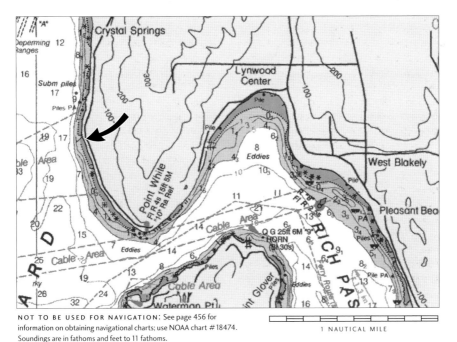

NOT TO BE USED FOR NAVIGATION: See page 456 for information on obtaining navigational charts; use NOAA chart #18474. Soundings are in fathoms and feet to 11 fathoms.

1 NAUTICAL MILE

389

ROCKAWAY BEACH

SHORE DIVE

SKILL
Intermediate and expert divers

All divers with guide

TIDE TABLE
Seattle

WHY GO
Life upon life upon life. Easy entry. Two boulder reefs to explore. And they might change from one dive to the next: Rockaway is on the Seattle fault line. The reefs originated with the Seattle earthquake in AD 900. Subsequent tremors – one a 3.5 on the Richter scale the month before I dived – add to the rubble that gives shelter to marine life.

We saw tube-snouts, a giant cabezon, quillback rockfish, egg cases of moon snails, and coonstripe shrimp leaping about like grasshoppers. Sea stars on the rocks: an orange dinner-plate-sized sun star. A purple striped one. A blood star. White plumose anemones. Orange sea cucumbers poking between the rocks. Red rock crabs in the kelp, some mating when we dived. We saw kelp crabs with pointed noses, an alabaster nudibranch, a small octopus with a large stash of crab shells outside its den. I missed the ratfish the others saw.

You might see harbor seals, blue-striped perch, painted greenlings – they're black and brown when mating instead of purple and gray. Lemon peel nudibranchs frequent this site. And look for brown-striped and leopard nudibranchs. On high tides, moon snails.

No taking of marine life, and take care when entering the beach not to destroy the fragile, grassy parkland. The entire area is a preserve. Avoid going closer to harbor seals than 100 yards (90 meters).

BOTTOM AND DEPTHS
Gently sloping sand leads to two rocky reefs – big clumps of fault-line boulders with sand all around. Sugar kelp glistens silver and red; in summer it covers the sand.

HAZARDS
Northwest wind, current and boats. The sound of the Seattle ferry is loud yet nowhere near you – not a hazard. But listen for smaller boats and fly a dive flag. Plan your dive: check weather and tides. Northwest wind creates surf – not the time to go. Best to dive on a calm day on a high tide when visibility is greatest at Rockaway. Complete your dive before the ebb or else dive with a low exchange, no greater than 6 feet (2 meters).

Evening dive at Rockaway

TELEPHONE

Eagle Harbor Drive and Bucklin Hill Road, outside Ray's Auto Repair Shop at head of the bay.

FACILITIES

Limited roadside parking for up to six cars; groups should carpool. Full-service dive shop with dive guiding in Winslow. Camping in summer at Faye Bainbridge State Park, north end of island.

ACCESS

Rockaway Beach is located on Puget Sound; it is at the southwest corner of Bainbridge Island, 15 minutes from Winslow city center.

At Bainbridge Island, turn off Highway 305 to Winslow city center; go on Winslow Way to Madison Avenue. Turn right; get into the left-hand lane as you go one block to the stop sign at Wyatt Way. Turn left. Go on Wyatt Way to the bottom of the hill where the road bears left and becomes Eagle Harbor Drive. At the head of Eagle Harbor turn left again; continue curving along the waterfront on Eagle Harbor Drive which becomes Rockaway Beach Road. From the head of Eagle Harbor go 3½ miles (5½ kilometers) to the "Welcome to Rockaway Beach" sign.

At Rockaway, enter through the gate, walk a few paces to a sign and down to the beach. When I dived, a fixed line was in place on the bottom making it easy. If the buoy is present, follow the line through the shallower boulder reef at 25 to 35 feet (8 to 11 meters) to the deeper reef at 50 to 60 feet (15 to 18 meters).

If the buoy is not present, snorkel out 50 feet (15 meters) and follow a compass bearing toward the Space Needle: or go down and follow a 60° heading to the shallow reef at 25 to 35 feet (8 to 11 meters); from there, follow a 90° heading to the deeper boulder reef at 50 to 60 feet (15 to 18 meters) and deeper.

Reach Bainbridge Island from many directions:

- From downtown Seattle, a 35-minute ferry trip lands you at Bainbridge Island; then turn left at the first traffic light to Winslow city center.
- Heading south on I-5 (Interstate Highway 5) from Canada or Anacortes, avoid some I-5 traffic: take the ferry from Keystone–Port Townsend and drive about 60 minutes; or Edmonds–Kingston and drive about 30 minutes. At Bainbridge Island, follow signs to the city center.
- From Bremerton drive via Highways 3 and 305 to Winslow – takes 50 minutes.
- After crossing the Agate Passage Bridge bridge to Bainbridge Island, continue on Highway 305 for 6½ miles (10¾ kilometers) and turn right to the city center.

NOTES

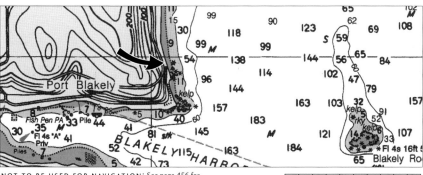

NOT TO BE USED FOR NAVIGATION: See page 456 for information on obtaining navigational charts; use NOAA chart #18449. Soundings are in feet.

1/2 NAUTICAL MILE

METRIDIUM WALL

BOAT DIVE
GPS
47°35.857′ N
122°29.699′ W

SKILL
All divers

TIDE TABLE
Seattle

WHY GO

A narrow rock fissure was created by an earthquake in AD 900. Since then it has been enlarged by many earthquakes. The most recent quake at the time of writing was in February 2001 – it created an enticing narrows just wide enough for two divers to swim through at its entrance. The laneway is decorated with fluffy white plumose anemones: Metridium Wall.

Inhabited by many fish – we saw painted greenlings, quillback and copper rockfish, kelp greenlings, a big lingcod, many smaller lingcod, a tiny grunt sculpin in a giant barnacle, a red Irish lord. In January and March look for egg masses of red Irish lords. Must be much more there that I

missed but I was captured by the bright white swim-way in the wall, the potential for change and the fish.

BOTTOM AND DEPTHS

Depth at bottom of the wall is 30 to 35 feet (9 to 11 meters) at low tide. The rock wall is short, about 30 feet (9 meters) long with more rocks scattered around, and a shifting shape and more rocks again as more earthquakes shake it up. Rock outcroppings below the wall extend to 85 feet (26 meters) at high tide.

Top of the reef above the wall where we descend on the anchor line is 12 to 20 feet (3½ to 6 meters) deep.

HAZARDS

Northwest wind and small boats. Check the weather before your go. And fly your dive flag.

TELEPHONES

- On the water: VHF radio; if no VHF, try a cell phone.
- On land: Bainbridge Island, Eagle Harbor. Telephone is visible from small, launch-ramp parking lot; walk a short way uphill on a paved path to the edge of the park in Winslow. The telephone is at the roadside, immediately across from Bainbridge Island Commons on Brien Drive.

FACILITIES

Charters out of Bainbridge Island. Full-service dive shop with dive guiding in Winslow. Launch ramps at Eagle Harbor and Fort Ward State Park, both at south end of island; and in West Seattle. Chemical toilets top of dock at Eagle Harbor.

ACCESS

Located in Puget Sound just offshore from Bainbridge Island.

Charter out of Bainbridge, Seattle or Tacoma. Or launch your own boat at Eagle Harbor or Fort Ward State Park in Bainbridge Island; or at West Seattle.

Metridium Wall

*From Rockaway Beach,
Seattle Space Needle
across water*

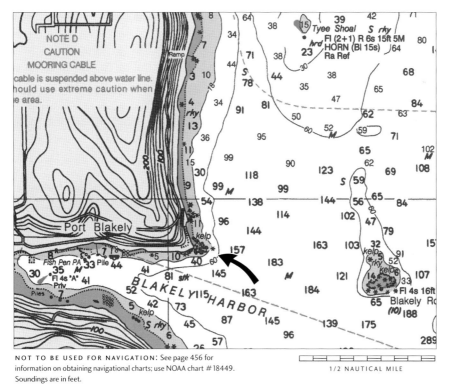

NOTES

NOT TO BE USED FOR NAVIGATION: See page 456 for
information on obtaining navigational charts; use NOAA chart #18449.
Soundings are in feet.

1/2 NAUTICAL MILE

SEACREST PARK

SHORE DIVE

SKILL
All divers

TIDE TABLE
Seattle

WHY GO

The wreck of the *Honey Bear*, treasure hunting and a bottom that drops off quickly are three good reasons to dive along this north-facing shore. And, it is usually protected from southeast winds.

Seattle's first settlement was here in 1851. Shortly after, many settlers moved into the area of Seattle now called Pioneer Square. They named Seattle after Chief Sealth of the Duwamish tribe. Later a ferry service connected Seattle and Duwamish Head in West Seattle. For years it was the only way between these two points.

Today two new parks, Seacrest and Don Armeni, occupy this historic strip of land offering excellent access to divers searching for bottles and other valuable old junk from early Seattle days. Even old Indian artifacts. The steep underwater cliff is unstable and periodically whole chunks fall away to reveal new bottom. It is a constantly renewing treasure-hunting ground. And the wreck of the small cabin cruiser *Honey Bear* is a popular attraction.

Seacrest is a perfect place for new divers. Many open-water certification dives are done here. Interesting, night and day. When the wind blows at Alki Beach, Seacrest is often sheltered.

BOTTOM AND DEPTHS

The *Honey Bear* is only 25 to 35 feet (8 to 11 meters) deep, depending on tide height. Beyond it, muddy bottom drops off steeply. Some bull kelp attached to pilings.

HAZARDS

Boats and broken fishing line are potential hazards. Listen for boats and be aware when they are present; more traffic in the summer. At the time of writing, the Elliot Bay water taxi loads and unloads passengers at the dock on the left of the *Honey Bear* from early May through September. Extra buoys are on the surface; underwater markers indicate the boundary of the dock. Ascend up a buoy line or anchor line

Boats and divers at Seacrest Park, Space Needle behind

or stay close to the bottom all the way to shore. Carry a knife. Always fly a dive flag at this busy location.

TELEPHONE
Outside café at Seacrest on Harbor Avenue side, beside restrooms.

FACILITIES
Parking, picnic tables, wheelchair-accessible flush toilets and a café at this grassy park at Seacrest. Launch ramps close by at Don Armeni Park.

ACCESS
Seacrest Park is on Elliot Bay in West Seattle off I-5 (Interstate Highway 5). From Seattle center drive south on I-5: 5 minutes to West Seattle Bridge turnoff.

From Tacoma go north, 30 minutes to it.

When heading south, take Exit 163A; heading north, take Exit 163 to the bridge. Go west onto the bridge; then move to the right-hand lane. On the far side of the bridge take Harbor Avenue Exit. Turn right: continue around the waterfront to the 1600 block Harbor Avenue SW and Seacrest Park. Multiple dives at Seacrest: from Cove 1, Cove 2 and Cove 3.

To dive the *Honey Bear*, enter from the beach at Cove 2: it is east of the café, boathouse and dock. Snorkel out between the white can-buoy and the first piling on the right-hand side. Look for the wreck in 25 to 35 feet (8 to 11 meters). Next dive, ask local divers about the sights at coves 1 and 3. Always lots of divers to meet at Seacrest.

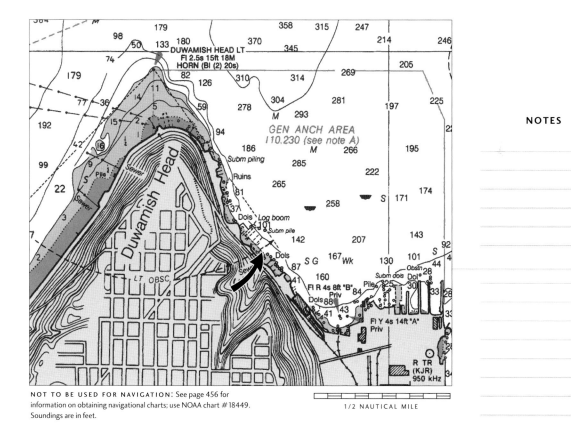

NOTES

NOT TO BE USED FOR NAVIGATION: See page 456 for information on obtaining navigational charts; use NOAA chart #18449. Soundings are in feet.

1/2 NAUTICAL MILE

— ALKI PIPELINE

SHORE DIVE

SKILL
All divers

CURRENT TABLE
Admiralty Inlet
• Slack before flood:
  Subtract 36 minutes

• Slack before ebb:
  Add 13 minutes

WHY GO
Popular for good reasons – Alki Beach is easily accessible and easy to dive. A good night dive.

The main attraction is the "tubular reef", or Alki Pipeline, at the south end of 63rd Avenue and Beach Drive around on the south side of Alki Point. Broken rocks are scattered over the pipeline that extends in a narrow 3- to 5-foot (1- to 1½-meter) wide pathway out over the clean white sand. We saw small pink swirls of tube worms, kelp crabs menacing us with their small pincers, sculpins, blood stars, sunflower stars, delicate nudibranchs on and under the long, low row of angular rocks. Orange and white plumose anemones tilt over the top of the "reef". A profusion of anemones is at the apparent end of the pipe about 200 yards (185 meters) offshore.

The pipeline reappears and actually ends about 50 yards (46 meters) farther out, I am told. To look for it, follow your compass and continue in a straight line. This area used to have great holes and caves and hid a large octopus in its dark depths under the pipe, but the caves are filling with sand. The end of the pipeline is supposed to be the most beautiful part of the reef and it is surely the least visited. Also difficult to find. I missed it altogether. Finding myself in an orange jungle of sea pens I didn't even mind. And I enjoyed the moon snails, flounders and tube-dwelling anemones on the sand around. You might see harbor seals. Do not go closer to them than 100 yards (90 meters).

Alki is a marine reserve beneath the sea as well as on land – no taking of shell-fish or fish, not even seaweed.

BOTTOM AND DEPTHS
A broken rock path, 3 to 5 feet (1 to 1½ meters) wide covers the pipeline extending out over clean white sand, gradually sloping to a depth of 25 to 35 feet (8 to 11 meters) at the end of the pipe. Some bull kelp.

HAZARDS
Surf. Shallow depth. Lion's mane jellies in the fall. Strong south wind sometimes

Tube worm feeding from current, about three times life-size

blows up the surf, making entry difficult at Alki Beach. A warning sign at the site: "Possible Sewage Overflows during and following heavy rains". Dive after dry spells. If you have seen jellies, check for stinging tentacles before removing masks and gloves. Weight yourself carefully. When windy, check nearby Seacrest Park which is sheltered from most winds.

TELEPHONE

Go to north end of 63rd Avenue SW. Turn right. Telephone is outside shop on Alki Avenue SW.

FACILITIES

Good beach for a picnic at the dive site beach, south end of 63rd Avenue SW.

Wheelchair-accessible flush toilets beside the beach, north end of 63rd Avenue SW and across the street from the telephone. Fast food too.

ACCESS

Alki Pipeline is on Puget Sound at Alki Beach Park in West Seattle. The site faces southwest into Puget Sound. Reach it off I-5 (Interstate Highway 5).

• From Seattle center, drive south 5 minutes on I-5 to the West Seattle Bridge turnoff, and take Exit 163A. Go onto the bridge and move to the right. Take Harbor Avenue exit.
• From Tacoma, drive north for 30 minutes to the West Seattle Bridge turnoff and take Exit 163. Go onto the West Seattle Bridge, move to the right and take Harbor Avenue exit.

At Harbor Avenue SW, turn right. Go 3¾ miles (6 kilometers) around the waterfront to 63rd Avenue SW, turn left and go to the end of Beach Avenue SW. Turn right and park beside Charles Richey Sr. Viewpoint at Alki Beach Park. Walk down the gently sloping concrete ramp toward the pumphouse, then right to the beach. Go a few steps to the left over cobbled beach, but not onto the privately owned beach property, and enter the water in front of the concrete pump station. Snorkel out to the southwest, lining up with the wall at the pump station, for 150 yards (140 meters) or so until you see rocks. The rocks mark the beginning of the "tubular reef". Easier to dive at high tide.

NOTES

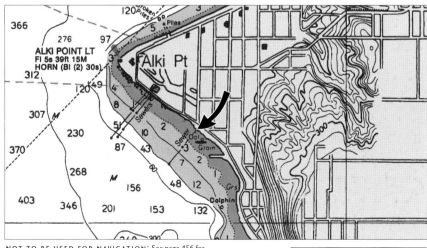

NOT TO BE USED FOR NAVIGATION: See page 456 for information on obtaining navigational charts; use NOAA chart #18449. Soundings are in feet.

1/2 NAUTICAL MILE

HARPER FISHING PIER

WHY GO

At Harper, you'll find a quick and easy dive in a quiet place. A shallow easy-to-find wreck. It's great at night. Uncomplicated. Good for new divers or anyone who wants to unwind.

The fishing boat sank north of the pier. The oak and cedar hull is 50 feet (15 meters) long and 16 feet (5 meters) high; it is tilted to the north on its port side. There is lots to explore around the outside – but do not penetrate the deteriorating hull. Marine life is excellent. Within six months, white plumose anemones and purple tube worms were on the wreck, an octopus had moved on board and poachers and shrimp were all over it. Two octopuses now live under it. Schools of slim silvery juvenile tube-snouts spurt forward in unison and seaperch swim through the wreck. Recently a skate was sighted beside it. Flounders are all around on the sand.

If the wreck should be towed away or if you still want more after the wreck, go sightseeing along the plumose-covered pilings of the pier. We saw pink anemones, lots of horse crabs, moon snails, horse clams and sea stars. This site is where I first saw an octopus shoot its ink. Popularity has not spoiled it, but for best visibility go on a weekday when fewer divers are stirring up the silt. Rain increases the silt. Good visibility ranges up to 50 feet (15 meters).

BOTTOM AND DEPTHS

The wreck rests on silty sand in 20 to 30 feet (6 to 9 meters), depending on tide height. The silty sand slopes gently from beach to wreck and end of pier.

HAZARDS

Small boats and transparent fishing line. Before diving, look for people fishing from the pier. When diving, listen for boats. Use a compass and swim close along the bottom all the way back to shore, or ascend up a pier piling. Carry a knife and be careful of fishing tackle, but do not disturb crab traps.

TELEPHONE

Outside store at corner of Southworth and Cherry at end of Sedgewick Road near the ferry terminal. Go 1 1/3 miles (2 kilometers) to it.

FACILITIES

Chemical toilet on Harper Pier. Air fills at Port Orchard, Bremerton and Tacoma.

ACCESS

Harper Fishing Pier is in Puget Sound near the east end of Yukon Harbor. It is on Highway 160, Kitsap Peninsula, north of Southworth and south of Bremerton. From Seattle by car ferry and road, 45 minutes to the pier. From Tacoma, 55 minutes. From Bremerton, 20 minutes.

Just north of Harper Fishing Pier, space for one or two cars to park beside the seawall. Climb three or four steps down the rocks piled beside the seawall to the cobble beach and snorkel to the dolphin off the end of the pier – it looks like a tepee. Descend on the north side of the dolphin. If you find a yellow polypropylene line at about 30 feet (9 meters), follow it to the wreck. It is 50 yards (46 meters) directly north of the end of the pier.

To get to Southworth
• From Seattle, Olympia and Tacoma by road: go on I-5 (Interstate Highway 5) to Highway 16. Head north on Highway 16 for approximately 35 miles (60 kilometers) to Highway 160, Sedgewick Road exit; go east 7 miles (11 kilometers) on Sedgewick to the end of it. The Southworth ferry landing is on your right. Turn left onto Southworth Drive: go 2/3 mile (1 kilometer); turn right and continue on Southworth Drive, a curving arterial that snakes along the waterfront for 2/3 mile (1 kilometer) more to Harper Fishing Pier.
• From Seattle by ferry and road: head south on I-5 (Interstate Highway 5) and take Exit 163A onto West Seattle Bridge.

Move left. At the end of the bridge, continue on Fauntleroy Way, following signs to the Vashon ferry and sail from Fauntleroy to Southworth. Off the ferry, go straight for ⅔ mile (1 kilometer) on Southworth Drive; turn right and continue on Southworth following this curving arterial along the waterfront for ⅔ mile (1 kilometer) more to Harper.

• From Bremerton, head south on Highway 3/16 through Gorst to Port Orchard, then southeast on Bay Street into Beach Drive and past Manchester State Park. At Manchester, turn left into Main Street and immediately right onto Colchester Drive. Continue on this arterial road that becomes Southworth Drive for 3 ¾ miles (6 kilometers) to Harper.

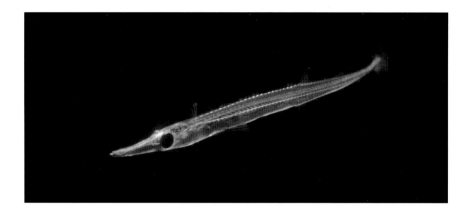

Tube-snout

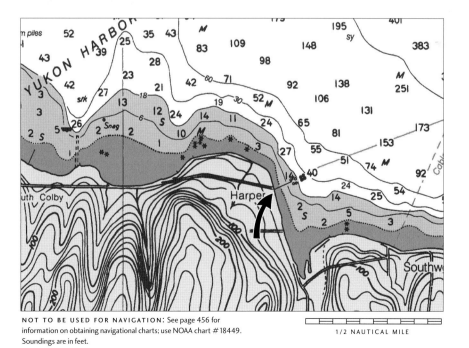

NOT TO BE USED FOR NAVIGATION: See page 456 for information on obtaining navigational charts; use NOAA chart #18449. Soundings are in feet.

1/2 NAUTICAL MILE

NOTES

SHORE DIVE

SKILL
All divers

TIDE TABLE
Seattle

WHY GO

Bottle garden, easy entry, shallow diving safe from boats. Sheltered in all except north winds. Great for night dives.

Plumose anemones on the pilings are lovely, but we pushed off for the bottle garden. Then forgot it when we saw a small octopus in the open. With arms spread, it was the size of a golf ball. We spent half our dive observing it, and my dive partner photographed it. This small species of octopus, often seen at bottle sites, is the *Octopus rubescens*. Its scientific name refers to its red color. At the surface, I laughed when my dive partner referred to it as "Ruby". I was rinsing a bottle I had picked up to show my partner when another octopus pushed its way out of the skinny neck of the bottle. Seeing these octopuses is one of the prime reasons I enjoy diving bottle sites.

Lots more marine life, too, at Tramp Harbor. Big day – a first sighting for me. We saw a skate. We also saw two ratfish in 13 feet (4 meters) of water. In summer, look for lion nudibranchs on the back of the kelp. In winter, Tramp Harbor is a stubby squid breeding ground.

BOTTOM AND DEPTHS

Flat sand bottom, with lettuce kelp, slopes gradually to a depth of 50 to 60 feet (15 to 18 meters), depending on tide height.

HAZARDS

Silt. Lion's mane jellies. Weight yourself for a shallow dive, and stay off the bottom. Best visibility is on outgoing tides. If you have seen jellies, check for stinging tentacles before removing masks and gloves.

TELEPHONE

Outside shop at northeast corner of Vashon Highway SW and 204th Street SW.

FACILITIES

Picnic table beside the dock. Parking space for 4 or 5 cars. Air fills in Tacoma.

ACCESS

Tramp Harbor Dock is on the east side of Vashon Island. It is a 25-minute ferry ride from Seattle; 15 minutes from Point Defiance in Tacoma; 10 minutes from Southworth on Kitsap Peninsula.

Once on Vashon, the dive is 20 minutes

Bottles, logs and frilly plumose anemones

from either ferry landing. Go on Vashon Island Highway to 204th Street SW. From there, 1¼ miles (2 kilometers) to the dive. Turn east down 204th Street SW, which becomes SW Ellisport Road, and curve downhill to the water. Turn right into Dockton Harbor Road and to Tramp Harbor Dock.

At higher tides, six or eight stairsteps to the beach and a few paces across it. Snorkel on the right-hand side of the dock to the ladder – about three-fourths of the way out the dock. Take a sighting

on Robinson Point on the right, set your compass and head down: 10 to 30 kicks and you're in the bottle garden.

To get to Vashon Island
- From Tacoma, take the ferry to Tahlequah at the south end of Vashon.
- From Seattle, go to West Seattle and take the Fauntleroy ferry to the north end of Vashon.
- From Bremerton, drive to Southworth, take the ferry to the north end of Vashon.

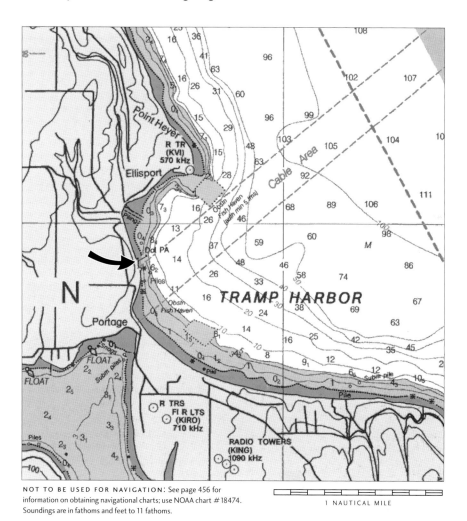

NOT TO BE USED FOR NAVIGATION: See page 456 for information on obtaining navigational charts; use NOAA chart #18474. Soundings are in fathoms and feet to 11 fathoms.

1 NAUTICAL MILE

NOTES

DALCO WALL

BOAT DIVE
GPS
47°20.020' N
122°31.118' W

SKILL
Intermediate and expert
divers on wall

All divers and snorkelers
in shallows

CURRENT TABLE
The Narrows

WHY GO

To plunge over a sheer wall – see undercut caves, columns sculpted by current, sandstone pitted like moonscape. Dalco is easy to get to. Good for deep divers making safety stops. Good for shallow divers, too, as well as snorkelers.

Wolf-eels abound. When heading down, we happened onto a mated pair in a shallow slot at 50 feet (15 meters). At least two more dens are along the wall. We dropped over the edge and hovered above darkness, enjoyed the vacantness, the space. It is stark. Then we started looking for things and saw a big lingcod, a tiny grunt sculpin, a ratfish. Swimming scallops at the base of the wall.

Gradually moving up, we passed columns of sandstone. Came to an old piddock clam area: the sandstone is pitted where piddocks have burrowed into it. In the kelp, we saw lots of piddock clams that were alive and well. Or we saw their paired siphons with dark hairs lining them – that's what you see of a piddock clam. In the shallows near the end of our dive, a great many big painted greenlings. Black-and-white pile perch. Striped seaperch. Schools of tube-snouts. Silver flashes of juvenile perch. A myriad tiny alabaster nudibranchs. One clown nudibranch. Tube worms. Shrimp all lined up beneath a ledge to defend themselves against us. Decorator, hermit and kelp crabs. A few white plumose anemones. And one water jelly. Later my buddy told me they glow in the dark when touched.

BOTTOM AND DEPTHS

Wall of glacial sandstone with till embedded in it sheers down to silty bottom at 120 to 130 feet (37 to 40 meters). Along the southeast end of the wall, depth at the top ranges from 30 to 50 feet (9 to 15 meters). There are plenty of big rocks and cubby holes for divers who just want to look over the edge. Heading northwest, we found undercuts and shallow caves at 110 to 120 feet (34 to 37 meters). At the center of the wall, the depth sounder shows 190 feet (58 meters).

Dramatic sandstone columns are near the northwest end. Then shallow rocky crevices and ledges riddled with piddock holes at 20 to 30 feet (6 to 9 meters). Near shore, sand bottom with starry flounders, moon snails and all that goes with it. An interesting place to end a deep dive. Good snorkeling too. Bull kelp, in summer.

HAZARDS

Current, small boats and bull kelp in summer; water jellies, spring and summer. Dive on slack. Good on almost any incoming tide. The current in Dalco Passage sets west or northwest almost constantly. Easiest to start your dive at the southeast end of the wall and drift toward your anchored boat. Before ascending, listen for boats. Carry a knife for kelp. If you have seen any jellies, check for stinging tentacles before removing your masks and gloves.

TELEPHONES

• On the water: VHF radio; if no VHF, try a cell phone.
• On land: Tahlequah ferry dock, accessible up a narrow trail on east side of the dock.

FACILITIES

Air fills, boat charters, rentals and launch ramps in Tacoma.

ACCESS

Dalco Wall is in Dalco Passage 100 yards (90 meters) offshore from Point Dalco on the southern tip of Vashon Island.

Charter, rent a boat or launch your own boat at Point Defiance Park and cross Dalco Passage. Go 1 ½ nautical miles to Vashon. Look along the shoreline: ½ nautical mile west of the Tahlequah ferry landing is a large home with a concrete retaining wall. Often a boat is moored in front of it. West of this home is an old shed, also with a concrete retaining wall.

Anchor near the shed in 30 feet (9 meters). Swim southeast out past the mooring buoy. Head down. A short underwater swim and plummet over the wall. Or, snorkel or dive in the shallows right around your boat.

At Point Defiance Park: diver and gear lowered in rental boat for Dalco Wall

NOTES

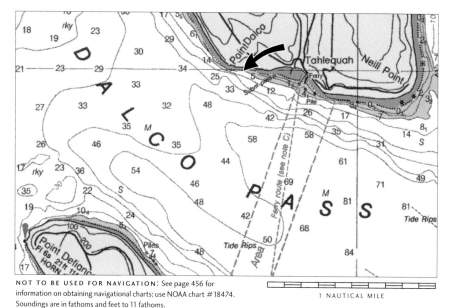

NOT TO BE USED FOR NAVIGATION: See page 456 for information on obtaining navigational charts; use NOAA chart #18474. Soundings are in fathoms and feet to 11 fathoms.

1 NAUTICAL MILE

SUNRISE BEACH PARK

WHY GO

Crevices in the wall hide wolf-eels, octopuses, mosshead warbonnets.

The most vivid red-and-white warbonnet I have seen was at Sunrise. And the wolf-eels were exceptional. We saw one mated pair and a pale peach-colored one. A red Irish lord. Swimming scallops. Pink encrusting sponge on the rocks. Grunt, sailfin and buffalo sculpins and white cucumbers. Beneath the overhangs, barnacles thickly encrusted with yellow sponge, purple plume worms, red slipper cucumbers. Kelp crabs and decorator crabs. You will see painted greenlings, blue sea stars, blood stars, nudibranchs, chitons, green urchins. Look for gunnels, ratfish, dogfish. In the sandy shallows look for orange sea pens, hermit crabs, seaperch and flounders. Mussels on the beach. So much in so little space at Sunrise.

Sunrise Beach is considered a marine protected area – no taking of marine life.

Early morning dive at Sunrise Beach

BOTTOM AND DEPTHS

The top of the wall is at 30 to 40 feet (9 to 12 meters), depending on tide height. The wall is 20 feet (6 meters) high, riddled with undercut ledges and crevices. Boulders are below it from 50 to 60 feet (15 to 18 meters) down to 130 feet (40 meters) and beyond. In summer, the top of the wall is marked with bull kelp. Sandy bottom with no handholds slopes slowly from top of the wall to shore.

HAZARDS

Current, small boats, long walk, bull kelp and lion's mane jellies. Dive on a day with tidal exchange of 8 feet (2½ meters) – not more, not much less. Dive at high water at the end of the flood. Start 1½ hours before *high slack* – do not dive at the end of ebb when it is almost impossible to predict slack and when there might be downcurrents. It is a circling current. The water almost constantly ebbs past Sunrise, flowing parallel to shore in a northerly direction through Colvos Passage.

Listen for boats; make your safety stop before leaving the kelp which is something to hold onto. Then stay close to the bottom almost to shore. Carry a knife. Past the kelp, you might need to "knife it" across the sand. If jellies, check before removing masks. If you have been swimming hard, take it easy walking uphill as the possibility of bends may be increased by overexertion after diving.

Divers who want a pickup boat or who want to avoid the long walk down the hill can go by charter to Sunrise; or launch their own boat at Gig Harbor Public Ramp – 15 minutes to Sunrise.

TELEPHONE

Outside a shop, near a flashing light: return ½ mile (¾ kilometer) past sharp turn from 96th into North Harborview Drive. If you reach the flashing light, you have gone too far.

FACILITIES

Picnic tables, chemical toilet in parking lot and lots of parking space The park closes at dusk: not only be out of the water at dusk but also have your car out of the park.

ACCESS

Sunrise Beach is on the west shore of Colvos Passage. It is just north of the town of Gig Harbor and 15 minutes off Highway 16 between Tacoma and Bremerton. From I-5 (Interstate Highway 5) and Highway 16 junction, 25 minutes to the dive. Plan to dive at the end of the flood – see current precautions in "Hazards" section.

From Highway 16, take Gig Harbor Exit to the city center. Go downhill on Pioneer Way to Gig Harbor. At the bottom of the hill, turn left onto Harborview Drive and follow it around the water to a flashing traffic signal. Turn right onto North Harborview Drive. Continue around the waterfront for 1½ miles (2½ kilometers) and turn right onto 96th Street NW. Go on 96th to a "T" junction and turn right onto Crescent Valley Drive NW for ⅓ mile (½ kilometer). At Dana Drive NW, turn

left up the hill. Follow this arterial road with many names: go 1 mile (1½ kilometers) to Sunrise Beach Drive. Turn right. Head down the long, steep hill to the park. Lots of space but park where directed. Walk on a well-graded footpath, 250 paces to a shed beside the cobbled beach. Swim south from the shed for 100 yards (90 meters). At the time of writing, you swim toward a tree that hangs out over the water. The north end of the wall is out from it. Past the tree, keep angling south as you start down. Swim across the sand and through the kelp.

To get to Highway 16 exit to Gig Harbor
• From I-5 (Seattle, Olympia or Tacoma) take Bremerton Exit 132. Follow the signs to Highway 16 West and Tacoma Narrows Bridge. From I-5, it takes 10 minutes to Highway 16 turnoff. After crossing the bridge, do not take the first Gig Harbor–Olympic Drive Exit. Take the second exit to Gig Harbor city center.
• From Bremerton, go south on Highway 16 East for 30 minutes; take Gig Harbor Exit to the city center.

NOTES

NOT TO BE USED FOR NAVIGATION: See page 456 for information on obtaining navigational charts; use NOAA chart #18474. Soundings are in fathoms and feet to 11 fathoms.

1 NAUTICAL MILE

Z'S REEF

**BOAT DIVE or
KAYAK DIVE**
GPS
47°14.869' N
122°36.280' W

SKILL
Intermediate and expert
divers from boat

Advanced kayak-divers

CURRENT TABLE
The Narrows

WHY GO

At the rocky reef, a great sculpin lazes on top of a ledge. During one dive, we see 10 great sculpins, two pairs of mated wolf-eels, one lone wolf-eel, swimming scallops on the rocks and a red Irish lord. My buddy flashes his light. Between some boulders he's found an octopus with large suckers. On the same dive, we see four more octopuses as well as sunflower stars, blood stars and copper rockfish. Purple tube worms are beneath the undercut ledge. Crabs wave their claws at us. We see painted greenlings, a valley of rock heaped with leafy hornmouth snails, a school of pile perch and a dogfish at the edge of deeper water.

Water jellies pulse around us over reef and sand like puffy, white cumulus clouds.

BOTTOM AND DEPTHS

An undercut ledgy ribbon of rock parallels the shore of the cove for 200 yards (185 meters). It is 150 feet (46 meters) offshore and up to 20 feet (6 meters) high. Boulders are scattered along it. Depth at its base is consistently 50 to 60 feet (15 to 18 meters), depending on tide height. Gently sloping sand stretches into Hale Passage.

*Paddling from Z's Reef
to East Wall,
Mount Rainier behind*

HAZARDS

Some small boats, current and stinging jellies. Listen for boats and, if possible, ascend your anchor line. The reef is in the shadow of the island on the ebb. Dive any time from high slack through the ebb, but do not dive during the last half of the flooding current. If you have seen jellies, check for tentacles before removing your masks and gloves.

TELEPHONES

- On the water: VHF radio; if no VHF, try a cell phone.
- On land:
1. Fox Island, East Wall, uphill from fishing pier outside restrooms.
2. Narrows Marina, east side of The Narrows, beside bait shop.
3. Titlow Beach on the east side of The Narrows, beside gear drop-off stall, beach side of park. It is immediately north of Narrows Marina.

FACILITIES

None at Z's Reef – not even a rock to stand on. Charters out of Tacoma Harbor.

ACCESS

Z's Reef is in Hale Passage off the eastern shore of Fox Island near Tacoma. It is in the second cove 1 nautical mile north-west of Fox Point where there are a few homes and privately owned yachts at anchor, but no public access. Z's Reef is only accessible by boat or dive-kayak.

At Z's Reef, the southeast end and closest to Fox Point is more or less marked by a swimming float. It is not intended to show the reef and could be moved or removed, so do not count on it. North-west of the swimming float, when I dived, were two private swimming floats held in place by pilings and rotating around them, and on the beach a small white building that marked the west end of the reef. Drop anchor 100 feet (30 meters) offshore and 100 feet (30 meters) east of

*Sampan unloads divers at
Tacoma Narrows*

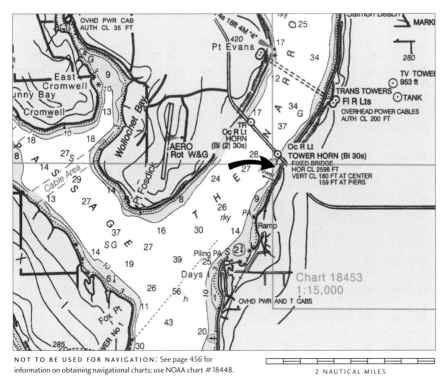

NOT TO BE USED FOR NAVIGATION: See page 456 for
information on obtaining navigational charts; use NOAA chart #18448.
Soundings are in fathoms.

2 NAUTICAL MILES

NOTES

TITLOW BEACH

SHORE DIVE

SKILL
All divers

TIDE TABLE
Seattle:
Add 20 minutes

WHY GO

Easy access to old pilings and natural ledges that provide attachment and hiding places for a great deal of life.

White plumose-covered piers of an abandoned ferry landing slip rise like columns of a Roman temple directly in front of the beach. They provide habitat for red Irish lords, cabezons, seaperch, giant sea stars. At the ledges, lots of little rockfish. Many giant octopuses used to hide here. Not so many now, but take a light for looking under ledges and into holes.

Always the chance for old bottles, too. And look for tiny octopuses in them, the *Octopus rubescens*. The total length of body and arms of a large one might measure up to 16 inches (40 centimeters); they have smooth skin. The scientific name refers to its color, which is red. And they make bottles their homes. Before removing bottles from the water, check them out for any residents to release.

BOTTOM AND DEPTHS

Pilings of the ferry landing provide attachment, sandy bottom around them, 25 to 35 feet (8 to 11 meters) deep, depending on tide height. Ledges and caves are beyond buildings on pilings, 25 to 45 feet (8 to 14 meters) deep. A few rocks and bull kelp, flattening to shell and gravel at 45 to 55 feet (14 to 17 meters).

HAZARDS

Current; fairly strong back eddy from The Narrows. Lion's mane jellies, in the fall. Dive near slack. If you see any jellies, you and your buddy should check one another for stinging tentacles before removing masks and gloves.

TELEPHONE

Beside gear drop-off stall, beach side of park.

FACILITIES

At dive entry, beach side of park: marine life information sign, cold-water showers for washing gear, and picnic tables. At park on other side of railway tracks: cooking shelters, playground and tennis courts. In summer, wheelchair-accessible restrooms near beach. In winter, no restrooms.

ACCESS

Titlow Beach is on the east side of The Narrows south of Tacoma Narrows Bridge in Tacoma. Approach on Highway 16. From Seattle or Olympia, 50 minutes to the dive; from Bremerton, 45 minutes.

At Titlow Park, cross the railway tracks to a gear drop-off stall near the beach. Return to parking space provided. Walk 15 paces down a shallow path to the beach. On your right, pilings of an abandoned landing slip. On your left, a building on pilings over the water. There are some pilings in front of it. Beyond this building and the pilings is a series of shallow rock ledges and small caves.

In summer, often two slacks close together during the day with low tidal exchange between. Then you can dive two times.

To get to Titlow Park
• From Seattle or Olympia, go on I-5 (Interstate Highway 5) to Tacoma and take Exit 132. Follow signs to Highway 16 West and Tacoma Narrows Bridge. Just before the bridge, take the Jackson Avenue exit. Turn left, crossing over the highway and go straight to 6th Avenue. Turn right and follow 6th down the hill to Titlow Park.
• From Bremerton, head south on Highway 16 East. When you reach the Tacoma Narrows Bridge, move to the right-hand lane; immediately across the bridge take the Jackson Avenue exit. Turn right and go to 6th Avenue. Turn right again and follow 6th to Titlow Park and the water.

High tide at Titlow Beach

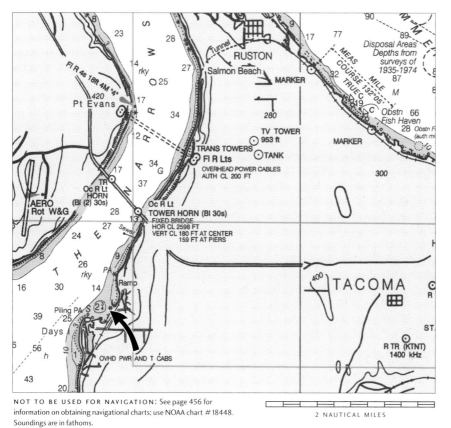

NOT TO BE USED FOR NAVIGATION: See page 456 for information on obtaining navigational charts; use NOAA chart #18448. Soundings are in fathoms.

2 NAUTICAL MILES

SUNNYSIDE PARK

SHORE DIVE

SKILL
All divers

TIDE TABLE
Seattle

WHY GO

A resident octopus hides under the pipeline. Orange and white plumose anemones, red rock crabs and encrusting sponge are at the pipeline – guaranteed. Beside the pipeline, tube-snouts slide in smooth jerks through the open water. Flounders swoop over the sand. Hermit crabs scuttle across the bottom. We see a moon snail. Black-and-white striped pile perch and other perch. Geoduck clams – pronounced "gooey duck" – suck into the sand as we swim over them. We see two lingcod, a white-spotted greenling.

A totally hassle-free dive. Easy, sloping, short walk to the beach at low and high tides, the shortest of snorkels. Current free. Good place for all divers to drop into any-time for a quickie dive on your way to any-where. Or try it at night – you might find the octopus in the open. Also, since I dived this site, a 32-foot (10-meter) trawler has sunk here.

Steilacoom (pronounced "still'a-coom") is a neat-looking Victorian town. And it's "for real". Incorporated in 1854, it is the oldest municipality in Washington State. In the 1850s and 60s it was the busiest port in Puget Sound. Probably bottle and artifact collectors could find rich hunting grounds nearby.

BOTTOM AND DEPTHS

Sandy bottom slopes very gently to one quick smooth slope close to shore, then almost flattens again at a depth of 25 to 35 feet (8 to 11 meters). An abandoned pipeline that is 2 feet (⅔ meter) in diameter provides attachment and hiding places for marine life. The metal pipeline appears offshore at a depth of 20 to 30 feet (6 to 9 meters) and gradually deepens to a maximum depth of 90 to 100 feet (27 to 30 meters). It goes far out; you could not swim to the end of it.

HAZARDS

Small boats might be in the area in summer. Listen for them. Return to shore close to the bottom along the pipeline.

TELEPHONE

In parking lot at Sunnyside Park.

FACILITIES

Parking – take dollars for the parking machine. Wheelchair-accessible flush toilets, cold-water shower for rinsing gear, picnic tables, volleyball nets.

ACCESS

Sunnyside Park is in the southeast corner of Puget Sound. It is 10 minutes off I-5 (Interstate Highway 5) in Steilacoom. The turnoff is midway between Tacoma and Olympia: from either, 25 minutes to the dive. From Seattle and Bremerton, 65 minutes.

From I-5, take Steilacoom-Dupont Exit 119 and follow signs to Steilacoom. When you see the U.S. Army, North Fort Lewis sign, keep going. Drive between tall trees. Head downhill; you will see a ferry dock. Turn right. Immediately across the tracks, pass cold-water showers, a picnic table and a broadleaf maple on your left, and volleyball courts on your right. Follow the short trail, three or four paces down a gentle gravel slope to the sandy beach.

Swim straight out and down. Near shore, the bottom swishes downward in a short quick slope. If you have a compass, follow a 270° heading. If you come to a submerged line, follow it to the right to a concrete block at the head of the pipeline. If the line is not there, swim straight out to a depth of 25 to 35 feet (8 to 11 meters), turn right and go to the pipeline.

Moon snail creeping across sand

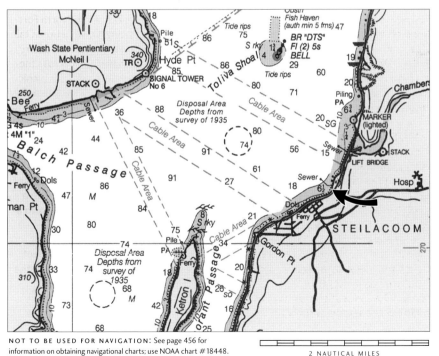

NOT TO BE USED FOR NAVIGATION: See page 456 for information on obtaining navigational charts; use NOAA chart #18448. Soundings are in fathoms.

2 NAUTICAL MILES

NOTES

SUND ROCK

SHORE DIVE or
KAYAK DIVE

SKILL
All divers

TIDE TABLE
Seattle

WHY GO

Easy access, no current to consider, fascinating at night – excellent flora and fauna.

Orange and white plumose anemones, sea stars and sea cucumbers are on the rocks. Red rock crabs scurry from their cracks. Tube-dwelling anemones blossom from the sandy bottom, pull in when we pass, and we see peach-colored frilly things. Blackeye gobies, shiner perch, copper rockfish and totally tame lingcod swim around us. Moon jellies drift through the open water; a videographer in our group recorded a red rock crab nibbling around the periphery of one, gradually, tidily consuming the moon jelly – we all saw the video after the dive. Sund Rock is locally considered a marine protected area, thus the lingcod population. No taking of marine life.

Many different dives are at this location. In addition to the popular option of paying a nominal fee to cross privately owned property to gain easy shore access, which I did, there is free public access from shore with a longer swim. Or divers can paddle dive-kayaks to their chosen location. Various dives available at Sund Rock: boulder garden and wall, a deep wall at the south end, a wreck, the fish bowl and the North Wall.

Best season for visibility is October through March. And, best to dive Sund with higher tides – at least 10 feet (3 meters); these occur in daytime in winter – you can plan it. We did a night dive in summer with a greater than 12 foot (3½ meter) tide. So much to see, I did not want to come up. I was still diving in 4 feet (1 meter) of water when my buddy tapped my shoulder to tell me we'd passed the entry/exit point.

BOTTOM AND DEPTHS

A boulder garden in 20 to 30 feet (6 to 9 meters). A stark rock wall bottoms out to silty sand at 55 to 65 feet (17 to 19 meters), depending on tide height. Bottom kelps are rich in summer, Turkish towel, sargassum – tall with berries, and eelgrass.

HAZARDS

Boats and silt. Listen for boats throughout your dive; surface up the wall or in the shallows – and look up when ascending. Establish good neutral buoyancy in each depth to stay off the bottom and reduce silt.

TELEPHONE

At roadside, in front of dive shop and resort ⅔ mile (1 kilometer) north of Sund Rock.

FACILITIES

Chemical toilet at the privately owned ramp entry to Sund Rock. Air fills at Shelton, Hoodsport and Lilliwaup. Accommodations in the vicinity include bunkhouses, RV parks, motels and campgrounds.

ACCESS

Sund Rock is on the west side of the Hood Canal beside Highway 101 between Olympia and Port Angeles. It is 37 miles (60 kilometers) north of Olympia; 83 miles (134 kilometers) south of Port Angeles and 22 miles (35 kilometers) south of Brinnon.

To select a date with high tides go to Water Level Tidal Predictions web site at www.tidesandcurrents.noaa.gov/tides07 (the year changes annually). Click Washington in the left-hand column, Hood Canal, then Union Predictions.

- Public access to Sund Rock is 2 miles (3¼ kilometers) north of Hoodsport. A small lay-by with a Sund Rock signpost is there, with space for 3 or 4 cars to park. Walk 170 paces down a steep, curving trail to the water, and swim 220 yards (200 meters) to the left to Sund Rock.
- Privately owned access to Sund Rock is 2¼ miles (3½ kilometers) north of Hoodsport, 1¼ miles (4 kilometers) south of Lilliwaup bridge. But first go to Hood Sport 'n Dive. It is 2¾ miles (4½ kilometers) north of Hoodsport, 1½ miles (2½ kilometers) south of Lilliwaup. For a nominal fee you will obtain a key to the gated road to the ramp, a

map of underwater features and directions to the ramp. Then go south for ⅔ mile (1 kilometer); around a bend on the left and immediately past a guard rail, turn sharply left down hill to the gate and ramp: space for 10 to 12 vehicles to park. Swim 30 yards (50 meters) to the right toward Sund Rock. Shortly before you reach the wall that is above water, descend to the boulder garden.

At Sund Rock privately owned access, divers gear up

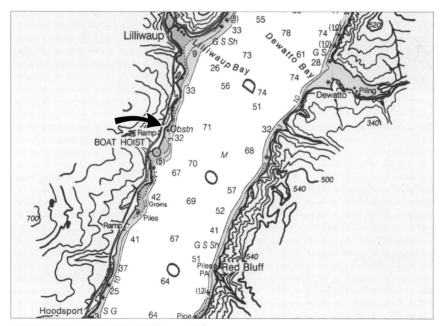

NOTES

NOT TO BE USED FOR NAVIGATION: See page 456 for information on obtaining navigational charts; use NOAA chart #18448. Soundings are in fathoms.

2 NAUTICAL MILES

OCTOPUS HOLE

SHORE DIVE

SKILL
All divers

TIDE TABLE
Seattle

WHY GO

Easy access, minimal currents and an attractive rock wall dropping from 30 to 60 feet (9 to 18 meters) make this a popular open-water certification site.

Octopus Hole is excellent for new divers. We saw rockfish in crevices, lots of bright orange encrusting sponges splashed over the wall, rocks capped with picturesque white plumose anemones, an octopus and sunflower stars. One weird invertebrate that was a "first" for me that day – a galatheid crab, sometimes called "tuna crab" or "squat lobster". Also look for another slightly unusual marine animal sometimes seen in Hood Canal that looks more like a giant tarantula than anything else – the hairy lithode crab.

Octopuses are cyclical and fewer are present in winter when lingcod move in to spawn; then the octopuses hide at other sites. Later return. At all times of year you have to look hard to find one of these shy creatures as many divers frequent the area. To find an octopus, look in holes and under ledges, look for small piles of bits and pieces of crab, telltale signs of the entrance to an octopus lair. You might find one or two wolf-eels, too. And I've been told, if you continue south of the wall after you think you are at the end of it, you will find sea whips.

Great place for new divers. But just look; don't touch. For many years the owners of the access trail have requested that divers voluntarily protect marine life at Octopus Hole.

Galatheid crab, or squat lobster

BOTTOM AND DEPTHS

Rocky beach gives way to silty sand bottom which slopes rapidly to a ledge at 20 to 30 feet (6 to 9 meters) that is marked by a buoy. From the ledge, the rock wall drops to 50 to 60 feet (15 to 18 meters), depending on tide height. The wall parallels the shore. Slightly farther offshore the bottom drops off quickly again. Very deep water in Hood Canal.

HAZARDS

Lion's mane jellies, in the fall. If you see any, you and your buddy should check one another for stinging tentacles before removing your masks and gloves.

TELEPHONE

At roadside, ½ mile (¾ kilometer) south towards Hoodsport – water side of road.

FACILITIES

None. Air fills in Potlatch and Hoodsport. Flush toilets year-round at Potlatch State Park picnic site. In summer, cold-water showers to rinse gear and hot showers to warm up in at Potlatch State Park campground – both are 7 miles (11 kilometers) south of Octopus Hole. A variety of motels and cafés are closeby.

ACCESS

Octopus Hole is on the west side of the Hood Canal next to Highway 101 between Olympia and Port Townsend. It is 35 miles (60 kilometers) north of Olympia; 60 miles (100 kilometers) south of Port Townsend.

The Octopus Hole access trail is owned by Mike's Diving Center in Potlatch. At the time of writing the owners make the access available to all divers with no fee. But space on the trail and beach is limited; two points to remember when accepting this courtesy:
• Before you go, telephone (360)877-9568 to inform the owners you wish to dive – they can tell you if other divers are there.

• When you go, honor this conservation area – no taking of marine life.

You will know you are at the access trail when the road comes down close to the water and you see four signs in the trees: "Octopus Hole Conservation Area, No Harvesting of any kind", "Welcome to Octopus Hole Courtesy of its Owners Mike & Shirley Smith, Mike's Dive Center", "Private Property, No Shellfish Harvesting", "Welcome to the Octopus Hole Marine Conservation Area, please do not take, feed or harass the animals".

Roadside parking for up to five cars at the lay-by on the water side of the road; fifteen cars across the road. Climb over the guard rail at the north end of the lay-by and walk down a few stairsteps to an easy path to the water. To find the wall, swim out to the wooden raft and go down the anchor line. Stay at the depth of the base of the anchor line and swim south. If the raft is gone, walk or snorkel south 75 yards (70 meters) from the bottom of the stairsteps before descending to find the wall.

To get to Octopus Hole beside Highway 101
• From Hoodsport, heading north on Highway 101: from the bridge in Hoodsport, measure the distance. Go 3¼ miles (5¼ kilometers) to Octopus Hole.
• From Lilliwaup, heading south on Highway 101: from the bridge in Lilliwaup, measure the distance and go 1 mile (1½ kilometers) to Octopus Hole.

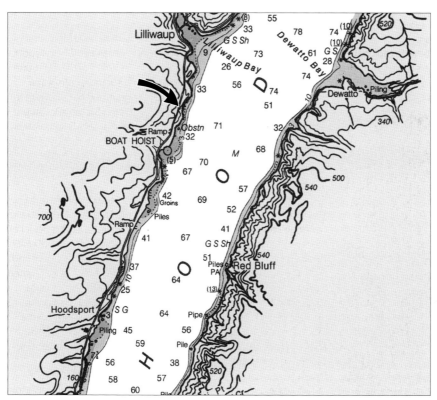

NOT TO BE USED FOR NAVIGATION: See page 456 for information on obtaining navigational charts; use NOAA chart #18448. Soundings are in fathoms.

2 NAUTICAL MILES

NOTES

—PINNACLE [BRINNON PINNACLE]———

BOAT DIVE
GPS
47°43.468' N
122°52.533' W

SKILL
Intermediate and expert divers

All divers with guide

TIDE TABLE
Seattle

WHY GO
Guaranteed life on this pinnacle, no current and, on the surface as well as beneath the water, it's a quiet peaceful place.

White and orange crevice-dwelling cucumbers light up the top of the Pinnacle. Brown sea cucumbers lounge on the rocks. Lots of little shrimp dart about. Galatheid crabs, or squat lobsters, scramble over the rocks. We saw lithode crabs. Lemon nudibranchs too. Painted greenlings, quillback rockfish, blackeye gobies darting about. Deeper, we saw many big lingcod swimming in the open, a wolf-eel in its den and a yelloweye rockfish – eggs of yelloweyes hatch within the female and then the young are released.

BOTTOM AND DEPTHS
Top of the Pinnacle is at 20 to 30 feet (6 to 9 meters), depending on tide height. Broadleaf bottom kelp is on it. The Pinnacle slopes off gently in all directions and bottoms out at 90 to 100 feet (27 to 30 meters). The wolf-eel den we found, and there are more – six at least – is at 73 to 83 feet (22 to 25 meters) on the south side. Lots of hidey holes for octopuses and wolf-eels in the rocks; take a light.

HAZARDS
Boats, depth and visibility. Go on a low tide. Winter is best visibility – but I dived it in midsummer and enjoyed 40 foot (12 meter) visibility. Ascend up your anchor line out of the way of boats, and make a safety stop.

TELEPHONES
• On the water: VHF radio; if no VHF, try a cell phone.
• On land: At Pleasant Harbor, outside marina store.

FACILITIES
None.

ACCESS
The Pinnacle is in Dabob Bay, which cuts off the northwest end of the Hood Canal, and is protected from most winds. Go shortly past the entry to Dabob, on the west side of the Hood Canal.

Yelloweye, bloated after a good meal or carrying young

Charter out of Pleasant Harbor or launch your own boat and go to Brinnon Pinnacle – use GPS locations and a depth sounder to find it. It is 4 nautical miles north of Pleasant Harbor; 6 nautical miles south of Quilcene Boat Haven ramp, and 2½ nautical miles south of Point Whitney ramp to the Pinnacle.

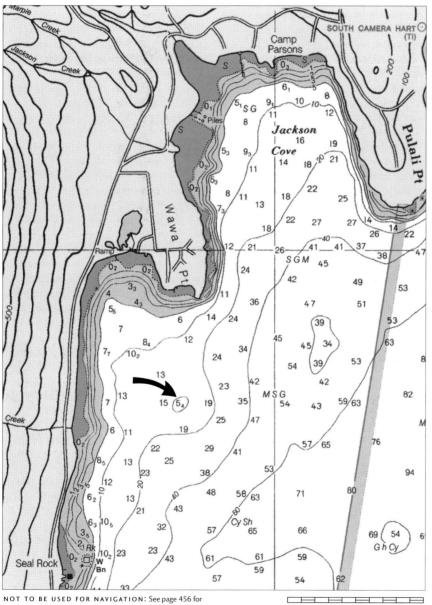

NOT TO BE USED FOR NAVIGATION: See page 456 for information on obtaining navigational charts; use NOAA chart #18458. Soundings are in fathoms and feet to 11 fathoms.

1/2 NAUTICAL MILE

NOTES

HOOD CANAL BRIDGE

SHORE DIVE

SKILL
Intermediate and expert
divers

CURRENT TABLE
Admiralty Inlet
• Slack before flood:
Subtract 1 hour,
3 minutes

• Slack before ebb:
Add 4 minutes

WHY GO
Where else can you dive from shore
and see such magnificent feather duster
worms? Fast currents feed these giant
purple bouquets. Elegant plumose
anemones, countless enormous sea stars
and other invertebrates are heaped
around the bridge piers. Not an inch of
concrete to be seen.

Swimming out to the piers and back,
we were fascinated with ranks of sand dollars studding the clean white sand. They
feed on fuzzy amber-colored diatoms
hanging quietly in grooves of sand while
current rushes over the top of them.

A wealth of invertebrate life, but
frustrating for the photographer because
the current stirs the silt and creates poor
visibility.

BOTTOM AND DEPTHS
Perfectly smooth, silty sand slopes gradually
to the bridge piers. At the first submerged
pier (which is the second pier), 10 to 20
feet (3 to 6 meters) deep. At the next
pier, 30 to 40 feet (9 to 12 meters) deep.

HAZARDS
Current. Dive on high slack. Sandy, smooth
bottom offers no handholds to grasp to
pull yourself along against the current.
You cannot, therefore, go far during the
very limited slack tide under the bridge.
Beyond the second submerged pier, a
pickup boat is advisable. Carry a knife so
you can "knife it" back to shore if all else
fails. But take care not to damage the
dark-colored sand dollars – they are alive.

TELEPHONE
At Port Gamble General Store, outside. To
reach it, go to Highway 3; turn left and go
north 1 mile (1½ kilometers) to Port
Gamble Visitor Info; turn left and follow
Museum signs to the General Store.

FACILITIES
Roadside parking for eight or ten cars at
Whitford Road. Camping with hot showers year-round at Kitsap State Park which
is 3 miles (5 kilometers) back along Highway 3 toward the Highway 305 junction
and Bremerton.

ACCESS
The dive is beneath Hood Canal Bridge
(east end) near the entrance to Hood
Canal. It is off Highway 104. By ferry and
car from downtown Seattle takes 1¼ hours
to reach it. From Bremerton, 35 minutes.
By ferry and car from Edmonds, 50 minutes. From Port Townsend, 30 minutes.

At Hood Canal Bridge (east end): go
north ½ mile (¾ kilometer) on Highway
104 and follow signs to Salsbury County
Park. Go down Wheeler Street which
curves back toward the bridge. Two roads
go from Wheeler Street to the beach. The
first one is Whitford Road to Salsbury
Point Park where you will find a huge parking area, boat ramps, picnic pavilion and
playground, as well as a flush toilet and
hot shower – both wheelchair accessible.
However, if you go to the second road end
which is ⅓ mile (⅕ kilometer) farther, the
swim is shorter. Snorkel 275 yards (250
meters) south to the bridge, and swim to
the first or second pier. For information
on Hood Canal Bridge traffic telephone
1-800-419-9025.

To get to Hood Canal Bridge
• From downtown Seattle: take
Seattle–Bainbridge Island ferry; 35 minutes to cross. Then drive north 21 miles
(34 kilometers) from Winslow to the
Hood Canal Bridge: go on Highway 305
and cross Agate Pass Bridge; continue
on Highways 305 and 3 following signs
to the Hood Canal Bridge.
• From Bremerton: go on Highway 3 to
Hood Canal Bridge.
• From Edmonds, north of Seattle: take
Edmonds–Kingston ferry for 30 minutes; then drive 10 miles (16 kilometers)
to the dive. From the ferry, follow signs

on Highway 104 to Port Gamble. From there, go 1 mile (1½ kilometers) to the turnoff to Salsbury County Park. This is the turnoff to the dive and is before the Hood Canal Bridge.

• From Port Townsend, 25 miles (40 kilometers) to the dive: go on Highway 20 to Highway 104. Then east on Highway 104 to Hood Canal Bridge.

Purple sand dollar

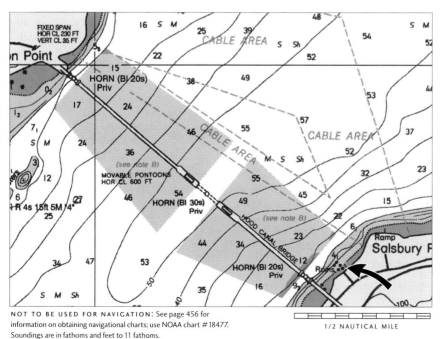

NOT TO BE USED FOR NAVIGATION: See page 456 for information on obtaining navigational charts; use NOAA chart #18477. Soundings are in fathoms and feet to 11 fathoms.

1/2 NAUTICAL MILE

NOTES

**BOAT DIVE or
KAYAK DIVE**
GPS
47°51.549′ N
122°38.503′ W

SKILL
Intermediate and expert
divers from boat

Advanced kayak-divers

CURRENT TABLE
Admiralty Inlet
• Slack before flood:
  Subtract 1 hour,
  3 minutes

• Slack before ebb:
  Add 4 minutes

WHY GO

Underwater pinnacles are incredibly rich in marine life. The Sisters pair is no exception. The color is intense.

Pink soft coral and transparent glass tunicates are around the rocks. We saw a clown nudibranch, red Irish lords, a bright green gunnel, a grunt sculpin. A sailfin sculpin was lying sideways in a slit in the rocks. We saw gray-colored sponges, keyhole limpets, large white plumose anemones and octopus dens, but nobody home. Rock scallops. And fields of juvenile white sea whips on the flat sand stretching out to forever between the Sisters and shore.

BOTTOM AND DEPTHS

Two small seamounts are at the Sisters site. The Big Sister is marked with a light; the Little Sister is northwest of it with a flat sandy stretch between that is 20 to 30 feet (6 to 9 meters) deep, depending on tide height. On the shore side at the Big Sister, rocky ledges with crevices and some boulders pyramid down to 70 to 80 feet (21 to 24 meters). On the channel side, the bottom drops to 110 feet (34 meters) and deeper. A great deal of marine life from the surface down to a depth of 30 to 40 feet (9 to 12 meters).

HAZARDS

Current, boats and transparent fishing line – we saw a net. Dive on slack on a small tidal exchange. Listen for boats. Carry a knife. If caught in fishing line or a net you can cut your way free. Kayak-divers who dive deep should rest before paddling back. Bends might be brought on by energetic exercise after diving.

TELEPHONES

• On the water: VHF radio; if no VHF, try a cell phone.
• On land:
1. Port Gamble General Store, outside. To reach it go by road to the east side of Hood Canal Bridge, turn left and go

1¼ miles (2 kilometers) to Port Gamble Visitor Info; turn left and follow Museum signs to the General Store.
2. Visitor Center is at the junction of Highways 104 and 19; go west from Hood Canal Bridge for 5 miles (8 kilometers), turn right and immediately left into the Visitor Center. Telephone is outside between Visitor Center and chemical toilets.

FACILITIES

Launch ramp immediately north of Hood Canal Bridge (west end) with extremely limited roadside parking – no toilet. Launch ramp and wheelchair-accessible pit toilet south of Hood Canal Bridge (west end) at Hicks County Park. Camping year-round nearby at Kitsap State Park with flush toilets and hot showers. It is 10 minutes away.

ACCESS

The Sisters site is near the entry to Hood Canal. It is ½ nautical mile south of the west end of the Hood Canal Bridge. A marker is on the Big Sister that breaks water.

Charter or launch at the ramp immediately north of Hood Canal Bridge (west end) and go south beneath the bridge to the Sisters. Kayak-divers can anchor close to the Big Sister with the marker on it and, at the end of the dive, ascend up the rock; larger boats anchor north of the marker. Take a depth sounder. Plan to be at the site ready to dive 30 or 45 minutes before slack. Currents whirl around the Sisters even on slack, but you can usually find a place to hide from it. Also hold onto the rocks. First trip, dive the Big Sister; second time, look for the Little Sister. One diver finds the Little Sister by watching diving birds. If you know your birds, you can go where the shallow-diving birds are and land right on the underwater pinnacle.

Kayak-divers can launch at the ramp beside Hood Canal Bridge – that's what we did. When diving at high slack you get help from the flooding current. It took us 15 minutes to paddle ½ nautical mile to the Sisters. If diving at low slack, you might paddle 1 nautical mile from Hicks County Park. I have not done that but it's worth a try. Allow time. It is a difficult paddle from Hicks County Park. With ebbing tides a counter-clockwise eddy forms in Squamish Harbor – you might have to break out of it.

Upping anchor after diving, Sisters Marker behind

NOTES

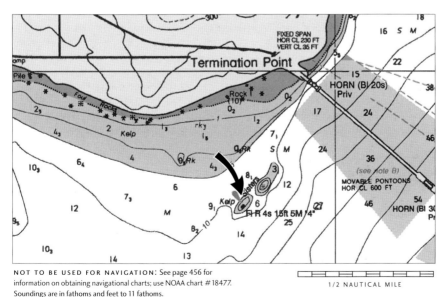

NOT TO BE USED FOR NAVIGATION: See page 456 for information on obtaining navigational charts; use NOAA chart #18477. Soundings are in fathoms and feet to 11 fathoms.

1/2 NAUTICAL MILE

FORT FLAGLER FISHING PIER

SHORE DIVE

SKILL
All divers with guide

Intermediate divers

CURRENT TABLE
Admiralty Inlet
• Slack before flood:
  Subtract 53 minutes

• Slack before ebb:
  Subtract 1 hour,
  13 minutes

WHY GO

Fort Flagler is off the beaten path – few divers visit this park. Wild roses crowd the roadside. Under water it feels like wilderness, too, untouched and remote. As you swim along the line to the artificial reef, gunnels dart from the kelp, flounders ripple away, iridescent blue kelp shimmers.

At the reef, it's rich, rich – so rich you cannot see the concrete cylinders that offer attachment and shelter for the life. On one dive we saw six red Irish lords, one big lingcod and four more small ones. We saw hermit, spider and Dungeness crabs. Moon jellies. Hard yellow sponges, flabby finger sponges, leafy hornmouth snails, gum boot chitons, a stinging jelly, kelp greenlings and lots of silvery fish. Quillback rockfish, painted greenlings, giant barnacles, swimming scallops, rock scallops, plumose anemones, Christmas anemones, plume worms, cemented tube worms, orange cucumbers and white ones, at the reef. Sea pens at its base. Egg cases of moon snails and pink anemones on the mucky bottom.

The current can be strong, yet the line to the reef, as well as the concrete cylinders themselves, give handholds to divers caught by surprise.

Behind pier, ship heading to Admiralty Inlet

BOTTOM AND DEPTHS

The sandy bottom gradually deepens to a depth of 40 to 50 feet (12 to 15 meters) at the reef.

HAZARDS

Current, fishing line and silty bottom. Dive on slack, best at the end of ebb as visibility is better. Carry a knife for fishing line.

TELEPHONE

Outside Museum, northwest corner. From the pier, return to the three-way junction, turn right to the Park Office and Museum.

FACILITIES

Flush toilets and picnic tables a short way uphill from parking space, across from the gun emplacements. Camping, summer only, in Fort Flagler State Park.

ACCESS

Fort Flagler Fishing Pier is on Admiralty Inlet. It is at Marrowstone Island but connected by a bridge to the Quimper Peninsula. Past the town of Hadlock, a bridge goes over the water from the Quimper Peninsula to Indian Island; the second bridge is a land-fill bridge from Indian Island to Marrowstone. From Port Townsend ferry terminal to the dive takes 30 minutes. From the Hood Canal Bridge, 60 minutes.

At Flagler Road, turn left. Go north for 8¾ miles (14 kilometers) – the length of Marrowstone Island – to a junction in Fort Flagler Park. Three roads: one goes to the campground, one to Marrowstone Point and the one on the right to the fishing pier. From this junction, ½ mile (¾ kilometer) to the pier. Walk down 25 stairsteps and 30 paces on the trail to the beach. Swim between the pilings. Find a submerged line at the eighth piling, 60 yards (55 meters) as you swim out under the pier. Look sharply; the line is covered with kelp. Follow the line to the reef, which is off the left-hand end of the pier and beyond it.

To get to Flagler Road
- Arriving in Port Townsend from Whidbey Island, turn left onto Water Street which becomes Sims Way then Highway 20. From the ferry, follow signs to Fort Flagler. Go nearly 5 miles (8 kilometers) to a traffic light – do not bear right on Highway 20 toward Port Angeles. Continue straight on Highway 19 South. Go 3½ miles (5⅔ kilometers) and turn left at Ness Corner into Highway 116 East following signs to Mystery Lake and Fort Flagler. From here, 2 miles (3¼ kilometers) more, passing through the town of Port Hadlock to Flagler Road.
- From Olympia or Port Angeles, go to junction of Highway 101 and 20. Head north on Highway 20 for 7 miles (11 kilometers) to the traffic light at High

way 19, and turn right. Go 3½ miles (5½ kilometers) and turn left at Ness Corner into Highway 116 East following signs to Mystery Lake and Fort Flagler. From here, 2 miles (3¼ kilometers) more, passing through the town of Port Hadlock to Flagler Road.
- From Hood Canal Bridge, head west on Highway 104 for 5 miles (8 kilometers) and turn right into Beaver Valley Road (Highway 19). Go on it 9 miles (14½ kilometers) to Chimacun Road. Turn right and go 1½ miles (2½ kilometers) to the town of Port Hadlock. Turn right onto Oak Bay Road (Highway 116 East) following signs to Fort Flagler State Park. Go nearly 1 mile (1½ kilometers) *west* and turn left into Flagler Road.

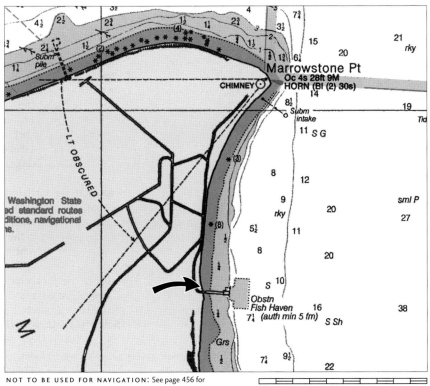

NOTES

NOT TO BE USED FOR NAVIGATION: See page 456 for information on obtaining navigational charts; use NOAA chart #18464. Soundings are in fathoms.

1/2 NAUTICAL MILE

FORT WORDEN SCIENCE CENTER WHARF

SHORE DIVE

SKILL
All divers and snorkelers

TIDE TABLE
Port Townsend

WHY GO

Elegant grandiose hallways – bright white plumose-covered columns rise from the dark world beneath the wharf, broken shells like sawdust on the floor of a market place. Wolf-eels, octopuses and dogfish at the edge of it.

The shell-littered bottom is rich with life. We see many sculpins. A sea lemon. A gang of hermit crabs tumbling onto and over a tire. An octopus hiding in it. We see two decorated warbonnets. Decorator crabs covered with stuff – "party" crabs, my buddy says when we ascend. We see orange cucumbers, a dahlia anemone, giant barnacles, yellow sponges. A white-spotted greenling, painted greenlings, a school of shiner perch flashing past. Sunflower stars. Lots of shrimp. A rust-colored juvenile wolf-eel stops in the open. Another juvenile wolf-eel follows. A pale gray dogfish lies on the bottom in sunshine at the edge of the wharf. Eyes me. Looks into cool darkness beneath the wharf. Another smaller dogfish swims slowly toward us, then away. A third, even smaller, dogfish

hurries past. After ascending at a piling, we snorkel toward shore, look down and see a sailfin sculpin.

BOTTOM AND DEPTHS

Bright white sand slopes gently from sandy beach strewn with silvery logs to silty bottom littered with broken shells and bottom kelp beneath the wharf. Depth at end of wharf is 20 to 30 feet (6 to 9 meters), depending on tide height. Gradually deepens beyond the geometric hallways beneath the wharf.

HAZARDS

Shallow depth, small boats, current and fishing line. Weight yourself so you can stay down. Listen for boats. If you hear one, stay down until it passes. Throughout your dive, keep the pilings in view because of boats and because of current – that is where the life is anyway, and ascend up a piling. Or stay close to the bottom and navigate by compass to shore. Dive near slack, especially with large exchanges. Carry a knife for fishing line.

Decorator crab

TELEPHONE

Cable House, outside; across road from the wharf.

FACILITIES

At the park: restrooms and cold shower for rinsing gear, behind Cable House; picnic tables and refreshment stand. Camping in the park year-round with restrooms and hot showers – by pre-registration. Overflow camping year-round at Jefferson County Fairgrounds with restrooms and hot showers. Air fills in Port Townsend.

ACCESS

Fort Worden Science Center Wharf is on Admiralty Inlet in the outskirts of Port Townsend. From Port Townsend ferry terminal to the wharf takes 10 minutes.

At Fort Worden State Park, turn left through the main gate opposite Cherry Street into Fort Worden Way and turn right on Eisenhower Avenue. Continue on Eisenhower to a large anchor; then turn left. Go downhill to the Marine Science Center. Parking is across the road. Walk

across the sandy beach *south* of the wharf, swim out and follow a piling down.

Wheelchair divers with dive-kayaks could paddle from the launch ramp around the wharf to the beach on the south side of it and go down: the distance is 220 yards (200 meters). Land your kayak on the beach at the south side of the wharf and go down.

To get to Fort Worden State Park
• Arriving in Port Townsend from Whidbey Island, turn left onto Water Street and go ½ mile (¾ kilometer). Turn right up Kearney Street and follow signs to Fort Worden.
• Arriving in Port Townsend on Highway 20 (from the Olympic Peninsula), head down the hill into town; Highway 20 becomes Sims Way. Go along the waterfront on Sims. Past the Chamber of Commerce you come to Kearney Street with a sign to Fort Worden – if you reach the ferry turnoff you have gone too far. Turn left up Kearney and follow the signs to Fort Worden Park.

NOTES

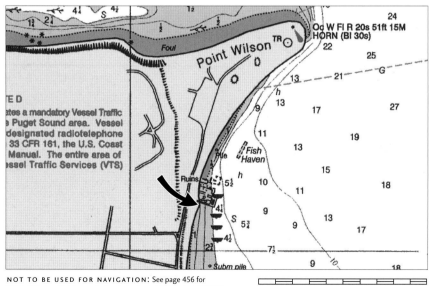

NOT TO BE USED FOR NAVIGATION: See page 456 for information on obtaining navigational charts; use NOAA chart # 18464. Soundings are in fathoms.

1/2 NAUTICAL MILE

POINT WILSON REEF

BOAT DIVE
GPS
48°08.840' N
122°45.924' W

SKILL
Expert divers

CURRENT TABLE
Admiralty Inlet
• Slack before flood:
  Subtract 1 hour,
  8 minutes

• Slack before ebb:
  Add 47 minutes

WHY GO

A rich dive on the few days of the year you can visit this current-swept, kelp-covered reef at Point Wilson. White rocks make a bright background for pale lavender anemones, dark red sculpins, hot pink and yellow-and-white striped dahlia anemones. Boulders crusted over with chitons and giant barnacles and capped with small white plumose anemones make good hiding places for wolf-eels. Mauve coralline algae and large yellow bath-like sponges fill any space that's left. Big lingcod are all over the place. Some divers say they have seen 60- to 70-pound (27- to 32-kilogram) lingcod at Point Wilson, particularly in the fall when the salmon are around. We saw schools of big black rockfish, copper rockfish and kelp greenlings on the reef. Loads of flounders between the reef and shore.

After the dive walk around historic Port Townsend, one of the oldest settlements in Washington State. Each Victorian home is as well painted as the day it was built. Signs on more than 200 homes indicate the date of building and original owner.

BOTTOM AND DEPTHS

The bright white rock reef is clean-swept with no silt, 25 to 35 feet (8 to 11 meters) deep. Some big boulders, scattered white sand and thick bull kelp.

HAZARDS

Extremely dangerous currents all year as well as bull kelp, in summer. The reef can only be dived on small tidal exchanges and exactly on slack. It is safest on slack at the end of an outgoing tide. All the water going into and out of Puget Sound pours past Point Wilson. Rip tides are vicious and could sweep you out into the big shipping lanes in Admiralty Inlet. Dive from a "live" boat at Point Wilson Reef. Carry a knife for kelp.

TELEPHONES

• On the water: VHF radio; if no VHF, try a cell phone.
• On land: Fort Worden Park, across road from ramp, outside refreshment stand.

FACILITIES

None at the reef. Launch ramp, fast food, campground with flush toilets and hot showers – both wheelchair accessible, beside the natural sand beach at Fort Worden. Plus historic remains of Fort Worden – including the Cable House refreshment stand and housing in old Victorian homes that were once officers' quarters. Many of the vacation homes are furnished with fireplaces and reproductions of Victorian furnishings. Pre-registration required for camping and vacation homes: contact Fort Worden State Park Conference Center, 200 Battery Way, Port Townsend, WA 98368. Telephone (360)344-4400 or fax (360)385-7248.

Wonderful wild beach walk from Point Wilson all the way to North Beach.

ACCESS

Point Wilson Reef is close offshore from Point Wilson at the entry to Admiralty Inlet. You can reach it from Fort Worden State Park in the outskirts of Port Townsend. It takes 10 minutes to drive from the ferry terminal in Port Townsend to Fort Worden State Park where you can launch.

Charter with a custom operation or launch your own boat. Go to the north shore of Point Wilson where bull kelp marks two reefs. The kelp is most easily seen at low tide. The best reef is 300 yards (275 meters) offshore under the kelp bed closest to the red buoy. Do not anchor. Dive from a "live" boat, leaving a pickup person to follow if you are swept away by the current.

*At reef closest to
red buoy*

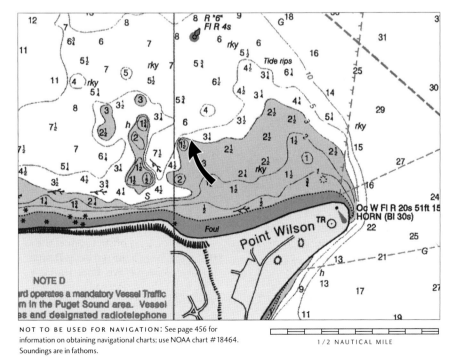

NOT TO BE USED FOR NAVIGATION: See page 456 for
information on obtaining navigational charts; use NOAA chart # 18464.
Soundings are in fathoms.

1/2 NAUTICAL MILE

NOTES

INDEX TO PLACES, MARINE LIFE AND DIVES,
DIVING ACTIVITIES, CONDITIONS AND FACILITIES

ILLUSTRATION CREDITS

ACKNOWLEDGMENTS

Technology has changed the world we live in – I have been running to keep up with it in both diving and book production. Old friends and new friends have guided me.

I will be forever grateful to Vic Marks, Hartley & Marks Publishers, who quietly lured me into the complex, powerful jungle of 21st-century book production. I jumped in eagerly, soon was alternately kicking and screaming with frustration and joy. Vic shared his support and expertise and that of many of his staff: John McKercher produced a flexible, exciting design for me to work with; do-everything Rocky Ingram sorted out infinite problems, even one entire New Year's Day; Supriti Bharma taught me to use my new computer and quietly provided continuing positive encouragement on all fronts. Lee Ingram provided excellent virus protection; Bill Hallam prepared nautical charts and helped me prepare the manuscript for the printers. Finally, and most importantly, Adina Costiuc and Sally Xu clarified my communications with the printers.

Vic also referred me to multi-talented artist Laura Redmond who did art work in the book, designed the index, tutored me in QuarkXPress and patiently answered my questions throughout book production; to sharp-eyed editor Glenda Wilshire who caught many errors and inconsistencies – however if any remain I claim them as my own. My heartfelt thanks to this exceptional team.

Stephen Hammet started pulling me into the 21st-century technical stuff creeping into diving in October 2002: evenings after our dives during the days at Seymour Inlet, Stephen set up my GPS and taught me how to use it. When I went for an air fill in Campbell River Kevin Bates nudged me to try nitrox. The following day I went south and learned the basics – ever since I've been diving with nitrox. Ron Akeson constantly helped me by answering questions about technical diving in detail and he taught me to use NOAA tide and current tables more efficiently. When we dived the *Capilano*, I was so thrilled with the wreck I forgot to take GPS readings; Ron shared his data from that day with me and you – this is the one GPS reading in the book that is not mine. Gary Mallender told me about early explorations at Seymour Inlet. Neil McDaniel and Andy Lamb helped me identify marine life.

I cannot name all of the divers and non-divers who helped me. Barb Roy was always ready to dive or help me find a buddy: a huge gift. When I wanted to kayak-dive at Neck Point she referred me to Corey Waldron: he was up for it – ask him about it! Pam Auxier often dived with me and found partners for dives in Puget Sound and the Hood Canal. One group included underwater videographer John Williams who recorded our night dive at Sund Rock, then, not only showed it to us after the dive but sent a copy to me. Good friend Gail Bauman helped me complete the index. It takes two. Unexpected gifts came from all directions: when driving home, I stopped for tea in Hedley and a Heritage Museum Society volunteer did scans for me, a total stranger.

Kevin Van Cleemput knows the waters from Juan de Fuca Strait to north of Port Hardy and he helped me in so many ways: the most important was when we dived Senanus Island Reefs. He taught me a way to dive that site to save the fragile sponges from being accidentally destroyed; that freed me up to write about it. Kevin also took me to a multitude of sites for GPS readings; to Pearson College to learn more about conservation at Race Rocks.

Others who generously lent a hand with diving and/or GPS locations in the Victoria area are Pierre Gagnon and Erin Bradley; in northern waters: Jim Witton, Bill Weeks, John de Boeck, Mike Richmond and Earl Rowe; at Hornby Island, Rob Zielinski and Amanda Heath; at Schooner Cove, Chris Turnbull – a friend from way-back-when – with whom I jumped off a bridge into the Athabasca River after our dive wearing full dive gear so I could become a member of the Jasper Rubber Ducks Club; in Nanaimo, Ian Hall and Ed Singer; in the lower mainland, Anthony Bing, Bob Bing, Craig Neil; at Sechelt, Tony Holmes, and at Pender Harbour the late Albert Hull; in Powell River area: Bob De Pape, Randal Drader, Dave Pollen and Bruce Randall; in Puget Sound and Hood Canal, Alan Gill, Jeff Rogers, Don Coleman; in the San Juan Islands, Henry and Jamie Powers and Ron Kinney. Thanks also to the many persons who assisted me but who are not named.

Thank you – each one of you – for your special contribution to this book.

AT HOME, PLANNING HER NEXT TRIP:
Betty Pratt-Johnson has dived every site described in this where-to-go guidebook. She loves to explore. You can go with her on easy dives for new divers as well as to more challenging sites to see sixgill sharks, cloud sponges, a heritage shipwreck, artificial reefs, gorgonian corals, Steller sea lions and the largest octopuses in the world.

She is an award-winning writer and photographer. Her accurate, lively treatments of outdoor topics have appeared in *Diver, BC Outdoors, Western Living, Oceans, Reader's Digest* and *The New York Times*.